EXIT
INTO
HISTORY

ALSO BY EVA HOFFMAN

Lost in Translation

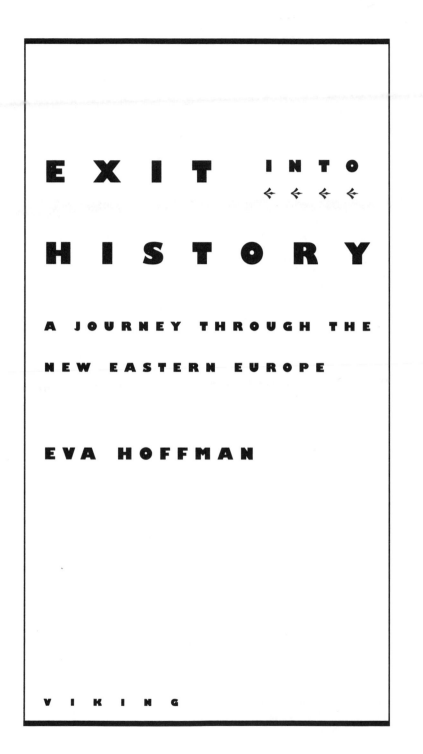

EXIT INTO
←←←←
HISTORY

A JOURNEY THROUGH THE
NEW EASTERN EUROPE

EVA HOFFMAN

VIKING

VIKING
Published by the Penguin Group
Penguin Books USA Inc., 375 Hudson Street,
New York, New York 10014, U.S.A.
Penguin Books Ltd, 27 Wrights Lane,
London W8 5TZ, England
Penguin Books Australia Ltd, Ringwood,
Victoria, Australia
Penguin Books Canada Ltd, 10 Alcorn Avenue,
Toronto, Ontario, Canada M4V 3B2
Penguin Books (N.Z.) Ltd, 182–190 Wairau Road,
Auckland 10, New Zealand

Penguin Books Ltd, Registered Offices:
Harmondsworth, Middlesex, England

First published in 1993 by Viking Penguin,
a division of Penguin Books USA Inc.

10   9   8   7   6   5   4   3   2

Portions of chapters one and two of this book first appeared
in different form as "Warsaw Days" in *The Yale Review.*

LIBRARY OF CONGRESS CATALOGING IN PUBLICATION DATA
Hoffman, Eva.
Exit into history : a journey through the new Eastern Europe / Eva Hoffman.
p.   cm.
ISBN 0–670–83649–4
1.   Europe, Eastern—Description and travel—1981–   2.   Hoffman, Eva—Journeys—
Europe, Eastern.   I.   Title.
DJK19.H64   1993
914.30004—dc20   93–19263

Printed in the United States of America
Set in Simoncini Garamond
Designed by Ann Gold
Map by Jeffrey Ward

ACKNOWLEDGMENTS
← ← ← ←

I've been fortunate in the attentive care which this book has received at all stages of its publishing. My special thanks to Pamela Dorman of Viking Penguin and to Tom Weldon of Heinemann for patience, intelligence, and tact in editing the manuscript; also, to all the people in both publishing houses who have worked with me with courtesy and good humor—particularly Paris Wald and Beena Kamlani of Viking Penguin and Sara Hannigan of Heinemann. I am truly grateful to Georges Borchardt, my literary agent, for his calm and wise guidance; and to the people in his office who have been unfailingly reliable and friendly, especially Alexandra Harding and Denise Shannon. Elzbieta Matynia and Ivan Sanders have given me valuable assistance in the early stages; Linda Bamber, Janusz Głowacki, Peter Hawkins, Ewa Kuryluk, Marta Petrysewicz, and Laurie Stone have listened and responded with insight and sympathy as the book took shape; Sara Bershtel's acute reading of the manuscript was enormously helpful, as was Sandy McClatchy's vigorous encouragement. Their support and interest has meant a lot to me.

The writing of this book has been greatly aided by a generous grant from the John Simon Guggenheim Memorial Foundation. An invitation from the Institute on East Central Europe at Columbia University to be a visiting scholar proved important, in part for giving me access to the University's libraries; and several weeks in residence at Yaddo and MacDowell Colony had a truly salubrious effect on my work. To all of them, my deep appreciation.

It is impossible to name all the people in the five countries through which I traveled without whose generosity, openness, and hospitality I could not have undertaken or completed my task. In a book such as this, the writer is more medium than actor, and I am immensely grateful to all the Eastern Europeans who carried me along on my journey as Sherpa guides, Virgils, hosts, and friends. I hope they will feel that this book is also written for them.

CONTENTS

Introduction   ix
Map   xxi
1 Poland I   1
2 Poland II   61
3 Czechoslovakia   120
4 Hungary   189
5 Romania   262
6 Bulgaria   346
Afterword   407

INTRODUCTION

← ← ← ←

Like all important undertakings in one's life, this one was over-determined. In 1989, when the revolutions in Eastern Europe began to reverberate like a series of powerfully plucked harp strings, I knew this was one historical event I wanted to see for myself.

"Eastern Europe" has been for me a notion potent with personal associations. I was born in Poland and got my primary schooling there, along with an intense early education in politics and the sentiments. I emigrated in early adolescence; but for a long time afterward, Poland—and by extension, Eastern Europe—remained for me an idealized landscape of the mind. Because I had loved and lost it, because I had been cut off from it summarily and, it seemed, irrevocably, it stayed arrested in my imagination as a land of childhood sensuality, lyricism, vividness, and human warmth.

To a great extent, Eastern Europe had stayed arrested in actuality as well. I had grown up in Poland under the aegis of Communism—the force that had provided, or inflicted, the ruling narrative on a large region of the world for more than four decades. The given of the "system" imposed certain unbudgeable conditions on the lives of several generations; it divided whole societies into bipolar oppositions between "us" and "Them." Throughout the various thaws and freezes, the liberalizations and the tightenings of screws, the basic elements of that overriding situation held in place. But now, in 1989, the meta-narrative met its abrupt end; nothing much was clear about what would happen next, except that Eastern Europe was going to be changed, changed utterly—and I wanted to go before that happened. This was the most personal urge behind my long excursion: that I wanted to see "my" Eastern Europe before it disappeared, but to see it, this time, without my childhood fantasies and projections. I wanted to make an attempt, at least, to understand it for what it was—from a larger, more robust, and more informed perspective. Happiness, Freud said, is the fulfillment of a childhood wish; meaningful knowledge, perhaps, is the satisfaction of a childhood curiosity.

But there was, behind my expedition, a less private—and undoubtedly more presumptuous—impulse as well. I was not immune to the kind of fascination that suddenly made the eyes of the world turn on Eastern Europe. It was clear, as the amazing events of 1989 unfolded, that history was happening there—and I thought that this was my opportunity to catch it in the act. I wanted to see how it took place day by day and near the ground; to understand what such a momentous social transformation means in the lives and psyches of particular people. In other words—aside from my very personal reasons for going there—I wanted to witness history in the making, to catch it *in vivo*, on the wing.

But to see any place for what it is is a famously difficult undertaking—and perhaps nowhere more so than in Eastern Europe. Our psyches seem to be so constructed that we need and desire an imagined "other"—either a glimmering, craved, idealized other, or an other that is dark, savage, and threatening. Eastern Europe has served our needs in this respect very well. For many centuries, it had been, to some extent cut off, separated, and—for all the insignificant geographic distances—strangely unknown. And for centuries, it had served as a stand-in for the exotic, the other. When Shakespeare wanted to indicate a fabulous never-never land, he called it Illyria (which, as a real place, used to be situated in what is now Bulgaria and Albania), or "the Seacoast of Bohemia" (that notoriously nonexistent geographic entity). And when he wanted to suggest a shadowy realm, somewhere on the outer margins of our political concerns, he made a glancing reference, at the end of *Hamlet,* to the kingdom of Poland.

The real Eastern Europe is a region of civilizations as old and strongly defined as those of the West. The Greater Moravian Empire, the ancestor of modern Czechoslovakia, was established about A.D. 800; the first Bulgarian kingdom rose to its height in the seventh century; Poland and Hungary can each claim a social and cultural, if not a political, continuity of over a thousand years; and Romanians still profess a kinship with the Dacians, whom the Romans found so hard to conquer that they celebrated the eventual victory for thirty years. But while the civilizations have survived and retained their identity, the national borders in this part of Europe have shifted in the last ten centuries with the capriciousness of a checkerboard puzzle being rearranged by a particularly wanton player. Poland, Hungary, and Bohemia all had their imperial, expansive phases before the seventeenth century; but more recently, Eastern Europe has been the arena for imperial struggles and expansion from both East and West. Partly because of their location on trade routes and partly because of geographic structure—several countries squeezed into a relatively small area—the nations in this part of Europe have been perennially subject to invasion, colonization, great-power bargaining, partitioning, and sheer conquest.

No wonder, then, that the region rarely achieved long periods of stability or economic growth, and that, in the imagination of the West, it never quite ceased being "the other Europe"—

less developed, less civilized, more turbulent and strife-ridden than the Europe we think of as the real thing. Even in modern times, when it became more accessible and better known, Eastern Europe tended to be seen as a source either of primitive savagery or of operetta entertainment. Still, during the interwar years of the twentieth century, some of the invisible barriers between the West and its sister Europe had begun to come down. Poland and Czechoslovakia once again became nation-states, with some admired political figures to represent them; the cultural achievements emanating from Eastern Europe were beginning to be appreciated as a salient part of modernism; and the region's capital cities became plausible places to visit.

But whatever penetration had become possible during that interval was abruptly curtailed by the eruption of the Second World War and the subsequent descent of the Iron Curtain. For the following forty-some years, Eastern Europe subsided into an even darker invisibility than before. To a large extent, normal communications and travel between East and West came to a halt. And ironically, while the literal distances became ever more trivial, the rifts of culture and life conditions widened. While the West, after World War II, started moving along a galloping accelerator of material development, Eastern Europe came close to an economic standstill, or even regression. And while the West, willy-nilly, had to experiment with various forms of democratization and pluralism, the East suffered a virtual stasis of political demagogy and centralization as well.

During those decades, Eastern Europe once again became a Rorschach test for Western wishes, dreads, and misunderstandings. To some, it was a repository of utopian ideological hopes; to others, a heroic region struggling against a demonic dystopia; but to most, I would hazard, "Eastern Europe" had become a lifeless, monochrome realm where people walked bent under the leaden weight of an awful System.

From growing up there, I knew at least that it wasn't the latter, that life was as multifarious and surprising in Eastern Europe as anywhere else, and just as impossible to summarize or reduce to a few concepts.

Nevertheless, before setting out on my travels, I made some working assumptions about what I was going to be looking at. I realized, of course, that the very notion of "Eastern Europe" is to some extent a fiction, and that the countries through which I was going to travel have distinct histories, traditions, identities. And yet I thought that the fiction was at least useful, and probably based on some measure of historical reality. This has been particularly true since World War II: the history of that period was largely unchosen, but definitely shared. The interval of Soviet domination created Eastern Europe, even if such an entity didn't exist before. And while I am well aware that the current debate about restoring the distinctions among Central Europe, Central Eastern Europe, and Central Southern Europe is much more than semantic, it did not seem crucial, for my purposes, to resolve it. For the sake of simplicity and convenience, I refer to "Eastern Europe" most of the time, though occasionally "Central Europe" seems clearly more appropriate; the same holds true for "Balkans."

The five countries through which I decided to travel—Poland, Czechoslovakia, Hungary, Romania, and Bulgaria—could all plausibly be said to have been part of the older Eastern Europe, as well as the postwar one; they were also the countries where "the revolutions" had already happened by the time I went there. I decided not to go to the places where the exit from Communism was following highly exceptional routes—i.e., Yugoslavia and Albania; and I left out East Germany from my trajectory because it had not been historically a part of Eastern Europe, even if it became a member of the "fraternal" bloc after the war.

But while I thought there were good reasons to speak of Eastern Europe, I also knew that this was a region full of its own social and ethnic variety. One of the myths imposed on Eastern Europe in the last forty-five years, and quickly abolished by recent events, was the myth of uniformity. Now that the stifling blanket of Communism has been lifted, the countries of Eastern Europe are once again revealed to be a mélange of ethnic groups, classes, and subcultures, many of which have survived the ideology of sameness with their identities—and, alas, often their antagonisms—seemingly intact. In my explorations, I tried to do some justice to these striations and distinctions. I traveled to peripheral villages as well as the capital cities, visited factories as well as editorial offices, talked to peasants and workers and newly uncloseted aristocrats, to Polish Jews and Hungarian Gypsies and Bulgarian Turks.

Though this was not part of my original plan, I made the journey from the Baltic to the Black Sea twice—once in the summer of 1990, and again in the summer of 1991. Partly, I needed to go back because I felt that seeing twice is believing. I needed to reassure myself of certain impressions and deepen others, to continue conversations that had gone unfinished, soak up the atmosphere of certain places more fully. But also, going back afforded me a glimpse of how "the changes" were unfolding in each country a year later. I've indicated the division into two journeys within each chapter.

As I made my way from the Baltic to the Black Sea, I listened to narratives of people's lives. Eastern Europeans do not yet have Cuisinarts, but they do have stories—historically embedded stories, intimately shaped by the turbulent events that have repeatedly swept through these small countries. History has often seemed thicker, more pressing, and oppressive in Eastern Europe; few lives have been disconnected from it, or unaffected by it. This was perhaps especially true in the last decades, when the question of Communism became a sort of controlling theme. In its various forms and guises, this subject infused and permeated everything, both as an idea and as a palpable, daily presence. There was no escaping it, no ignoring the large public events perpetrated under its aegis, or the private consequences of those events. The system was indeed very systematic, and it was one of its accomplishments that it nearly abolished the distinction between the personal and the political—an achievement that must surely throw some doubt on the desirability of such an equation.

What this means, however, is that individual biographies are often more intelligible—and representative—in Eastern Europe than in the more radically fragmented societies. Obviously, there is a qualitative disparity between an individual life and the life of a nation. Yet, as I observed the social landscapes around me, I was surprised by the consistency of certain patterns; by how often certain kinds of stories recurred in each country, and how much they mirrored each country's history and situation. Countries, cultures, societies are organisms, after all; and the parts do, to some extent, reflect the whole.

And if story is closer to history in Eastern Europe, it's also closer to moral drama—for it was another of the system's accomplishments that it forced people to make difficult, risky, *ethical* choices often and under considerable pressure. Just about everyone had to decide, at one time or another, whether he or she was for or against, whether to raise a hand at a meeting to approve someone's destruction or to leave it at one's side, thus approving one's own; whether to inform on a neighbor, sign a dangerous petition, stand by silently during an anti-Semitic campaign, or risk imprisonment by protest.

It often seemed to me that human character was more strongly defined in Eastern Europe—both more strongly formed and more strongly deformed—by such pressures. Of course, I met people whom I liked more or less, of whom I approved more or less wholly; but most often, I was impressed by the resilience, the strength, and the open-eyed consciousness with which Eastern Europeans are confronting the changes. The obstacles under which they labor are enormous; the X-factor of human energy and inventiveness makes almost anything possible.

How do societies go about overturning all their institutional arrangements at once? How do people adjust to the dismantling of a worldview that may have been hated but that deeply conditioned their lives? How do they reposition their daily and long-range methods for living? In the countries through which I traveled, the changes were almost universally desired, almost entirely nonviolent (with the exception of Romania) and accomplished with nary a protest from the ruling powers. As historical change goes, this is a best-case scenario, revolution in its most velvet guise. And yet the deeper transformations taking place there are profoundly dramatic and often disorienting. The landscape I saw after the changes was accordingly a mix of tonalities and moods, of calm and passionate conflict, optimism and wariness. It was also an eerie mixture of epochs, somewhat like a newly excavated and upturned archeological site, in which the relics from various historical strata have all been brought to the surface in a simultaneous jumble. Eastern Europe today is haunted by its various pasts, pursued equally by its memories, its amnesias, and its willful deletions. There is the immensely complex legacy of the Communist era, of course, but also the nearly palpable presence of earlier periods, whose ghosts were supposedly slain by Communism. Once the false unity of the system was breached, a congeries of attitudes, antagonisms, customs, and even political parties were resurrected wholesale from earlier eras—a strange reiteration of the past released from its artificial arrest.

If the past is very alive in Eastern Europe, the future is very uncertain. We have no ready names, no precedents for the experiment taking place in Eastern Europe today. We know it is of historical significance; but history tends to dissolve as you get closer, to fragment into a billion bits of ordinariness. Except for very heightened moments, and sometimes even then, we are usually, in relation to history, in the position of Stendhal's Fabrizio at the Battle of Waterloo: on the outskirts, missing the main event. Most of the time, one does not see it happen; what one does see is particulars.

At the time when I made my trips, Eastern Europe was within the very center of the turning gyre, but the patterns emerging from it were, as yet, difficult to discern. Moreover, any observer's experience is filtered through her, or his, own lenses and quirks, and all travelers are at the mercy of haphazardness and chance. And so, while the subject and the territory of a book such as this are large, the claims for it have to be very modest indeed. What follows is an account of a particular journey, and of one person's encounter with a region of the world at a particular historical juncture—a series of meetings, conversations, reflections, and impressions from which, as from fragments of a mosaic, the larger shape and picture can, I hope, not inaccurately emerge.

EXIT

INTO

HISTORY

ONE
← ← ← ←

POLAND I

"The *unexpected,* the divine unexpected, is better found elsewhere," Stendhal wrote in one of his journals of provincial peregrinations. The hit of the unexpected is what we travel for. I am traveling to an elsewhere that was once my home, but still I feel the raised pulse of anticipation as the LOT airplane dives into Warsaw and the milky morning. No more than two years have passed since I was last in Poland, but in my mind my native country has become defamiliarized. In the interval, dramatic events have taken place there, events that have provoked enormous headlines: REVOLUTION, END OF COMMUNISM, END OF AN ERA. In my mind, these headlines have become superimposed on my private images of the country where I grew up. Poland has taken a leap away from me, not in distance but in time, and somehow I expect it to be altered in ways I can't quite imagine.

But on the bus ferrying us from the plane to the airport, I instantly find myself in a familiar atmosphere. As we're about to disembark, a man's voice declares with a cutting flourish, "The flower of Polish culture returning to the Polish soil!" and everyone breaks into knowing laughter. Most of the people on the flight are probably working-class emigrants of the last decade—people who usually left Poland on political pretexts, but really to try to improve their lot in the land of supposedly universal opportunity. They're hardly noble exile types, and this is what the sharp, shared self-deprecation acknowledges. It's a mode of humor I know well, a sort of signature of the local character—and I experience a small pleasure of recognition at seeing it so spontaneously adapted to new circumstances.

The woman at the passport control makes an effort at a smile. It's obviously strained—her facial muscles are quite unused to being set in this position—but I note it with appreciation nevertheless. Better the pretense of civility than the sincere glower that used to greet me here. In the tiny, single terminal of the truly primitive Okęcie airport, there are actual porters—and they're hustling as I've never seen anyone in Poland hustle before. The one who grabs my luggage, with a bow, no less, is so eager to do his job that, after depositing my bags on the sidewalk, he clicks his heels and runs for the next customer before I manage to take my "greens" out of my purse.

But the city, the city of course looks unchanged, as I drive through it with Zbyszek, a filmmaking friend who has come to pick me up at the airport. On this early May morning, it's unseasonably chilly, drizzly, gray. Zbyszek is preoccupied by a terrible, but perfectly prosaic, toothache. Warsaw looks perfectly prosaic, too, a city that defines the nonexotic. It's positively antiexotic, tending to reduction rather than excess, to understatement rather than extreme effects. We pass quiet neighborhoods of low, gray stone buildings, a stretch of tree-lined promenade along the Vistula river, children with leather satchels strapped to their backs, on their way to school.

I detect in myself a slight disappointment at the quiet spectacle, and simultaneously upbraid myself for this odd reaction. Just what unexpectedness did I expect? Banners announcing the triumph of the revolution? Less grayness, more light? Or did I think that the pollution would be blacker just because it has been recently more publicized? On some level, I did, I guess, even though I had been here fairly recently, for such is the great power of headlines and selective images—that journalistic Heisenberg effect by which our contemporary perceptions are so strongly formed.

To right my balance, I ask Zbyszek about his sense of what has happened here.

"Oh, I'm more pessimistic all the time," he briskly informs me. "Things are falling apart."

"But are they falling apart more than before?"

"It doesn't matter whether they're falling apart more. Before, it gave me pleasure when they fell apart; they were falling apart for *Them.* Now, it's all closer to me. I won't say it's mine exactly, but I feel for these people who can't seem to manage."

I know that for a Pole to lose his pessimism is to lose his honor, so I prod a little further. "But has anything good come out of all this so far?"

"Well, I was in this provincial town recently, and there are fewer of those horrible mugs in which They specialized—you know those faces I mean."

"I wonder what has happened to those mugs."

"Oh, those mugs can change!" he declares resolutely. "If such a mug begins to care about something, or stops to drink, the mug begins to look different. Those mugs are somewhat re-formable, you know."

I'm intrigued by the notion that people's very faces can undergo change; but now we're approaching the place where I'll be staying. I've accepted a generous offer from a friend who's abroad, an apartment that appears to be situated in one of those ubiquitous blocks called "anthills" in the local jargon. This complex, no different from so many others, looms in a graceless mass of vertical boxes, sticking out of the bare ground with no lawn or shrubbery to soften the effect, and eying the world with bleak, stingily crowded windows. Behind, a muddy stretch of untended field. In the parking lot, some kids are learning to skateboard; on a cement path, two rough, brawny men stroll about not too soberly, arms clasped around each other in half-drunk camaraderie.

I've never stayed, or lived, in an "anthill," but the apartment is of a kind I've visited often: a generic Polish apartment. It's tiny, decorated in a generic beige, constructed out of materials that to a Western eye look insubstantially thin. It is in such apartments that much of Polish—of Eastern European life—has happened; it's for such apartments that people waited and bribed and hoped. In this one, every bit of available space is filled with books; Polish literature, learned journals, translated American classics. Zbyszek peruses them with approval. Then his toothache becomes more acute; he winces with pain and says goodbye, leaving me alone in my new quarters. I scan them with some nervousness. Automatically, I start running myself a glass of water, and then stay my hand. I have been warned not to drink the tap water on pain of poisoning or dysentery. Fortunately, a neighbor, who is supposed to ease my entry here, arrives to see how I'm getting on, and makes me a gift of bottled spring water—though she surrenders it with some reluctance.

I decide to walk around the neighborhood a bit to get my bearings, and to look for signs of change. None is in evidence. Architecturally, Warsaw has suffered from being built mostly after the war, in the most dreary decades; and this part of town bears all the marks of the almost willfully pedestrian socialist-collectivist style. There are no restaurants, posters, or neon lights, nothing to reassure one that the passing show of urban life, the refuge of a well-lit space or a good cup of coffee, is nearby. Only the broad streets, the depressing buildings, and the gray.

I know this grayness; I even used to love it, as part of the mood and weather with which one grew up here, and which sank into the bones with a comforting melancholy. Why, then, does it seem so much more desolate than before? I guess I'm looking at it with different antennae, without the protective filters of the system, which was the justification, the explanation for so much: even for the gray. Indeed, the drabness was partly Their doing, a matter not only of economics but of deliberate puritanism. Being no fools, They knew very well the connection between esthetics and desires—and the use of bright colors on public posters, for example, was restricted by censorship, lest such hues summon dreams of a more colorful reality.

No one has put up colorful posters yet, and now this neighborhood is just what it is, bareness stripped of significance. Something momentous must have happened here after all, to compel this altered reading even of the simple scene before me.

Back in the apartment, I make myself coffee and try to make a few phone calls. This turns out to be an exercise in sheer futility. Two times out of three, the phone refuses to give a signal or connect. When it does, often there's a busy signal that might, or might not, indicate that the line is busy. Briefly, I nurture a fantasy of calling someone in New York, but after reaching the long-distance operator through sheer persistence, I'm told it'll take four to six hours to get a connection.

I give up on making contact with the outside world and crawl into bed under several layers of blankets. The drizzle outside has turned into serious rain, and inside the apartment it's piercingly chilly. This, this is Eastern Europe, not the headlines, not history; how could I let myself in for several months of it?! I reach for a book, and remember why books led such an intense life here. Of course, during the dark ages of disinformation and censorship, they often brought more trustworthy news than the press; but also, books were an antidote to all this, a resting place for the mind, an assurance that reality wasn't circumscribed by these thin, unsteady walls, that one could temporarily escape not only into fantasy, but into other kinds of worlds and truths.

History is a hyperbole, I keep thinking as I walk around Warsaw's streets. Where is it happening? Has anything happened here at all? But closer to city center marks of change do appear. To begin with, there are the inconspicuous signs, affixed to shop façades or hotel entrances, announcing foreign currency exchanges. I walk into a makeshift shack bearing such a sign, as well as one announcing the sale of vegetables. Inside, next to bins of carrots and potatoes, there is a blackboard with official exchange rates listed in chalk. Such is the hold of habit that I'm tempted to look over my shoulder as I accomplish this once-illicit transaction. The money changer, of course, is quite used to this by now; the sums he calmly hands over are grotesque, bombastic, Weimarian. For my $50, I get nearly half a million zlotys. I feel momentarily very rich, but I can see how the heady descent of the currency's value might have given people some discomfiting moments.

"Well, but now it's stable and a man can give a lady real money," the changer says when I ask him about this. "A man could do O.K. for himself now, if only they would leave him alone."

"They? Who're they?"

"Oh, what can I tell you—shady groups. They want to control this business. With guns. Me, I'm an independent. But they're mafiosi, that's all they are, and you may be sure half of them are from the *nomenklatura.* Or from the militia. Who else has guns around here?"

The low-built streets near the central New World artery are crowded with improvised stands and with people selling a few jumbled items directly off their car hoods, or from newspapers spread out directly on the sidewalk. A pair of thick panty hose, a Hawaiian shirt, a bottle of vodka. Some bananas, some strawberries. These are the seeds of a new economic order. But how shabby it all looks, how poor! The objects, shorn of their context or glossy packaging, have a kind of sub-surrealist melancholy—fortuitous juxtapositions minus the poetry.

At the nub of downtown, dusty, overbroad avenues, perfectly dull buildings, crowded sidewalks, people coming out of a gloomy restaurant in good humor. I pass the Communist Party headquarters, another boring structure trying to look imposing through insistent stolidity; darkened windows. Two men with briefcases stand in whispered conversation in front of it. I wonder what goes on in there now. Then more fruit and vegetable stands, more tired-looking people inspecting the carrots and oranges carefully. I know that I'm supposed to see all this as jaunty, hopeful symptoms of entrepreneurial energy and venturesomeness. Instead, after my quick tour, I feel the same sort of letdown as yesterday. Before, there was a presumptive dignity in the deprivation; the utter absence of everything was like an absurdist joke in which one could take a certain sort of morbid pleasure or even malicious satisfaction. But now, as with the dismal architecture, this is what there is; and the meagerness of the improvements points up the pathos of the background. This is what Poland is starting from as it enters a brave new age—this ground zero, this trampled field.

I meet my friend Renata in an utterly ordinary cafeteria, and order a sandwich and a salad. An old woman has been contemplating the sparse offerings for some time, and as she sees what I order, she mutters, "Some people have enough money in their pockets to fill their bellies."

"See what's going on?" Renata says when we sit down. "This never used to happen here. People didn't envy each other on this pathetic level. What was the point? They knew that nobody had anything much. This is going to become a different country."

Yes, undoubtedly; and for a while it will combine the syndromes of poverty with the pathologies of capitalism. I tell Renata about my own sense of dismay at first impressions. "Melancholy of transition, that's what you're feeling," she informs me. "You're just getting a tiny dose of it, but we've all been through it in spades. Or I should say we're all going through it. I mean, nobody knows what to expect. We have to relearn the whole ball game from the start."

"You don't mean, of course, that things were better before."

"No, of course not. Not better—but they were simpler. Us, Them. It was a predictable game. Now we're in an utterly open situation. We don't know how things are going to turn out from day to day. I mean, we don't know what'll happen to our jobs, or who the anchor will be on evening news tomorrow, or whether the local child-care center is going to close. It's all up for grabs, and there's no one to blame. It does incline one to melancholy."

"But isn't open better?" I ask.

"Come on, don't sound so much like an American," Renata chides me. "Yes, better, undoubtedly, except what do I get out of it? My salary is now worth about half what it was before it all happened. And the shopping takes longer because I have to go from place to place to compare prices. It used to be, you bought an egg, you paid for an egg. Now they all think they can charge whatever they want!"

At this, her voice rises in something like indignation. Renata teaches biology in a high school, has three children, and little time to do comparison shopping.

On the way home, I decide to do some shopping for basic provisions myself. The time of severe shortages is clearly over, though food hardly comes in Western abundance or variety. One kind of cheese, one of salami, and in the vegetable store, a few tomatoes and carrots; that'll do very nicely, thank you. The prices, however, given the average Polish salary, are daunting. In my adopted neighborhood, putting together even a few items involves going to several stores, rather inconveniently set apart, and I've forgotten that nobody gives you bags, and so, since I haven't brought my "net," which people use for shopping, I end up struggling with several unwieldy packages, loosely wrapped and about to slide out of my arms. On the way back home, on a nearly empty street, a military man in uniform and high leather boots saunters contentedly, two enviable shopping nets neatly balanced in his hands and bouncing against his shins. And then, as if from nowhere, an old, bent-over woman in a scarf comes toward me, and recites a singsong plaint: "Everything hurts me," she complains in a sweet voice. "My neck hurts me, my back hurts me, my legs hurt me . . ." O perennial Eastern Europe, I think, you're still here, though probably not for long. She's not bitter about her pains, she looks into my eyes so trustingly, her eyes are baby blue, and she's sure she can tell me what hurts her because we're all human, and all the same.

I look in on a meeting of the Writers' Union, which takes place in the Old Town, a picturesque section of Warsaw, reconstructed from utter ruin. At first saunter, the Old Town looks like a well-conserved section of a typical European city, with winding, narrow streets, Renaissance and Baroque townhouses lined up neatly around a large market square, the requisite number of churches, and a royal castle extending serenely on an escarpment of the Vistula. But for all its convincing patina of age, the Old Town, except for a few pieces of authentic old stone, is a very recent creation.

It was one of Hitler's ambitions to make of Warsaw "a second Carthage," and during the city's two-month uprising in 1944 he almost succeeded, with the Germans bombarding the city literally to rubble, while the Soviet Army stood on the other side of the Vistula and watched; the Germans, after all, were doing the work of subduing the Poles for them.

The reconstruction of the Old Town began almost immediately after the war was over. Surely, in their devastated city, the inhabitants of Warsaw needed basic housing or medical facilities more urgently; but there must have been something unbearable about this bloodletting in stone, this abrupt loss of so much accumulated history. And so the Poles, who had put up a strenuous resistance to the Nazis, and who suffered devastating human losses as well, set about the beaver labor of reconstructing an area of the city that took centuries to accrete naturally—an act of dedication to memory that took place not only in the imagination and partisan polemics, but in brick and mortar.

To tell the truth, I'm not enchanted with the Old Town, not right off. Perhaps because I'm conscious of its newness, it strikes me a bit as a stage set. Or maybe it looks like that because of its careful preservation, its incongruous, well-maintained prettiness in the midst of Warsaw's grit and grime. Anyway, I'm not taken with the kitschy art mart in its central square, or the touristy shops in antique-seeming interiors. But as I begin to notice its details, the mullioned windows and the wrought-iron door handles, the heraldic ornaments and the arched cellars, and as I contemplate the work that went into making them, the Old Town begins to gain layers, not so much of history as of meaning.

There's something about this dedication to the past, this stubborn loyalty to what was cherished and defeated, that seems as romantic to me now as it did when I was growing up here and was being inculcated into the ethos of heroic Polish moments.

And the work was tremendous. The reconstruction of Baroque façades and Gothic churches proceeded from photographs, prints, drawings. To accomplish an accurate rendering of the Castle, with its marble galleries, its intricate wooden inlaid floors and tapestries, its period furnishings and glittering chandeliers, battalions of Polish craftsmen reeducated themselves in forgotten skills, and abandoned quarries were reopened for the right kind of stone. One of the painters consulted by the postwar architects was Bernardo Bellotto, the nephew of Canaletto, who had done for Warsaw what his uncle did for Venice. Bellotto's views of eighteenth-century Warsaw now hang in the royal castle, whose reconstruction was in part based on those paintings. If history goes on long enough, the life of a culture and its art start mingling like old, cross-fertilizing compost.

The sentiments that energized this enormous effort cut across all factional lines. The rebuilding of the castle itself didn't start until twenty-five years after the war, and was underwritten by a Communist government, for whom it might have seemed ironic to be engaged in recreating royal residences; but probably there were very few Poles, even internationalist, Communist ones, in whom all vestiges of patriotic feeling had disappeared. And everyone must have felt that in a country that had suffered so many violent ruptures; signs of continuity have a value that is more than "only symbolic."

The Literary Club itself is a comfortably elegant building—one of those refuges that made life chic and bearable for Poland's prophets and scribblers. Like everything at this pivotal moment, the meeting, too, has the extra charge of a historic occasion. It's the first one After. Even the location is steeped in significance. When martial law was imposed in Poland in 1981, there was a split in the Writers' Union between those who decided to cooperate with the government and those who would have none of it. The dissidents, who of course represented most of Poland's legitimate literature, were barred from the comforting premises of the Literary Club, and they're here for the first time in ten years, vindicated on a grand historical scale.

All this is alluded to in a dignified and understated address given by the outgoing president, a man with the gravitas and sturdiness of an oak tree. The meeting itself is quite formal, marked by the extreme courtesy of all declarations, dialogues, and hallway chat. There's none of that feyness, or impishness, or pleasure in provocation that is the expected accompaniment of such gatherings in the West. Polish writers rarely style themselves as *enfants terribles* or anti-bourgeois terrors. Perhaps because the antibourgeois position was claimed by the Communists, it didn't have the same inversely snobbish appeal here as in the West. And perhaps because of the enormous importance writers have always been accorded in Poland, there has never been the same drawing of lines between middle-class philistines and the chosen avant-garde few. The writer was supposed to speak for the nation, and was supposed to do so as a serious person, and not as some blithe hippie or naughty subversive.

But the conditions of being a writer are, at this very moment, about to change quite radically. The manners in this room are impeccable, but literature is hardly mentioned. The talk is all business. Culture in Poland is about to be thrown into the belly of that dreaded and worshiped beast, the free-market system— and the agenda of the writers at this Congress is to figure out whether the beast will feed them or will swallow them.

The latter seems much more likely. "Do you mean that some people will get paid more than others for the same amount of writing?" someone asks in a perplexed tone, after the rules of capitalist publishing have been unfolded from the lectern. "And what about these advances, will they be calculated per page? No? Then how?" "And then sometimes you can get paid twice, once before the book is published and then afterward?"

An elderly man from Łódź, who has apparently just figured out the implications of all this, stands up and declares, in a shocked voice, that, under the new system, it's possible that good, serious books may make less money than mediocre or even very bad ones.

Not possible, likely! I want to inform him, with the perverse pleasure of superior knowledge and longer suffering. But my momentary malice quickly gives way to sympathy. Some of the dignified and cultivated people in this room, some of the less adaptable or the less savvy, the ones who are too attached to the old, coded style of writing, and also those who hid their lack of talent under a veneer of political seriousness, are in for a very bad time.

And, though they have suffered as much as many, they have more to lose than most of their countrymen. For all the trials of censorship, the written word in socialist Poland was not only highly valued but also, in effect, subsidized. It's true that writers had to resort to unwieldy allegorical maneuvers in order to get around the censor, and that at certain times, the honorable among them refused to be published officially; but much of the time, their writing—of no matter what quality or popularity— was compensated like honest labor, at uniform, fairly privileged, per-page rates. Moreover, to make up for the scarcity of titles, books were issued—by Western standards at least—in stunningly large editions. Then there were those gigs in the West—an interview in Germany, a lectureship in Denmark—which yielded precious, hard-currency fees exchangeable in Poland at highly advantageous black-market rates.

All that lost. As a culmination of the morning's proceedings, a deputy minister of culture—a Solidarity man—arrives to defend the policies of his governmental body. His speech stirs something close to a commotion at this civilized gathering. Words and questions fly, though their purport is roughly the same: How can the ministry cut subsidies to, of all things, culture—the culture that has preserved Polish identity when everything else was going straight to hell?!

The deputy pleads with the assembled litterateurs to think it all through with him, all together. There's simply no money to support culture on the same scale as before, surely they can understand that? But the market system will create its own prosperity—that's the point. That's exactly the point. Real talent will always rise. And if popular books are popular, well, who's to say they shouldn't be? Anyway, that's how things are done in normal countries—and surely we all want to be a normal country, don't we?

But alas, solidarity can no longer hold. The deputy is one of the smart young men—well-trimmed beard, the supple movements of someone not used to an official persona or a suit—who fought the good dissident fight, and who probably never had a public job, or even any regular job, until recently. He undoubtedly has many good friends in this audience. But now he has crossed the power barrier, and the laws of power, and its divisions, are taking over with astonishing speed; and by their inexorable logic the deputy minister is all of a sudden on the other side. By that logic, also, and for all the good will in the world, there's an intrinsic incompatibility between the broad and the individual view, between planning for the whole and the interests of a particular group. Not surprisingly, the writers' anxieties aren't allayed by the deputy's appeals to the larger picture.

Luckily, there's always lunch—lunch, the saving grace of conferences. This one is served in a modest dining room downstairs, known for having nourished generations of literary luminaries, and it is served by Krysia, a combination hostess and waitress, whose doubles I've seen in many Polish institutions. Krysia, whose pretty face is severely framed by pulled-back gray hair, has been at the Literary Club so long that she seems to be its most stable embodiment—and she has a no-nonsense way with its famous and almost famous members.

"Patience and humility," counsels a woman at my table when some of us get fidgety from hunger and long waiting. "You don't want to irritate Krysia." The food, when it finally comes, is delicious—delicate, tart pickle soup, light blintzes filled with cheese, and sweet apple crepes with a wonderful soft consistency.

At very low prices, these, too, have been among writerly perks and privileges.

Afterward, I go upstairs to have some tea in a pleasant sitting room. The room empties quickly, leaving only me and a writer whom I briefly met earlier.

"They wouldn't adopt a resolution about respecting Polish values, can you imagine that?" he informs me.

I shake my head mutely; what follows then is an astonishing verbal avalanche. The writer is a small man, but all that I really see emerging from the deep armchair is his head, which is large and rather beautiful, in a Polish way—regular, chiseled, with dark, deeply set eyes and a neatly trimmed beard. His mouth twists a little when he becomes impassioned, giving him a slightly mad look; but he speaks in precise, controlled, though darkly intense tones.

"Why are we so ashamed of ourselves, why do we feel so guilty, why do we have to beat our breasts about being Polish?" he queries rhetorically. "Why is it that this country is the whipping boy for the whole world and that we consent to being whipped? Are we so much worse than anyone else? Have we done such monstrous things? We're accused of being anti-Semites from birth, we're accused of having behaved terribly during the war. But for God's sake, this country was in a terrible situation! I'm an engineer as well as a writer; the language of mathematics speaks to me. I've looked into this and I know it was statistically impossible for Poles to save all the Jews, given that there was a death penalty for anybody harboring Jewish people. But people did save Jews—my family . . . oh, well, I don't want to tell you personal stories. I deeply regret that most of the Jews have left. Believe me, I was heartbroken when some of my Jewish friends felt they had to emigrate. I studied the history of Polish Jews, and it was a unique, a wonderful *marriage*" (he pronounces this word in the French manner), "the *marriage* of the vital Polish culture and six thousand years of Jewish wisdom. My favorite literature is written by Polish Jews . . . it was a wonderful *marriage*!"

"But you must admit . . ." I begin. I signaled to him at some point that I'm Jewish, to give him a chance to stop or change tracks. But he is honest enough not even to pause.

"Yes, I know, there's a lot to admit, but why are criticisms allowed in only one direction? If you want a real conversation, brother, you must let me have my say! And Lithuania? Now we're being blamed for the woes of Lithuania because we helped the Soviets defend them from the Nazis at the beginning of the war. What harm did we ever do to Lithuania? Not enough to scrape under a fingernail!"

I'm quite overcome by the sheer brio and conviction of this tirade, but I decide to interrupt, this time more firmly. "If you were to defend the honor of Poland," I ask, "what would you particularly point to?"

The answer surprises me. "I would defend what I know," he says. "The feats of Polish engineering in the 1920s and '30s and that much misunderstood September defense of 1939. It's simply not true that our army acted like quixotic buffoons."

And then he's off again: "We're supposed to be a nation of irrational fools, we're supposed to be dirty, noisy, barbarian. Is that what you see on our streets? I recently visited an aunt of mine in New Jersey who now feels very superior because she thinks she's made it into the greater world. But believe me, Newark is not more cosmopolitan or beautiful than many Polish towns!" (I believe him.) "And what about this Old Town, where we are? I don't come here often, I'm from Łódź, but yesterday I walked around, and for heaven's sake, it makes you feel warm, it wraps itself around the heart. . . . But I must stop," he says abruptly. "Perhaps I have bored you."

"Not at all," I tell him, quite sincerely.

"It was such a pleasure to talk to you," he says, not smiling at all, looking at me very directly and shaking my hand forcefully. And then he walks away, a tormented incarnation of a beleaguered, proud Polish patriotism, the writer as the knight of the nation's honor indeed. As I look around the sitting room, still empty, but now grayed by the dusk, I'm not at all sure whether he has walked back into today's Congress or into the pages of a nineteenth-century Polish epic or historical saga.

On the street in front of the Literary Club building, there are several long tables covered with books. Stands like this, mostly tended by determined-looking young people, have appeared all over Warsaw, and they seem to me the only genuinely cheerful symptoms of the new capitalism. On the other hand, I see from them what the writers inside the Literary Club are worrying about. From living my bookish life in America, I know that a book is the most mobile, the most easily produced, the most demystified of contemporary commodities. So, to some extent, is literature. On these stands, the process of demystification is proceeding apace. The potpourri of titles, the mix of high and low was unthinkable before. There are biographies of starlets, cookbooks, soft porn, and hard thrillers, the latter mostly imported from America and referred to as "the Ludlums," in a bow to the extreme popularity of Robert Ludlum's productions. All of these are brought out by dozens of independent publishers, who have quickly caught on to what the appetites of the moment might be. Junk writing, like junk food, has an instantaneous appeal, perhaps by its very definition, because it requires least effort and offers least resistance. And Western junk is doubly irresistible here right now, because it has the added glamour of the new; for while the *ancien regime* produced, by command or reaction, a perfectly adequate amount of drivel, it was earnest or serious drivel, and almost never the frivolous kind.

Well, of course I'm a bit sorry that literature is going to lose its exalted status—but at the same time I find myself impatient with Western pundits who are quick to shake a metaphorical censorious finger at this instant absorption of Western trash—as if Eastern Europeans were somehow supposed to be better than us, our impoverished but nobler conscience.

The new frivolity hasn't entirely displaced seriousness, though that too comes in new varieties. There is a striking absence of important new fiction, and a predominance of autobiographies and other personal documents: sagas of suffering within the Soviet gulag, memoirs of formerly closeted aristocrats, and confessions of Communist potentates. An account of his years in power by Edward Gierek, a former prime minister, has been a runaway best-seller. The first need, in these new times, seems to be for the new; the second, for a recovery of history. These are the basic chronicles, journals of the plague years, the documentaries. In new times, the chronicle always comes before fiction; imagination, inventive reworking, will have to wait till later.

In the meantime, there's the basic fact of variety and confusing choice. In the more monolithic times, people stood in long queues whenever a "hot" title came out; everyone read the same books and discussed them with some passion. It made for a kind of community of reading and, I fancy, for a deeper engagement. But now, how does one choose among these indiscriminately mixed goods? What to read, when, how thoroughly? What book to buy, given that there are so many of them, and why buy a book in the first place, now that there are so many other kinds of goods beckoning? What are the chances that somebody else will read the same book? Sheer quantity—that most pervasive contemporary force—is beginning to exercise its effect, and reading is bound to become a more consumerist, and a more private, endeavor.

Sunday in Warsaw. A church on New World Street overflows; there are people standing outside, straining to hear the sermon, and kneeling on the pavement to pray. I take a taxi to Łazienki Park, one of the oases of the city. The taxi driver, like most drivers here, sits very straight, talks politely, and drives unflappably. He multiplies the sum on the meter by two hundred to account for inflation. On the streets, family groups in Sunday dress and people carrying bunches of flowers. One doesn't go visiting without a bouquet, no matter how bad things are. Łazienki Park is one of the most beautiful city parks I know, enormous and varied; there are ponds and picturesque bridges, dipping hills and

formal *allées,* and various royal buildings dating from the eighteenth century—pavilions and gazebos and other pretty architectural caprices. In front of a dramatic statue of Chopin, children
play. It's quiet. It's one of the striking things about Warsaw, the
quiet—going counter to all stereotypes of noisy, badly behaved
Poles; going counter, even, to my preconceptions of temperamental and explosive people. In fact, I've rarely heard raised
voices in public places, and I'm beginning to note something
downright imperturbable in the Polish manner—though whether
this comes through being subdued by circumstance or through
having learned to maintain sangfroid in any circumstance is hard
to tell.

I visit the offices of *Gazeta Wyborcza,* Poland's first post-
Communist newspaper, established by Solidarity during the
Round Table talks, which ushered in the transitional government
now in office. In a quiet courtyard, an inconspicuous sign points
to a hard-to-find door. Inside, a look of barely controlled disarray. In the rush of events, *Gazeta* has taken over a space previously occupied by a kindergarten, and the offices—though the
word seems a euphemism, like so many terms imported from
wealthier and more stable climes—have incongruously childish
dimensions and the charm of improvisation. Tiny desks made of
unvarnished wood, people huddling round them in twos or
threes, sharing computers, telephones, and cigarettes. On the
walls there are Solidarity posters, of course, but also some photographs of the Pope and one of Lenin, with a Solidarity button
affixed to his lapel. The image, in this setting, seems to have produced an almost conspiratorial wink; remember me, it seems to
say, I'm the old familiar ogre of everyone's kindergarten past.

I go quite unnoticed, and this in itself is notable. I remember
visiting languid offices of yore, where everyone was in effect on
a low-level strike, and a visitor was an instant excuse for a long,
leisurely coffee break. Here, energetic young people walk about
with a look of drop-dead seriousness, fully absorbed in what
they're doing. At an editorial meeting, people wander in and out,

and so do several house dogs. Not a jacket or other bit of formal wear in sight. The meeting is led by Adam Michnik, one of the genuine heroes of the underground, and now editor-in-chief of *Gazeta*. Aside from his other attributes, he's known as a charmer, and he conducts the proceedings with informality and humor. There seems to be none of the pecking-order anxiety often prevailing in comparable American establishments. Jokes fly, and so do mundane journalistic matters. How should a headline sound, what should be explained in an article, how to maintain the sound of impartiality? Everything has to be decided from the ground up—and somehow it's done without pomposity, with that sharpness and wit that the Poles identify with style.

But the nonchalance of manner is deceptive, for even in the few months of its existence *Gazeta* has become an utterly serious organization, as well as a highly successful newspaper. There are pages of advertising—a practice defunct for several decades in Poland—plans for expansion, for offering competitive salaries, for employee shareholding. I'm startled, and impressed, by the speed and the sophistication of it all—but perhaps I shouldn't be. *Gazeta* is run by hip, well-educated younger people; why should I think that they couldn't cope with the new conditions? There's been a sort of assumption in the West that post-Communist Eastern Europe is in an adolescent phase, from which it'll have to grow into "our ways" awkwardly and slowly. But the ways of the West aren't that mysterious after all, and Eastern Europe isn't made up of bumbling teenagers. As I contemplate the hustle and bustle around me, I think, This is freedom, this is its prosy sound, the concentration and crackle of real work—not pretend work, or enforced work, or boycotted work. It seems to me, from the energy and intelligence in evidence here, that everyone had been poised in preparation for this during all those cynical years, ready to spring and go at the moment of release.

After I spend a few days in Warsaw, Krzysztof Kieślowski, a filmmaking friend, invites me on a short excursion to Szczytno, a provincial town some 150 kilometers north of Warsaw. He's going there with a friend to complete the purchase of land on which they've built their country dachas, and which they were leasing until now.

"You must be ready at five-thirty in the morning," he instructed me when I said I'd like to go.

"You must be kidding," I said, but he wasn't, and so now I'm staring out the car window through early-morning bleariness at the flat, moody countryside. The road is marked by willows and corridors of poplars, quick reference signs that to me say "Poland." Occasionally, a horse-drawn plough makes its slow way along the border of a field. At village crossings there are roadside chapels—lovely, pastel-colored folk artifacts, in which a wooden saint, usually a Madonna, stands in a small, roofed enclosure, as in a nest, surrounded by symmetrical, neatly carved patterns and flowers. For better or worse, this has remained.

It must be typical of the confusions of this period that Krzysztof and his friend disagree about whether this is the first moment when they could have bought the land legally, or whether they could have done so some time ago. In Krzysztof's village, we meet his peasant landlord, a strapping, tall blond man with somewhat watery blue eyes, and his wife, who's dressed in an odd assortment of clothes—a purple flowered skirt, a blue striped blouse, a heavy red sweater. These must be the best items of clothing she owns, and she has put them all together for this special trip to town.

At the Szczytno courthouse, rows of farmers, with ruddy faces and few teeth, sit on long benches waiting their turn. The deputy judge calls us in rather quickly—privileges of the city intelligentsia, no doubt. She is a pleasant, vivacious woman, who chatters at us spiritedly and without cease, all without interrupting her task of filling out enormous forms (with several carbon copies) on an antique typewriter.

"It's complete chaos right now," she assures us. "A mess of gigantic proportions. From one day to the next, everything changes. People come here to ask me about selling land or buying something, and I don't know what to tell them. And do you think over in Warsaw they know what they're doing? They're in chaos too—look what they send me practically every day." And she shows us little slips of Xeroxed paper with clumsily typed directives about some new fillip in the legal regulations.

"And this?" she points to a bookshelf. "They'll have to rewrite all of this too!" I peruse a bookshelf of legal tomes. The prospect of rewriting, or even rereading, the thousands of onionskin pages of rules and regulations seems quite hellish; an Augean-stables labor of turning over the social soil. But our amiable deputy judge doesn't seem overwhelmed; her dismay is too vigorous and eloquent for that.

A girl of about ten, who is the judge's daughter, comes in to report on her morning in school. Her mother greets her delightedly, and then instructs her to sit quietly while she goes back to her oversized forms. Somehow, from this image of an easy continuum—the judge chatting with such immediate, frank friendliness, the little girl following her usual routines—I begin to sense one way in which people get through this period of deep, fundamental change: just this way, step by step, coping with what's in front of them, and commenting all the way, knitting the present to the past even before a larger picture can emerge.

Our business completed, Krzysztof's landlord wants to stop by at a local watering hole to celebrate the sale, which has just been signed and sealed. Krzysztof agrees without much enthusiasm, and when we go in, I understand his reluctance. Thanks to our merciless starting time, it's only about eleven o'clock, but the inn's interior—dirty, unadorned, with naked cement floors—is filled with drunken men. Not congenially or reservedly drunk, as they might be in an English pub: these men reel across the floor, shout, stare at each other with glazed eyes and vacant, toothless faces. There's something quite infernal about the spectacle, and slightly comical, too—the drunks look so much as if they were play-acting the classic drunk. But Krzysztof thinks that they are seasonal alcoholics: farmers who have very little to do at certain times of the year, and who come here while the women cook and clean.

We leave our peasant host to his buddies and vodka, while we go to look at the land Krzysztof and his friend have just purchased. The cottages themselves are modest affairs, built from prefabricated materials and set right next to each other; but there are fresh fields, hens waddling about, a crisp brook nearby—and now it's theirs, all theirs.

When we go back to pick him up, the landlord emerges from the inn weaving. Somewhat weavingly still, he bends to kiss my hand when we drop him off—for this is one of the gallantries that has never died, not even under Communism. It was everyone's small protest against comrade-style egalitarianism, and it's the farmer's way of saying that he has as much class as any cultivated city person.

On the way back to Warsaw, driving through a pleasant rural stretch, we're arrested by a curious sight. At the edge of a dewy, unmown field, a group of peasants have gathered around a small foldout table placed directly on the grass. On the table there's a red rug, and on the rug a powder-blue statuette of a Madonna.

"We're having the field sanctified," a ruddy-faced peasant, with bony, precise features, tells us in response to our inquiry. "It's time to go back to old customs, don't you know."

"Do you remember doing this a long time ago?" I ask.

"Well, no, I can't say I do," he answers cheerfully, "but the priest remembers, he does, he knows what it's about."

"And where is the priest?" I ask, wondering whether we should wait for the ceremony itself.

"Ah, he's running late, he stops by at each village and sanctifies the field and collects money. Everyone has his bit of interest, don't you know." And he gives a good, hearty laugh.

And there's a bit of Poland as well, I think—with its respect for tradition, its religiosity, and its sturdy, irreverent skepticism about both.

Back in Warsaw, I have a visit scheduled with Bronisław Geremek, one of the new cadre of politicians whose worldly positions, in a short span of time, have shifted as radically as the positions of the planets in a new astrological phase. Geremek is a highly respected medieval historian by profession, and until recently he was one of the main intellectual advisors to Wałęsa, a member of the highly subversive opposition. Now he's ensconced at the very heart of power, as the leader of the Citizens' Clubs, one of those improvised political formations that emerged all over Eastern Europe in the heat of the changes. This makes him, in effect, the leader of the parliamentary opposition, and even more than that: although the Communists were guaranteed two-thirds of the Parliamentary seats in the current government, they've been keeping a surprisingly low profile; General Jaruzelski has made it clear that he will resign before the next elections. In effect, the reins of power are in Solidarity's hands. And in the interim elections, many of the Solidarity candidates were writers, artists, and other intellectuals, resulting in a rare spectacle of a government, if not of philosopher kings, then at least of the intelligentsia.

I visit Geremek in the Parliament, or Sejm, a pleasantly unassuming, modernist structure, which happens to be one of the two buildings in downtown Warsaw to escape destruction during the war; the other was the National Museum. Inside, the hushed hubbub of significant action. The foyer of Geremek's office is full of people waiting to see him, among them a writer-turned-senator, whom I've met before, in the old days when he spent his late mornings not in Parliamentary corridors but in coffee houses frequented by the Warsaw literati. He's an impressive-looking personage—broadly built, with a big, handsome head, a shock of white hair, and thick, overhanging eyebrows. It's a thunderous face, a face from which streaks of lightning could come. But when I ask him how he likes his new role in life, what comes out is a deep rumble of complaint, accompanied by eloquent gestures of his large hands.

"I tell you, if I had known what this job is like, I'd have never taken it," he says, with quite disarming frankness. "I can't wait till the term is over so I can get back to writing. I'm exhausted. I can't keep up . . . ah, it's too much."

"Do you have an office staff to help you?" I ask.

"Office, what office?" he asks with rhetorical sarcasm. "We have no offices. I've been answering all my letters myself. Do you know how many letters I get? And of course you have to answer some pensioner in the provinces who's worried about his retirement pay. Now I've hired a nice lady, she comes to my house and she's going to do it. And my poor wife, she's been doing nothing but answering the phone. I'm lucky to have a phone, of course, but that's not what she wants to do with her time!"

But in the middle of this tirade, his name is called, and so he waves it all away with a resolute flick of his broad wrist, kisses my hand, and strides into Geremek's office.

By the time it's my turn to go in, I expect to see a very harassed politician, but Geremek is one of those people who, though he's presumably under considerable pressure, has the gift of acting as though he has all the time and attention in the world to give you. He is a compact man with precise, vigorous movements, and he speaks with a measured orderliness. The central matter on his mind right now is the new constitution, which is being drafted under his supervision.

The constitutional committee, he points out, has a long native history to hark back to; contrary to their reputation for political backwardness and ineptitude, the Poles have an unusually long and at times unusually advanced democratic tradition. By the beginning of the thirteenth century, various regions of Poland had assemblies called *sejms,* or parliaments, which used the voting method to decide important issues. From the end of the sixteenth century, Polish monarchs were elected, and the voting privileges were gradually extended from a small group of magnates to all of the *szlachta*—a class, or caste, that included small nobility and gentry, and that comprised a considerable portion of Polish society. During the Renaissance, the constitutional law of the then-extensive Polish Commonwealth included remarkably liberal clauses providing for religious freedom and individual rights.

"And, of course, we have our Constitution of May 3rd,"

Geremek says—for this is a document of which the Poles are very proud. Drafted in 1791, it was the first written constitution in Europe, and it was celebrated all over the world; Edmund Burke called it "this great good" and Thomas Paine acclaimed it as a breakthrough in the advancement of liberty.

But in their effort to forge an up-to-date document, Geremek says, his committee will also study American, French, and Spanish constitutions. And they'll also consider what to retain from the current Polish constitution, bequeathed by the Communists: the right to work, for example, or the right to education and medical care.

I'm impressed by his calm, unpolemical relation to the past— even the near past. Of course, constitutions are only blueprints of the best intentions, and this one won't guarantee what it promises anymore than others; but it may be an advantage to have a historian in charge of a founding document.

On the way out of Geremek's office, I look more carefully at the dented antique plaque he has affixed to the door. For a small object, it's rife with symbolism. First of all, it features the old, prewar Polish eagle with its royal crown still on—the original tiara on the original bird, which must have been preserved in some attic chest. At the bottom of the plaque is an archaic word, *soltys,* which means something like "village chief." I leave the Sejm hoping that both this amiable self-irony and the senatorial senator's impulsive frankness can survive the constraints of official politics.

I am taking a gift from New York friends to people I've never met, and a friend drives me to where they live, in a block on the outskirts of Warsaw. In the lobby, bare cement floors, bits of wire hanging from the ceiling, smell of urine, no light. The architecture of diminishment. "Harlem," my friend briskly opines, and despite the gloom of the surroundings, I'm somewhat bemused by the incongruous ring of the word in these precincts.

I ascend in a stuttering elevator, a cramped box made of

dented metal. But the apartment I enter has been made decently neat, and my hosts have put out a Polish version of afternoon tea, with several kinds of cookies and cakes—those cakes that are the last things to be sacrificed in the Polish diet. Zofia, a plump woman with a broad face and a braid coiled around her head, has the slightly stilted manners of someone trying to affect the best manners possible. Her husband, Jurek, is gaunt and tired-looking. Inevitably, the conversation turns to the one subject on everyone's minds nowadays: what is it like now; and how the changes have changed things for them.

Oh, not for the better, not at all. The fortunes of these people have declined just as rapidly as some others have gone up. Jurek has just lost his job, which he describes as protecting old buildings from vandalism. This probably means that he was in the low rungs of the militia, though more exact descriptions aren't forthcoming.

"Now they're writing wise articles about how quickly a person falls into a depression after he loses his job," he says. "How you get up later and later in the morning. They don't have to do studies, they could ask me, I'll tell them!"

Why did you lose your job? I ask, though in this case I don't expect a complete answer. "Oh, you think they were fair about it? I tell you, these new people are just as bad as the old. It's all patronage, they don't care who's competent. It's a new elite. So O.K., so I walked into some of the buildings where a Solidarity strike was going on. I wanted to do my job. Wasn't that what I was supposed to do? But no, they looked at me as if I was some kind of monster."

"They're giving me trouble too," Zofia throws in. "I do my job well, better than some. But all they want to know is, Did you belong to Solidarity. I'm willing to leave them in peace, if they just let me be."

"Were you in the party?" I ask Jurek. "Well, yes," he says, "I was in the party. I grew up in a family of real workers. My father was a railroad man. But I wasn't any sort of fanatic. I went to some meetings, that's all. They didn't even ask you to do very much. This party wasn't much of anything in the last years. I'm more a believing Catholic, anyway, though I don't go to church. So you see, I'm a believing-non-practicing Catholic, and a practicing-non-believing Communist. What can I tell you, this is not a normal country.

"You see, we try to live a decent life here," he continues in an angry rush. "We made this little world for ourselves. We listen to music, we go to the movies. Zofia went to America once, to work for somebody. Why do they want to bother us?

"I even voted for Solidarity in the elections," he goes on, "because I thought having an opposition is good, it shouldn't all just be one party. But I tell you, if things don't get better in this country, I'm going be out there on the streets, beating them." I'm surprised again, this time by the venom in his voice.

"But who are you going to beat?" I ask.

"Whoever is beating me," he responds furiously, and I sense the full force of his bitterness, this new down-and-outer whose privilege didn't amount to much in the first place, and who has now slipped off whatever social ledge he was holding on to—a perfect candidate for politics of resentment and disaffection and extremism.

For me, one of the entertainments of being in Poland is watching the Polish language itself as it spawns new expressions and zestful slang. These are some of the things that crop up in conversation these days:

"The road to Europe" is the ubiquitous formula, more slogan than slang, and like all slogans, too multipurpose by half. Getting to Europe is the great unquestioned desideratum, but what it means depends on who you are and what you want. It means the pure free market to the shock reformists who want to move to capitalism as briskly as possible, and social democracy to "the Third Way" people who want to combine the best of free market and socialism, and ethnic homogeneity to the nationalists, and pluralism to the progressives. I've heard "the road to Europe" invoked by a bishop, speaking on television, as a justification for introducing religion in schools. According to him, the mixing of church and state is an all-European idea.

Then there's "joint venture." Ah, the permutations of the joint venture! If "the road to Europe" is the ideological sine qua non, the joint venture is the libidinal object of desire. Probably the road to Europe is paved with these beautiful, shimmering, ineffable business propositions, which, of course, have to involve a respectable Western partner—though "Western" has come to include Japan and Hong Kong as well.

"Man of money" is probably someone who has succeeded in a joint venture already. Given the vagaries of Polish vocabulary, it's really "person of money," which is certainly more accurate because women are beginning to make fortunes too. "Person of money" is uttered with respectful gravity and with no insult or irony intended, the way Poles say "person of the theater," or "man of the cloth."

In an antithetical relationship to "persons of money" are "beautiful souls"—those poor exalted spirits who keep believing in social utopias, or the life of the intellect, or art for the sake of art. Even people who could have themselves been "beautiful souls" till yesterday pronounce this phrase (or rather word) with considerable condescension. After Communism, the thing to be is a tough-minded pragmatist, and not a wimpy transcendentalist.

Aside from these personae, there are "sweating men in pursuit of power," a phrase coined by a young politician to express contempt for politicians who're in it purely for what politicians in "normal countries" are usually in it for. I myself think these sweating men are a nice counterpart to those American men with briefcases, who, of course, never sweat.

"Our Polish hell" is both perennial and always new. This Polish version of hell is a caldron of quarrels and fragmentation, of anarchic individualism and telegrams and anger—all with slightly domestic overtones. It's an almost cozily familiar condition, and everyone thinks there's a bit more of it just now, when everybody can say what's on his or her mind, and they all seem to have minds of their own.

On the other hand, there's the resolutely antimelodramatic "prose of life." Do I only imagine that this lovely expression comes up more frequently than before? "It's just this prose of life," people say when they explain some mundane task they have to perform. Or, contemplating an ordinary day before them, of which, after all, there are so many—"Well, it's time to go back to the prose of life."

The express train to Cracow is crowded, though very quiet. "You must try it, it's so convenient, it's like something in the West," Renata urged me before I left. Well, not quite—it's too nostalgically smoke-filled for that—but the seats are comfortable and the dining car serves some very acceptable canapés; in the corridor, people chat in muffled voices.

Cracow is where I grew up, and I am half nervous about going there. It is the place that is the root and model for my notions of Poland and Polishness. And so I find that I don't want the changes to violate the Cracow that was so changeless during the last few decades. I want change to come in just the right measure there, or perhaps I don't want it to happen at all. There's an incipient regret I sense in myself—though I hardly want to admit it even in thought—for the Poland that is about to pass; for that familiar, reduced reality, for the safety of very slow time. Perhaps I simply don't want to lose my memories; but I have sensed this in other people here too—an unspoken and inadmissible ruefulness about the passing of something hardly loved but nevertheless known.

It's been fourteen years since I was last here; but once I start walking around Cracow, I quickly refind something of the peculiar, gnomic magic that the city had for me in my childhood. Cracow's layered age, its cobblestoned streets, its surprises, are both a soothing potion and a liberation. There are stone townhouses dating from the fourteenth, sixteenth, and eighteenth centuries; historic churches; statues that burst the bounds of stone. What a comfort this all is, this excess, this going beyond function and necessity! Oh, reason not the need, I keep thinking. There's a level of material meanness that renders our souls mean, makes us shrink to fit the surroundings.

The squares and courtyards where footsteps echo and old gentlemen take pensive walks; the old pharmacies with the medicinal fragrances and the orderliness of tinted glass and dark wood; the caprices of clouds and lively light—they seem, once again, to be at the heart of something; perhaps of Central Europe. Here, even the rain comes with a *gemütlich,* old bourgeois sound, rather than with a harsh post-Communist starkness.

As I walk about, I am caught in a sudden downpour, and I run for the first shelter I see. I run straight into the past. The doorway in which I'm huddled belongs to a movie house I used to come to as a child, but haven't seen since; I got conned here once, by a man who talked me out of some money when I was ten years old, and the memory comes full and unbidden, sharp as day. I really did live here once, in a long-ago world.

The new looks better here too, within the context of the old. There's less merchandise on the streets, and more in lovely nineteenth-century shops with arched vitrines and chrome-handled doors. The old Galician connection shows up in shops full of Austrian and German cosmetics, which I never saw in Warsaw. In an archway between two streets, an accordion and violin duo play kitschy melodies. In one of the more frequented downtown spots, Russian women stand in a row, selling gold rings—dozens of them, displayed on the merchants' fingers, or strung on wooden rods. The women have come here to sell their wares for the suddenly valuable and fully convertible Polish *zloty;* but judging by all that gold, even the woebegone Russian economy must have a few hidden resources.

None of this disrupts the quiet continuity of the city. Ancient Cracow can absorb these new sights without being fundamentally altered by them. But of course, deep change is brewing here as well. In the afternoon, I meet Zygmunt Matynia, whom I last saw in New York. Soft-featured and soft-spoken, Zygmunt is one of those people for whom integrity seems to be not a choice but a necessity, whose sensibilities are palpably bruised by vanity or lies. I think he suffered more than most under a system that made lies into an institution, he thought about emigration, decided to stay, but resigned his job as a professor of legal theory at the Jagiellonian University because of the compromises it required him to make.

Now Zygmunt has been asked to participate in Cracow's "self-government," and he approaches the prospect with enthusiasm and with a great deal of informed intelligence. "Self-government" is a new institution in Poland, and Zygmunt talks about possible arrangements for it, and the problems it will face, with a sort of sweet and open reasonableness. He has thought about the respective merits of the French and American models; about the dangers of too much central government control and too much regional independence; about which of Cracow's historical buildings should be considered private property and which national legacy. Cracow's local government is, at this point, at that most hopeful of stages—*in potentia*—and one can unfold philosophical thoughts about it with a nice tingle of anticipation.

Part of our conversation takes place at Michalik's, one of Cracow's famous coffeehouses. Early in the century, this cozy, cavelike interior was a gathering place for the Cracow bohemia, and the dimly lit walls are decorated with frescos in rich red hues, and with pungent caricatures and paintings donated to the management by grateful artists in lieu of more usual payments. In the back, there's a small recessed stage, and, next to it, a display of adult marionettes—really, witty satires of various classes and types—used in the cabaret performances of yore. In the absence of political power, cabarets and satire have always thrived in Poland.

Zygmunt and I choose a room with tiny marble-topped tables, and odd, manneristic chairs whose unnaturally high, curved backs provide a playfully exaggerated frame for the sitting figure. On weekends, Cracovians take their afternoon tea quite seriously, and we spend a leisurely interlude there. Afterward, we stroll over to Cracow's ancient and stately main square. This cobblestoned expanse, with its Renaissance merchants' hall named Sukiennice, its Gothic thirteenth-century Church of St. Mary, and a tower from which a broken trumpet tune is played each day to commemorate the advent of Turkish armies, was one of the centers of gravity of my childhood. Pigeons used to hold great convocations here, and the archways of Sukiennice echoed with dusky emptiness. Now they're crowded with shops, stalls selling wooden folk crafts, Russian *matryoshka* dolls, and ghastly tourist trinkets.

This afternoon, the square has been turned into an enormous outdoor church, through which a procession, celebrating a religious holiday, moves slowly. The sculpted saints borne on people's arms are taking an old, traditional route from a nearby church through the square. Children in colorful regional costumes follow the statues; and they, in turn, are succeeded by a poignant group—aged resistance fighters, in uniforms encrusted with medals, with hunched shoulders and worn faces. This is probably their first appearance in public in a long time, since they were in effect forced from one underground into another as soon as the war was over. It is odd for me, almost eerie, to see these old warriors, whose existence was only whispered in my childhood, in their living regalia—a few frail threads of continuity between the old era and the new. So much past has been preserved in Poland, behind closed doors, by a stubborn cleaving to memory. It is so difficult, after all, to erase any part of history entirely.

In the evening, another kind of spectacle. Cracow is in the throes of a festival dedicated to Slawomir Mrożek, a playwright, cartoonist, and satirist, who left two decades ago under political pressure and is now returning for the first time. Returns—this is a time for them. There are performances, receptions, press conferences; the staid, ancient city-hall tower in the middle of the main square has been wrapped in a large natty tie—Mrożek's trademark—which goes sooty from pollution within a few days.

People wait on the street for hours to catch glimpses of the shy author himself. Mrożek is one of the native sons who has made good abroad, and his considerable fame is even further inflated from this angle back home.

The Slaughterhouse, the play I go to see at the Stary, or Old Theater, is a sharp satire of the Polish propensity to worship art, culture, the Higher Values. There are strong traces of the war in its revelation of brute physicality—meat, blood, slaughter—behind the formalities and good manners. The production is top-notch, the acting precise and strong. This is the side of Polish temperament I find most invigorating—this acerbic, dark skepticism, this puncturing of the vanities and of mystifications.

On the way back to Warsaw, in my train compartment an elderly man keeps asking confused questions of his wife, who answers him with scalding sarcasm. "Where are we?" he asks. "How fast is the train going? When are we going to get there?"—and each time, she chastises him without mercy. Toward the end of the trip, he dozes off and then wakes up abruptly. "Has the Uprising started?" he asks anxiously. "Are we in time for the Uprising?" The Warsaw Uprising, he means. This time, his wife doesn't answer.

History; where is it happening? Partly in the great rush to the past; a reverse tug of the current. The emergence from Communism is partly a retro revolution. It seems sometimes that Poland is trying to take a great leap backward, over the last forty years. Millions of royal crowns have been painted on the previously bald Polish eagles; Communist street names have been erased, to be replaced by older ones, and aristocratic residences are once again referred to by their former owners' names. There's a strengthened cult of Marshal Pilsudski, the interwar leader who presided over Poland's brief period of twentieth-century independence, and an intensified consciousness of the Polish Commonwealth, which from the fourteenth to the eighteenth century extended over large, multinational territories and to which many now refer as Poland's golden age.

"Myths, that's what they're going back to," my friend Renata says with disdainful impatience. "They think they're going back to tradition, or history, but they're falling for mythology. They put crowns on eagles, they put on some funny hats, and they think it means something. It's a chimera, a charade."

"But I suppose people are looking for some kind of identity, some symbols. . . ."

"And you think that painting a royal crown on the Polish eagle is going to give people an identity?"

"Well, but what is? The very meaning of being Polish is up for grabs. I can see why they would fumble around for some signposts."

"Well, they're not going to find them in the Polish Commonwealth," Renata interrupts. "The Commonwealth wasn't as great as they make it out to be anyway. The Poland they think they're going back to never existed in the first place. As far as I'm concerned, being Polish right now means getting down to work and not worrying about crowns on eagles or cults of dead heroes. Think about the present, that's what it means. The past will take care of itself," Renata concludes high-mindedly.

But Renata's is a minority view. The Poles have a tradition of tradition, a talent for historical memory—if only because for so long they had to live by it alone. They preserved their identity through memories of Poland, and through a potential ideal of Poland during more than a century of partitions, when the real Poland was virtually wiped off the map. It's partly where the Poles' strong sense of themselves comes from—this defiant maintenance of memory. They sustained themselves on unofficial versions of their history during the Communist decades, when the official versions tried to wrest their idea of Poland away from them. From growing up here, I remember how teachers tried to sneak bits of real history into the tedious, obligatory Marxist narrative—and how much such morsels of risky information mattered. I remember from my later visits the night-to-dawn discussions that the Poles call "compatriots' nocturnal conversations," and from which "the question of Poland" was never absent.

But each beginning needs to construct its own history. The

changes have thrown all of the Polish past into new perspective, just as a sudden rounding of a bend in a road reveals the vistas we've just crossed in an entirely new configuration. In the newspapers and daily debates, different notions of Poland are being invoked: there is a nationalist story of Poland and a liberal one, and new emphases on the history of a mercantile Poland, and even of Poland as a "normal country," which has always belonged within the mainstream democratic tradition of Europe.

But in addition to the reclamations, appropriations, and revisions of the old past, there's the problem of the brand-new past, just produced by the latest division of time into "before" and "after." For this, too, is at the heart of the events that have taken place here—that four decades have been added to the category of history. Moreover, it's a chunk of history that was largely unwanted, and already a debate is stirring about the proper stance to take toward it.

The first post-Communist president, Tadeusz Mazowiecki, has enjoined the Poles to draw a "thick line" between the past and the present. The "thick line" has caught on, and is repeated in many articles, conversations, and graphic representations. It's a nobly intended motto, urging against bitterness and for forgetting—for getting on. On the other side, there have been some urgings of revenge against the former Them—though fortunately, so far, they've been rather muffled. And everywhere, the impulse to cancel that unfortunate time is evident: in the toppling of the statues—of the Lenins and Stalins and the Dzierżyńskis; and in those attempts to revert to the symbols and rituals and putative glories of earlier times. Indeed, it could be said that the reversion to that further past is a form of repressing the more recent one.

In the meantime, there's the ongoing recovery of suppressed knowledge of the darkened decades. Almost every day, the newspapers carry articles based on archival discoveries: about the Soviet occupation of Eastern Poland at the beginning of World War II, about the Soviet-Polish relationship since the war, about the history of the Polish Communist Party.

But of course, memory is not so easily controllable. The release of the older past from its artificial arrest has produced monsters as well as glories—extreme nationalism, anti-Semitism, the gamut of unpleasant social tendencies. As for Communism, neither the physical infrastructure it left behind nor its internalized inheritance—the daily habits, the modes of thought—can be smashed as easily as the statues. Still, there's a lot of healthy discussion on all these matters, and sufficient appeals for moderation and sanity. Indeed, for now, the fervors seem marginal; the center seems to be occupied by an almost strange calm.

I've been staying for a few days with an elderly lady I know. She's been squeezed tightly by the economic reform—her pension money goes only half as far as it used to—but she's managing, in the Polish way. There are relatives abroad who send some dollars—one of the secret sources of the Polish economy. There's a helper who bustles in once a week, bringing cheese and meat purchased at very low prices—she has her ways, too, probably consisting of relatives on a farm. Still, Mrs. Ranicka, my hostess, dispenses her Sanka and her pieces of ham very carefully.

There's a tenant in the apartment, a young man who comes and goes very quietly and negotiates his movements around us with unfailing politeness. He's a film technician, and like everybody, he's worried about losing his job; without subsidies, the film industry is likely to suffer quite badly. For now, his film "cooperative" is keeping afloat somehow, though his salary has hardly kept up with inflation.

One evening, they both come into my room, which has a television, to watch *Interpelations,* a program of debate on which a leading public figure is interrogated by political opponents and counterparts, and by a group of ordinary citizens. Television has quickly become a public forum for debate, "our big new café," in Renata's phrase; and *Interpelations* has the entire country glued to its sets each Thursday night. The discussions tend to be brisk, sharp, and, in comparison to the stammering rhythms of American political debate, highly articulate. So far, they're not yet fruitlessly, polemically polarized; the point still seems to be to figure out what is best to do, rather than to court popularity or show yourself politically correct; blessedly, for the moment, nobody knows what politically correct *is*.

This time, the program features Leszek Balcerowicz, the engineer of Poland's drastic and tough economic reform, and the subject of the discussion is whether to accelerate the "shock reform," as it is called, even further, or whether to slow it down. This is the hottest and the most salient issue of the day, and the stakes are high. The reform is meant to generate fast-forward movement toward free enterprise, initiative, the creation of wealth; its failure would result in more unemployment, galloping inflation, an even greater misery for an already devastated country. Both my hostess and her tenant have suffered from the reform already; and yet they both view the situation with a philosophical acceptance.

"Doesn't the thought of further acceleration make you nervous?" I ask, thinking it would make me very nervous indeed.

"Oh, my dear, I well remember the reform in the twenties," Mrs. Ranicka replies. "That was much worse." And then, to my amazement, this woman in her eighties, who sometimes gets confused about what she did yesterday, recites the details of the various monetary reforms she has lived through, complete with rates of inflation and changes in her salary. The inflation during the twenties' reform was so extreme that, on payday, she picked up her father's salary and went shopping immediately, because the money would be worth much less after lunch. And then there was the war, with its terrible troubles. "Anyway," she wraps up her recollections, "I guess they won't let a person starve."

"Of course, I don't love it, but it's necessary," the young man avers. "And anyway, it's not working so badly. The capital is beginning to circulate. You've got to take the longer view, you know."

This is the mood I've sensed in most of my conversations here: a sort of stoical sobriety. Oh, of course there are the dark comments, the self-criticism, the gusto of disgust. But almost nobody I talk to is panicked, or angry, or bitter. We must get through this somehow, is the message I keep hearing over and over again; we're in it together. Amazingly, there've been no strikes, no protests, no large-scale violence. Amazingly, so far the government continues to have a very high approval rating, despite the fact that it has been performing a painful operation on the country, without anesthesia.

The calm—while it adds to the strange sense that maybe nothing has happened here at all—seems to me to be one of the most interesting things that *have* happened. It takes a certain political maturity, after all, to exercise patience and restraint in bad times, or to refrain from blaming one's elected representatives even for inevitable ills. But this is an exceptional moment, and the curious quiet is probably the payoff of the exceptionally turbulent Polish history. My hostess, who has lived through the war and a few other things as well, isn't going to be easily shaken by several zeros being added to her banknotes; and the young tenant has experienced not only the hardships of ordinary life here, but also the outbursts of protest and violence that have punctuated the Polish postwar period like eruptions from an exceptionally active volcano: 1956, 1970, 1977, 1980, 1981. And of course, 1989.

In omniscient retrospect, one might speculate that these eruptions probably constituted an excellent preparation for the present pass. There was no country in which the opposition to "the system" was more widespread than in Poland; and over the years, a kind of oppositional culture grew out of the grassroots activity, out of *Samizdat* and unofficial education and inventive local tactics—out of the direct political education. This is the useful, usable past—and it seems to be paying off in the odd phenomenon of a patient Polish population.

This is undoubtedly a pause, a lull—a moment that cannot last. But I find that I want to say, "Please notice this. Please note what hasn't happened as well as what has, and that for once, even if for the briefest moment, the situation isn't as bad as it very well might be." That's probably too much to ask. But if I were queen, I think, indulging in a bit of wish fulfillment instead of sober analysis, I would move Poland forward to a certain point and then I would stop. I would give it a few neon lights, but not enough to make for the tacky garishness of Times Square, I would put a few more cars on the street, but not enough to create traffic snarls; I would provide the incentives of private enterprise, but not enough to produce glaring inequalities; and I would keep some of this moment's stoicism, and its sense of a common situation, in the more democratic, and undoubtedly more fragmented, future.

A Saturday evening; I meet a friend for dinner. Janusz Głowacki is a playwright who comes from here but has lived in New York for the last few years. He looks more restless than usual in his native city, and stands on the street for a while turning this way and that, trying to figure out where we could possibly get dinner at the unorthodox hour of nine o'clock. We begin with the Victoria, a hotel mostly frequented by foreigners; no places left, we're told by the impassive maître d', though infuriatingly, we see several empty tables. We stomp off to the Europejski, another hotel. No tables in the small restaurant. We go to the big one. It's not big, it's gigantic. The ceilings are too high, the tables too large, and all of it is bathed in a yellowish light. In front of the room, a stage has been set up. Janusz and I sit down and settle in for a long wait. The waiters don't look as though they'll be easily persuadable in the matter of service. "They make ten times the ordinary salary because of their foreign currency tips, why should they bother with us?" Janusz says. But we're in for something else. The front of the room lights up glaringly; TV cameras are wheeled out, and a folk-dancing group makes its way onto the stage. Their colorful costumes, their heavy makeup, their fake cheerfulness, and the merry sounds of the music are so depressing that Janusz and I look at each other and, as one, get up and make for the door.

Out on the street, we stand once again, not knowing in which direction to turn. "We could go to P.'s, there's always something to eat there," Janusz says. That's how Polish social life is conducted, in people's homes, where one can always casually drop in. But since I am reluctant, we begin to wander through the dark, empty streets. No cars; no neon lights. About the only person we come across is a decrepit drunk. Two restaurants are closed for the evening. Finally, Janusz remembers one that might be open. It is. Of course, most items on the menu are gone, but there's shashlik and Janusz says, "Please note that it is good." He seems genuinely satisfied by this small victory. I am so depressed that I drink two vodkas. I begin to understand the genesis of Polish drunkenness. "See, this is how life has been here," Janusz says. "These have been our accomplishments and victories. If you found a good meal, or got your shoes repaired, you felt you'd moved mountains and you returned home in great triumph. How else were you supposed to do anything else?"

One evening, I spend some time talking with Helena Łuczywo, who coedits *Gazeta Wyborcza* with Adam Michnik. We're driven to her home by the newspaper's "chauffeur"—though the disheveled state of his car belies his dignified title, and his conversation with Helena had nothing of a boss-employee formality. This bit of instant privilege notwithstanding, Helena lives as modestly as almost everyone here does, though her block is one of the nicer ones in Warsaw, with tiny bits of garden outside. She has told me that people are beginning to accuse intellectuals like her of not knowing enough about the real conditions of Polish life. "But, frankly, I don't know what they're talking about," she says, and it seems to me she's right. The reductive Communist pseudo-egalitarianism had some genuinely equalizing effects; and Eastern European intelligentsia has not suffered the sense of remove from ordinary people that occasionally assails their Western counterparts.

Once we have settled in her small living room, and her daughter has brought us some brandy, Helena breathes a great sigh of relief. In the last few months, *Gazeta* has become one of the most successful newspapers in Poland, and since much of the time she is in charge, she works relentless hours, at a relentless tempo.

Helena is part of the new intellectual elite that has just emerged from the underground, and that has had such a crucial role in shaping recent history. The larger circle, which includes her and others I know, is probably the real magnet that keeps drawing me back to Poland, and to Eastern Europe. Every immigrant has a second, spectral autobiography, and in my revision of my own history I would have stayed in Poland long enough to become involved in the oppositional politics of my generation. The postwar intelligentsia in Poland met an enormous historical challenge with panache and moral power, and they got to live out something that for Western intellectuals of that generation was the great, unlived romance: they made a revolution, or at least they were in its vanguard. The social movement they sparked seems to me one of the most inspiring anywhere or anytime, propelled as it was by lots of intelligence and inventiveness, and by political ethics that were both uncompromising and unfanatical.

In any case, their version of dissidence constitutes *my* favorite Polish tradition. I've met them over the years and heard them talk, with high vivacity and wit, about their shared history of common action and clandestine study groups, of strategy sessions and periodic imprisonments. But behind the irony and the brio, one can glimpse qualities for which only certain old-fashioned terms seem appropriate—terms like integrity and courage and moral commitment.

Certainly Helena had her moments of great risk, of defining decisions. She is a small, soft-featured woman, with a quick, warm smile, a rapid-fire way of speaking, and a resolutely antipompous manner. Helena's father was a member of the Communist inner circle, or at least, as the deputy chief of propaganda, the inner circle's outer fringes. Helena says she knew few specifics about his work when she was growing up. Neither was there much talk about the fact that they were Jewish—partly because her father was a principled internationalist to whom such facts didn't matter. For people like him, ethnic self-identification was a retrogression. In any case, Helena thinks it's just as well that these subjects remained unspoken. "I don't believe in this American system of endlessly talking about everything," she says crisply. "That's not what it's about, anyway." But she attributes her optimism and basic security and strength—for she thinks of herself as a strong person—to being very well loved by both of her parents.

Nevertheless, Helena knew certain things. She knew she was Jewish clearly enough to be sickened by herself when she was sent to a summer camp and attempted to hide the fact. This episode was one of those decisive points in her self-knowledge, for she resolved never, never again to fall into such bad faith.

And she could sense, from early on, that something was rotten in the state of Poland, and of Communism. There were features of her family's situation, for example, that struck her as incongruous with what she was taught—for after all, whatever was discussed at home, her education was heavily permeated by ideology. She noticed the kinds of facts that may be particularly transparent and grating to a young person. Although equality was supposed to prevail, her family lived in special housing reserved for the *nomenklatura,* which was luxurious by Polish standards, and that they enjoyed other privileges as well. Certain historical discoveries distressed her. When she was in high school, she heard a budding dissident talk about the killing of various nationalities by Stalin—a horrifying revelation. On the other hand, when she first went abroad and got her hands on the émigré publication *Kultura,* she was dismayed by the frankness of its anti-Communist language; at that point, such criticism still had the force of sacrilege. Occasionally, ideology reared its head even within her family; for example, she remembers how her father struck her physically on the street when she was already quite grown-up, because he found out that she had crossed out the names of all the candidates in the voting booth as a protest against the falseness of the elections. "And he really adored me," she reminds me, showing no resentment toward him. "He just went mad for that moment."

Helena's conscious politicization, however, didn't start until 1967, when she was already twenty-two. That year, there was a double shock of events that shaped the consciousness of her whole generation. There was the Soviet invasion of Czechoslovakia; and there was the Polish government's campaign against Jews and intellectuals, which, according to the Polish custom of referring to dramatic historical punctuation marks by the months in which they happened, came to be called "March."

"I considered March an utterly senseless show," Helena says sharply. "But it was utterly impossible not to get involved." Perhaps what made detachment impossible was the extreme virulence of the anti-Semitic campaign. Many Jews left then, in an emigration consisting largely of the political elite and the intelligentsia. Helena was among those who didn't think of leaving. The reasons for such choices are always partly rational and partly adventitious. Helena never experienced anti-Semitism personally, and her future husband, who wasn't Jewish, was here. Like many Polish Jews of her generation, she was powerfully formed by Polish culture; and, though she might be loath to use such words, her subsequent actions can't really be understood without the spur of solidarity and love of her country, without something like patriotism.

But, in her nascent politicization, the subliminal messages of her upbringing may have been taking effect as well: Helena, after all, grew up in a climate of social engagement, in which certain ideals, though they were regularly violated, were nevertheless professed. As it happened, her initiation into political activism repeated, in form if not in content, her father's political baptism some forty years earlier. Just as he, a young Communist, printed and distributed illicit leaflets—an action for which he was promptly thrown in prison—so Helena, with a friend, printed leaflets appealing for worker-student solidarity, and dropped them in the factory settlement of Ursus.

Helena got away with her bit of agitation; and after this first spurt of involvement she forgot about politics. She went on to get married, have a child, work in a bank, and then study English so she could get away from her dull job. Until, that is, the next tremor of the Polish ground, and the next moral turning point. In 1976, Jacek Kuroń, a friend who later became one of the charismatic oppositional leaders and, later still, a member of Parliament, asked Helena to help KOR, a new organization formed in response to the persecutions of workers and one of Solidarity's seeds. Kuroń wanted her to act as an English translator for a Swedish TV team doing a documentary in the same Ursus factory where she had once dropped her illicit leaflets.

At first she refused. The action carried a considerable element of hazard. Most of all, she was worried about "anti-Semitic shit in the press"; she simply didn't want to be subjected to something so ugly. And so, with another friend, who also went on to become an important Solidarity leader, Helena "deliberated" about what to do. "For three days I deliberated," she says, "and on the third day, I started feeling revulsion, against myself and against my friend. If I agreed to work with KOR, I was convinced they'd throw me out of work, start another campaign against me—but I came to the conclusion that I couldn't refuse. That's not how you behave. The people at Ursus really got a horrible kick in the ass, and I knew I couldn't turn away. That's just not how you behave. And once I made that decision, I never turned back."

From then on, she and her husband, Witek, devoted their best energies on KOR. Jacek Kuroń, in his wonderful memoirs, conveys something of the intense involvement, the fearlessness, and the strategic brilliance that went into dissident politics in the KOR days. The great breakthrough of KOR politics was to go, in effect, public, and to protest all persecutions of workers on purely legal grounds, thus calling the authorities on their own rules, and beating them at their own game. This was the period when thousands of people knew Kuroń's phone number, so that, when an arrest occurred in a public place, someone could call him immediately. He, in turn, could notify Radio Free Europe or other useful organizations. It was a period, also, of forty-eight-hour weekend detainments, which became so routine that Kuroń and others would tell their friends to call back on Sunday night, after they got out of the clink.

Helena and her husband helped out wherever they were needed—putting together KOR's information bulletins, or contacting Western media. "It turned out that we were great at whatever we had to do," Helena says, with an objectivity that comes from a well-balanced ego. She tends to speak about herself as she would about others, praising or criticizing herself without false modesty or false vanity.

The Polish difference—the unique feature of the Polish "revolution"—was that, largely owing to KOR's efforts, the fabled alliance of workers and intellectuals, the Marxist *summum bonum,* actually occurred here—though, of course, in opposition to the Marxist state. When Solidarity started up, Helena became the editor of its *Information Bulletin;* Witek worked on the production side. She worked "unbelievably hard" on it, she says, harder than she does as editor of *Gazeta.* "There were two hundred pages of information, it came out twice weekly, and it had no mistakes."

In the 1981 crackdown, Helena and Witek narrowly avoided arrest. On the night of December 12, on which martial law was declared, they stopped at their office on their way back from a movie—"the first movie we had seen in a year." By the time they arrived, the phones in the office had been cut off; so had the telexes; when they looked out the window, they saw troops of militia approaching from the front and the back. Some of their colleagues who were in the office wanted to defend it, but Helena thought that this was heroizing "nonsense," and that the only solution was to run. She and Witek made their getaway and ducked for shelter in a nearby building—they were instantly gathered in by a concierge—just as the troops were entering the building.

For the next two years, they lived on the lam. Those were the conspiratorial days of the underground, and it is only through the details of Helena's account that I begin to understand what that darkly glamorous notion actually entailed. Helena and Witek couldn't go home; they would have been picked up by the militia immediately. They hid in other people's apartments, which they changed every two weeks, so that it would be harder to track them down. Their daughter, Łucja, who was then seven, was taken in by Helena's mother; they saw her once a week, usually on a walk in a park. It was during this period that the marriage broke up, when Witek got involved with one of his women hiding companions. Through it all, however, they never interrupted their political activities. With several friends, they produced *Mazowsze,* the main underground journal, under conditions of extreme hardship. Helena shared her hideouts with two women friends; they slept three to a sofa, with their legs extended on chairs. "I slept in the middle, because I could always sleep, no matter what the circumstances," Helena says. "My resilience really passed the test then. When others couldn't go on, it seemed I could." She could work through the night, or fall asleep under a table while somebody was typing on it.

The most exhausting aspect of hiding, for Helena, was having to act like a guest all the time. The apartments in which they took refuge were small, their owners ordinary people eager to talk, to find out what was going on. "But they were all so nice to us," she adds, "I really owe them a large debt of gratitude." When I ask if the fleeting tenants paid for their hostelries, however, she is shocked by the very idea. "No way, of course not, it wouldn't even occur to us," she protests in her machine-gun style. "This is some kind of an American question. Nobody here would have thought of it."

And apparently nobody would have thought of mistrusting their hosts, or each other, or themselves. "This was one of the characteristics of hiding here," Helena says, "that in this country we knew who to trust. We thought there were practically no informers."

Indeed, this must have been the defining condition of dissident life in Poland, and one that distinguished it from other countries in Eastern Europe. The breadth of the opposition, which unified most segments of society, and the trust that people could accord each other at least in this respect, surely enabled many ordinary people to take extraordinary risks.

And there was an ethos of bravery that goes deep in the Polish tradition, deep enough to have the force of an imperative. While Helena didn't have the experience of prison, she, like almost all of her comrades-in-arms, had her share of apartment searches and secret-police interrogations. Helena says that everyone developed his or her own technique, a style of response. "Jacek Kuroń carried on some discussions with the cops, to keep from being bored; and besides, he thinks that one should talk to everyone. Adam Michnik was ironic, or tried to convince them that they were wrong. I didn't say anything, because I didn't feel like it. I knew all their tricks, and it was dull as dishwater. It went on for hours. It wasn't dramatic at all, just small potatoes. The cops knew we were nonstarters; they didn't have a prayer with us."

But for all of Helena's nonchalance about the dangers of being a kind of outlaw, there were occasions, she says, when she felt she was in *The French Connection*. On some evenings, on the way to work on her journal, for example, she abandoned several cars en route to her destination, or zigzagged her way, or ran under viaducts, in order to put potential pursuers off her scent. But eventually, the conspiratorial season came to an end; the political air changed, and Helena and others judged it was time to surface—though she still had to use considerable ingenuity to avoid having charges pressed against herself. Eventually, in the late eighties, Solidarity regained some of its strength and began negotiating with the government again—although they were unprepared for the extent of their triumph.

"It was utter lack of imagination on our part," Helena says—for while Solidarity was appealing for no more than official status as a union, the Communists had already seen the handwriting on the wall, and were ready to give up part of their total power.

But if they were taken by surprise, they were certainly quick on the uptake. *Gazeta Wyborcza* was launched even during the 1989 Round Table talks, in which the shape of the transition government was negotiated. Helena was asked to join the newspaper by Adam Michnik; since then, she's become the publisher as well as the deputy editor. She seems quite undaunted by her new role, or the entry into the thickets of capitalism. I've seen her presiding over the disheveled offices of *Gazeta* with quiet self-assurance, and trying to figure out how to arrange housing loans for her staff from an American bank. On a TV documentary about *Gazeta* she said, in her soft, decisive voice, that if you really want to do something, difficult circumstances are no obstacle. You can always find a way, with whatever means and materials are at your disposal. Her plans for the newspaper are grand, though I sense that her ambition is not yet purely personal; it's still for the cause, and for *Gazeta,* which she wants to make competitive with the best newspapers in the world—"a sweet little miracle."

And while such attitudes might seem practically American, after talking to her I can see that their provenance is more local. In a way, the underground provided perfect preparation for the more open world Helena has now entered. For while dissidence emerged out of a high idealism, it was also a training in taking enormous risks, making quick, hard decisions, and assuming difficult responsibilities. Helena is one of the lucky ones for whom the transition from one era to the next has been almost seamless, not only in her work, but in something perhaps rarer—an untroubled continuity of conscience. She has no dross of self-reproach to carry forward with her, no guilty secrets to stuff away or regrets to leave behind.

Does she feel there are particular difficulties in being a woman in a position of such power and responsibility? "No, that's not any kind of problem," she says. "That's why I couldn't understand American feminists when I spent a year in the U.S. But you see, in Poland it's different for women. On one hand, they're in a worse situation—all those queues after coming home from work—but on the other hand, they're better off." They're better off, she thinks, because of the Polish tradition, which includes a long lineage of female activism and authority. Women took part in the many uprisings and conspiracies when Poland was an endangered nation; they participated in the resistance and later in the underground. It's possible that the commonality that came from fighting for the same fragile cause was a stronger force than the polarizing stereotypes of gender; it accounts in part for the formidable examples of feminine strength I've encountered in Helena and others.

It's getting late, and Helena's daughter, Łucja, who has been doing her homework, comes in to ask her mother about a detail of English grammar. Helena told me that the most painful aspect of hiding was "thinking about Łucja, worrying that you'll skew your child's life. But Łucja is all right. There are certain personalities that get strengthened by such experiences." Indeed, Łucja doesn't seem like a young person whose life has been skewed. She's a slight, very attractive girl of sixteen, with a saucy face and light movements; Helena is delighted with her daughter's beauty, with her resilience during those difficult times, and with her work as a general girl friday at *Gazeta*. Now, though, she upbraids Łucja energetically. "Come on, Łucja, stop being so lazy, you can figure it out, just exercise your brain a little!" Her tone is sharp but fond, and I can see that Łucja doesn't mind being so challenged or taken to task. There seems to be no animosity or generational gap between them. And in this little exchange I fancy that Łucja is being initiated into that Polish system of relations that I still remember from childhood, in which people manage to treat each other with affection but without sentimentality—because they are all equally subject to certain common expectations, to certain ideas of what is required from themselves and each other. Perhaps it is some such sense of a shared dignity that is ultimately at the core of solidarity and of Helena's strength.

On the way out, as Helena accompanies me downstairs to help me find a taxi, I put to her what I know is another "American question." Why, I ask her, did she do it all, why did she put herself through such strain and hardship with every chance of punishment and so little chance of reward?

"Oh, come on, Eva, give me a break," she says, as I expected. "Well, you know." She pauses in some embarrassment. "From a sense of duty. To maintain myself in some sort of dignity. One doesn't descend into such shit. I'll tell you," she says in a different tone, as if she finally hit on the real explanation. "This reality here was odious. It was impossible to accept it. Now, some people don't like us, because they knew what ass lickers they were. I didn't go for that—I didn't want to lie, didn't want to lead a double life. And perhaps people have an intrinsic moral sense after all; they know when they aren't in the right, and they know when they are. One doesn't behave in certain ways, that's all."

When I was growing up in Poland, on the social and literal peripheries of Cracow, They were remote figures, and one wanted them to stay that way: They were, after all, the limbs and parts of that great monster, of the thing that governed our lives for ill. Later, I read memoirs of Communists who lapsed, or reformed, or struggled with their demon; I read accountings of conscience and researches of the soul and analyses of the God that failed. But I hadn't met Them; one didn't, in the natural course of events, not in the Poland that I inhabited. Aside from the Iron Curtain, there was an internal one as well.

It was a porous curtain, of course, and in certain circles people walked through it regularly—though always with the sense that they were, indeed, crossing an invisible border, or peering behind a veil with a slightly voyeuristic excitement. They were a nation within a nation, in a sense, a quarantine minority, Bluebeards trapped in their own castle.

But as I talk to my dissident friends, I discover an interesting twist on this schema—for it turns out that many of them are Their children. Helena is not exceptional in this respect; the number of leading Polish dissidents whose fathers and mothers were among the early, leading Communists is quite striking; the crème de la crème giving rise to a sort of anti-crème—or vice versa.

My friends are often a bit vague about just what their parents did; perhaps they prefer not to know. But while they heartily dislike what the older generation stood for, they tell fond, bemused anecdotes about their actual parents.

There's, for example, an episode my friend Marta recounts— this is one of my favorites—from the time she was held in prison in 1968. Perhaps because she was the daughter of a prominent Communist, Marta received a letter from the then-premier of Poland offering her release on the condition that she make certain concessions and statements. While she was struggling with how to answer the premier, her father came to visit her in prison, and told her a story about his own father, who, before the war, had come to visit him in prison, where he was then serving a sentence for Communist activity. There had also been an offer of amnesty, on similar conditions. "I don't know what you're going to do," Marta's grandfather said to her father. "As you know, I'm not a Communist, and I do not agree with you. But as for mercy—we do not plead for it." After receiving this message, Marta knew what to do; she refused the premier's offer.

Of course, the dissidents' parents were the early Communists, who often began in idealism, even if they ended in corruption and abuses of power. One day, I finally meet one of Them—Helena's father. Right off, he puts me incongruously in mind of a minor character in one of Tolstoy's novels—an outmoded Enlightenment rationalist who has outlasted his time, and who continues to putter in his private laboratory, ignoring the world that has overtaken him, and performing his pointless scientific experiments with great clarity of mind and sturdy cheerfulness.

Helena's father, Ferdynand Chaber is a small man, thinned out in the way of old people; but at age eighty-four, he has retained full agility of movement and robustness of speech. He's proud of his age and his vigor. "I lead a rational lifestyle," he tells me happily, and with a marked touch of didacticism. "I eat healthily; I have done exercises every day of my life, half an hour in the morning and half an hour in the evening; I work on my garden plot; I never watch television, because it's chewing gum for the mind. I lend myself to others. To stay healthy, you need to have thought, and you need to have action. Also, I should add that I have very optimistic temperament."

When he gets excited, Chaber's voice rises to great oratorical decibels, and he punctuates his sentences with rhythmical gestures. He seems, sometimes, to be speaking to the masses, or to an invisible audience he needs to rouse, as much as to a person sitting next to him at a table over cookies and tea.

But then, Chaber's eyes are still—always—on the Cause and some entity like Mankind, as much as on the cookies and the present. We've hardly begun talking when his voice gains rhetorical force, and his finger begins to tap out each phrase on the table, as he peers into the still messianic future. "Right now, we're living through a turning point in the long revolution. America has won the Cold War—but the war before us is harder—a war against cholera, the destruction of jungles in the Amazon, hunger, and famine. I don't want to exaggerate, but this is the last hour, and we need the Communist Party to help shape the new consciousness. I would like to live till the year 2000, when Communism will regain its historical mission."

The fate of the party has always given Chaber's life its shaping narrative, and its purpose. His story has all the elements of a panoramic Communist saga from which Soviet film epics used to be made: conspiratorial meetings and fiery illegal speeches, prison sentences and close escapes, a tour of duty in the Soviet Union during the war, a rise in the party ranks, and eventual expulsion. Like many old activists, he has a formidable, a passionate historical memory. He can still recall, with intense partisan excitement, the factional fights and ideological arguments of fifty years ago.

Helena's father became a Communist the way many young people did in the prewar period—because he was scandalized by the poverty he saw in villages where he spent vacations with his well-off parents, and because, in the roiling, industrializing, impoverished Poland, he thought that Communism provided an answer to these and other social ills. He joined the then-illegal party in 1920, and within a year, he was writing illegal leaflets—just as, forty years later, his daughter would write leaflets against the regime in which he had come to play an important part. He was promptly arrested, and received a four-year sentence, the first of six he would serve in his lifetime.

Helena suspects that during his career, her father went on to do "monstrous" things; and she has spent much of her life fighting the doctrine to which he remained faithful. And yet there is a continuity of posture, and partly of fate, between them. Ferdynand Chaber thinks he got ejected from his highly positioned party job because of his children's subversive activities. In the late 1960s, both Helena and her brother participated in student protests led by a reformist Communist youth organization called The Commandos. The group was a target of particular party ire, as family dissenters usually are, and Chaber was asked by his superiors whether he would criticize The Commandos publicly. "Criticism" was a highly charged word in those days. Good Communists were supposed to engage in "self-criticism," and were promptly punished for it; they were required to "criticize" others on command; the refusal to "criticize" could be deadly. Chaber refused, and defended his children to his comrades; he said that's how he brought them up, and he was proud of them and their ideological spirit. "Internally," he says—for internal reactions are for him clearly a separate and a secondary reality—"I was happy that my children lived for a cause."

Living for a cause: that certainly has been as true of the important dissidents as it was of the early, believing Communists. The content of the cause has been quite different; while the Communists hardened their convictions into dogma, the children became principled moderates, skeptical of all militant ideology. I asked Adam Michnik once what he thought had really gone wrong with Communism. "I'll tell you one thing I learned from it," he answered. "I'll never try to make anyone happy by force."

Yet both generations have been involved in the same drama: they've been locked in an agon whose nature they both recognize. This is the drama that has now come to an end. But perhaps, just as parents often pass on to their offspring not what they are but how they ideally imagine themselves, so the early Communists may have passed on a sort of social ego-ideal of a political morality and social engagement—an ideal that ironically carried the seeds of its own reaction, and their eventual defeat. But that ideal, and that drama, may also be one clue to that firmness of personality, that straight-backed, strong scaffolding of character that I sense in so many people here; whether that will survive the more diffuse and complex circumstances of the new era is as yet unknown.

One afternoon, I make a visit to a fortune-teller. This is not anything I would do in my ordinary life, but I tell myself I'm going to see her out of socially redeeming interest. All kinds of people go to fortune-tellers in Poland, and to spiritualists and alternative healers. There's been a massive rise in this kind of thing lately, perhaps because other explanations are failing so massively.

This one lives on the Avenue of the People's Army, and she's a perfect crone, bent and toothless and swathed in kerchiefs and sweaters. She takes out a stubby pencil, an oily piece of paper, and an ancient deck of cards. "You'll come into a lot of money, lady," she intones, "but first you have to wait out this goddamn shock reform." A politically informed soothsayer! "Your heart, it's all right," she assures me, "but it never hurts to get an EKG." I haven't given her any clues as to who I am, and when I inform her, toward the end, that I am an emigrant, she throws me a sharp, furious look. I've cheated! In retaliation, she charges me four times her usual fee—though by international standards, she's still a bargain.

Walking into the Marriott Hotel is a jolt; instantly, one is in San Francisco, or Connecticut, or the Midwest. The marbleized floors and mirrored surfaces, the long leather couches and the careful flower arrangements, all emanate a kind of carefully modulated, luxurious neutrality that assures one nothing bad can happen here; nothing much can *happen*. The hotel was built just a few years ago, and it's become the premier elegant place in a town in which such places may still be counted on the fingers of one hand.

I'm meeting an American journalist for a drink. The bar is filled with foreigners, and Poles returning for their post-Communist visits, and high-class prostitutes, and the new persons of money. A vodka—a Polish vodka, for heaven's sake!—costs ten real American dollars. In the dusky lobbies, men in tacky suits bend over low tables, talking joint ventures. Others just wait for something like a joint venture to appear, and there's a phrase for them already—"the Marriott sitters."

The journalist is relieved to be at the Marriott, which to him is about the only bearable spot in Warsaw; when he's here, his movements take on the confidence of someone who's at home. He's come with a friend from California, who has a theory that the reason the Poles aren't smarter is because they have an unhealthy diet. It doesn't seem to bother her that she has hardly talked to anybody Polish.

I've been relieved to be here myself on occasion, to relax from shabby, spiky Warsaw, to sink into the comforting vapidity of the carpeted restaurant, into the comforting *comfort*. This evening, however, the place seems slightly monstrous, stifling; a slap in the face of the city outside. A *chanteuse* sings an international medley, including several Yiddish melodies; they seem to be very fashionable this summer. Overdressed Poles come in, looking as if they want somebody to notice them, and a group of underdressed Israelis. More American journalists join us, and gripe about what an impossible, dreary place Poland is. I feel surprisingly defensive, surprisingly implicated.

The break in Solidarity comes not exactly with a bang or a whimper but with a resounding crack. By chance, I learn of it practically as it happens, when I visit *Gazeta Wyborcza* again and look in on Adam Michnik.

Michnik is a shortish, surprisingly mild-faced man, whose

hair is as mussed as his shirt and whose grayish-blue eyes are perpetually lit up by alertness and irony. His famous charm, which
seems to me to be made up of partly of a sort of elegant playfulness, partly of a talent for directness, for saying unguardedly the
simple, true thing. This is perhaps also one source of the enormous moral authority he has exercised—albeit in a charmingly
casual manner. The stories about him are by now part of Polish
political folklore. When he was about fourteen years old, Adam
founded something called The Club for the Quest of Contradictions, which, high school affair though it was, became one of the
seeds of Poland's later, mature opposition. This group, with its
discussions about democracy and Marxism and Polish history
and ideology, was such a thorn in the regime's side that the
then-premier of Poland paid the teenage Adam the enormous
compliment of singling him out for a reprimand.

From then on, Michnik, whose first ambition was to be a historian, proceeded on a career of activism, imprisonments, and
writing—the last of which owed much to the time provided by
his stints in jail. Many of his exploits and utterances have become legendary. There is a much-repeated anecdote about how
Michnik, finding himself accidentally in the midst of a violent
crowd, got up on an improvised podium, and—despite the dis-
advantage of a marked stutter—managed to quiet the rioters and
stop them from attacking the policemen in their midst. He did
this, even though there was no love lost between the police and
himself; but Adam profoundly abhors violence and vengefulness.
He has written about how, when he was in prison during the
martial law period, he was given the offer of "a Christmas on the
Côte d'Azur" from the government, which preferred to be rid of
him rather than have the embarrassment of his presence. He answered in a series of biting epigrams whose stylishness to me has
the sound of true grace under pressure. He wrote: (1) "To admit
one's disregard for the law so openly one would have to be a
fool." (2) "To offer to a man who has been held in prison for
two years the Côte d'Azur, in exchange for his moral suicide, one
would have to be a swine." (3) "To believe that I could accept

such a proposal is to imagine that everyone is a police collaborator."

During the early Solidarity days, Michnik was one of Wałęsa's main advisors, and the two became great personal friends. It was a friendship with a high symbolic content—for it was a particularly attractive, distilled expression of that alliance between intellectuals and workers that made Solidarity such a unique phenomenon in its fighting days. There are many images of Michnik and Wałęsa literally putting their heads together and whispering in urgent consultation, while the president, or prime minister, or another personage representing power waits for their statement.

One could not have asked for a better pair to personify the larger collaboration: both very energetic, funny, and very smart. Smart and charming in different ways, which was part of the romance. Wałęsa claims to be entirely unlettered, speaks a salty, peasant-inflected Polish, is publicly devout, and has shown brilliant, unerring instincts for handling heated situations, crises, and crowds. Michnik's manners have a touch of the old Polish formality; he's the complete intellectual, with a tutored sense of history and the big picture, and is said to have been the strategic brain behind Wałęsa's tactics.

There was, of course, great romance to Wałęsa's and Michnik's friendship; but now, as is so often true in romantic relationships, the differences that brought them together are breaking them up. This afternoon, Michnik has received a letter from Wałęsa asking him—or rather, ordering him—either to resign from his job as the editor of *Gazeta* or to remove the Solidarity logo from the newspaper's masthead. Michnik quickly fills me in on the background of this startling gesture. The fracture line that led to this outburst has been increasingly pronounced during the last few months. Partly, the split is personal. *Gazeta* has published articles critical of Wałęsa; there was a survey of public opinion that included some unfavorable remarks about his manners and his ignorance of French, to which Wałęsa took particular exception. These were "the intellectuals" casting aspersions on a man of the people; and Wałęsa's vanity is known to be easily wounded.

Still, ordering Michnik to resign is an extraordinarily high-handed act, and one that can only spring from Wałęsa's assumption that he is Solidarity's embodiment and imperial head. "Solidarity, c'est moi," is essentially his letter's message, and the irony of that has too many potential consequences in Polish life to be merely amusing.

I must confess that I don't want to lose my notion of Wałęsa as a sort of genius of a place and a people, risen to fight not for himself but for all of Poland. I still have fresh images in my mind of him goading his opponents brilliantly, finding just the right repartee, the right stance, in the midst of the most confusing melees, speaking as if inspired by the collective fury and intelligence of all those fellow workers, and fighting for them—what else did he have to fight for? In leadership, Wałęsa never seemed egotistical. But perhaps, just as some people are corrupted by power so others can be corrupted by powerlessness. During this transitional year, Wałęsa has had no way to fight, or to act. In the division of power over which he presided during the Round Table talks, he neglected to give any role to himself; and for the last few months he's been living a private life, and clearly fuming all the way. For the first time in his career, this man, who has never lost his political balance, has made awkward gestures, as if not quite able to square the enormous importance he actually has in Polish life with the ineffectuality to which he's consigned himself.

Michnik shows me the letter he has drafted in response to Wałęsa. It's written in a tone of dignified informality, as if he were trying to recall Wałęsa to the spirit of their friendship, while stating with a sort of regretful firmness that he, Michnik, has no intention—even no right—to fulfill either of Wałęsa's requests. *Gazeta* is a cooperative, he reminds Wałęsa; the editor is appointed by his colleagues and important decisions about logos are made collectively, too.

"Is it all right, what do you think?" Michnik asks me, with a touch of writerly gratification at having penned a forceful document. But he seems quite deeply saddened by this turn of events, and I feel the gravity of it as well; this quarrel, after all, involves much more than an argument between old buddies. The rift is larger than that, and has been growing in the last few months. There's been a widening split between "Gdańsk" and "Warsaw," between the populist part of Solidarity and the intelligentsia. There are beginnings of mutual reproaches, and of polarized character casting: in this new scenario, the Gdańsk people are presented as nationalists, with tendencies to potential demagoguery, mixing Church and state, and insufficient diplomatic savvy. The intellectuals are castigated for the usual things for which intellectuals get castigated: their superiority complex, being out of touch with the people, and—what else?—being soft on the Communists.

From the observer's point of view, it seems fairly clear that there's a sort of structural logic, a political fatedness, about these developments. Now that its common enemy has been, to all intents and purposes, defeated, Solidarity, with an almost mathematical predictability, is splintering, as if no longer held in place by a great magnetic field. Without that unifying force, people turn out to have different opinions, temperaments, wills—the usual symptoms of human nature.

But inevitable or not, I can understand why the breakup of a friendship, which is also the breakup of Solidarity, would be exceedingly painful for Michnik. "Wałęsa is the godfather of my child, you know," he says, and looks, again, genuinely sad. The period of history that brought them so close also brought out the best in many others: a capacity for camaraderie, courage, and a mature criticism of power. But that terrible, heroic chapter is over. What comes next is multiple interests and the unavoidable conflicts between them: competition, election campaigns, sloganeering, and struggles for power—the prose of democracy; prose of life.

A few months later, I see Wałęsa in person, at a meeting of television employees. In the intervening summer, he has announced he will run for the presidency, and his appearance at the television station is, in effect, one of the first salvos in his campaign. The room is packed to the rafters and hot with anticipation. When Wałęsa comes out, he immediately announces that he has a cold and a sore throat and has to leave for another engagement in an hour. He looks pale and tired and pudgy; and his speech, when he isn't addressing the issues, is an odd mix of defensiveness and vanity. And charisma—the all-important X-factor. It's in the energy and the horse sense and perhaps even in the vanity itself; it's also in the way he plays with the audience, once the back and forth begins. That's when he's at his most brilliant, quick, sure-footed, and salty; this is clearly what he loves. He's impulsive; he takes risks. He alludes to his Nobel Peace Prize much too often, but then makes self-mocking remarks; he teases people sharply, makes colloquial jokes. This is not yet the cautious politician. Among other things, he accuses the new team of treating him too harshly. The new head of television explains that they're simply playing by the rules of nonpartisan journalism; they can't single out Wałęsa as their fair-haired boy. But I can see how, in the Polish context, the notion of impartiality might be hard to swallow. There *is* something unnatural about the idea that the withdrawal of personal passion and opinion and preference is a value in itself—and after the ardent fights and the high-minded partisanship of the last few decades, it'll take some getting used to.

In the meantime, there's still lots of passion and engagement in this room. At the end of the hour, Wałęsa's assistant says it's time to go, but Wałęsa brushes him off, saying he'll go on. He loves this; he's in the action again. He talks about what kind of a president he'll be—"a president with an axe," cleaning out the previous *nomenklatura.* This is meant to be a contrast to the gentle Mazowiecki. It's highly probable that Wałęsa will be running against Mazowiecki, the man whom he in effect designated as the prime minister less than a year ago. The new battle is joined; the next stage begun.

T W O
← ← ← ←

P O L A N D   I I

It's almost exactly a year since my first visit when I land in Warsaw's tiny airport again. It's May again, but the city looks different to me this time. I catch the tune of its muted charm—its extensive parks, its no-nonsense ordinariness, its quiet side streets, where one can hear the clicking of a lone walker's heels. I've come with less apocalyptic expectations; but also, since then, I've traveled through Eastern Europe and, my mental antennae have become accustomed to a different urban esthetic, a lower level of stimulation and of visual noise. I have remembered what I used to know from growing up in this part of the world—how little such external stimuli correspond to the real interest of the human scene, how much drama and variety and pleasure can take place on this less garish stage.

But the stage itself has visibly changed as well. New World Street, running through the city's center, is lined with boutiques, some of them quite elegant and quite expensive. The Toyota salon that opened a few months ago can't keep up with the demand for its $10,000 product. Somebody mentions a new club for wealthy women. In a many-chambered, shiny Greek restaurant, there's a plaque downstairs saying FOR MEMBERS ONLY. Nobody takes it seriously, but such an exclusionary sign of privilege would have been unthinkable a little while ago. There are a Japanese and a Middle Eastern restaurant as well. In every restaurant the waiters have become more polite. They use softening diminutives for everything—"Would madam like a little cup of coffee or a little glass of vodka?"—and their manners have become so feudally formal that I sometimes wish (such is the incurable perverseness of human nature) for their old, unsubdued orneriness.

Or course, this is the surface, though it's not meaningless that the surface has become a bit more glossy. Glossy and tacky at the same time. There's a Klondike sleaziness aspect to the new Eastern Europe, and the unregulated opportunism of a Wild East. Right next to the Palace of Culture there has sprung up an enormous bazaar of mind-boggling messiness. Ramshackle, plastic-covered stands spill with strawberries, cream, cigarettes, answering machines, children's clothing, and computer parts. The woebegone trading posts of last year have burgeoned into this anarchic energy.

As for the Palace of Culture itself—that reviled and mocked symbol of Soviet vulgarity and power—I think I detect in its wedding-cake structure, and the campy stern lions seated on pediments in the plaza, touches of postmodernist playfulness. What was ever so wrong with it, except its significance?

The Communist Party headquarters has been converted into a stock market. *Dances with Wolves* is the big cinematic hit of the season. There's not a single Polish film playing in the movie houses. Not one.

In the center of the city, several money-changing booths have put new signs in the windows that say WEAPONS. I stare with incredulity. Actually, the authentic-looking revolvers displayed under glass-topped counters inside are Mace guns; but they're a symptom of something suddenly in the forefront of many conversations: crime. Stories of robberies and muggings and ingenious embezzlements have supplanted accounts of erotic liaisons for primal interest.

Unemployment statistics are now recorded regularly; on the streets, I pass a few familiar figures of contemporary woe: people sitting on sidewalks in poses of desolation, with signs that say they're homeless, or that they have AIDS.

One afternoon, as I sip a cup of coffee in the foyer of the Europejski hotel, a young man, strikingly handsome and dressed in a slick silk jacket, approaches me with an obvious con. "I was robbed and my daughter is very ill and hungry, won't you give me some money, I'm not talking about big sums," he demands in a peremptory tone, while his eyes let me know brazenly that he's lying. I shake my head severely. But when this unconvincing beggar approaches a group of Poles sitting at a nearby table, they engage him in a conversation. "Show me your veins," says one of them, and the guy, with deliberate slowness, rolls up his sleeves. "It's obvious you want the money for drugs," the interlocutor concludes. "No," the guy says, "I want it for my daughter." "Then what do you prick yourself for?" the man confronts him. "You want to die, don't you?" "That's just it, you want to destroy yourself," someone else throws in angrily. Nevertheless, they give him some money, and as he walks away, they launch an animated discussion about whether anyone can help such a person, or whether he can only help himself. The personal engagement of this exchange would be unlikely in New York, but the rest of the man's behavior seems imported from other contemporary capitals. Is it that in our small world even the symptoms of pathology are imitative, even cons dispersed through international television networks?

One evening I go to a party in a villa on the outskirts of Warsaw. It's given by one of Warsaw's nouveaux riches, who has made his money importing computer parts from Thailand. The setting is a charmingly overgrown garden, which has been decorated, for reasons indecipherable to me, with American Indian motifs. There are photographs of totems, and a papier-mâché imitation of one. Little light bulbs have been strung up from tree to tree. Inside the house—"the manor," as the host likes to call it—there are spacious rooms, all the modern appliances, and a very respectable collection of Polish Impressionist and Romantic paintings. The music is slanted heavily toward Little Richard, and beautiful young people dance to it with enormous energy and almost balletically articulated movements; no languid cool for them yet. Two gay men have come dressed in dandyish white outfits and straw fedora hats.

The host, who is a mathematician as well as an entrepreneur, tells me how the illicit computer trade grew in Poland. About ten years ago, he started going to Southeast Asia to bring back computer parts, which he and his colleagues needed for their work. From parts he progressed to whole computers; from just one or two, to several dozen per trip. Many of his countrymen were doing the same. He remembers one woman he met on the plane (the whole *sub rosa,* private trade was possible because of very cheap charter flights from Poland to the Far East) who asked him what a mainframe was. A year later, when he went back to Thailand, she had a shop set up and was doing a brisk business in computers. There were whole hotels for Poles in the Philippines, whole clothing markets run by them. My host isn't in the least self-conscious about this past, nor does he find it incongruous with his current, high-class respectability. He's still teaching mathematics at the university, but he thinks that the commercial instinct is a healthy thing—and that, in fact, the illicit computer commerce helped bring down Communism by creating an alternative, and uncontrollable, business infrastructure. From growing up here, I know that most Poles have always done a little business on the side—undoubtedly, that's partly why they are taking to the initiatives of basic capitalism like fish to water.

In another group, a woman artist wants to know how I "made it" in America. Did I come from a rich and influential family? No, I say, hardly. Then, she asks, her eyes opening wide with curiosity, did I have to climb? Rung by rung, I tell her, but I'm not sure she understands that I'm teasing her. People who are capable of most refined subtlety in other areas of life still have a sort of raw eagerness about wealth, careers, ambition; they're not yet embarrassed by their hungry desires.

I get tired earlier than the others, who undoubtedly are going to go at it till the dawn dampens the grass; I'm still jet-lagged. How they do go at it, though, in every way, I think. This Polish *dolce vita,* or "ostentation," as it's called here, is not yet decadent; it's too full of energy and aspiration for that, though I can't help but juxtapose it with those other sights on the street. Well, I can't put it all together; I'm not sure it can be done, not as a mathematical equation. I remember what a historian friend once said: history is a process of double-ledger accounting, with each gain balanced by a loss; and this is to some extent true even in post-Communist Eastern Europe. My host summons his chauffeur for me, and I'm driven home in comfort through the still-quiet Warsaw night.

Quickly, I get reinitiated into the group around *Gazeta Wyborcza,* and Helena invites me to a dinner party. These comings and goings are becoming easier, in both directions. Helena was in New York recently; the host of the evening has come back to live in Poland after two decades abroad; someone else just flew in from Paris for a few days. The barriers are rapidly coming down, and I register a small pang of regret even for this—for the excitement and poignant specialness that used to accompany these reunions when they were rare and dramatic. Not rational, I know, but there it is, together with the more proper pleasure at the new state of affairs.

But the informal, spontaneous vivacity of such encounters hasn't faded away. The apartment is tiny, untidy and charming, the chairs oddly assorted. The little group gathered around the table is part of the new elite. They are still young, they have excellent dissident credentials and they are all intellectual professionals. A year ago, they were part of the united Solidarity front. Now—the wheel of fortune turns fast in these first days— they're part of the new opposition. Since I was here last year, the rifts that began with Wałęsa's letter to Michnik have deepened. In the interval, there were the presidential elections, and now Wałęsa is president, and any number of parties opposed to him have begun forming. The group in this room is firmly on the anti-Wałęsa side of the fence. They paint him as a bit of an ogre, with a giant ego and dictatorial leanings. It's he who is likely to betray the fledgling democracy, they think, not they, the putative elitists.

These dark forebodings, however, don't seem to have dampened anyone's high spirits. Everyone teases each other mercilessly and affectionately, and everyone smokes ferociously. Helena declares that she's tired and starved and energetically upbraids the host for the lateness of dinner. A senator from a district near Warsaw, who with his regular features, blond hair, and forthright blue eyes looks like a poster advertisement for the ideal new Polish politician, launches into a spirited account of a recent battle in his district. The local garment factory, which has been one of the major employers in the area, had to let go about a thousand people. A German firm wanted to open a factory of its own, which would employ these one thousand people and more. These obvious benefits notwithstanding, the citizens of the district said, in the senator's somewhat mocking paraphrase, "Never, we're not going to let the German lord it over us." The senator, who takes the approved liberal position on foreign ownership—that there's nothing wrong with it—had to use all his powers of persuasion to get the locals' approval for this potentially very profitable employer.

The German firm has been understandably grateful to the senator for his efforts on their behalf, and the senator casually wonders whether he should ask them for the $2,500 he needs to support his campaign. "Are you kidding? They'll laugh at you! Ask for $250,000 minimum!" says someone who's been in the West more often, and who knows that over there they respect people who think big. Only at the mention of the bigger sum does it occur to someone else that it might not be politically correct to solicit a contribution from such an obviously interested party. How is it done in America? someone inquires. Probably very discreetly, I answer, giving in to a momentary jadedness. But there's no reason, anyway, why the people in this room should automatically follow American rules. At this stage, the rules have to be invented, from the ground up.

After dinner, the conversation veers to other matters. A news bulletin about a new food store where you can get such rarities as Camembert is followed by a discussion of recipes, enthusiastically joined by the men at the table. The senator remembers a moment of youthful erotic awakening. "Keep your tone!" his wife warns, but he recounts his anecdote about his first awareness of attraction, to an older woman, quite lyrically. Then some reminiscences about old friends. "Did he sit [in prison] in '68?" somebody asks about X. "Yes, just a few weeks, remember, but he had that rough interrogation." The underground was, for the people in this room, their formative adventure, their college and graduate school, and that's how their biographies will always be parsed. But the adventure is in the past now, on the other side of the historical divide. From my occasional visits, I remember the all-night convocations that used to go on here when there was plenty of time and nothing much to do except discuss, discuss, discuss. "Compatriots' nocturnal conversations," people used to call these Polish chautauquas. This gathering is so close to them—and yet, of course, everything has changed. But I keep being surprised at the lack of surprise in this room; at how much people take this enormous tidal shift in stride, as if it were the most natural thing in the world, rather than the most amazing; at how quickly they're getting on with their new conditions, new business. Perhaps living in a state of ongoing astonishment is impossible; perhaps the amazement can only be registered later, from a distance, after the necessary groundwork of change is done.

▌ decide to go to the Gdańsk shipyard in the spirit of pilgrimage; it is, after all, the birthplace of Solidarity, and therefore, in a sense, of the new.

It's a perfectly gray day when I arrive in Gdańsk and find my way from the airport to the local Solidarity headquarters. A building like so many others in Poland: dank, dismal corridors; an indefinable smell of damp. In the office where I wait, a buxom, energetic woman entertains all manner of questions and complaints with great good humor. "You know how it is, democracy-bureaucracy," she tells one man rhymingly when he gripes about baffling new regulations. She's really after retirement age, she tells me in her strongly marked regional accent, but she had worked in the shipyard more than thirty years and was an early Solidarity activist, "and so my chums arranged something for me, a part-time job, so I can be with them."

My appointed guide through the shipyard is Edward Szwajkiewicz, a compact man with a short, pointed beard, a leather jacket, and without the shadow of a smile or social pleasantry in his face. Partly, the unglossed earnestness seems to be a local trait, which I notice in others as well, the pleasing frankness of the provincial personality that hasn't acquired the graces or the affectations of the capital. But Szwajkiewicz is the leader of the regional Solidarity union, and his initial reserve, I later realize, also comes from a well-cultivated suspicion. "There are some people to whom I can never talk openly," he tells me à propos of his Communist coworkers, "and I know it within two minutes. Just as I knew within two minutes whether I could talk to you."

Szwajkiewicz takes me to a conference hall where the first accord between Solidarity and the Communist government was signed. It's an enormous, dull room, redolent of soc-realist pomposity and endless lengths of tables and green-backed chairs, but as I stand in it, I feel a certain *frisson* of history nevertheless. I remember images of meetings that took place here, of tired, heated workers shouting defiant, impudent things at suddenly defensive government officials, and I am moved to be in this undistinguished space as one is moved by certain landmarks of human achievement.

Still, one doesn't walk through the shipyard these days in a spirit of triumph. If this is the point of origin, it's also the site of decline, the place where Solidarity may yet be defeated through its very victory. Szwajkiewicz tells me that its economic situation is dire, and that the rescue of foreign investment has failed to materialize. "Most of the foreigners who come here, they think they're on a safari," he tells me. "We're interesting, but we're exotic. They don't take our concerns seriously. They don't offer to do business with us."

The space covered by the shipyard is enormous, but it emanates the special futility of dilapidated industrial sites, of construction that was always formlessly functional, and that is no longer filled with the bursting energy of activity. We walk among rundown buildings and over rickety bridges and under enormous looming cranes. Economically, Szwajkiewicz explains, the shipyard is a casualty of the very changes it fought so hard to bring about. Until two years ago, 20,000 people worked here; now there are 8,500. In one of the docks, a completed ship stands by uselessly, a victim of a double bind. On the one hand, the shipyard is no longer fully subsidized, and, in a proper capitalist manner, has had to borrow money at interest to pay for the construction of the stranded behemoth; on the other hand, the company that ordered the ship in the first place cannot afford to pay for it, and there's no way to force it to do so. Like so much of the Polish economy, the shipyard is caught between two systems—"rotting Communism and raw capitalism," as people here say; and moreover, it's struggling with the legacy of unreal Socialist economics, which allowed it to become this rundown and uncompetitive in the first place.

The enormous metallurgy workshop is one of the world's satanic mills; but Szwajkiewicz leads me through its infernal noise and the poisonous, chemical smells quite casually. After even a quick walk through it, the smaller and quieter electricity shop is a relief. The few men who are working there wear dark blue overalls, and they look like an advertisement for the noble worker: they all have intelligent faces and blue eyes whose clear, direct gaze suggests some form of honesty, or at least resoluteness.

We stand about, among the pell-mell of machinery parts, while they talk—which they do readily, and with a sort of sharp, colloquial eloquence. Has anything changed for the better? I ask. Ah, things could be better, they say, if it weren't for Them. Yes, still the same Them, the middle-level *nomenklatura,* who, by and large, have remained in the very same positions they occupied before.

"And They like the old rules," one man says. "It's these guys who stop this place from getting anywhere."

I've heard about this repeatedly now: the highest level of Communist management has been relatively easy to unseat; the middle level—that mainstay and passive layer of any bureaucracy—remains tenaciously entrenched, a human infrastructure as difficult to remove as the physical infrastructure of outmoded industrial plants and housing projects.

"We have such a one here," an older man says. "All the time he informed on us, and all the time he kept saying he wanted everything for the best. Can you beat it? When the man who persecuted you works next to you—well, it makes you furious."

"If he has a conscience, he feels awful now," the youngest of the three men suggests.

"What sort of conscience?" another one responds. "All of them are starting joint ventures with the stuff they stole from here, right out from under our noses. And there's nothing to do to them because now we have new laws. Democracy. Just in time to let them off the hook."

"Hey, you want to talk to him yourself?" another man asks, clearly delighted at the possibility of taking even a small revenge. "You could ask him a few questions right in front of us."

But somewhat to my relief—I'm not good at conducting hostile interrogations—the man doesn't appear.

It's only before I leave that the youngest man—he has worked here seven years—declares, almost defiantly, that something *is* better now. "We have the consciousness now that we're working for ourselves. When we take a lunch break, we come back after only forty-five minutes, and that's enough. Because now one wants to work."

The others look at him as at a young pup who hasn't learned the hard lessons of life yet. I understand their accumulated frustrations more fully when I talk to Marian, a metallurgist who has spent close to forty years in the shipyard. He is a small, lithe man with delicate, chiseled features, the supple movements of a much younger person and a great courtesy of manner. I am touched by this grave refinement in a man who has worked in such rough conditions. And his story, as it unfolds, is rough indeed, and so full of typical events that it could serve as a cameo of the true, rough history of the working class in a workers' state. In 1970, when the army was turned onto the striking workers of Gdánsk, Marian was mauled by a tank rolling through the city's streets; one of his kidneys was destroyed, and for months he urinated blood. Then, in 1980, he participated in the first round of Solidarity strikes and continued to do clandestine work even after martial law was imposed; as a result, in 1982, he was interned on the slimmest of pretexts.

"Speaking generally, this is how it was," he says in his soft, restrained voice. "In the internment camp, I got so tough that I'm not afraid of anything anymore, except betraying Jesus Christ. If somebody put a revolver to my ear and said, Talk, give us some names, or we'll shoot, I'd say, Go ahead, shoot." This is a man who had plenty of opportunities to measure his courage and his powers of resistance; in the camp, where he stayed for close to a year, inmates were badly beaten; when Marian came out, he was so sick that, for the first time in his life, he was given time off from work.

In 1988, there was a new round of strikes, and Marian was on the barricades again. "This was the hardest one of all," he says, because this was a period when people had lost hope and had become afraid; only eight hundred shipyard workers participated this time. "On one side, there was the secret police," Marian remembers, "and inside, all these informers among us. That's why we're so bitter about them now."

As I listen to his story, I wonder at his seemingly endless sources of resilience and hope; I wonder why he kept doing what he did, in the face of such odds.

He smiles a little at my question. "I'll tell you why," he says simply. "The injustice was so terrible, that's all. We were exploited and exploited and exploited. I have seven children; sometimes I worked sixteen hours a day just to feed them. It wasn't right. We just knew it wasn't right.

"And it's still not over," he continues just as simply. "Not over. They're still among us, still holding the shipyard back, and now we need to fight them by other methods. Legally. But I'm of good thought. We'll do it somehow—so at least my children's children will have a better life. Speaking generally, that's how it is."

Before we part, Szwajkiewicz wants to take a picture of Marian and me; and Marian stands very upright for it, almost at attention, the way peasants or generals used to pose for photographs; then he kisses my hand good-bye and goes off at a half-run back to his shop. I'm sorry to see him go; I'm touched by something in him, perhaps by the quiet dignity of his personality; perhaps by the thought of how much dignity he has retrieved from his bleak conditions.

After we leave the shipyard, Szwajkiewicz, who has finally relaxed into quiet friendliness, offers to show me another symbolic spot—the ancient church of St. Brigid's, where many Solidarity strategy sessions took place in the most secretive of times. "It's not that everyone was so religious, necessarily," he tells me. "Some of us weren't at all. But we knew that the informers wouldn't come here. It really was a sanctuary."

Gdańsk (or Danzig), like so many other history-haunted Eastern European cities, has two radically different personalities, ruptured from each other by the war. World War II began when Hitler issued Poland the ultimatum to return this free port to Germany, and the first shots of the war were fired when Poland refused. The violence that followed was severe.

As a result, the drab, postwar urban character predominates. St. Brigid's, however, is in the Old Town, another feat of accurate reconstruction. The church is one of twin Gothic structures, and it shows marked German, or Hanseatic, influences, for

Gdańsk is one of the cities where German and Polish destinies were inextricably and often horribly entangled. During its thousand-year history, Gdańsk changed hands between the Poles, the Teutonic Knights, and the Prussians so often that its history reads like centuries-long tales of Beirut.

The harmony of architecture ignores clash and conflict, and the interior of St. Brigid's is lovely, with delicate brick lines marking the edges of the crossing arch patterns within the ceiling. Below, however, temporal woe has been allowed, or rather invited, to leave its traces. The priest who officiates over this church must be a man of iron courage. During a period of severe repressions, he erected, in plain sight, memorials to the then most taboo subjects of Polish history. There's a chapel with a sculpture devoted to the memory of Katyń, where thousands of Polish officers were murdered by the Soviets; and there's another chapel honoring the resistance fighters of the National Army, those who later fought the Communists as well.

After the notorious murder in 1984 of Jan Popieluszko, another Solidarity-supporting cleric, the priest of St. Brigid's received a chilling warning, one worthy of the Mafia: his chauffeur was found murdered one morning. But he refused to be intimidated, to soften his sermons, or to cease giving shelter to Solidarity people.

It was this kind of behavior that gave the Church its continuing and enormous authority in Poland; and for all my ambivalence about it, I cannot help but admire the evidence of this priest's sheer nerviness. During the difficult 1988 strike, Marian said in his homely way, the small group of strikers felt bereft of moral support; but "Lech Wałęsa was there, and by then we knew that the Holy Father was with us, and somehow the Communist power buckled."

As we walk through the Old Town, I ask Szwajkiewicz what the Solidarity union, in its now official guise, can do for the shipyard's workers. Not all that much, he admits. Some of the people who have been laid off are in bad trouble, and the wages for those who are working have gone down in real value. But he is very conscious of the limits on his actions. They are discussing various options, he says, but Solidarity has to move very carefully now, because they don't want to weaken Wałęsa's government.

There's no bitterness about Szwajkiewicz, only a sort of level realism. There seems to be no bitterness in Marian, either. But as I consider the injustice—poetic injustice, at least—of their situation, I marvel at their discipline. Solidarity has accomplished this much. But I wonder what promise the new Poland holds for these men.

From Gdańsk, I make a brief sortie to the nearby town of Sopot on a small commuter train, of which the locals are very proud. It's a primitive enough affair, but it functions, it's clean, it runs on time, and it has a clear diagram of various stops, copied from the Paris Métro. In my car, there's a group of German tourists, talking at a normal conversational pitch, which stands out only because everyone else is quiet and they're speaking German. Suddenly, a woman's voice, loud and insulted, fills the car. "You Germans—not so loud!" she commands, in a strangely formal Polish locution. "In your country, you can behave like that, but not here! It's very irritating to the average passenger!" Perhaps this is reflexive revenge for the ill treatment Polish traders have been receiving in Germany; or perhaps an older reflex. Fortunately, the average passenger seems to have a sense of humor, and people roll their eyes discreetly at this outburst. The German tourists pause for a moment, understanding that these remarks are addressed to them, and then resume their conversation without any change of tone.

After this spurt of international tension, Sopot exudes a most pleasing languor. There's a fresh, mild breeze at the train station; young people disembark with knapsacks; my *pensione* is on Chopin Street, in a gently hilly, tree-lined part of town. There I meet Agnieszka Osiecka, a friend who is here to attend a rehearsal of her new play, and she leads me down to the seaside promenade. Agnieszka is a statuesque woman with a serene manner and unfailing conversational resources, who's a genuine cult figure in Poland. Aside from writing for the theater, she is a poet, novelist, and songwriter, whose lyrics have accompanied an entire Polish generation, the way the Beatles did in the West. This, together with her stormy romantic life, has made her the kind of celebrity you would get if you crossed Bob Dylan, say, with Dylan Thomas. As she leads me around Sopot, Agnieszka is full of anecdotes, history, landmarks. She knows Sopot, and many other towns, as well as her own Warsaw neighborhood. Though she would never speak about patriotism, Poland for her is truly a familiar, well-loved home, with favorite corners and crannies, memories and cherished bric-à-brac.

I can see how I might adopt Sopot as a favorite spot myself. It's true that the quirkily designed, pastel villas have been cut up into socialist-size apartments, and that the Baltic waters are polluted from the nearby industry. But the slow, sunny streets still hold some of the lazy charm of those interwar watering holes where the clientele was international, and where burghers and bohemians felt equally at ease. The promenade has an elegant, lengthy sweep, delineated by formal rows of trees with their crowns shaved flat, in the French manner; and the boardwalk juts far out into the hazy sea, emanating, on this late spring day, a warm, mingled smell of old wood and ocean.

For dinner, we stop at the Grand Hotel, which has indeed managed gallantly to hold on to its former grandeur. Its tall French windows give out gleamingly onto the sea; inside, an art-nouveau staircase forms a spiral winding stunningly up through several stories; and the furnishings of the main restaurant come in two shades of green, to match the ocean on a sunny day.

Unfortunately, while the decor is prewar, the service is distinctly post. Sleepy waiters lean against counters, looking way past the few customers who have gathered here off season. While we exercise forbearance, Agnieszka reminisces about the long, leisurely family vacations that used to be a Polish middle-class ritual, and about a famous café near here, where the inspired, the beautiful, and the alcoholic used to gather. Polish artistic society is still small enough to be intensely interconnected, and Agnieszka knows just about everybody in it.

In the evening, we make our way to Gdynia, another coastal city in a "tri-city" area, where Agnieszka's play is being produced. The theater is one of those regional companies with a serious repertory that have long thrived in Poland, and which are facing much tougher times now that the subsidies are vanishing. But despite economic endangerment, the mood is as loose, workaday and friendly as it should be in the theater.

During a pause in the rehearsal, a round of cognac appears for everyone. The set designer entertains us with anecdotes of directors he has known and mishaps he has witnessed. American plays are the trickiest to stage, he tells us, because they often call for such odd props and accessories. He recalls an American director who worked here for a while, and who, in his innocence, chose to stage a Sam Shepard play that called for twelve carefully orchestrated toasters. The director should have known better. First of all, it was downright impossible to get twelve toasters in all of the tri-city area. The director compromised on six. Out of these, two didn't work. Two were stolen. One was smashed to smithereens by a temperamental actor. The play, despite the central importance of a dozen toasters, was produced with one. "Such things act as a spur to invention," our raconteur concludes.

The rehearsal goes very well, although Agnieszka is unhappy about a scene in which she wanted a stageful of actors to move like mechanical robots, and instead "they keep flinging their hips about in this provincial way." After she registers her complaint, we set off with several people to the Polonia restaurant, an establishment that exudes the stodgy, funky, funny atmosphere of the fifties. The waiter swings toward us in his black suit like a character in a comic movie. Vodka and delicious cream herring are served all round. On a raised dance floor, a woman wearing spike heels and a tight, low-backed dress and a man in an overlarge suit move slowly to the sounds of a live band playing

"Never on Sunday." Ah, I remember this, from Poland and from my American adolescence and from the movies; and it puts me in a very good mood, as perhaps the past always does when we have safely outgrown it, and can therefore look at its reappearance with an indulgent smile.

The conversation, like the tide under the pull of the ever-present moon, turns to current economics. The theater has been heavily hit by budget cuts; the actors are worried; they're faced with the unprecedented prospect of being fired in the middle of the season. But the manager, who has come with us, has a few plans waiting in the wings. In the theater's large foyer, he wants to build a bar and a cabaret; after all, Poland has a wonderful cabaret tradition to draw on. The costume department will produce uniforms for a local factory, and the woodcutting department will make stereo tables, which are in great demand. Best of all, an unknown benefactor has appeared from nowhere and has offered to buy a piano for the cabaret. "In America, he would be called an angel," I say, and they agree that that's exactly right, he's a veritable angel.

I am impressed by the manager's determined ingenuity, but Agnieszka declares that she's tired of profit rates and tax percentages, and other paraphernalia of capitalist accounting around which so many conversations suddenly revolve. Instead, she launches into an anecdote about working on a new Polish soap opera. This is not exactly a native art form, and the producer, in his zeal to be positive and cheerful and American, apparently wants to banish all traces of sadness from the series. I point out that this is a misunderstanding of the very essence, the weepy, meretricious heart of the genre; and Agnieszka points out that positive thinking goes right against the Polish grain. But, by virtue of an international misunderstanding, the first utterly upbeat soap opera on record may be produced in post-Communist Poland.

I've brought along a collection of Thomas Mann's stories, and on the train back to Warsaw I decide to reread *Death in Venice*.

I must be led to it by a process of subterranean association. Though Venice was the appropriate symbolic setting for the novella, the meeting of Aschenbach and Tadzio was much more likely to have taken place in Sopot. It is on the white Mediterranean beaches that Mann's duty-bound, severely disciplined, and deliberately sublimated artist encounters the sublime, sensual beauty of a Polish boy and is undone by it. But mundane versions of such encounters, of the curious gazing that is Aschenbach's main activity, must have taken place on Sopot's Baltic beaches every day. They lived so close together, the Poles and the Germans, and yet, to the Germans vacationing on these shores, the Poles to a great extent remained the Other. A despised Other, for the most part; eventually, only a bit less despised than the Jews. But in Mann's story, they're a noble, glowing, infinitely attractive Other; Tadzio's family has great elegance and almost majestic manners. And they have something—some wisdom made up of dignity and ease—that Aschenbach wants.

But of course, in Mann's fiction, and undoubtedly in reality as well, to travel toward Otherness, even if it is most ardently desired, is to risk disintegration; it is to lose the firm certainties of yourself. Not at all coincidentally, Mann's parable could be read as a cautionary tale about the dangers of travel. It is the figure of a traveler, ambiguous, slightly sinister, and evocative of primal jungle imagery, that beckons Aschenbach toward his glorious misadventure. Perhaps I should take warning; except, of course, Mann's Otherness is, in some degree, my notion of home; and in my travels, for all their hardships, I'm pursuing the essence of the familiar—though that too, after long separation, can become oddly elusive.

Back in Warsaw, a friend takes me through Praga, Warsaw's old working-class district, and now one of its poorest parts. And it's very poor. Buildings with crumbling masonry, smashed windows; discolored patches on the façades of buildings where the balconies have fallen off; some of the still attached balconies look as if they're about to crash on our heads right now. It's Sunday, and quiet; but this is a district of nineteenth-century factories, where people still work in Dickensian conditions; of bazaars with the cheapest goods; of pimps, prostitutes, bootleggers, criminals, con men. A police car—with its sign freshly changed from MILI-TIA to POLICE—stops in front of a building, and within moments the police drag a man from the entryway and shove him into the car; a large canister goes into the trunk. A bootlegging arrest, undoubtedly. Corpulent women lean over the parapets to watch the scene; kids run after the car.

Zbyszek is attached to this district because he grew up here, and his parents had a pharmacy, which was confiscated in 1949, and which he still misses. He remembers when this was a neighborhood of Jews and Byelorussians; he remembers a bazaar of his childhood, with its familiar eccentric, who came supposedly to sell birds, but every time someone wanted to buy one from him, he'd let the bird out of the cage, and let it fly away. . . . We come to a courtyard where young boys in short pants are kicking a ball around. I respond to the shabby appeal of this place; I grew up in a neighborhood not unlike it, in Cracow. But Zbyszek says that since Cracow had been part of the Austro-Hungarian Empire, it was never as poor as this part of Poland, which had been under Russian occupation until World War I. The Russian occupations, he says bitingly, were always the worst. Accumulated injuries of history, rankling still.

On a wall of a decaying building, there are faded traces of signs in Russian, left over from old food and liquor shops. A few blocks down, scrawled in ungainly letters, is a still-fresh sign on a small wooden shack that says OUT WITH SHACKS—a bit of self-referential graffiti criticism that cheers me right up.

For a few weeks now, the newspapers have been full of an upcoming vote on a bill to outlaw abortion. A great number of articles are written by priests and other spokesmen of the Church; the Church altogether dominates the debate. Its moral authority is such that it has nearly everyone intimidated into silence or assent. Even my oppositional friends, usually so pesky on almost any issue, seem to be subdued into ambiguous half-statements.

A few days before the vote, I stop at a small demonstration in front of the Sejm building. It consists of a handful of women, dressed with casual chic, some of them carrying placards with slogans protesting the bill and some distributing leaflets. Still, it's startling to see them. This kind of demonstration, legal and directed toward a government to which you feel some loyalty, is very new in Poland, where opposition took place either on a massive scale or in people's apartments. Moreover, several of them identify themselves as members of feminist organizations—and feminism, insofar as it exists here, is a target of reflexive scorn or disapproval. For one thing, like socialism, feminism was coopted and corrupted by its association with official ideology. It will undoubtedly take a while before it recovers from this past and might be understood in a different vein.

I talk to a few of the women afterward over coffee. It turns out that they belong to two groups, and I sense some tension between them. One of the women is the president of the League of Women, which has taken over from the old Communist organization; she explains quickly and perhaps a touch defensively that she's trying to reform it, and attend to the actual problems of working women. The others at the table are free-floating intellectual feminists; one belongs to a group modeled on American consciousness-raising endeavors; some are *au courant* with Western feminist theory.

All of them are worried, of course, that the situation of women in Poland will take a turn for the worse; that the power of the Church will work against them. But it is clear from their conversation that the feminine dilemma here is interestingly different from the American situation. In some ways, they're starting from a rather more advanced point—that is, if we envision history as a progress toward our notions of progress. Or perhaps it's more accurate to say that they're starting from a different point entirely, from a different cultural context.

For one thing, Poland never went through an equivalent of

the American fifties, with the cult of domesticity, and suburban isolation. Under the Communist dispensation, women were expected to work, and they did, in nearly the same proportions as the men. Higher education was more discriminatory by class than gender—discriminatory, that is, against the upper classes—and women entered the professions in relatively large numbers, and reached high levels of authority, if rarely the highest. "In this, Communism really did achieve something," one of the women admits, though with some reluctance.

Of course, that meant that women usually carried the double burdens of work and housework, and the task of running a household in the times of shortages and long queues was truly daunting. But whatever problems they are facing—and the problems are not to be underestimated—the feminists to whom I'm speaking hardly seem to understand the concept of female weakness. They look uncomprehending when I talk about the fifties' stereotypes of passive, ornamental femininity, of the half-childish, doll-like women. "I've met a woman once who tried to style herself as a sort of doll," somebody says, combing the recesses of her mind to come up with an example of this, "but she was hardly passive."

Indeed, in public life and in private, I keep encountering women whose spark and strength and personal authority seem quite formidable. Altogether, in the elusive realm of cultural values, there seems to be less of a division between "male" and "female" virtues here—and female valor, intelligence, and strength of personality are as highly prized as the male versions.

Perhaps that, too, harks back to the political tradition, and all the uprisings, rebellions, and insurrections in which women strove side by side with men as their comrades-in-arms. This, of course, continued on the postwar underground, and in Solidarity. "Well, you know, we've had all these problems we had to deal with together," one of the women says when I inquire about it. "We've always had to struggle, and in some respects, we tried to help each other."

The women here worry that if the power of the Church becomes too great they may suffer a regression. Already, apparently, there have been suggestions—unbelievable though they seem—that women's education should be different from men's. Already there's a pull toward what we would call a "division of roles."

"I don't know what's going to happen now, if lots of women stop working. I can't imagine how a marriage would work in such a setup—he comes home full of his problems and interests, and she's been out shopping? They would live in two different worlds; I don't know what they would have to say to each other." Such "setups," so recently familiar to women in the West, may indeed be on the horizon, as some people make enough money to live on one income, I've talked to a number of younger women who believe that for them the prerogative not to work would be the essence of freedom. Still, I find it revealing that this is a problem that Polish women are just encountering, rather than one from which they are trying to emerge.

During a visit to a publishing house, I mention to Bolek, a friend who is an editor there, that I would like to meet someone who used to work as a censor.

"No problem," Bolek says, though I thought I had presented him with a tricky task. "There's somebody here who used to know such people. He'll arrange something." Within a few minutes, a thick-set man with a stiff briefcase walks into Bolek's office. He works in the commercial department of the publishing house.

"You want to meet an ex-censor?" he asks, after Bolek presents my request. "You need go no further. You have one before you." And he gives a smart bow.

"I'm terribly sorry, I had no idea . . ." Bolek mutters, and I never learn whether he really didn't know or was pretending ignorance to save everyone's face.

It's one of the minor mysteries of life why people so often look as if they were trying to fulfill their professional stereotype. Perhaps our work changes the set of our faces as much as long years of living with another person; but certainly, Michał Malicki could be cast as the ideal type of the *nomenklatura* functionary. He is beefy, has a large paunch, and moves clumsily in his ill-fitting suit; his hair is cropped down practically to a crew cut and his eyes are almost imperceptible behind very thick glasses.

But once he starts talking, over dinner later in the day, my sense of him changes considerably. He's impressively articulate, precise, witty, and logical. He speaks in a fast-paced monotone, and with a sort of sharp dispassion that he applies equally to himself, his career, and just about every sacred cow on the former and the current scene. I've noticed this tone in other Communists as well; to some extent, the training in the "objective" view of human actions must have taken effect. Not once in our lengthy conversation does he make the slightest attempt to gain my sympathy, or offer even the pretense of embarrassment or apology. On the other hand, his attitude toward his work as a censor is one of perfectly conscious irony. In effect, he paints his own portrait as an utterly unrepentant, and utterly skeptical, *apparatchik.*

"Perhaps it's not nice of me to admit this," he begins, his gray eyes showing just a flicker of amusement. "But I treated my work at the firm . . . well, as a game. A circus. It was such a comedy, a cross between Kafka and Mrożek. Of course, a comedy can border on tragedy, but at first the comedy prevailed. Later, the laughter faded on one's lips."

I am instantly amused myself, by the apt literary allusions, and by "the firm"—the same word that British spies use for their secret service. But why did he enter it in the first place? "Well, you know how it is," he says. "So much of life is a matter of happenstance." In college, Malicki majored in geography—not a field that offered many job opportunities. So when he saw a small notice on the college bulletin board advertising a job in the Bureau of Censorship, he applied—"half because I needed a job and half out of curiosity"—and was accepted.

I wonder what kind of training he received for what must have been, after all, a fairly intricate job. What rules were overt, what hidden? "Oh, of course we had codexes enumerating the rules. Generally speaking, we had three areas of prohibition: the military, where secrecy is completely justified, though it was exaggerated; the economic, where information harmful to national interest was forbidden—and this had some unfortunate consequences, for example, when we held back data on industrial pollution; and the cultural, where the criteria were of course more political. But this was the meat-and-potatoes kind of stuff. The real nuances and subtleties you could learn only by watching the older censors."

Among the censors, he distinguishes several kinds. "There were the old convinced Communists, who practiced their work for its own sake; the ones who were in it for a political career; and the cynical Communists. The director, I would say, was a 'declared cynical Communist' "—here, he indicates quotation marks around the phrase with his fingers—"a man of truly Satanic intelligence. His specialty was the history of the Church, and the conversations he had with some of the priests whose manuscripts he handled—well, his erudition was amazing. He could really run rings around the good fathers.

"Then, of course, there were the idiots, the targets of everyone's mockery. There was for example a woman who refused to allow the word 'Germany' in a book about geological formations of forty thousand years ago, because the rules said you had to say East or West Germany. That kind of literalist stupidity."

I ask him what his own attitude toward the subtleties and nuances of the rules tended to be. Again, he answers without hesitation and in the same changelessly understated tone. "From the beginning, I preferred not to censor wherever possible, not to intervene. I also preferred not to refer my decisions to my superiors—first of all, because I liked the feeling of power, and second, because passing the buck upward took too long. But my basic attitude was that I was on the writer's side. Of course, I respected some of them more than others. . . . Sometimes, let me tell you, I was very surprised to see the manuscripts which came in from our most distinguished pens. They could have done with some editing."

If he saw himself as the writers' ally, I pursue, how much could he—on their behalf—get away with? How much leeway did he have for bending the rules?

This time, Malicki's answer surprises me. "You know," he says after a small pause, "it was all a matter of interpretation, and I can interpret anything in the way I want. I can make anything mean one thing and its opposite. Because in literature, you see, anything can mean anything."

Anything can mean anything. The sentence has an incongruously familiar ring. Somehow, from his hermetic office in the firm, Malicki managed to come to a conclusion strikingly similar to the ideas expounded by the most sophisticated literary critics in the West. Nothing means anything, or everything means nothing, they might rephrase it; but it comes to pretty much the same thing. This is a level of critical savvy surprising in a former geography major with no early love of literature. But then the firm was clearly an excellent school in applied literary criticism. The censor's job was to manipulate texts—and manipulation is the quickest way to demystification. There was a point where such real-political games and critical games of multiple interpretation met—though of course, the consequences for the writer were somewhat different. In place of critical ascendancy, the censor had the more concrete superiority of power; and through his practical alterations, he could quickly learn that there was nothing absolute about the meaning of literary artifacts.

From his vantage point, Malicki could even engage in a sort of underinterpretation, and ignore meanings that were clearly intended. The coded, Aesopian language to which writers in Eastern Europe so often resorted "passed its exam," he says, as a method for getting round the censor—himself—though not because the censor didn't know what was going on. "But the point is," Malicki explains, "that you could always say to your boss, 'There's nothing underneath this, there's no subtext. It simply says what it says.' And then maybe both you and your boss could pretend there was nothing there. After all, life under socialism was supposed to be one big stretch of sunny happiness; there was not supposed to be a dark layer to anything. So it was perfectly possible, even advisable, not to notice anything under the overt surface."

Yes, Malicki's literary education was good. And, like any dedicated critic, he began to live in a closer and closer symbiosis with the writer. He liked the writers he was assigned to; he had high ambitions for them; he was disillusioned when they fell short of his standards. So at some point it was natural that he should start edging closer toward the boundary separating him from the other—that is, the writers'—side. His withdrawal from the firm began with an appearance at a students' club, which invited him to participate in a panel on censorship. He asked the firm for permission to accept the invitation and was refused. He decided to go anyway. Did he think he was taking a big risk? "Risk, risk, one exaggerates these risks," he says acerbically. "What could they have done to me? Put me in jail? At most, I could lose my job."

He wasn't, however, at all happy with what happened at the club. "By all means, I understand that our work should have been criticized; undoubtedly it should have. But the criticisms should be based on accurate information. The people there, though—they weren't interested in the truth; they still aren't. They wanted to demonize. Of course, if you demonize the enemy, that gives you a certain importance." He shrugs. "They really wanted to figure me out personally. How could a person do what I did, they wanted to know? I tried, insofar as I could, to be polite, to talk civilly, to smile. The next day, in a student article, my smile was described as cynical. Because, of course, if you're a censor, your smile has to be cynical."

This is the one note of bitterness, of sarcasm, that steals into his speech, though his voice hardly changes register. It was after this peccadillo that work at the firm became uncomfortable for him. For a while, he toyed with the unlikely idea of starting a Solidarity cell right within that organization. But, he says, punctiliously making sure that I don't overestimate him, "This was not a job for me. I'm not of a fighting or a revolutionary temperament." Instead, he decided to take an editorial job at a Communist youth magazine.

After the changes, he took another small step to what is after all the most proximate profession, and started working at a prominent publishing house. He doesn't think it compares all that favorably with his former employer. "The firm had its problems," he says, "but it was more efficient. There's no ethos of work at this place. It's horrible. My colleagues can only carry out strictly defined tasks—and then only after a cup of tea. Everyone is scared to make the slightest decisions. But I guess I shouldn't be surprised. Existence precedes essence, after all, and this is what their existence has taught them."

And I guess I shouldn't be surprised by what he says next. "I keep telling them that they have to be more commercial, that they have to publish what will sell—but this doesn't meet with approval. I'm afraid they're still suffering from the legacy of Communism—they think their function is to publish literature if it's good. And where the money comes from . . . well, they're too elegant to worry about that. One doesn't talk about money in the salons."

I shouldn't be surprised, because Malicki is clearly a man who is accustomed to playing well, no matter what the rules of the game he's involved in. The game is what there is. He has seen through all the beliefs of the former system, including the beliefs of the antisystem; including the belief, shared to a great extent by both sides, in the holiness of literature. With regard to the makers of literature, his critical faculties haven't lost a whit of their sharpness. "These days, there's a certain playing at martyrology," he says. "There's a well-known writer—everyone knows that his big tragedy was that he wasn't interned during martial law. Everyone else was, but for some reason he was passed over. He was practically running around pleading to be interned. Sometimes I'm embarrassed to see how some artists make heroes of themselves, when I know how they came to us and changed what we asked them to change without special fuss. The greatness of these artists shouldn't depend on their being victims."

All right, then, he's seen everything from both sides of the fence, from within, without, the middle and the margin. But what, when all is said and done, does he now think about his role in the past? "One must judge," he responds with his unhesitant dispassion, "but one must judge within the standards and atmosphere of the time. Communism was accused of being dialectical, of claiming that socialist morality was different from other moralities. But unfortunately life is dialectical." Then he adds, "You see, I'm not a doctrinaire person. I'm against reductionism and dogmatism. There are no absolute values, after all."

With that last twist, our conversation comes to an end. We're about to say good-bye when Krzysztof comes in, and greets me. As I usher Malicki out of the restaurant, he looks back at K. with something like increased interest. "Mr. K. probably doesn't remember me," he says, "but I used to work with him. That is, I used to censor him. A wonderful filmmaker. I respect him very much."

"No, I don't remember him," K. says after Malicki leaves. "They were not exactly people with whom one wanted to make personal acquaintance."

At least one didn't until recently. The meeting is mere coincidence, and yet I fancy there's a telling symmetry in it, for in Communist Poland, K. could be thought of as Malicki's perfect antithesis. While Malicki was playing his games of expedient interpretations, K. was making movies on squarely moral themes. They are very dark films, usually; they take into full account the degradations and the lies and the cynicism of socialist reality. But they are also about people's responsibility to each other and the failures thereof, about the power of attachment, and love, and even something like faith. K.'s films are unique; but the emphasis on responsibility—on a morality not of abstract values but of concrete human relations—recurs again and again in the thinking of Polish and Eastern European postwar artists and writers. It comes, perhaps, out of Catholicism, which many intellectuals embraced, if only in reaction to the prevailing ideology. But an ethic of responsibility also constituted a strong antidote—a kind of irrefutable answer—to the amorality of rules and games and systems and the system. Anything can mean anything, except what we do to each other.

This moral turn—the specific Eastern European humanism, which included a very modern horror and irony and complexity within itself—was a riposte to the lies and cynicism; it came out of the lived knowledge of what people can do to each other in the name of ideology and power. The question is what happens when there is less need for a strong answer because the provocation becomes less clear. What happens when the censor is no longer on "the other side," but works in the publishing house, and it's hard to tell whether he's a free-market cynic or just a practical man? In one fundamental sense, this is at the heart of "the changes" in Eastern Europe. Whether or not to publish more commercial pulp in order to keep an enterprise going is an issue on which reasonable people may disagree; and Eastern Europeans are exiting the era of grand moral drama, and entering the era of issues.

It's too early to know what will follow when the Eastern European intelligentsia collides with the realities of competition and the messy ambiguity of "normal" life. In the meantime, I muse somewhat selfishly on what interesting art K. and others might produce—without the hazards or benefits of censorship—out of the transition to a new, and confusing, moral territory.

I spend the better part of one afternoon talking to a woman whose biography I find fascinating. Anna Branicka-Wolska comes from one of the great aristocratic families in Poland, and her story is one of those in which Poland and Eastern Europe specialize—of a life so tested, wrenched, and molded by stormy events that it seems to have the design of an all-too-unlikely, or all-too-stereotypical, historical melodrama. I first met Anna at a meeting of the Landowners' Association—one of the brand-new entities on the Polish landscape that have suddenly arisen as if from the swirling mists or the watery depths of the past. The association was formed just a few months ago and is comprised of aristocrats, squires, and small gentry who used to possess certain minimal acreages of land. It counts in its ranks about seven hundred members, for a year after the demise of Communism, it appears that Poland has a full-blown aristocracy, with its hierarchy of princes and countesses and somewhat lesser personages quite intact.

Of course, it would not be accurate to say that the aristocrats ever disappeared from Poland, though this was not for lack of efforts to destroy them, or at least erase their identity. Poland always had a large aristocratic class, divided into the great families and the *szlachta,* or small-fry nobility, which gained its right to vote very early, and which became gradually known for its anarchic divisiveness. But it's been a long time since Polish aristocrats were the masters of their universe; during the partitions, when Poland was swallowed up by the neighboring empires, they were subjected to domination more than they were dominators of their subjects; the *szlachta* grew impoverished and dispersed. At the same time, while Poland didn't exist on the map, it continued to live in the aristocratic homes and heads, in the mansions and manors, where the physical Polish traditions were preserved, and in people who embodied a certain idea of "Polishness" even when they were forced into exile.

After the war, an aristocratic pedigree became a near guarantee of poverty and persecution—and, therefore, of a kind of nobility. The aristocrats, once again, came to represent a vanquished but, to many people, true Poland; they never had a chance to become figures of farce or of decadence. During my childhood, occasionally I'd hear how someone with a great "name"—and names never lost their class significance in Poland—was coping with admirable bravery in reduced circumstances. I've heard of peasants who never ceased to call their village's newly christened People's Culture Center by the name of the building's former, aristocratic proprietor—the Radziwiłł house, or the Zamojski place. I've heard of farmers recognizing the same Zamojskis or Radziwiłłs as they came back for a nostalgic walk under the family trees, and paying them respectful, secret homage.

Today's meeting of the Landowners Association takes place in the Polytechnic, an impressive nineteenth-century white marble structure, whose central pentagonal courtyard is surrounded by several stories of arched arcades. This is the building where the First Congress of the Polish Communist Party took place; hence, its site is called the Square of Unification. I've heard people, though, refer to it by its old name, the Square of the Savior.

The people gathered in the large meeting hall might be mistaken for a crowd of robust English gentry, or farmers. They look so vigorous and so unglamorous; in a country where overt chic is highly prized, they dress with resolute plainness. Among them, though, there are faces of such delicacy that they might be made of parchment, or etched in fine ink. Mostly, they are older faces, though the younger generation isn't entirely absent. The opening address is delivered by a very old man whose voice is shaky but beautifully inflected with tones of gentleness and courtesy. "We are emerging from the half-dark," he begins. "For the first time in a half-century, we can admit who we are and where we've come from." It is tempting, and easy, to view a meeting of newly uncloseted Polish aristocrats as a sort of comedy; but, as always, I find something moving in the story of suppression and survival encapsulated in the old man's sentences. Before the meeting started, another old man told me—it mattered to him intensely that I know this—that the aristocrats mounted such an effort of resistance during World War II that they sustained the greatest losses of any class or caste of Poland.

It is all these echoes that make me a captivated listener to Anna Branicka-Wolska. We meet at the Europejski Hotel in a sleepy coffee lounge, into which Branicka-Wolska strides with great energy. She is one of those who might be mistaken for a healthy, corpulent farmwoman in late middle age, except for her mild, warm voice, and an expression in her large blue eyes so sanguine and undefended as to suggest a clement day. Her ancestors came from the border regions in the northeast. I've seen the beautiful Renaissance palace in Bialystok, which was the seat of the Branicki family, and which in the eighteenth century housed a Polish and a French troupe of actors, as well as a corps de ballet. Branicka-Wolska herself, however, grew up right outside Warsaw, in Wilanów, in a three-wing Baroque palace built as a royal retreat in the late seventeenth century, but converted after the war into a highly popular museum cum tourist spot. "It had such a wonderful location," Anna says, remembering her young years. "That's why everybody came—politicians, international diplomats, artists."

All that changed utterly when the war came. Anna summons up quite fantastic scenes of resistance activity in Wilanów. The enormous rooms of the palace were used for target practice by young men training for underground fighting. Anna was only fourteen when the war started, but by the time she was sixteen, she joined her two sisters in running arms, acting as couriers, helping to hide people. The palace acted as a refuge for escaped POWs and peasant partisans. When the bombing of Warsaw began, crowds of young people came to spend nights at this safer place, and Anna remembers merry nights, with rows of mattresses set up in various rooms.

It was during the Warsaw Uprising, at the war's culmination and endgame, that the Branickis' greatest hardships began. First, they were caught and arrested by the Germans; but the Germans were almost immediately succeeded by the Russians—who, three days after they marched into Warsaw, arrested the Branickis again, with three other aristocratic families.

The group of sixteen were destined to spend the next three years in close proximity, "in slavery," as Anna puts it. Overnight, they had been turned into class enemies, the force of whose potential threat to the Communists had just been demonstrated by the strength of their resistance to the Nazis. The group were first transported to the Lubyanka prison in Moscow, whose dread reputation made them quite sure they were going to their executions. As it was, they were detained there for only two weeks. During that time—such are the details that stand out in memory—Anna remembers a Pekinese dog, probably the only such creature ever to survive Lubyanka, which was allowed to accompany her because it had amused a Russian soldier who

thought it was a pet monkey. Then the group were taken to a settlement in Krasnoyarsk, where for two years they lived under
close guard, sixteen of them squeezed into three rooms. During
the first year, they were not allowed to go outside; later, the regulations were relaxed and they could walk in a small garden, or
chop wood for their jailers. After the second year, for no apparent reason, the group were transported to a more severe labor
camp for prisoners of all nationalities (Anna particularly remembers a whole phalanx of Japanese generals); and then the wheel
of Soviet caprice turned again, and in 1948 they were released
and allowed to return to Poland.

I ask Anna whether the years of imprisonment were a period
of despair, but she assures me that they were not, that though
people were afraid of illness, and though sometimes they quar-
reled, on the whole they showed great resilience. "The ambition
of this class of people was to show that we could manage in bad
circumstances just as well as in good," she says with her pleasant
smile. "We took pride in improving our cooking and sewing
skills. We gave lessons to the children. My father recounted
whole plots of Polish classics, so that the kids wouldn't have
gaps in their education.

"And I," she continues, smiling pleasantly, "I wrote letters to
my beloved." The letters were never sent, because the young
man to whom she was writing was a leader in the resistance,
and in the vicissitudes of war his whereabouts were unknown.
Anna was writing partly to have a record of her astounding
experiences, which she could share with him when the war
was over.

This was not to be. "I thought he'd wait for me," she explains with great simplicity, "but when I came back, it turned out
that he was married and in London. This was my great tragedy,
just when I was supposed to be at the height of happiness."

The letters, however, were published many years later. They
are a rich chronicle of terrible events, full of vivid detail, astute
observations, and affection for fellow prisoners; full, even, of a
sense of happiness, which, Anna writes, didn't entirely leave her

even at the hardest moments. She was, however, to be sorely tried. The return to Poland held other calamities, aside from the loss of her "beloved." No sooner did the group of sixteen cross the Polish border than they were arrested again, this time by the new Communist authorities. Most of them were released in a few days; but Anna's father was among those who were detained longer—and the blow to his patriotism, to everything he stood for, was terrible. Anna remembers that he said, "I can survive in a German jail, I can stand a Russian labor camp. But I can't bear to be imprisoned in Poland." He didn't stay in jail for very long, but he died soon afterward, and Anna attributes his death to this episode.

In one of those well-aimed meannesses in which they specialized, the Communist authorities forbade the returning aristocrats to live even in the vicinity of their old homes. Anna and her mother moved to Cracow, where they tried to start a new life. It was hard: they had no money, and they were now such undesirables that people began to be afraid to be seen with them. Some of their fellow aristocrats went so far as to change their highly recognizable names—"not many," Anna hastens to assure me, "but you had to get along somehow."

For a while, mother and daughter were reduced to the most extreme poverty. They slept on other people's couches, ate at the poorest cafeterias, and often didn't have money for the tramway. As I listen to Anna, it seems to me that this demotion within the country which had been so much "theirs," this prolonged state of supposed, terrible normality, might have been even harder than the clear and encapsulated injustice of the prison. But when I suggest this, Anna smiles mildly and says that people make too much of hardship and poverty. "And anyway, people who never experienced it, who were never down and out, seem to me somehow unfinished, unripe, don't you think?"

Eventually, Anna got a degree in sociology, and after being turned down for fourteen jobs—in a country that did not recognize unemployment—she was taken in by a literary research institute. She was interviewed by the director, who said to her—she remembers this vividly—"Ever since I was sixteen years old, I fought against people of your kind." But for some reason he decided to take a risk on her nevertheless.

Eventually, also, she was married, to a man who was not an aristocrat—despite everything, such distinctions mattered—and who is a professor of genetics. "And, well," she says, "we've been married thirty-eight years. He was very much in love with me—and I liked him and respected him. Our love is of a quiet kind. There are so many kinds of love, don't you think?

"And so I want to convey the message," she continues, in a somewhat didactic locution, though without any didacticism in her tone, "that you should never fall into despair. Somehow, things fell into place for me. I think I have a sort of knack for life." Certainly, she never stopped being engaged in the world. Like most people in "the milieu," as she refers to it, she worked actively for Solidarity. "Oh, the number of parcels of medicine from you I've unpacked!" she says, meaning parcels from America. She has founded the Sibyrians' Society, which helps people who served time in the most dreaded part of the gulag. She works for it with a sense of mission. "I understand what they went through," she says. "I have utmost sympathy for them.

"Right now, I feel in the very middle of life," she summarizes, in her sunny voice. "I feel needed. I have gained some understanding of human affairs, and I try to squeeze the juice out of everything as from an orange. That's my religion of life. What's important is that the shoemaker should make good shoes and the writer should write well. That's how it seems to me. And thinking of others, that's also important and it's my job. You know, there've been times when I thought that I'm too old, too fat, that my heart is bothering me. . . . But now that I occupy myself with others, none of it bothers me. But that's how I was brought up, after all, to give the most of myself."

That's both sentimental and not at all so; not at all, because it has been so clearly proved in action, in the living. Despite my democratic prejudices, which make me hesitant about the very notion of aristocracy, I've allowed myself to get past my reservations. I like this woman, with her unironic romanticism and unaffected manners, her old-fashioned ideals and her knowledge of the worst of the world, her strong sense of who she is and her strong sense of a common humanity. She contains within herself so many periods of history, so many epochs of sensibility and experience.

And now, in another unexpected twist of fortune, the past, so long frozen in memory, is undergoing a strange revival. Anna, now in her late sixties, is thinking of reclaiming a part of her childhood home at Wilanów—"only a small part, it would be wrong to take any more." She would like to convert some of the outlying buildings into a retreat for old people who want to return from abroad, and use another part for a restaurant. She also mentions a more improbable development. Recently, she tells me with an unusual blush of pleasure, she has been initiated into something called the Order of the Knights of Malta. I give a small mental balk at this name, which sounds suspiciously like something made up by Umberto Eco. But this ancient order, which admits only aristocrats with several centuries' pedigrees, is currently very active—lest the comedy of historical incongruities should ever cease—in Eastern Europe. As Anna explains it, the Knights have a long tradition of charitable work, and they're planning to open a hospital for people with AIDS in Poland— something in which she would like to help.

Still, as I remember the mostly aging faces at the Landowners' Association meeting, I wonder what "aristocracy" can possibly mean in Poland from now on. Paradoxically, this group has remained intact, not in spite of, but because of, Communism. The system acted as a sort of historical freezer, in which aristocratic identity was preserved in a conserved state. But I wonder whether the aristocracy, or any number of other, artificially preserved social phenomena, can survive the opening of the freezer and the collision with the present. What will it mean to middle-aged professionals with inherited titles who have never lived on their estates and can't afford to reclaim them, or to the scion of one of the great families who manufactures women's underwear, or to the few younger people at the meeting, once they start moving freely in the contemporary world in which titles have genuinely ceased to matter?

Branicka-Wolska is level-headed on this subject. "In the older generation, yes, the aristocracy exists," she says. "We know each other, we meet at weddings and funerals—sometimes these occasions are practically blue from all the bluebloods. But in the younger generation? Oh, maybe there are pulls in that direction. Maybe there are sentiments, snobberies. And there's some continuity with the past. That was our whole system of upbringing—we talked a lot about the past. But will all this amount to a real Polish aristocracy? I doubt it."

I doubt it, too. My friend Agnieszka professes quite without embarrassment that she "adores" the aristocrats. She loves them because they're always in a good mood, she says, and for their insouciance and good manners in daily living, and because they are excellent company, and until now haven't cared about making money, or about proving anything to anybody. There's something of that attractive aristocratic ease about Anna Branicka-Wolska; habits of early satisfaction die hard, and so does a strong sense of identity. But I wonder whether even her sort of personality will be possible in the new world, driven by its new living values. There will be different "best people" from now on, and the pull of ambition and new choices. The memories of the old Wilanów will always hold their meaning for Branicka-Wolska, but the new Wilanów will never regain its former grandeur or heroism; even if she reclaims it, part of it will be used as a plain place of business.

Except on the page, the past can never be recaptured, or repeated—and this is what give the Polish scene nowadays a touch of the surreal. All these returns from the Rip Van Winkle sleep of Communism are both concrete and ghostly. This is partly because individuals and social phenomena are incommensurate with each other. There's nothing faded, or outmoded, about Anna Branicka-Wolska. But as for the once noble notion of Polish aristocracy, it can only come back in an altered form—a fainter version of itself, apt to dissolve into the full-blooded reality of the present.

On an excursion to Żelazowa Wola, Chopin's birthplace near Warsaw, the taxi driver, a young, well-groomed, and ceaselessly loquacious fellow, starts a line of inquiry that somehow leads to the Jewish question. Once he ascertains that I'm Jewish, there's no stopping him. "Just the other day, I had Jewish passengers from America," he informs me. "They were very nice people, very nice. We talked very frankly, because that's the way I am, I like to talk frankly. I think I may say we became friendly. They told me they thought Poland is an anti-Semitic country, and I tried to tell them it isn't. I'm not an anti-Semite, I count myself as a civilized person, but my problem, you see, is that I don't know any Jewish people, I grew up after they all left. . . . So I only know what I've been told about them."

And what have you been told about them, I want to know. "Well, you see, they played such an unfortunate role in our history. They were such great capitalists, you know, they owned most of the factories in Łódź, and that's where the Industrial Revolution happened. I heard that they were very stingy, it was terrible to work for them. And they didn't like to help their own, either."

I haven't had my morning coffee, I'm groggy and thick-headed, and the pollution on the industrial thoroughfare is making me miserable enough. Do I really have to take this on? I guess I do. On this matter, I have my Historical Obligations. So I start from the basics. "Do you know that most Polish Jews lived in small towns and barely eked out a living?" I ask. "That, on the other hand, there's a great tradition of mutual help and philanthropy among Jews?"

"Really?" he says in genuine surprise. "You see, that's our problem, none of this was taught in our schools and there was nowhere to discuss it." And so it goes for a while, until he drops me off.

Żelazowa Wola is a modest manor surrounded by a beautiful park with dipping hills, weeping willows, luxurious flower arrangements, and a winding, albeit polluted, stream. It's picturesque, it's melancholy, it's everything I love, and Chopin is one of the top gods in my pantheon; but somehow the conversation with the taxi driver interferes with the charm of the place. It's not so much his gullible opinions that disturb me as the odd way he addressed me as a court of appeal on them, as if there were a cognitive disjunction between a Jewish person in front of him and his vague ideas of Jews.

But that's the way reports of the new anti-Semitism have struck me as well. Although the taxi driver is the first person I've heard parroting anti-Semitic views, talk of the Jewish question is all around me. People express chagrin and outrage about the reappearance of anti-Semitism. Other people express chagrin and outrage about Poland's being branded as anti-Semitic. Adam Michnik, who is half-Jewish himself, has used a term "secondary anti-Semitism," to describe Polish reactions to such accusations. So there are anti-Semitism, secondary anti-Semitism, anti-anti-Semitism, and undoubtedly tertiary phenomena as well.

The purveyors of anti-Semitism themselves remain elusive; nobody ever seems to meet them, but everybody knows they exist, because somebody puts words like *Judenfrei* on walls of buildings and swastikas on the austere stone monument marking the site of the Warsaw Ghetto. Then there are people who discern Jewish origins in Catholic priests and bishops with progressive leanings, and even in the former prime minister, Tadeusz Mazowiecki, whose Catholic provenance is perfectly clear. For it is a distinctive feature of the new anti-Semitism that it can be directed at just about anybody, regardless of actual Jewishness or its absence, as if the term "Jewish" were a pure minus sign denoting whatever the speaker dislikes, suspects, or disapproves of.

On the other side of the ledger, there are stories of increased interest in all things Jewish, and a sort of nostalgic Judeophilia. I've heard of Poles flocking to performances of the Yiddish theater in droves, of students learning Hebrew and making pilgrimages to Israel, of a man who has taken it upon himself to be the caretaker and the archivist of an old, neglected Jewish cemetery in Warsaw.

If the aristocracy is the return of the suppressed—of a group kept down politically—anti-Semitism is the return of the repressed, of attitudes that had gone underground. But there's an obvious irony in the recurrence of the Jewish obsession right now, since, as everyone keeps repeating, "there are no Jews left in Poland." Well, not quite; there are a few, probably more than the seven thousand or so that the official statistics indicate. There are those who stayed here through everything, the sad, vanishing remnants of the prewar communities; there are people who, for various reasons, have never made anything of their Jewishness, nor mean to in the future.

And there are people like Konstantin Gebert. Konstantin, or Kostek, as he is known to his friends, is among the younger Jews of the postwar generation who grew up without knowing about their Jewishness. Their parents masked, or at least downplayed, this part of their identity because their memories of the Holocaust were too painful, or because they didn't think that Jewishness was to their children's advantage, or because they were, like Kostek's parents, committed internationalists. So Kostek didn't learn he was Jewish until his early adulthood. Once he did, he discovered, by an almost comically circuitous route, that there were others in his situation. In the 1970s, Karl Rogers, an American psychologist who conducted seminars all over the world, came to Warsaw and announced a workshop on Jewish identity in Poland. Kostek went, expecting to find an empty room; instead, he found half of his friends gathered there.

After this moment of recognition, Kostek started a group whose purpose was to administer to itself a measure of Jewish education, and possibly to recover a measure of Jewish identity. The young people involved in it had to start from the basics: none of them had ever seen a Sabbath service at home, or had been to a synagogue. But, bit by bit, they learned the Sabbath rituals, read, studied the Torah, gave seminars to each other on such subjects as Provençal Jewry in the Middle Ages, or the Hasidim in nineteenth-century Poland. Some of them learned Hebrew; some became religious; a few emigrated to Israel.

Kostek stayed, and continued his work as a journalist and a brilliant political commentator, writing under a pseudonym, Dawid Warszawski. He was active in Solidarity. He often comments on the Polish-Jewish question.

I have sometimes used Kostek as a sounding board on questions of Jewishness and anti-Semitism, because I find that his views on these matters have a reassuring sanity. And I find that, on these matters, I need the benefits of sanity rather badly. If I came to Eastern Europe in part to understand it as an adult, then I find that the Polish and Jewish parts of my history, my identity—my loyalties—refuse either to separate or to reconcile. At the very moments when my attachment to Poland, my admiration for all that is powerful in its culture, is strongest, I upbraid myself for insufficient vigilance on behalf of those who suffered here—on behalf, really, of my parents, who survived the Holocaust in awful circumstances. Every time I hear Poland described reductively as an anti-Semitic country, I bridle in revolt, for I know that the reality is far more tangled than that.

I am visiting Kostek shortly after my conversation with the taxi driver. He lives on a quiet midtown street, in an apartment with a large courtyard—almost a little park. Kostek leads me into his comfy study, lined with books in several languages, and sits cross-legged in his armchair, puffing on his pipe. It's probably true, he says, that the taxi driver's ideas are entirely secondhand. In part because ethnicity was supposed to evaporate under Communism, the question of Jewishness hasn't been discussed publicly in a long time. This doesn't mean, of course, that the Communists weren't capable of deliberate anti-Semitism, but to a great extent, the active, articulated knowledge of the complex Polish-Jewish history was arrested at its prewar point.

As for the current wave of anti-Semitism, Kostek carefully distinguishes between several shades of it: standard religious anti-Semitism, an old-fashioned folk anti-Semitism, and a new

kind of anti-Semitism, which is really a camouflage for anti-
democratic feelings, for the resistance to openness, and uncertainty and pluralism—for the fear of change. It's this last variant
of anti-Semitism that led people to brand any number of members in the first post-Communist government as "Jewish." Kostek
says, with some amusement, that when he asked ordinary people
why they thought prime minister Mazowiecki was Jewish, he got
some very interesting answers. "Because he's so sad and prays
too much," one old woman said, showing a truly inventive ability to mix stereotypes. And when Kostek brought up some evidence to the effect that Mazowiecki clearly wasn't Jewish, a man
protested, "Well, but he got to be Prime Minister after all!"

A few days after our conversation, I happen to see Kostek on
Interpelations, which this time is conducting a debate on Polish-
Jewish relations. Kostek is the MC, and the honored guest is the
Israeli ambassador to Poland. The ambassador, an ursine figure
with a kindly manner and Russian-accented Polish—he grew up
in Lithuania—answers all questions, no matter how unpleasant,
with unruffled politeness. Two of the interrogators represent
right-wing nationalist groups, and they come out with prejudices
that are nearly embarrassing in their staleness. They both happen
to be thin and excitable, and one of them has a prominent
Adam's apple which bobs with bantam aggressiveness, as he suggests that Jews were responsible for Communism, for the secret
police, for control of Poland's image aboard.

The ambassador addresses himself to these questions
patiently—but then comes the seesaw's swing. As the camera
pans to a Cracow group, one of the guests, a writer associated
with a well-known Catholic journal, bursts into a rather amazing
speech. "Gentlemen," he shouts at the previous speakers, gestur-
ing furiously, "what you say is odious. I'm ashamed to be on the
same program with you. I have to assert that you're just simple
anti-Semites." I'm impressed with the sheer intensity of his
speech; nobody on the cooler medium of American television
would speak with such uncontrolled movements, or such naked
fervor.

But what really interests me amidst these displays of passion-ate convictions is the seemingly small matter of Kostek's yar-mulke. Kostek wears it everywhere, and he says he has never been directly confronted with an anti-Semitic remark. This is very different from what would have happened in my childhood, when you never talked Yiddish on the street, and nobody would have dreamt of displaying such an obvious sign of Jewishness as a yarmulke in public. A yarmulke, then, was exactly what would have provoked anti-Semitism; a yarmulke now seems to ward it off.

But then, a yarmulke makes the wearer's Jewishness quite clear, and the current wave of anti-Semitism, in the virtual ab-sence of actual targets, seems to thrive on uncertainty and vagueness—like a transference neurosis, in which a free-floating anxiety is trying, rather impotently, to find an object and a cause. And, like all neuroses, this one seems to have been lifted whole and unchanged from the past. A friend has shown me a carica-ture of a Jew that she tore off a city wall where it had been put up during the last elections; the image was clumsy, ugly and mean—and copied straight from the prewar era. Certainly the sort of Jewish person depicted on the flimsy piece of paper—with a long beard, black caftan, sidelocks—hasn't been seen in Poland for the last several decades.

So far, Polish anti-Semitism has had no public ideology, or any real consequences. It seems to be a symbolic matter, a rever-sion to an old language to name unnamable new problems. Per-haps symbolic "Jews" have become a substitute for the partly symbolic "Them," who had become so necessary to the Polish psyche, who were the ubiquitous explanation for so many pains and dark problems. Now They are gone, but explanatory views aren't overturned so quickly; the need for dark secrets remains, and the language of anti-Semitism is convenient for this purpose. This might be why overt Jewishness is not the real object of this peculiar attitude—for once Jewishness is admitted, open, it doesn't serve the need for a veiled and sinister mystery.

In certain villages, I've heard, peasants visit old, abandoned

Jewish cemeteries at night to pray for the fulfillment of their wishes. They've heard that wise men, magicians perhaps, are buried under the indecipherable stones—as if the Jews of Poland, so recently gone, belonged to a time of myth.

In the meantime, the actual history of Polish-Jewish relations remains largely untaught and unknown. It is a long and complicated history, including long periods of fruitful coexistence as well as times of prejudice and persecution, including a rich Jewish culture that grew and perished here, and that was interestingly cross-fertilized with the mainstream Polish culture. The process of reconstructing the centuries of this story—particularly its recent chapters—is bound to be convoluted and painful. But, as the return of the repressed demonstrates again and again, the work of memory needs to be done before unconscious ideas stop exercising their force, before current reality can be faced on its own terms. Apparently history needs to be remembered before it can move on again. At the same time, history in Poland had to begin moving before it could be accurately remembered. Now the movement has begun, and the discussions of the Polish-Jewish question with it. This is one issue on which I cannot attain an observer's detachment. But it seems possible to me that the odd, reiterated, unreal anti-Semitism pervading the Polish air may not survive a thorough examination; that, like other phenomena that have been removed from the Communist freezer, it will wilt when exposed to the present actualities—which certainly have very little to do with the "Jewish problem," or the few remaining Polish Jews.

Tykocin is a town on the Byelorussian border, about one hundred kilometers northeast of Warsaw, and I decide to go there to see how change comes to the periphery, and also because I can catch a ride with Agnieszka, who has been invited there—to read her poetry and talk about literature and song writing and theater and many other things that she talks about so well. On the way, she talks indefatigably as well. She tells me about how she has had to retrain her manners several times in her rich life. When

she was a young woman, she was very involved in a student theater, and at social gatherings she would tell people about its
problems—until an older mentor said to her, in effect, that's not
how it's done. At parties, one makes graceful chitchat, one
doesn't talk about professional matters. And so, years later, when
she came to New York, that's what she tried to do. But all her
refinement fell on deaf ears. "What do you do?" people kept
asking her, and that was clearly what she was supposed to ask
back. "They didn't realize I had exquisite manners; they thought
I was a fluff head." She laughs.

It's just as well Agnieszka is so entertaining, because the
landscape is almost perfectly flat and monotonous. Occasionally,
marks of that melancholy I used to love as a child appear: long
colonnades of poplars, farms and meadows that always manage
to look more disheveled than in the West. The towns we pass,
however, are depressingly graceless—subfunctional architecture, bedraggled vehicles, and shabbily dressed kids. We stop in
one of these towns, hoping to get some food. We get out near
grandly named Roosevelt Street and Woodrow Wilson Square.
But food stores—such as they are—are closed for lunch, and in
any case, all we can see are some parsnips and carrots, and in another one, some bread. The "café" to which we are directed is a
dismal, kitchen-size place, which serves only a sticky, orange-
flavored liquid.

Tykocin, however, is a soul-gratifying place, a cross between
a timeless village and a small historic town. On this sunny day,
the winding paths and warm cobblestones look like an invitation
to slow your step, and the abundant flowers in small garden
burst luxuriously against the wooden fences. The houses, some
made of wood, some of stone, stand low and long, covered by
sheltering, sloping roofs. On Tykocin's northern side, garden
gently segues into riverbank and the serene, broad Narew River,
and beyond it, into flat, languorous, tall-grassed wetlands—as if
the transition from civilization to nature were an easy, indeed a
natural, process.

It might seem that the growth of civilization here was natural too. On the outskirts of Tykocin, there are traces—no more than a hilly mound and a few stones—of an early settlement left by Slavic tribes who arrived here in the nineth century. On the further bank of the Narew, overgrown foundation stones of a castle, built as a royal retreat in the sixteenth century, stand as a reminder that Tykocin was once a prosperous and important seat of independent princelings. In the mid-eighteenth century, a local guide explains, Tykocin "received a Baroque spatial composition," with a "monumental church" as its balancing axis. The church and several other Baroque buildings still calmly dominate the town, with their mild curvatures and creamy yellow and white façades.

But Tykocin has a second focus as well, for it still bears the marks of its old division into two sections, Polish and Jewish. The houses lining the Jewish streets tend to be narrower and taller, since the ground floor was reserved for little shops from which the nonfarming inhabitants made their livelihoods. The dominant building in this part of Tykocin is a synagogue, of a stately Renaissance design, which has stood here since 1642.

Nor were Poles and Jews the only inhabitants of the town. Once upon a time, Tykocin was an example of that multi-ethnic diversity that existed in this region of Europe long before it arrived at the doorstep of the West. There were Lithuanians here and Byelorussians and some Saxons and Tatars. According to respected historians, these mixed populations managed to live together quite amicably until the Second World War.

Almost nothing remains of this fertile mix; through a succession of border changes, migrations, and wars, Tykocin has achieved a nearly complete homogeneity. Agnieszka and I walk into the synagogue, which has been turned into a well-restored museum. On the walls, Hebrew inscriptions from the seventeenth century thank the wealthy merchants of the day for their patronage. Once we enter, somebody turns on a recording of a Hebrew chant, swooping, trembling, falling through its long and sorrowful lines, till we feel that the presence of the synagogue's ghosts is very near.

My meditations, however, are interrupted by a stout, buxom woman who runs up to me and presses me to her breast, tears in her eyes. They have nothing to do with the spirit of this place. "Madame is a friend of Madame Agnieszka," she says breathlessly, and introduces herself as the caretaker. "We're so honored." That's what literary fame means in Poland.

The museum's curator is a plain, pleasant woman, who, like many people who live in close contact with the past, talks about her piece of it—the history of the synagogue and of Tykocin—with an almost domestic familiarity. She and her colleagues, none of them Jewish, fought hard before the changes to have the synagogue recognized as a Jewish landmark and to maintain it in proper order. They're a quiet, amiable group, and their dedication to the lost world over which they are guardians is clearly deep: one of them has studied Jewish history abroad, and the curator travels to Warsaw twice a week to take lessons in Hebrew. The little world they have created in the present, in their corner of Tykocin, seems orderly but alive with their involvement. Not for the first or the last time in these travels, I think, Lucky are those who have a task to which they can be devoted. The curator shows us a model of Tykocin as it looked in the 17th century; the Baroque church is not yet in the picture, but the synagogue is; and the symmetrical farm plots, she tells us, have remained in the same configuration till today, even down to the names of the owners. The "old families" have held on to their power, and to their feuds, even through the Communist times.

Clearly, change comes slowly to Tykocin. But its first sign appears in the middle of town, in a little rectangular park whose straight paths are protected by the spread of dark-leafed, murmuring oaks. There, a manly statue of Stefan Czarniecki, an heir to the Tykocin lands in the seventeenth century, fronts the world in a proud and graceful pose. The nobleman is styled as a Cossack hetman, or commander, and in his extended hand he holds a bulbous scepter. This object gleams with fresh gold, which contrasts oddly against the aged stone. Indeed, it is a recent addition, and it was given to the statue by a candidate in the first democratic elections, in a bid to win the Tykocin citizens' hearts.

The bid was successful, and the candidate is now Tykocin's alderman and the talk of Tykocin. We hear about him from the museum curator and a woman who invites us into her tiny grocery shop, and Janek, a teacher at the local technical institute. "Ah, this alderman of ours," they all begin, and then go on to say he doesn't understand what democracy is; he's selling off common property on the sly, he doesn't consult anyone about his decisions, and won't even hire an accountant so that nobody will see his books. "A clown, a real mountebank, you'll see," Janek's wife tells me. "And he likes to play the buffoon, too."

I meet the alderman in his very bare office, in which a rickety table and two wobbly chairs serve for furnishings. He's a ruddy-faced, corpulent man, whose gruff demeanor has a certain grace of masculine self-assurance. "Ah, the people here, they don't know that times have changed," he tells me as soon as I sit down. "They haven't figured out that nobody will think or pay for them anymore. Frankly, you can't tell them too much about your plans; it's just better to go ahead and do things."

Democratic manners are very new in Tykocin, and he's not at all embarrassed about the peremptory use of power. A hotly contested building, which the schoolteacher wanted to turn into a kindergarten, has already been disposed of, he tells me in a confidential tone. It's been bought by an American businesswoman who wants to convert it into a small hotel. The World Bank will probably give him a loan to improve the phone lines and build an antipollution plant. "We need a better infrastructure here," he says. "That must come first.

"But you see, I have one principle," he adds, giving me another confidential look. "Money should move. That's American, isn't it?"

I allow that it is. Indeed, this alderman might as well be the boss of a small southern town when the bosses were still thriving; he even speaks with a deep singsong lilt, a good Polish equivalent of a southern accent.

Afterward, Agnieszka and I are invited for dinner to Janek's house, where his wife has cooked a great, hearty meal. Agnieszka and I get the cushioned seats at an improvised table, and we're joined in the little room by another schoolteacher, a Byelorussian, whom Agnieszka privately dubs "the Byzantine," because of his soft, long face, his liquid, dark eyes, and a black, black beard, which might indeed come out of an old Byzantine mosaic. Janek, a shy, intelligent man, has opened a bookstore in Tykocin with the Byzantine's help, though he doesn't expect to make any profits from it. "It's just so that people have something to do here," he says almost apologetically, "so that something interesting should happen." Then the conversation turns to the alderman and his nefarious ways.

But are there no checks on his power? I ask. Janek waves his hand impatiently. The people here don't care, and wouldn't know what to do; they don't even know what their rights are. For all the formal changes, they're still caught up in an old-fashioned system of personal power and personal feuds; it'll take some time before the actual methods of governance, and of citizens' participation, catch up with the new electoral laws.

After dinner, we drive to another little museum next to the synagogue, where Agnieszka will be making her appearance. It's only when we're nearly there that Janek informs me that I've been included in the program as well! The poster on the door confirms this; my name is on it with Agnieszka's. "Eva Hoffman, from America," it says, as if that were enough of a claim to fame. I try to protest—I am utterly unprepared for this—and point out that I'm wearing sneakers and a T-shirt that has seen better days, but Agnieszka says briskly, "You're American, you're allowed to do anything you want," and so I find myself on stage in Tykocin.

The event takes place in a lovely oblong room with parquet floors and a piano; the audience is surprisingly well-dressed and unprovincial. Fortunately, Agnieszka carries most of the show splendidly. For the younger people in this room, she's part of the romantic history of Polish theater and they ask her intensely in-

terested, well-informed questions that she answers through anecdote after anecdote, character sketch after character sketch.

Then they turn to me with a few queries about America. This
is what they want to know: how are race relations shaping up in
the United States, what about the drug problems, how difficult
is it to publish a book over there? And also: Do I think Polish
people can understand Woody Allen's humor? I'm a bit flummoxed by the last one, but fortunately the evening draws to a
close. Agnieszka and I are presented with two beautiful bunches
of flowers and taken to a room upstairs in the museum, where
we're to spend the night. No hot water is in evidence, but there
are two tiny clean towels, and the beds are comfortable. I've
learned to feel grateful for such amenities.

The next morning, once again in my capacity as "the visitor
from America," I'm invited to attend the year-end ceremonies at
the elementary school. My entrance in the tiny auditorium is
greeted by considerable ado. The proceedings are interrupted,
the students all stand up and intone a rhythmical "Good day,"
somebody hands me yet another bunch of flowers, and the principal makes a little welcoming speech. A measure of formality, of
hospitable courtliness, has always been part of Polish culture,
and it has survived even the interminable tediousness of socialist
rituals.

This ceremony is not without charm. The graduating students have composed poems to the various teachers, which they
recite with some pomp, but not without humor; there are skits
about the dramatic highlights of last year, touching equally on
fledgling romances and building renovation; there are recitations
of poetry and songs. Throughout it all, several rows of kids, in
sizes graduated down to first-grade small fry, their heads as uni-
formly blond as a field of wheat, sit in unfidgeting silence, showing round-eyed interest in the proceedings on stage. A tiny noise
from the first-grade row brings a reprimand from a vigilant
teacher.

When it's over, I'm taken to the principal's office for conversation and cake. The principal is an attractive blonde woman,

whose stout, upright figure exudes a feeling of strength and rectitude. She's none too happy about the new state of affairs in Poland. "They're not delivering new textbooks; we have no curriculum for next year. It's disorder and it'll get worse. Democracy is all very well, but it's got to have a goal, a discipline."

But when I tell her about the problems American schools are facing—problems, partly, of pluralism, unimaginable in this homogeneous spot—she looks pleased to be where she is. "We do our best," she says proudly.

After we leave, the Byzantine tells me that she's a Communist, but that everyone respects her because she brings so much energy and dedication to her work. He offers to show me a few sights in Tykocin, including his prized spot on the Narew River. The excursion involves getting into his car, which is something I've already learned to fear. The car, if such it can be called, is not much more than a shaky box with a motor in it; and after the difficulties of sliding in and folding yourself into the requisite position, there's the problem of starting it up. The Byzantine seems to accomplish this routinely by turning on the ignition, leaping out, cranking up something or other in the area of the motor, letting the car slide downhill, and then running after it and jumping in.

My heart is rather close to my throat, as I contemplate hurtling into any number of trees in the car's path, but the Byzantine goes through these motions without really interrupting his conversation; and the place to which he brings me is worth a few nervous moments. Here the wetlands grow wilder and seem to extend forever, till the tall grasses and the gray mist and the river deliquesce into each other, and into an uncanny whole whose shapes and substance are as ungraspable as the shapes of the mysterious creatures that arise out of mists and waters in fairy tales. Nearby, on a thatched cottage roof, storks stand tall and straight out of their circular nests; and the Byzantine, in his gray windbreaker, looks as much a part of the landscape as they. This is what he loves best, he tells me in his soft voice; to come fishing here, to be alone in his canoe. This is why he stays here, even though he is the only Byelorussian around and some people look at him oddly.

Back in town, as I walk down a lazy street, an old woman begins chatting with me and then invites me into her house nearby. She's thin and wiry and strong-looking, and she tells me three grotesque tales, one right after another, looking merry all the time. The first is about maidens who went off into the wetlands by themselves and were attacked; and who knows what it was that attacked them, except it was hairy all over. Then there was the thief who tore earrings off women's ears—and once he cut off a lady's earlobes; and well, that hurts, and the lady screamed and cried. And also, there was the man who held up a bus, and jumped in—and then this hand fell off! And it was made of metal, and out of that hand fell jewelry and gold. . . .

"And you'll see," she concludes these modern tales of werewolves and highwaymen, "when they permit everything, as they do now, people will do even worse things, they will."

I emerge from her dark house onto the sunny street, and sit quietly on a low stone wall near the synagogue. Old peasants sit on their house stoops, chatting; the clip-clop of a horse drawing a long cart makes distinct sounds on the cobblestones; the cackle of hens and the protesting plaints of geese float in the warm air. The Industrial Revolution never really reached the Polish countryside, and slow development has created this premodern mix of barnyard noises and high architecture, of peasant superstitions and mannerly schoolteachers.

On the way back, we pass the grim towns again. Polish—Eastern European—landscape is beginning to arrange itself in my mind into a thin, vertical foreground of rickety socialist constructions and a deeper background of towns like Tykocin, with their strata of age and beauty, part of an older Europe that never disappeared and that is still surprisingly alive.

In Warsaw, I've been staying at the Ursus Hotel, and after several days the clerk behind the desk decides that he can abandon formality and engage me in conversation. The only notable thing about this ordinary, inexpensive hotel is that—so I am told—this was where many meetings between Solidarity and the government took place, and where Wałęsa took his famous "naps." Apparently, whenever the talks reached a particularly tricky point, Wałęsa took the ordinary man's privilege of having ordinary needs, and claimed that he was terribly tired. Then he went upstairs to figure out his next move.

When I mention this to the clerk, it turns out that he doesn't much appreciate his president's common touch. "To tell you frankly, I have enough of this Wałęsa," he says disgustedly. "Do you know how he behaved when he went to visit the English queen?" I know, because the anecdote has been widely repeated—how, after staying the night at Windsor Castle, Wałęsa informed Her Majesty that there was something wrong with the electrical wiring in her household, and offered advice on how to improve it. Most probably, the queen was charmed, but not so Wałęsa's fellow citizen. "Is this how the president of a normal country behaves?" the clerk rhetorically inquires. "What will they think of us in the West? A president of a real country should have manners, he should know how to talk. He should be a gentleman, a professor."

This brings back familiar echoes; I know, from my early years here, that the politics of personality in Poland was never egalitarian; that a hierarchy of manners, and notions of what it means to be a "cultured" person, were respected by everybody, no less by those who were lower on this particular ladder than by the "better" people. And now these remnants of an old feudal code are probably most honored by people like the hotel clerk, who haven't caught on to the fact that in the West—the West whose judgment matters to him so much—such hierarchies have become outmoded, or even inverted.

"I tell you, I'm sometimes ashamed of what these foreigners see when they come here," he confides, lowering his voice. "I mean, take this hotel. . . . Would this be acceptable in a normal country?" As a matter of fact, I find the hotel perfectly adequate, though modest. But the clerk has an obscure sense that in the

West standards are so unimaginably superior that the reality prevailing here cannot possibly measure up.

"I try to lead a decent life," he confides. "I keep clean. Every evening when I come home, I wash myself. But when I think of all this filth and poverty that people see at the train station . . . When people come here, I want them to feel they're in a normal country, not a rich one, just a medium normal country."

He exaggerates, of course. Filth and poverty are not the first features that strike the foreign eye, accustomed as it has become to more spectacular forms even of these phenomena than drab, reduced Poland can provide. But the hotel clerk has never been in the West; and for him, as for many others, it continues to be more an imagined location than a real entity. Until recently, the forbidden West was an obscure object of desire, and a place of glittering magic. Now, it is being turned into something else—a sort of severe super-ego, used by the Poles to castigate themselves for their own insufficiencies. The "road to Europe," in the hotel clerk's mind, is a road to "civilization" on its simplest plane—to cleanliness and better train stations and manners. But it is also a road to a mythical realm of social seamlessness and prosperity, a place that heightens his rankling sense of inferiority, and exists only through it.

What's happened here? The paradoxes, the contradictions, the costs and benefits, the pros and cons, the appraisals and critiques—they're enough to give you a sort of moral toothache. Things are better, but things are worse, things are moving forward but they are regressing, things are desperate but very hopeful. The diagnosis, the analysis, and the prognosis are constant. There's freedom, but there's unemployment, there're beginnings of wealth but there's poverty, there are options but there is suffering. History is a process of double-ledger accounting, I keep reminding myself, but that's a cool view, possible only from some distance.

I have a brief meeting with Adam Michnik before leaving Poland. He's worried about Wałęsa's potentially dogmatic tendencies, and about "séances of hate" against the former *no-menklatura*. Michnik has always advocated politics of reconciliation. While he was in prison, he wrote essays in which he urged the inclusion of everybody, even the quiet person who never made a strong oppositional stand, under Solidarity's umbrella. He has looked at the elements of the liberal Russian tradition that might be useful for Poland; he has tried to lessen the traditional antagonism between the left and the Church. In the reversals of post-totalitarian politics, he's coming under criticism for counseling forgiveness toward his former enemies and jailers.

He is less tolerant toward his former friends who now hold the reins of power—and he's sure that they dislike him intensely. But then, in his current conflict, Michnik is one of the engaged actors and has to retain his critical sharpness.

From a more detached perspective, what the conflicts are about, or along what lines of division they run, is sometimes harder to discern. The Polish political scene keeps reconfiguring itself with kaleidoscopic speed. Since last year, new parties have sprouted, wilted, fractured, and consolidated as if by multiple mitosis. People worry about the "Weimarization" of Polish politics, or the undermining of democracy through fragmentation; they worry about "Iranization," that is, the collapse of the separation between Church and state.

Certainly, the old categories of left and right are insufficient to the occasion. For one thing, the Communists were until recently the conservative force in Poland, and so everything opposed to them was progressive. By this logic, the free market is a progressive force, and the most liberal people are the most for it, though just about nobody seems to be against it. In the meantime, the Communists are reclaiming—oh, ceaseless paradox—some of the positions traditionally considered progressive, such as notions of a mixed economy, solid social services, internationalism reclothed as pluralism and, *mutatis mutandis,* anti-anti-Semitism. Yet new progressive and conservative positions are crystallizing as well, out of the unified mass of anti-Communists.

The conservatives are more nationalistic, respectful of the Church, intent on calling the Communists on the carpet. The progressives are pluralist, less resistant to foreign investment, and in favor of drawing that "thick line" between the *ancien regime* and the current era.

But, *sub specie aeternitatis,* the differences between the important political parties and actors in Poland do not yet seem so enormous. Among the significant actors, everyone wants to get on that road to Europe, and everyone professes decent liberal values, at least in public. For all the fears of his demagoguery, Wałęsa has acted well within the limits of constitutional democracy; and for all his noises about smoking out the Communists, no formal measures have been taken in that direction. Nor, for all the praise of an unencumbered free market, has anyone moved to dismantle free education or the health system, or to privatize the industrial behemoths so quickly as to cause massive unemployment. For all the sound and fury, extremism has not won the day. Perhaps this is because there are circumstances in the Polish situation that act as a sort of reality principle, an antidote to extremism. There is, of course, the dire and pressing state of the economy, which, no matter what one's ideological stripe, provides an urgent and clear task. But there are also the watchful eyes of the West, which demand a certain kind of good, moderate behavior, in exchange for approval and those desperately desirable hard currencies. And, no matter what ghosts, demons, and specters emerge from the past, the reality principle, after all, holds considerable sway.

In the meantime, there's the new Babel of pluralism, the views, voices, compromises; parties trying to identify their constituencies and politicians trying to figure out what would please the public. Polling and ingratiation—the special bad faith of democracy. Poland is becoming a normal country after all, in the contemporary way of normalcy. That—so it seems to me—is really what has happened here, the modest meaning of this nonapocalyptic and difficult "revolution"; though whether "normalcy" can ever be recognized as such by people who are experiencing it is another question entirely.

The evening before leaving for Prague, I drop in on a gathering at a friend's apartment. Some talk of the spiraling real-estate prices, the deteriorating situation in Yugoslavia, a new audience-participation play. Also, of the *matura,* the high school graduation exam, which everybody here takes very seriously. "Are you taking it this year?" people ask each other, as if they were taking it with their kids. There are articles about it in newspapers every day; one father has come back from abroad to be with his daughter during this ordeal.

Some of the guests drink. Good God, how they drink! They drink without interruption, ceaselessly, for hours on end. Have Poles developed a special gene adapted to the vodka environment? Eventually, a woman breaks into fragments of patriotic song, and loudly tells some indiscreet anecdotes. I'm a bit disconcerted, but no one else is; they're used to this, and give more latitude to all manner of human foibles; perhaps there's a kind of sanity in this, in not ejecting people too quickly from the circle of normalcy.

Someone who works at a sociology institute tells of cutbacks he'll have to make, and how of course he should start by firing a few *nomenklatura* people. "The damn thing is, though, that some of them are good at what they do. What am I going to say to them? I mean, I hate them, of course I hate them, but what can I tell you, I feel sorry for them."

"Let's not deceive ourselves, it'll take decades to straighten out this mess," somebody says, for my benefit. "It'll get much worse yet before it gets any better. How can you think this is a normal country? Now Czechoslovakia, that's a different story. You'll see. They've always been a civilized place, and they know how to do things. And they've had a bit of luck with their Havel, he's so popular with the West."

Several hours into evening, the inebriated woman emerges from the bedroom, where she had been sleeping it off; she seems quite lucid and fresh.

On the way to Prague, I make a brief stop in Cracow. The tramways have been painted pink! Some of them are covered with

pictorial ads and sixtyish, psychedelic designs; color is returning
to Eastern Europe.

I meet Zygmunt Matynia in the Cracovie Hotel restaurant,
for some vodka and creamed herring. Within the last year, he has
undergone several reversals of conscience. After starting his job
in the city government, he discovered to his chagrin that much of
it involved standard, unreformed power struggles. There were office factions, intrigues, firings of disloyal employees—all of it
starkly high-handed, because there are no new restraints yet, either of law or etiquette, on managerial imperiousness. Zygmunt
was terribly disappointed. In a way, the new nastiness was more
wounding to his idealism than the familiar old nastiness; this was
not what he was hoping for from the new Poland about which
he was so happy. So, for a while, he quit; then he went back, deciding that the city government was the place where he could
best do something useful, after all.

"What disappoints me now," he says, "is that the best people
aren't choosing public service, they're becoming private businessmen instead. You know, with all these conflicts, and sharp
words and sometimes even . . . aggressiveness, they're discouraged from going into politics." I know that Zygmunt is an unusually gentle person, but still I'm amused by a notion of
political life in which aggression is an almost unmentionable distortion of decency.

As last year, we walk through the central square, which once
again has been turned into an enormous church. A resplendently
clad bishop is saying mass from a balcony over the square. "For
a Polish saint," Zygmunt whispers to me. The square fills to the
brim and overflows with a quiet, reverent human mass. A pure
line of Gregorian chant rises into the air, followed by a response
from the square that sounds, despite the hundreds of voices,
sweet and quiet. Then the entire crowd kneels. They kneel in silence, on the cobblestones, as one person. It's a powerful, unset-
tling moment. There's so much unanimity in this crowd, so much
public assertion, so much certainty. The square has been entirely
taken over by the worshipers, and I stand up awkwardly among

the kneeling figures. Zygmunt, I see, hesitates about what to do, and then decides to keep me company in my upright stance.

Before leaving Cracow, I meet a friend, Jan, in a coffeehouse. Jan is a writer and an editor, and one of the great talkers one meets here—irrepressibly lively and humorous, throwing darts of irony quite freely at everyone and everything. Over vodka and creamed herring, he talks a blue streak about the current "situation," and how fed up he is with the new literary politics and the intrigues and infighting and the cliquishness of the new Warsaw crowd. "Our little Polish hell," he concludes.

Then, when I tell him that the next leg of my journey is Czechoslovakia, he shifts gears and launches into an unstoppable commentary on Polish-Czech relations in this region in the time of the Austro-Hungarian Empire. The memories of that time are hardly abstract for him; he remembers stories told by his parents' generation quite well—and none of them were apparently favorable to the Czechs. "The Czechs were terrible bureaucrats, believe me," he says, with actual venom. "The worst in the Empire. They were officious and hard. They extorted bribes. And they were always on the side of the imperial powers. For the Austrians, for the Russians. We knew them, believe me." So here it is—the Polish prejudice against the Czechs, which I've heard about, though it's always seemed to me one of the more inexplicable emotions in the lexicon of national biases. A regional prejudice, perhaps, springing from the old Hapsburg Empire to which Cracow belonged, from a seemingly irrelevant past whose long-buried conflicts can still send up these living embers.

And so, armed with several preconceptions, I set off for Czechoslovakia.

THREE

← ← ← ←

CZECHOSLOVAKIA

I am met at the Prague airport by Martin, a Czech friend who has lived in America for the last fifteen years. He has come with two friends, a rather scraggly-looking couple, both with longish hair, jeans, T-shirts. As soon as we begin driving in, Martin begins to ask me how I like what I see, with a touch of proprietorial anxiety. This is his first time back. We're passing rather nondescript peripheral neighborhoods; but soon we enter Prague proper, and I enter that state of primitive astonishment—of helpless appreciation—that is occasionally the traveler's reward.

Nothing I know about this other city of seven hills has prepared me for its extravagance and abundance and endless visual surprises, as if, somewhere beneath its ground, there were a constantly replenishing reservoir, or a geyser, from which beauty springs. The eye cannot move without encountering a stunning piece of statuary, or painted decoration, or ornate architectural detail, or a Cubist thicket of chimneys. The parts meld into a whole that yields a sort of esthetic overcharge, an organic effect that is more than the sum of its components. Baroque jostles against Gothic, sinuous art-nouveau fresco against delicate iron-work grille; on one side of the Vltava River the city rises in tiers of terra-cotta roofs and lush parks, and at the top, the castle gently dominates. Joining the two parts at its center is the breathtaking Charles Bridge, with its perfect proportions of supporting Gothic arches and its rows of majestic, serene saints bestowing benedictions from both balustrades.

I wonder what beneficent, self-assured power is expressed in this bridge, from whence springs the love of beauty and sensuality and pleasure everywhere visible in Prague's architecture. The history of Prague has hardly been as harmonious as its urban mien would suggest. Charles Bridge, for example, was originally commissioned in 1357 by Charles IV, the king of Bohemia and Moravia and the Holy Roman Emperor, who indeed presided over the Czech nation's great age. But the statues, mostly added in the eighteenth century, come from the era of Hapsburg domination, which lasted three centuries, and during which the Czechs almost lost their separate identity and their language. The Baroque style of those statues, as of so many churches and palaces, was imposed by foreign princes and by Jesuits, who conducted a particularly militant counterreformation in Bohemia, to retaliate for the fiery reformation conducted under the populist leadership of Jan Hus.

Still, even under foreign domination, Prague saw uninterrupted epochs of prosperity and development, and, aside from natural catastrophes like the great fire of 1541, the city never suffered physical destruction on a large scale. As I walk through its ancient quarters, I have a fanciful notion that the urge to save their gorgeous capital might have acted as a subliminal restraint on the Czech resistance when the Germans invaded in 1939. I know this is only an imaginative conceit, and yet I can see that it might have been as unbearable to think of the destruction of Prague as to contemplate the bombing of Paris.

Martin guides me around some of the central parts of the city. "So what do you think?" he keeps asking me, and he's as delighted by my clearly sincere approval as if I were paying him

a personal compliment. In the mid-seventies, Martin made a dramatic, illegal escape from a country that had become unbearably
stifling, involving a jigsaw puzzle of borders he crossed without
a passport—one of those anguished acts that already seem less
than credible tropes of a distant Dark Age. Like so many of his
countrymen, he has come the instant travel restrictions have been
lifted, and the intensity of his return is equal to his previous
shock of rupture. His has been an exile that belongs to a certain
period as surely as a sonnet does; and indeed, it was an exile that
created a literature of its own, marked by a yearning and lyricism
that were fed by a sense of irrevocable loss.

Now that his banishment has come to an end, Martin is beside himself with the pleasure of rediscovery and the triumph of
finding Prague as glorious as he remembered it. "I saw a small
boy with a knapsack the other day," he tells me, "and I thought
of myself at that age, walking around Prague, not knowing what
I had. I wanted to ask that child, Do you know how to see what's
around you? Do you know how exceptional, how beautiful this
is?"

He leads me toward Wenceslas Square, really a vast, broad
boulevard, where enormous crowds gathered to listen to Vaclav
Havel and register their disdain for their old leaders. The Velvet
Revolution was an event with a central site. For a while, we stand
on the steps of the Natural History Museum, from which Havel
spoke; by some acoustical fluke, the voice apparently carries extremely far from here; and the boulevard ascends toward the
other end, like a theater. A natural space for political drama.

A few months after the changes, what a contrast with Warsaw! The place is mobbed, mostly with young people ambling
idly with their knapsacks and guitars, looking, like all tourists, a
bit bored and dyspeptic. One hears every language in the book,
though mostly German. This summer of 1990, Czechomania, or
Czech chic has overtaken the youth international. Each of the
Eastern European revolutions has the equivalent of a designer la-
bel affixed to it, and of them all, the "Velvet Revolution," with
its philosopher king, its humor, and its rock bands, has been

seen as the sweetest, the gentlest, the most hip of them all. The perfect revolution for a summer vacation.

The nearby Na Příkopě Street is overhung with celebratory banners, but also lined with restaurants and stores that have been here all along. There're whole rows of shops next to each other, displays of jewelry (admittedly of the most tacky sort, and admittedly always the same), attractive Bohemian glass and china; in one window, though I can hardly believe it, I espy a gleaming white Cuisinart. After Poland, this looks practically Western to me, though Martin assures me that this is purely a trick of my severely altered perceptions.

Also, plenty of restaurants and coffeehouses, some of them with attractive outdoor terraces. Martin decides we'll have lunch in a place famous for slinky art-nouveau panels by Mucha. He takes an almost personal pride in the ornate, gilded interior; but when he tries to convince me that the food is as good as the decor, his credibility comes to a halt. The duck has hardly any meat on its bones, and what there is has the consistency of leather; the famous dumplings, which accompany just about every Czech meal, are puzzlingly dry, and since the only merit of the always bland dumpling is its plump, moist texture, these are rendered quite pointless. No vegetables accompany this meal, and when I ask about a salad, the waiter, already sullen, practically rolls his eyes with impatience. Martin tells me I must understand; they had no incentive to behave better under Communism; but I wonder how the incentive to better cooking got so entirely lost as well.

And what has happened to the esthetic sense, for that matter? En masse, and on first impression, the latter-day inhabitants of Prague look a dowdy, plumpish lot, without much sense of style. But though the Czechs may not look fashionable to me, they apparently find each other irresistibly attractive. On the streets, young couples nuzzle and caress and gaze into each other's eyes; on the steep, speedy subway escalators, they stand in tight embraces or fall into trances of exploratory sensuality. Given the untroubled, pervasive eroticism of so much Czech writing, I wonder if for some reason undetectable to the foreign eye, this is indeed, as Milan Kundera somewhere said, a sexual paradise.

The subway is a model of urban transport—impeccably neat, infallibly functional, and very well designed, with a tubular motif repeated in the escalator banisters, the ceilings, and the gleaming stations, whose walls are covered with ceramic tiles. The subway was designed by the Soviets, who were, for some reason, very good at subways.

After a day of being a tourist, I retire gratefully to my quarters, which I have rented from an elderly couple; a hotel room is just about impossible to obtain. The Zákons seem to me beautifully to fulfill every stereotype of Czechness I have acquired from Czech movies and novels. Mr. Zákon is a short, pudgy, walrus-faced man, with a mustache and a sharp twinkle in his eye, which I find immediately endearing; there's nothing like a gleam of humor to reassure you that a fellow human being is ticking inside a strange face. Mrs. Zákon is plump and matronly, and smiles calmly through all difficulties. She's very concerned about what I'll have for breakfast, but it seems we can understand each other just enough across the Polish-Czech barrier to settle a few basic matters—and we both take great satisfaction in this feat of international communication.

Mr. Zákon is teaching himself English from a book—everyone, it seems, is learning English this summer, for everyone knows that the road to Europe leads in large measure via America—and though his vocabulary is minuscule, his pronunciation is very exact, and there's a funny elastic bounce to all his simple sentences.

"Would you like to see your room, madam?" he asks with mock formality. "I hope you'll find it very . . ." He stops, raises a wait-a-moment finger, and proceeds to look quite calmly through a dictionary. "Comfortable," he enunciates. "I hope you'll find it comfortable."

The room is comfortable, and large, though marked by an almost willful drabness of decor. A beige rug, brownish bed covers made of some indescribable furry synthetic, a coffee table in a sub-Swedish style, dim, yellowish lighting; I am in Eastern Europe, after all. But there are fresh towels set out on a chair and a vase of flowers by my bedside—soothing modest signs of civility. When I discover that the hot water runs with some regularity and in adequate supply, my satisfaction is quite complete.

The next morning, however, it transpires that our sense of having achieved a cross-linguistic understanding was, alas, illusory. Despite my insistence that I eat almost no breakfast, Mrs. Zákon has set out before me a meal that throws me into a state of profound gustatory discouragement. On the small kitchen table there are several kinds of ham and salami and cheese; eggs and sausage; tomatoes; and two kinds of cake. Mrs. Zákon hovers over me solicitously, and wrings her hands when she sees what a poor customer she has in me. It takes some strength of character on my part not to stuff myself silly just to please her.

Mr. Zákon comes back from a fishing expedition on the Vltava. He gets up at dawn to practice this national pastime; and again, remembering the many fishing episodes in Czech novels and stories, I experience that small pleasure of recognition that people weaned on books feel when a fictional motif appears faithfully reproduced in real life.

Since I have discovered that my grasp of Czech cannot be trusted, I decide to go to the local Associated Press office to make inquiries about translators. There a secretary says that he can provide one, and, after doing some quick calculations with a transparently shifty look on his face, he mentions a truly extortionary price for such services, a price that would be high in Manhattan or London. I feel faintly insulted, both by being placed in the role of a rich, gullible Westerner, and by the alacrity with which this man is willing to exploit his country's new modishness. I say no thank you, probably too curtly.

An English-speaking journalist who's working in the office invites me for coffee and quickly launches into a long, acrimonious gripe against Havel. The journalist is tall, gangly, with long hair coming off a bald spot, and I can see that he derives a great deal of energy from having found a new critical stance. Havel has no economic program, he says bitingly, and surrounds himself with fellow dissidents who don't know the first thing about economic reform; and besides, there are too many Commies in the cabinet. So all right, so the guy wrote a few plays—let's not talk about how good they are—and nice-sounding moral essays, but this is business! "How would you like to have a playwright as the leader of your country?" the journalist rhetorically concludes, as if the answer to that one were self-evident.

"Perhaps better than having a politician for one," I answer much too glibly.

The New Criticism, however, seems to be firmly installed in Prague, or at least in its inner circles. Later in the day, I talk to a man whom I'll call Ota, who has been close to Havel through the dissident years. In the first few months after the changes, he also worked hand in hand with Havel in the Civic Forum— the political body, not yet a party, which, for the time being, is the umbrella structure for non-Communist politics. Now, he has resigned from the Civic Forum, in fatigue and disaffection. He says he has always been suspicious of Havel's flamboyance, of his tendency to theatrics, of his high-handedness. When Havel was the acknowledged opposition leader, Ota charges, he preferred to meet in restaurants and other dangerously open spaces; he exposed people to unnecessary risks. As the acknowledged moral leader of the underground, he made decisions by fiat—and he still does. In the meantime, he has no idea of economics, and is dithering on announcing any economic reform—they're falling behind the Poles, for heaven's sake! Moreover, Ota continues his complaints, Havel only listens to "his boys," buddies from the dissident days, who give him bad advice and unquestioning admiration—which shouldn't be surprising, he concludes, since Havel never suffered criticism gladly. All of this has caused tensions between the Forum and the Castle, the seat of the government, where Havel now resides—the beginnings of a fault line in the short-lived coalition.

The honeymoon is over so quickly! It is possible that dissident politics, which thrives on charismatic personalities and moral authority and abrupt decisions, is, in some ways, a poor preparation for the ordinary politics of pragmatic compromise. Still, I keep wondering just how exempt from human faults our politicians are supposed to be. Shouldn't Havel get more benefit of the doubt? We are pleased to think nowadays that suspicion is the best avenue to truth; but I find that I am becoming suspicious of the suspicious impulse itself.

In the streets, no disillusionment yet. Portraits of Vašek, as Havel is called here, are everywhere; in shop windows, his framed photographs have supplanted the ubiquitous Eastern European photos of Lenin and local Communist leaders.

Walking through Wenceslas Square, I come upon an incongruous scene: a small crowd of young people have gathered around a singer with a guitar, a very clean-cut, blond American guy; he's belting out, in a beautiful, smooth voice, a rousing religious hymn. After finishing his performance, he and his equally clean-cut assistants flash sunny smiles and hand out leaflets advertising their branch of the Baptist Church: the missionary spirit sensing, instantly, an ideological vacuum.

In the plaza of the National Theater, a free concert of another kind. There's music everywhere in Prague these days, lending a celebratory sweetness to this transitional season. In the evenings, sounds of Mozart and Monteverdi emanate from a central island on the Vltava; on the Charles Bridge, amateur bands try their Beatles mettle, and in various jazz clubs, serious-looking young people dressed in unwavering black, imitate Greenwich Village bohemians of the early sixties. In the plaza, popular actors and musical personalities perform light *Schlagieren*—sly, creamy hits of another time. A brassy orchestra breaks out into "Oh When the Saints," and near me, a round-bodied woman with a small, heart-shaped mouth lipsticked very red sways and bounces with a look of unadulterated pleasure on her face—an image of jolly, oom-pah-pah *joie de vivre*. Prague has always been a city of musicians, though that might change, too. "Until now, everyone wanted to be a musician," Ota said to me. "Now everyone wants to be a businessman." Reflecting the mood and the needs of the times, he made this observation with considerable satisfaction and approval, but I myself hope that, in this respect at least, the changes will be good and slow.

To rest a bit, I walk into a pub, that other motif found in every Czech film and novel. Though it's early afternoon, the dim stone interior is as full as Polish bars at any time of the day. But unlike the Poles, the men here—for they are all men—aren't drunk. They sip dark liquid from tall tankards slowly and look as though they could go on this way forever, and probably do. Of course, nobody bothers me, but they all look up with frank curiosity as I come in, and I can stand my double oddness of being a woman and a foreigner for only so long. I terminate this part of my investigations quickly, leaving my beer nearly undrunk.

A friend has arrived from New York, and I meet her in the Praga Hotel, on the outskirts of the city. A strange place: enormous, empty foyer, a ceremonial marble staircase leading to an equally empty bar and terrace, oversized leather chairs; the style of gigantism. A high-level *nomenklatura* hotel, where meetings with such people as Arafat and Qaddafi took place; the murky East-Mideast connection. The hotel is strategically placed on an isolated hilly promontory, to guard against attack.

Later, in the deepening dusk, I walk with my friend toward the Castle, that gorgeous complex of buildings and courtyards that began to rise over Prague in the eleventh century. The way up leads over deserted, steep cobblestoned streets, lit only by the golden glow emanating from the pubs and by the whiter illumination streaming serenely from the Castle. Ordinarily, I might be fatigued, or out of breath, walking up such long, steep hills, but now I seem to be in a state of enchantment, which pulls me toward the Castle as if I had forgotten I was a corporeal creature. Such must have been the feeling of awe, or of beauty, that convinced the more credulous populace of an earlier time that the monarch inhabited the realm of the sacred.

And now, the Castle is the location of real events that seem half fabulous. Havel's progress from prison to the Castle—surely that has elements of fable. But already he's undergoing a hard test of mundane political realities. One thing that is being tested is his own idealism. In his powerless days, Havel wrote stirring essays on the power of morality in collective life; on the efficacy of personal truth in changing the world. How much of his purist humanism can survive pragmatic politics? This is certainly one interesting question posed by these well-intentioned revolutions: what are the limits of good—of the best—intentions?

For now, it seems fitting that the playwright-president should have a setting so magnificently staged. Havel seems to like the pageantry of state; one of his first acts in office was to put colorful prewar costumes on the palace guards, and start driving in a Rolls-Royce once owned by the adulated interwar president Tomáš Masaryk.

The Castle's courtyards, irregularly shaped and drawing one in through a sequence of different epochs, are white-illumined and empty, except for a lone roller skater gliding in graceful circles around a straining, burgeoning statue. His figure, swooping in insouciant dips and turns against the night sky traces, for me, a lovely, teasing signature of Prague's dark-light magic.

The stories I hear of the shuttered decades begin to shade Prague differently, until it begins to seem an ironically beautiful setting for a dark fairy tale, a story in which a curse fell upon the city and arrested its citizenry in a long, fantastic nightmare.

There is, for example, Anna's story. I first met Anna Grusova at the Slavia, an ornate, large coffeehouse that was once the favorite hangout of Prague's literary crowd. Here, Jaroslav Seifert wrote, poets gathered and looked out at the miniature model of the Eiffel Tower you can see jutting out of one of Prague's hills, and at the river winding its way through the city, and in the poem's words "it was the Seine, yes, it was the Seine"—and the poets could imagine they were in Paris itself. Now, the Slavia is full of tourists rather than poets, and not even its great decorative charms can counteract the gloomy atmospheric effects created by the surly waiters.

Anna is a woman in her late forties, with a tough, bony body and a worn face. But when she begins to talk, she becomes quite beautiful. It's not that her face is mobile; but her large blue eyes fill with emotion as if with a palpable interior pressure. She is deeply moved by what has happened to her country; she remembers going into the subway in the week after the Communist regime had resigned, and seeing the faces of people coming up on escalators, "and those faces were different. I have seen those faces every day for twenty years—those closed, angry, downward-looking faces. Now they had changed. People were straight; they looked at each other; there was some trust, some hope."

But for her, Anna says with a quiet sadness, it all happened too late. Why, how can this be? I keep asking, for in my acquired repertory of American thinking, it's never too late, and this is not a phrase I like to admit to my consciousness. She had already been disappointed so often, Anna answers with quiet dignity. People older than she, who were already successful "before," can make a comeback; and younger people have a chance to begin anew; but people of her generation, who were stymied before they even got started, have very little chance, she says. She had been through her disillusionments and her reckonings and coming to terms; and she doesn't think she has the energy to start the process—not only of new actions, but of hope—again.

It is only after we talk at length and I learn the particulars of her biography that I begin to comprehend the weight of conditions that converged on her life, and to see how astonishing it would be if she did *not* feel weariness, and some wariness, too.

The burden of Anna's circumstances was, almost from the beginning, determined by her being her father's daughter—for the Stalinists who reigned over her childhood and youth closely followed the "Macbeth" principle that if you punish the parents, you had better punish the children as well, especially if you have no justice on your side. Anna was ten years old when her father, Edward Goldstücker, disappeared. She was deeply attached to him and to her mother, both of whom had been early Communists of the most idealistic stripe. He was a translator and a literary essayist, who was active in Czechoslovakia's wartime resistance in England; and he worked in the Ministry of Foreign Affairs after the war. In 1949 he briefly served as Czechoslovakia's ambassador to Israel—the first and the last until 1990. Neither this post, nor being Jewish, would serve him well in what was about to come. After returning to Czechoslovakia, Goldstücker taught at Charles University in Prague—but that wasn't really why he had been summoned back from Israel; and one day he simply disappeared.

When Anna's father didn't return for the weekend to the country cottage where they were then living, her mother went to look for him in Prague; she had no idea what had happened to him. But when she inquired after him at the reception desk of the hotel where he had been staying, the hotel clerk, in his eagerness to please the powers-that-be, notified the authorities that the wife of a man they had just arrested had shown up. By the time she returned to the hotel, in the hope that her husband was there, two security policemen were waiting for her. The Slanský trials were on.

The documents about the show trials in Czechoslovakia make for almost unbearably grim reading. As in the Soviet Union and Hungary, the Czechoslovak terror came in two phases. The first stage took place in 1948, when Stalin, after the expulsion of Tito from the Soviet Bloc, ordered a series of "purifying" purges within the Eastern countries. In Czechoslovakia, the trials were instigated by Rudolf Slanský, secretary-general of the party in charge of security. However, the grotesque proceedings were directed by Soviet security agents, who supervised the tortures and interrogations, and who, in truly Orwellian lingo, were called "teachers." In this phase of the terror, thousands of Communist Party officials were tortured and sentenced, and hundreds of non-Communists were executed.

A year later, it was Slanský's turn. In another piece of perverse logic, the Soviets decided that, to justify the purges of small-time *apparatchiks,* they needed highly positioned scape-goats to persuade the populace of the enormity of the anti-Communist danger. In Czechoslovakia, Slanský himself was cho-sen as the appropriate figure, and, in order to make charges of conspiracy plausible, thirteen other senior members of the gov-ernment and the party were put on trial with him. Eleven of the fourteen defendants were Jewish; eventually, eleven were exe-cuted, eight of them Jews.

It is also grim to reflect that while these horrors were going on, Western ideologues were debating the merits of the Commu-nist experiment; and that some were still deluding themselves with fantasies of an Eastern utopia. For the actual subjects of these fantasies, the experiment was conducted on their lives; Communism was turning not only into the god that failed but into a macabre deity that mutilated and devoured its children.

Like all relatives of the accused men, Anna and her mother heard the trials on the radio. After an interrogation and a house search, Anna's mother had been released. But they had not had word from Eda Goldstücker for ten months. Now they listened to him confess to acts he had never committed. And, like other wives who listened to their husbands reciting the deadly litanies in monotone voices, Anna's mother understood that her husband was repeating a memorized script. It was only much later that they learned about the torture and the breaking of personality, which led to these acts of utter self-betrayal.

Eda Goldstücker was relatively lucky; his part of the trial took place in March 1953, after the deaths of Stalin and Klement Gottwald, Czechoslovakia's obedient president, when executions were supplanted by sentences of lifetime imprisonment.

Anna vividly remembers going to visit her father, more than a year after his disappearance, in the old fortress of Leopoldov. "It was a peaceful village on a Sunday morning, people going to church in peasant costumes; road, water, bridge, trees—and then nothing but the black earth and the fortress rising out of it. Then, very thick walls, and somewhere in the middle of a dark entrance tunnel, big bars. On one side of the bars, about a meter away from it, there were the prisoners; on the other, women with children."

She remembers trying to act cheerful so that her father would believe that everything was all right; and she remembers feeling terrified, at the mercy of the guards who were watching her every move. Ever since then, she says, she has been pursued by the knowledge that your fate is not always your own, that in certain circumstances there are people who have the absolute power to decide it by mere caprice.

These were the formative events of Anna's youth, as they were for an entire generation—for even those who were less directly affected lived within the black cloud of fear that emanated from the terror. For most, alas, the show trials were a convincing lesson in the necessity of submission.

There are several memoirs that came out of that terrible period. Two of them—*Under a Cruel Star* by Heda Margolis Kovaly and *Love and Freedom* by Rosemary Kavan—were written by wives of accused men. They are beautiful books about abysmal events; but one of the most dispiriting features of both women's experience was the isolation into which they were thrown after being branded as wives of traitors. For the most part, Czech society drew its skirts tightly around itself; Anna's mother was thrown out of her job the day after her husband's "confession," because, as the head of a small dairy where she was an accountant explained, "to work with such a person is unbearable for the working class." Anna, who was in elementary school, lived with the consciousness that she had no chance of being admitted to high school, even if she was the best student in her class.

Anna's father spent four years in prison, eleven months of it in a solitary cell, with nothing to read or to write on. He told Anna later that what kept him sane was doing mathematical puzzles in his head. After being transferred to a cell with other prisoners, he taught his cellmates, some of whom had never been to high school, about painting and literature. Anna recalls a young man coming to visit her father later and thanking him for what had been his only education. Lucky were those who, in prison, could draw on such resources of memory and knowledge.

Eda Goldstücker was also lucky in that he lived to see the beginnings of de-Stalinization. In one of those sentimental gestures to which for some reason the crueler rulers are prone, he was released on Christmas Eve. Anna remembers his colorless face and the happiness they all felt when he reappeared as unexpectedly as he had vanished four years before.

Despite everything, it was difficult for Anna's parents to shed their beliefs. Anna's father is Jewish, her mother Catholic; but both of them, Anna says, were brought up in deeply religious households, and made a very conscious break with religion in their early youth. It was the very strength of their reaction, Anna thinks, that led them to invest all their need for a system of belief in their next faith. Like many committed Communists of their generation, they continued to think that the unspeakable things that had actually happened to them were a deformation of the original idea. For many of them, it took the Soviet invasion of 1968 to give up that forlorn form of idealism too, and to reject their philosophy at its very foundations.

There was, however, for all of them, an interlude of hope. After his release in 1957 and official "rehabilitation," Anna's father went back to teaching literature, translating from German and writing criticism. Anna married Jiří Gruša, who was to become one of the best-known Czech novelists, and they soon had a child.

On the political front, there were enormous changes as well. The icy Communist monolith was showing signs of strain, and the increasingly bold attempts to pry it apart—mostly from within the party itself—culminated in that great burst known as Prague Spring. Anna's father was once again at the center of events, since he was at that time the chairman of the Writers' Union, which became one of the main forces behind the thaw. That was the time when writers were the acknowledged legislators of the oppositional polity, and the speeches made at the famous 1968 Congress by Ludvik Vaculík and Milan Kundera among others sounded a clarion call for this brief revolution. Alexander Dubček, the Slovak leader of the liberal faction within the party, became first secretary; for eight months, there was exuberant activity in the streets, and attempts to institute "socialism with a human face" from the top.

Anna speaks with even precision, but as she talks about the importance of that time, and the defeat that followed, her voice becomes halting and muted. The difference between before and after was a difference between "a perspective of hope" and a sort of blackness in which the horizon of hope disappeared. "It was as if a screw was turning slowly," she says. "The space for breathing was less and less."

It was dismaying to many that the Soviet tanks rolled into Czechoslovakia basically unopposed; on the other hand, the lessons of the bloody crushing of the Hungarian Revolution in 1956 were still quite fresh. To give me a sense of the impact of those events, Anna tells me that, until then, she thought literature was the most important thing in the world. After the Soviet invasion, reality so overwhelmed imagination that for a while she couldn't read anything at all; all literary description and form seemed annoying and false, insufficient to the swallowing blackness of what had happened.

After 1968, it was almost impossible to be an idealistic Communist anymore, and those who entered the party afterward did so out of opportunism and careerism. For most of Anna's generation, there was only rage or resignation. Anna's parents, for whom the situation had become dangerous once again, managed to emigrate to England. For Anna herself, as the daughter of her parents and the wife of her husband—he had also been a prominent activist in the Prague Spring—there was small, unspoken, soul-eating persecution. At the technical institute where she worked, she was boycotted by not being given anything to do for weeks. She quit, to maintain her dignity. At one of the places where she subsequently applied for a job, the director was so terrified of her very presence that he made a personal appeal to her to make herself scarce. At an accounting firm, she was told that she would get a low-level job if she agreed to inform on her fellow employees. "After I went out of there," she remembers, "I felt like somebody from whom a dog wouldn't take a piece of bread."

It was then that Anna started choosing what the Czechs called "internal emigration"—that strategy of decamping psychologically, which many adopted as a way of preserving their sanity. She started working as an assistant in a dress shop, and she stayed there for fourteen years. It was a hard period. By that time Anna was divorced and had two children. Her job started early in the morning and required her to stand on her feet all day long. But there was also an emotional adjustment to make. "In the shop, I had to check the words I was using," she recalls, "because people reacted to my vocabulary as if I were trying to be something better. There were times when I came home and wrote a few lines of anything—just to remind myself that I still had this other language. But I understood that from then on I had to live in two worlds, and that those worlds would never be integrated."

In all these years, I ask her, was it impossible to find a job in publishing, for example? "Once, at the beginning," Anna answers quietly, "I dropped by to see friends who worked in a publishing house, and they were very nervous. I realized they were worried I'd ask for a job. And on the whole, it was very funny to meet people on the street who pretended not to know me. After a while, I formed a policy that I never addressed anyone unless they addressed me first. But what I really hated were the complaints of people who remained within the official structures and made careers within them, all the time talking about how hard it was for them to compromise and to adjust. I felt it was their choice; it was possible to remain outside the structures."

When Anna got married again, after ten years of being alone, she did so in almost comically Czech circumstances. She met her new husband because he was one of the few lawyers daring enough to defend her ex-husband, Jiří Grusa, who was in prison on the charge that his celebrated novel, *The Questionnaire,* was pornographic. Grusa was released after three months—

imprisoning a well-known writer generated too much bad publicity in the West.

Anna's new husband was also habitually harassed, since he took on cases of dissidents and other unpopular people; he was subject to weekend detainments in jail, and their house underwent frequent police searches. This was the period of "normalization"—that is, the deep entrenchment of oppression—in which intimidation sufficed in place of execution or torture.

Still, whatever the costs of her own situation, she thinks she was better off in her "internal emigration" than the great majority who made their accommodations with the system. "You see, this was something that I chose for myself. No one forced me to do it. If something happens due to your own decision, it's easier to bear. And I always felt that we—that is, the people who somehow stood on the outskirts of the society—were more free. We didn't have to go to May 1 processions, or to write reports on our fellow workers. And we could act according to our convictions, and that was a great luxury." In the latter part of the Communist epoch, the game of life and death was supplanted by a pettier business of lies and corruption and daily, blatant abuse. I try out the thought that perhaps she could have gone along with that, could have made her compromises in order to gain a small measure of comfort. But as I imagine the thousands of small, rubbishy acts that Anna would have had to swallow and commit in order to stay within the structures, I begin to understand that for her the choice to stay outside was not only an act of moral high-mindedness, but a matter of self-preservation, of keeping her identity alive.

I spend some time with her in Prague. We walk around the city, which she knows like the back of her hand and loves with that attachment so often found here, where people spend lifetimes, and generations, in one place. She points out an especially beautiful courtyard here, a monastery garden there. As I get to know her, I think about how gracefully she carries her experience, and the hard wisdom it has imparted to her. There is about her a kind of permanent gravity that she does not try to mask by any false, jovial cheeriness.

We talk about American television—CNN is widely available here, and Anna follows it closely. Currently, she is astonished by a couple who came on and talked about their private lives in front of the camera. "I think it's a sort of self-alienation to talk about yourself in this way," she says quietly, and I reflect how, in all her hardships, or perhaps precisely through them, self-alienation is something she avoided. All her choices were designed not to betray herself; and they have paid off in her having all of herself, even her pain.

Eventually, Anna had another child, a daughter who is now ten years old; eventually, she got divorced again, and found another partner, with whom she lives now. In the last few years, she has worked at a job more appropriate to her qualifications, translating medical articles from English for a hospital library. Anna's daughter—by the law of punishment unto the third generation—was kept out of the university, and has had to wait until the changes to have her status as persona non grata reversed. Her parents, after twenty-one years, have come back, exchanging the comfortable conditions of their Brighton home for these rather harder ones. I think of Hester Prynne, and her desire to live out her life where her fate was; for so many Eastern Europeans their countries have been something like fate.

An excess of fate, however, breeds fatalism, and I can see how Anna, whose circumstances have been so in excess of the normal conditions of human unhappiness, might not feel unalloyed joy at the start of yet another new era. While it might be tempting, for the casual outsider, to see her whole story in the light of the recent events, and to shout, "Hurrah! Happy ending!" Anna cannot divest herself of the burden of her life, or of the kind of wisdom it has taught her. On this level, there is a radical incompatibility between the goals of an organism as large as a nation, and one as individual as a human being; for while the country needs a jump start into a new age and a selective forgetting of the old, Anna has to move into the future as herself, while all the time living with the past.

Joseph, the man who is now Anna's companion, is an editor of a new journal, *Central Europe,* and one evening I am invited to their editorial meeting. The apartment where this takes place is dim and full of ornate, very dark furniture, age-worn rugs thrown about on tables and sofas, and mounds of books, manuscripts, paper. Once everyone comes in and gathers, round the rug-covered table, I have the impression that I'm at a Dutch guild meeting, or maybe in a Frans Hals painting, rather than at a modern editorial conference. The men are all thick-bodied, with enormous, broad faces, beards, and loose shirts with open collars and rolled-up sleeves. Just to show that they're in the twentieth century, though an earlier part of it than obtains in New York, for example, they all smoke like chimneys, and the room soon fills up with hazy cloudlets of smoke floating in the dim air.

In a sense, they *have* been part of a secret guild. Opposition was much less widespread in Czechoslovakia than in Poland, and more dangerous. Charter 77, the founding document of Czechoslovak dissidence, was signed by fewer than two thousand people; and many of the signatories paid a harsh price for their gesture. Dissidents lived in fear of being informed on; and several of the people working on *Central Europe* were consigned to enforced labor of sorts, as stokers or bricklayers—the preferred method of punishment for uncompliant Czech intellectuals. But their real lives revolved around their underground journal—one of the few that came out in Czechoslovakia after 1968; *samizdat* was also less widely disseminated here than in Poland, and its methods were less developed. Each issue was typed with multiple carbons, and about one hundred copies were distributed by hand to a trustworthy few, who in turn passed them to other readers. Already, this painstaking mode of production seems as remote and unlikely as medieval feats of stone ornament.

Now they are official and they have a computer, of which they are very proud. But they worry about the new Eastern European problems: funding, buying paper, getting issues printed on time.

And what is the idea, the vision of *Central Europe* in their title? Well, it's a squarely neo-conservative concept, they explain with Anna translating. They are followers of Milton Friedman, and were great admirers of Ronald Reagan; they think that Czechoslovakia needs a very strong bourgeoisie, a class that accumulates and produces wealth.

None of this surprises me too much. The combination of dissident temperament and neo-conservative convictions is becoming an Eastern European specialty, bred, like so much else, by local Communism. The first turn of mind, in opposing the ideology of centralization, the reality of totalitarianism, and the sentimentalities of the noble worker, is to reach for their polar opposites—the unhampered free market, personal liberty, and the virtues of middle-class individualism. Moreover, all such terms have a different meaning in the Eastern European context. To talk of a free market in a situation in which there is none has different implications than to talk of it in a country where it already rages. Here, the notion of the market represents a redress of an extreme imbalance; and if Eastern Europeans can't always see the ultimate implications of following Milton Friedman's vision, I don't see how they can be expected to. Certainly I'm not tempted to lecture to them at this point about the dangers of wealth or the diseases of the rich; for all my private thoughts on such matters, it would seem presumptuous to me; they, I'm sure, would think it a pure affectation.

Late in the evening, though, I am surprised when the discussion turns to the actual state of post-Communism. I am surprised by the vehemence of opinions that fly around the table, by the bitterness. Havel is running a pseudo-"red" government, somebody says, and everyone seems to agree; there are some nasty Communist types near him, and then there are all those pinkos, his buddies; he always had socialist ideas in the first place. Nothing has really changed yet; everything can still revert to the former state. "They" haven't given up an inch of their real power, and They are waiting for Their moment.

This is an early moment in the transition to the unknown;

and I sense, in such views, the pull of a worldview that offers the comfort, at least, of familiarity. Anna, with her quiet acuteness, offers another explanation. These opinions have little to do with ideology, she thinks; they reflect "our anxiety about what to do next. Now, things really could get better, and we really have to take responsibility. And we don't want to become too hopeful, not yet."

Later, I read one of Joseph's articles, which has been translated into Polish, on "the idea of Europe," in which the idea of Central Europe is, of course, included as well. Joseph belongs to a species almost unknown in the West, but frequently found in Eastern Europe—the declared religious intellectual—and the general point of the essay is that the moral underpinnings of Europe are to be found in Christianity, and that without Christian beliefs Europe is fated to fall from its high civilization and its political strength.

Milan Kundera has somewhere written that the only good Europeans nowadays are Central Europeans—those who have been so painfully exiled from the Europe to which they feel they rightfully belong, and for whom, therefore, "Europe" has remained a meaningful and unsullied ideal. But what I find both poignant and a bit startling about Joseph's article is that even its ideal of Europe belongs to a rather faraway past. It could only have been written in isolation, both from the realities of contemporary Europe and even from Europe's discourse about itself. I ask him what he would do, within his scheme, about a large population of Muslims now living in Western Europe. Should they be included in the idea of "Europe"? Are they European, even though not Judeo-Christian? He hasn't thought about it, he says; but then, this is not a problem that would have naturally occurred to him. Ideas do, after all, arise from our experience, and both the realities and the consciousness of ethnic and religious pluralism were strictly suppressed in Eastern Europe in the last several decades.

This is terribly ironic in a part of Europe that used to be a veritable bouillabaise of languages and nationalities. But the memory of a former multiculturalism—of the original Central Europe—has been effectively erased in Czechoslovakia in the last few decades. It may be significant that the only mention I hear of Mitteleuropa comes from someone who is, so to say, an official representative of this idea. Vladimír Železný could himself be a fine embodiment of it as well; he's a man in his early forties, with highly chiseled, intelligent features, great literary erudition, and an education in astrophysics. He is the new spokesman for the Civic Forum, but he also heads a recently created Kafka Society and has plans for establishing the Central European Culture Museum.

His notion of Mitteleuropa has to do with the burst of strenuous creativity that took place here between the wars. At the turn of the century, the compressed, variegated map of Central Europe gave rise to a moment of an almost fabulous cultural intensity. A certain kind of brooding, brilliant modernism could be said to have been born in this region. Not only Kafka but Freud, Mahler, Husserl, Franz Werfel, and Max Brod came from within a close radius of Prague. Železný thinks that the complexities of their perceptions were generated by the "vital tensions" among the three points of "the cultural triangle"—the Czechs, Germans, and Jews who lived within the Czechoslovak territory. I imagine that there was some interplay of difference and familiarity, of proximity and otherness among these centuries-old neighbors that gave the old Mitteleuropa its peculiar energies.

But after the war, the same region experienced another mode of modernity—modernity of massive scale and cultural monadism. Železný thinks that social homogeneity is unhealthy, as well as boring, and that the disappearance of the Jews and the Germans from Czechoslovakia helped pave the way for totalitarianism. But the new modernity systematically destroyed the memory of the earlier modernism. In history books, Mitteleuropa went unmentioned, and only now, Železný says, is the first textbook on this topic appearing, entitled *What Was Omitted from Your Textbooks*.

I doubt that the cultural Mitteleuropa can be resurrected *in vivo,* as Železný would wish; the setting—the gorgeous setting—is still here; but too much else has vanished. But I can see how Kafka's once-banished prophetic presence might be useful in interpreting the recent past—his future—and how reinserting the memory traces of Mitteleuropa might counter the monolithic imaginings of the last decades.

And in the meantime, intellectuals like Joseph have yet to make their encounter with the contemporary versions of heterogeneity: with the kind of coexistence and interpenetration of cultures from which the extreme Western relativism springs—a relativism that contends not only with questioning an opposing belief system, but doubting your own. Latter-day Eastern Europeans are used to skepticism about Them; but not yet to the more radical skepticism about the I. They haven't started deconstructing themselves. In that, undoubtedly, lies a certain strength, the integrity—in both senses of the word—of self that they have so much needed. With their exit from isolation, though, they'll once again have to begin navigating in more open and less charted waters.

I have found an excellent, amiable translator in Wendy, as she calls herself for Westerners' benefit, and she has invited me to come on a country outing—a ritual in which a large proportion of her countrymen participate each weekend. And so, on a beautiful Sunday morning, I wait for her and her husband Ota in the Castle area. For a while, there's a Sunday serenity and freshness, as if the dross of the week had been swept away. Then, the cobblestoned streets fill up with milling tourists—mostly German tourists, some of them dressed in dirndls and Lederhosen, as if they were returning to a place arrested in prewar time, a quaint outpost of their former empire. On the hour, church bells ring in a wonderful range of timbres.

Wendy and Ota arrive in their Russian Lada, and we're off, into the mild, rolling Bohemian countryside. After Poland, this, too, looks like the West: the roads consistently asphalted, the village houses built mostly of stone and brick, the farms neat as a pin.

Our first stop is a small hamlet of dachas, where Wendy and Ota want to drop in on some friends. A small settlement, its dimensions clearly visible: several rows of almost identical, cabinlike houses divided from each other by dirt paths nicely overgrown with wildflowers. The friends are a personable young couple who are clearly very happy with their tiny dwelling and little yard. A merry bustle greets our arrival, the couple's son urinates against a tree, the next-door neighbors bring over a large basket of beautiful sour cherries, and the whole scene somehow arranges itself into a vignette from a Czech movie. Only a brass band, or a chamber group, is missing.

The hosts tell me how hard they worked to put their cottage together. Materials were terribly hard to find, but they saved and scrimped and did everything themselves. Many others did the same; these country houses have been a Czech obsession, the *folie* to sweeten the bitterness of things; practically everybody has one, including workers, who are often paid better than teachers, or doctors, or other professionals. For many people, these little retreats have been the antidote to the small filth of daily politics, the privileged retreat where one could withdraw into "internal emigration" and one's real life.

The center of social life in our little hamlet is, of course, the local pub. We amble there after finishing our cherries, along the sunbaked, unpaved lanes, toward the river. It's before noon, but the large picnic table outside the pub is already crowded with people who have clearly been at their beer mugs for a while. Down at the riverbank, several boys are fishing.

Inside the pub, there's an array of old-fashioned and very crude pinups above the counter. From my Eastern European travels, I've become used to these; but I'm still surprised by the next bit of decor, which consists of several very ugly brassieres suspended on a clothesline. Some kind of joke, apparently.

Later, after we've finished our beer and have said our good-byes, I ask Wendy whether this display doesn't annoy her. She seems annoyed by my question instead. This is a specific kind of humor, she tells me rather brusquely, and it's not meant to give offense to anybody. I should understand. Well, I do understand that it's meant to be a joke, but a line of yellow brassieres seems to me too crude to be funny. Wendy is a free-lance journalist, and in many ways a kindred spirit; but here, a culture gap opens up. This must be another impenetrable aspect of the sensuality I've seen in Prague's nuzzling couples, which is present in so much Czech literature. When it's controlled by the carefully calibrated humor of Josef Škvorecký's fiction or the cinematic talent of Miloš Forman, the eroticism can be wonderfully sly, robust, comical; but without the brakes of artfulness, it can apparently descend into this pub drollery, which to me—these are the limits of my sensibility!—seems irrefutably and dully vulgar.

We step back from our little misunderstanding quickly. By midafternoon, we arrive in the country house that Wendy and Ota share with her parents. This one is in an older, more prosperous settlement, and has a spacious yard surrounded by tall pines of the adjoining forest, though still no indoor plumbing. Wendy's parents are both plump and comfy-looking, and they spend the afternoon puttering in the flower garden. Wendy soon produces the first delicious meal I've had in Czechoslovakia, of vegetable soup and salad, and a wonderfully moist plum cake. She seems perplexed by the extent of my gratitude for the greens on my plate. I was beginning to wonder if they exist here, but they do, though they're apparently regarded as an inferior part of the human diet—fit for private consumption, perhaps, but almost universally disdained in public establishments.

Wendy's nine-year-old daughter takes me around the yard, showing me her favorite spots and hiding places, and speaking to me in Czech all the time, in perfect confidence that I'll understand her. Perhaps because of her childish vocabulary and intonations, I do. She's a serious little person with a lovely, dimpled smile, and Wendy treats her very much like an adult, as parents here tend to. The children seem happier for that, less coyly "childish," and friendlier in facing the grown-up world. Wendy's son arrives, with some high school friends, and they try to converse with me in English, though to little avail. Like all their peers, they are trying to learn English quickly; they consider it their card of entry into the modern world. Then they go off into the forest, for one of those long, two-day hikes that the Czechs—who are great campers and fishermen and aficionados of their countryside—do with a passion. The sound of a boom box accompanies their departure, and Wendy looks disapproving. "See?" she says. "Pretty soon, they'll forget how to make conversation."

Then it's time for us to go too, and we set off in the Lada into the pinkish sunset. A day in the country, Czech style. It's not exactly Renoir, but there's something of the French cult of *le petit plaisir* in this relish of small, daily enjoyments. The pub, the country house: they were antidotes to the system, and I can see their legitimate appeal. They represent a less heroic model, perhaps, than the barricades; but after all, it is—or should be—the goal of every revolution, or social transformation, to allow people to enjoy just such satisfactions, to achieve some order of things in which the little pleasures of life can take their normal place.

Back in Prague, I meet Martin and his friend Jiří, and together we take a cable car to a restaurant at the top of the Letenske Gardens, way up in Prague's verdant hills. There we sit at a terrace table won for us through Jiří's "connections" with the head gorgon of the place, and eat the usual fattening fare, and look down on Prague's red roofs and gold spires, sweeping majestically down toward the river and beyond it; a spectacle of beauty and historical texture rivaled by few places in the world.

Jiří is a handsome, blond man, a graphic artist and homespun philosopher, in whom the mildness of the Czech personality has been refined into a positive virtue. Martin and he reminisce about their common Communist upbringing the way lapsed Catholics reminisce about their schooling at the hands of nuns, with a combination of robust satire and wistfulness; it's all over now. They laugh at their memories of the People's Olympiads, in which tens of thousands of citizens gathered in Prague from all over the country, to show off the physical prowess of the collectivity. Enormous formations of comrades, dressed in white athletic outfits, marched and performed exercises in a giant sports stadium, for the greater glory of the people. But Jiří remembers his brother, who kept stumbling and falling out of step; and Martin recalls how, during one rainy Olympiad, the white outfits became a ghastly splattered mess after a round of pushups in the mud. The people making a mockery of the People. After these official spectacles, Martin and Jiří fondly recall, the parks of Prague became a coupling ground, as the citizens from various provinces lustily fell upon each other and the police relaxed their guard in acknowledgment of an unstoppable carnival.

But Jiří grows pensive as he talks about his situation right now. In a way, he's afraid of the opening to the West, of the new availability of the world. The minor arts—the less politically threatening ones, like illustration, posters, prints—have thrived in Czechoslovakia, since they were allowed pretty much to go their own way. But Jiří has ambitions to be a painter as well, and painting—like all art that depends on pushing the limits of vision and experiment—has suffered in Eastern Europe from the limitations imposed upon it. Jiří has a lovely atelier, for which he pays almost no rent, and which is the kind of thing the previous regime provided. But the same regime also insisted upon strict isolation, and now, for all his curiosity and aspirations, Jiří is half reluctant to come out of his esthetic cave and look at what has been happening in the wider world all this time. Like a person who's been fasting and can't start eating too rapidly, he's wary of sudden overload. "We'll have to go slowly," he says. "We can't take it in all at once. There's only so much I can really understand at one time. I'll have to have time to think, digest."

This is not the heroic attitude of the Promethean artist; but I find something very appealing in his modesty, and in his self-knowledge. He understands what it really means to take something in, and he knows that to do that he needs to go slow.

Jiří has lived quietly in Prague, in a fashion that almost harks back to a prewar world. He has painted, taught, gone to concerts in Baroque churches, sung in choirs. The gentleness, the civility of his personality are of a piece with this, created by it, no doubt; and I can see why he might not want to be jolted out of his well-defined frame too suddenly by all the shocking disorder of the art made in the last several decades.

We finish our dinner and drink our *beherovka,* a bitterish liqueur, and look at the mellowing light of Prague. Jiří talks with a touch of envy about a fellow artist who has succeeded in America, "just because his uncle knew somebody who knew somebody." Then he says, "Well, but instead, I got to stay here. I didn't lose Prague. Maybe, all in all, that's what I prefer."

"We're a nation of petit bourgeois," the Czechs often say about themselves. "And we have bourgeois aspirations." This confession is made half in self-satisfaction, half in self-deprecation. Being petit bourgeois means being earthbound, concrete, and sensible, as well as cautious and limited in aspirations. Czechoslovakia is a plebeian nation—so the standard explanation goes—because it has had no aristocracy for several centuries. One of the watershed dates in Czech history was 1618, when the Czech nobility was eliminated in a wholesale massacre by the Hapsburg armies in the battle of Bílá Hora, or White Mountain. That event instigated three centuries of Hapsburg rule, of cultural Germanization and the near-obliteration of Czech language and identity. During that time, the Czechs were relegated to the lesser roles of merchants and farmers and functionaries—especially the latter; Czechs served as clerks and bureaucrats representing the crown throughout the Hapsburg Empire.

"We're not a nation of Švejks," is another thing the Czechs say. Or, more rarely, "We are a nation of Švejks."

The Good Soldier Švejk, Jaroslav Hašek's archetypal creation, is the consummate articulation of the plebeian sensibility—shrewd, self-protective, sly, and profane. The novel recounts the multiple adventures of its eponymous hero as he evades all attempts to be enlisted in the Austro-Hungarian army during World War I. I confess that, though I know it's a great work, in fact I dislike it. I am uncharmed by the petty cynicism of its protagonist, who is willing to play the utter fool and subject himself to any degree of humiliation in order to save his skin. Of course, I know that while playing the fool he's exposing the idiocy of war and foiling an absurd bureaucracy—but I would prefer him to fight these evils in a more high-minded (and undoubtedly self-defeating) way. Polish prejudices, no doubt.

Hašek and Kafka: both were part of a founding generation of Czech literature, which burgeoned seemingly out of nowhere after centuries of quiescence, and which also included Karel Čapek, the creator of fictional robots and prophetic totalitarian fantasies. Hašek's and Kafka's life spans overlap almost exactly (they were both born in 1883; Hašek died in 1923, Kafka in 1924) and they are the two literary reference points the Czechs use most often (at least when talking to foreigners) for explaining their country, or their situation, or themselves.

Hašek was a man of the people, who wrote in Czech, lived the life of an adventurer-tramp, defected from the Austrian Army, and got regularly soused in neighborhood pubs. Kafka, of course, was a Jew who lived a sequestered life and wrote in German. Their sensibilities couldn't have been more opposed. But it could be said that, in their very different veins, they wrote about the same subject: bureaucracies gone berserk, bureaucracies as edifices of darkly absurd, or just stupidly absurd, menace. I wonder if it's not too fanciful to think that this was because they both lived at one of the pressure points where bureaucracy and irrationality converged most intensely. Their formative years coincided with the apogee and the decline of Franz Josef's empire, when Czechoslovakia was a near province of Kakania, as Robert Musil renamed Austro-Hungary—that monstrously static kingdom governed by rafts of clerks, a love of hierarchy and respect for formalism. At the same time, the Czechs were a subject nation, which never quite lost its sense of smallness, or the instinct of at least passive resistance, a stubborn

disagreement with the condition of oppression. It was a conjunction that must have heightened the feeling of disproportion between the ordinary, small person and the bloated tiers of
Hapsburgian institutions. Or, to put it another way, Prague must
have been a good vantage point from which to observe the neuroses of the bureaucratic personality.

A Czech friend of mine talks about a rhythm in Czech history, an alternation of near-submission followed by a burst of
highly moral response. The latter was evident in Jan Hus, with
his early attempt at reformation, mounted in response to the excesses of an essentially foreign church hierarchy; and in the phi-
lologists and philosophers of the late nineteenth century, who
tried to restore Czech identity through translating Shakespeare
and other classics, and through sweetly reasoned arguments
about the rights of nations; and in Tomáś Masaryk, surely one of
the most humane and broadly educated politicians ever to attain
presidential office. There were Prague Spring and Charter 77.
There is Václav Havel, of course, who has the rare daring to continue writing in a quiet, civil voice about his own inner history
and about his country's new moral quandaries even while he oc-
cupies the seat of power.

The other response to overwhelming domination has been
that mix of accommodation and withdrawal characteristic of the
Communist period: the Švejkian response to a Kafkaesque situation. Havel wrote somewhere that the trouble during the time of
"normalization" was that the Švejks took over; they were the
ones who imposed their moral tone, their seeping cynicism, on
the whole society.

I must confess that in my daily encounters with waiters and
travel agencies and the post office, with clerks whose expressions
are fixed in a glum "horseshoe mouth," as the Czechs call it, I
feel the Švejkian presence acutely. One morning, I walked into a
store and asked the saleswoman if she could let me have a cardboard box I needed for mailing something. She arranged her expression into a disdainful indifference, and shrugged her
shoulders. This doesn't concern me, her demeanor said; I'm not

going to lift a finger. There was a stack of boxes near me. I pointed to them; I asked if I could pay for one. She deepened her look of disgust and turned away.

But then, there's the endearing side of the Švejkian sensibility: the relish in small pleasures I sense everywhere; the ripened irony that I hear in Jiří and Martin's conversation; the constant jokes and Mr. Zákon's humorous twinkle, which says, "It's all right, somehow we can fool the world, and get some enjoyment out of it all yet." The sense of the absurd lives on and may be a saving grace in this time, as at any other.

Mr. Zákon knocks on my door on a quiet morning, and summons me to the living room to watch a historic moment on a big color television set, with the rest of the family. Havel is being inaugurated as president. Plump Mrs. Zákon is there, and their son, who has come over for this occasion, and also the son's girlfriend. Havel walks down the aisle jauntily, trying to keep down an irrepressible smile that threatens to break out with perhaps less gravity than is required of the moment. Mr. Zákon points out various MPs—who is quarreling with whom; the Slovak deputies, standing in a separate cluster. Beginnings of troubles can be clearly read. But Havel's unruly smile continues to get away from him, as he signs the swearing-in document with a long, ceremonial pen. He looks as if he were not only pleased but utterly amused by the event in which he's participating: perhaps by its wonderful improbability; or by its staginess. The playwright turned main actor and producer in the theater of reality.

The ceremony over, the elderly Mr. Zákon leaps up from the couch and shakes everyone's hand. "Congratulations!" he shouts. "We have a president!" We—for the moment at least.

A year later, there's the pleasure of rediscovery—of moving around Prague with ease, of looking more closely at details that were lost at first in the overwhelming whole. The Prague of stone and history is thankfully changeless, and its golden luster remains untarnished. I still pause breathlessly at the vista of the Old

Town Square, and look up with an epiphanous sensation at two slender obelisks bracketing the entry to a bridge, topped by two beautiful angels about to take flight from water and stone straight into the empyrean.

But, more surprisingly, the commercial Prague of today seems relatively unaltered as well. In contrast to the Toyota salons and the computer boutiques in Warsaw, the store windows here still face the street with the same state-produced fashions and Bohemian glass. Even the book-selling stands that in other Eastern European capitals have sprouted like mushrooms after the first free-market rain, are still absent here.

One afternoon, I walk into an "international" bookstore supposedly specializing in translations, in the center of town. I've run out of reading matter and my need for a book has become quite as urgent as my need for dinner or sleep. Travel apparently restores to one the meaning of literature, and if I ever doubted the uses of books, I am now very sorry. I begin to understand why travel writers are always alluding to what they've been reading, even as they are scaling a glacier or plunging into a deadly swamp. Faced with the unformed world before me, with the plethora of places, personalities, and accidental encounters, I crave the shapeliness, the ready-made order, of a written world.

So I enter the "international" bookstore with high hopes. These are soon crushed. The English section features *Treasure Island, Robinson Crusoe,* and *Little Women,* all in children's-book format, with cardboard covers and large print; plus three books on Chinese acupuncture. In my famished state, I buy *Little Women,* which, in my Eastern European childhood, I hadn't read, and *Robinson Crusoe,* which I had. At the counter next to me, a middle-aged American tourist is buying *Robinson Crusoe* and *Treasure Island.* His desperation apparently equals mine.

I also visit Iván Gabal, who is the head of the presidential office of opinion polls, and who confirms my very cursory impressions about the early progress of the Czech economy. I've met Gabal before, but he has changed jobs since I last saw him, and he's now ensconced in what must be one of the best office spots in the world, in the third courtyard of the Castle. I wait for him downstairs in the large waiting area, among a motley group. There's a scraggly, long-haired man who clearly styles himself a hippie, and an elderly gentleman who takes a cigarette out of an elegant silver box; the receptionist, in an elaborately designed Italian sweater, looks immaculately overdressed; a woman in rubber boots and a babushka is taking children's shoes and apples out of a paper bag and showing them to a man next to her. The old Central European *gemütlichkeit* was created by the mix of Slavs, Austrians, Jews, artists, peasants, scientists, in a lively common intercourse; the new Eastern European *gemütlichkeit* is made up of coexistent epochs so easily coming together in one room.

A young woman, munching an apple and moving languidly, takes me upstairs to Gabal's office. Gabal is a dark-haired, pleasant-looking man who tends to wear buttoned-up shirts and ties and good tweed jackets. There's a smoothness of manner about him, an easy self-confidence and a worldly savvy that come from having traveled a bit and, perhaps, from knowing that he counts. He is a member of a new cadre of technocrats, who are internationalist in manner and outlook, and whose expertise will be crucial in the reconstruction of Eastern Europe. Each age breeds its dominant personalities, and young men like him have appeared all over Eastern Europe—men with neatly trimmed hair and a rational air about them, and a tone of held-back, restrained objectivity; men whom I recognize because they look so American, as if together with America's mode of know-how, they've imbibed the corresponding style.

Gabal says he is disappointed by the quick breakdown of political consensus. The Civic Forum, following the seemingly ironclad logic of post-Communist politics, has split into three quite hostile factions. Havel, so far, has tried to stay above the fray, though it is widely known that he favors the group called "conservative"—the word here is used with the kind of approbation usually accorded in the West to the word "progressive"— which wants speedier transition to the free market.

The official plans for economic reform, though they came tardily, are in some ways more far-reaching here than in Poland. But Gabal says that the government has been discouraged by the passive attitude of Czechoslovak citizenry toward privatization. The reform program has been set in motion, but there are very few applications for new businesses, or proposals for what to do with outmoded factories. The process of reversing agricultural collectivization has also met with resistance from farmers, most of whom, it seems, have no desire to go back to private ownership. "People are more cautious than we thought," Gabal says.

A strain of caution among the Czechs has been noted before by Czechs themselves. In his autobiography, a document of rare and temperate humaneness, (it was dictated to Karel Čapek), Tomáš Masaryk upbraided his countrymen for a tendency to a sort of temperamental conservatism: "The mere desire for material serenity, preferably in a Government post so as to be sure of a pension," he wrote, "I see fear in all this, fear of a life of enterprise, of responsibility, of mastery. It is true that we lack a seacoast, we lack the consciousness that there is another world on the other side of it; we sit like frogs in a pond croaking to one another."

In my conversations with people, I have sensed some such initial timidity, a reluctance to step outside the prescribed bounds of action. "It's too late for me," people frequently say. Or, in effect, "Not yet; we're not ready to begin."

I talked to a young man, Jan, an engineer who's worried about losing his job if his factory becomes privatized, as it might if the economic reform takes off the ground. His dream is to start a business to import tools from Austria. The trouble is, he explains, the rules for starting businesses aren't yet set down; and besides, nobody has any money, so even if he started a business, who would buy anything from him? And then, the Communists are still around, and who knows what they'll get up to; he doesn't want to invest in a business only to have it confiscated. No, all of his friends are waiting until the situation clarifies itself much more.

An American journalist who lives here told me a small but telling anecdote about trying to have the windows washed in her apartment. She called a friend and asked him how to go about it. "It's impossible," was his fatigued response. "What do you mean?" she protested. "They do it only for commercial buildings. No one will come to do windows in a private apartment." "How can it be impossible to have your windows washed? There must be a way," she insisted. He was pessimistic. The funny thing was that he used to wash windows in his dissident days— this was the punishment to which he had been consigned. The journalist eventually called up the company in which he had worked, and after long negotiations persuaded them to send somebody. But "this business of the impossible" is still very much entrenched, she says, though she sympathizes with its causes.

But then, the Czechs have had good reasons to become wary in the last forty years, for this long period has been exceptionally discouraging, even by Eastern European standards. There was the deep totalitarianism of the Stalinist era, the most brutal series of show trials in Eastern Europe, and the ruthless crushing of the Prague Spring. Instead of the periodic liberalizations of the seventies and eighties that took place in Poland and Hungary, the last two decades were characterized by unrelieved repressiveness. There was no elbow room for individual action, almost no interstices in the grid of the system. The black market, the second economy—these were nonexistent in Czechoslovakia. Agriculture, which remained almost entirely private in Poland, was almost totally collectivized here.

The Poles, in their years of illicit activity, became very accustomed to bending the rules, or acting outside them or without them—or, of course, against them. For the Czechs, taking risks and initiative and banding together outside bureaucratic structures were subject to severe punishments. And though the system has suddenly changed beyond anyone's boldest expectations, the habit of hope cannot be acquired overnight, the customs of caution aren't easily discarded.

But there are, of course, people like Gabal, for whom the winds of change are whirling almost confusingly fast. When I last saw him, Gabal was launching an independent sociology institute, which was to distinguish itself from the old, official institute by its empirical methods of collecting data—an innovation in a country where data were unabashedly bent by ideology. Gabal's enterprise soon became so successful, that Havel offered him his current job as the pulse-taker of public opinion. Now he works much too hard, and really, he says, the work isn't as interesting as his own institute, which was "my love, my everything"; but still, somehow, he finds his new position irresistible. His wife, a museum curator, is working in the United States, which makes them chic pioneers in what will undoubtedly be a new breed of East-West commuting couples. But Gabal finds that the glitzy package has its unglittering aspects. "I work morning till night, from Monday till Saturday," he says, looking a little baffled, and even, for someone as composed as he, a little tormented. "And then I come back to my apartment and fall asleep. It's terrible to do it without family background."

Welcome to Western lifestyles, I comment silently; for, along with the excitement of their new international stature, people like Gabal have been catapulted into a whole new order of problems, which his Western counterparts know only too well. They'll have to calculate how much glamour and prestige are worth at the cost of pressure and stress and constant hurry; what they really, really want to do, when options are multiple and there is nothing but personal preferences to guide them; what job will lead where on a career ladder, and what a worthy occupation means in the first place in a world where jobs become more ambition-laden and more value-neutral.

When I visit Anna again, I find her in a somewhat altered mood. A year later, she allows herself a tempered optimism about the future, as if it has taken a while for her to really grasp that the conditions of her life have changed. Or perhaps—as is true of so many—it has taken her a while to get over the anxiety of change: anxiety about how she could respond to the new possibilities. She doesn't plan any dramatic alterations in her life. She wants to stay at her job until she can collect her pension, but afterward, she muses, perhaps she can finally do some literary translations—something she has wanted to do since high school, and which would have been so simple in more normal circumstances. "I can still do that, fortunately," she says. "But think about a singer who missed her best years, or a theater director who couldn't work when his imagination was at its most energetic. There are people who literally missed the best years of their lives, from whom they were taken away."

In the meantime, it has already made a difference to her that her boss, who until recently knew all too well that he was one of the few who would hire her, understands that now she has less reason to feel so deeply beholden to him. There's also the relief of knowing that if she sees ominous-looking men ambling down her street she needn't assume that they are the secret police; and neither does she need to assume that her phone is tapped, though she had become quite accustomed to the thought that it was.

I'm with Anna when she receives the news that her oldest daughter has been admitted to the university, after having had her entry barred. Anna looks quietly happy; her daughter is young enough to begin again, to make up for lost time.

Anna reiterates that she doesn't regret her own past; that she chose her life as a free agent. I have heard this tone of affirmation in others. A philosopher I talked to, a man who has suffered more than most, and whose response has been a reinforcement of his Catholic faith, quoted a rabbi to me. He said that if we had a chance to choose a second life, we would always choose exactly the same one we had.

I didn't quite believe that, I said. And yet . . . one cannot *not* choose one's life; one cannot reject it. And I can see how retrieving the sense of having owned one's life might be terribly important right now, both to the philosopher and to Anna. For how do you come to terms with a life in which you have been the subject—the victim—of plain injustice, of bald lies, of black absurdist farce? The alternatives are either a debilitating bitterness or a gesture of acceptance that is tantamount to choosing what has happened to you, perhaps even what has been done to you.

And in the meantime, there's ordinary life, one's own, unstealable personal life. I spend some time at Anna's house, where she cooks me an old-fashioned, labor- and cholesterol-intensive chicken dish, requiring several stages of sauce, butter, and milk, though my untutored palate fails to appreciate all its nuances. She chides Joseph for not doing his part of the housekeeping and gripes about the condition of women, but she says she's not a feminist; she believes women have a different destiny, because they have children. She scolds her daughter, a dimply ten-year-old who seems to me a model of good behavior, for a small transgression.

Anna worries that children like her daughter have become excessively private and solitary—paradoxically, because they have been overfed on collectivity and child-care centers. She worries, too, about adolescents who have grown up without any experience, any actual memory, of democracy, and who have been given a mendacious version of their own history.

But in her family's case, the compact between the generations has held strong. Anna's bonds with her parents, she tells me, have always been intense. During the time of their greatest troubles, she was her mother's confidante; now, at the age of fifty, she says pensively, she still turns into a daughter when she visits her parents. Her own older daughter, in turn, took on the role of moral and practical helpmate when Anna was in her time of great need; but now, Anna says, she becomes gratefully irresponsible when she comes to visit. In the extremity of the experiences that families such as Anna's were undergoing, generation gaps were surely less pertinent than in milder or more comfortable circumstances. Whatever the price of stymied adolescent rebellion, or premature maturity, they have paid, the prize that Anna and her parents and children seem to have retrieved is a sense of each other's common humanity, a kind of vertical solidarity through time.

Another weekend, another conference. In the midst of transition, Eastern Europe is undergoing an orgy of conferences about transition, as if historic change nowadays couldn't happen without instant self-analysis. There are conferences on the transition to democracy and the transition to freedom and justice and capitalism; on the virtues of democracy and the costs of democracy and the pitfalls of democracy; on the road to Europe and the path out of totalitarianism; on nationalism, patriotism, chauvinism, ethnic identity, and imperialism—and, of course, on that ideal conference subject, the situation of literature. A stream of letters, faxes, invitations, and paper proposals—all in English, the new regional Esperanto—flows ceaselessly between the Baltic and the Black Sea, though mostly to the same addresses. A jet set of conference-hoppers, ferried tirelessly from Bucharest to Vilno and from Sofia to Madrid, is emerging as the newest new class.

The subject of this weekend's gathering, insofar as one can make it out, is the situation of literature in Czechoslovakia after Communism, and, beginning with the mind-bending title (Divorce Between Politics and Literature: Preparations for a Wedding in the Country), the conference makes as little sense as any. The proceedings are presided over by a member of a growing Western tribe for whom Eastern Europe, now that it's hot, is becoming an interestingly exploitable career opportunity. A prize for translation is awarded. Seemingly numberless writers, among them several distinguished visitors from foreign countries, sit on a podium and make entirely unrelated remarks about the putative subject under discussion. An aging Czech *enfant terrible* makes an excited, provocative speech about either Communists or anti-Communists, I'm not sure which, translated in a deadpan voice into the earphones. The audience roll their eyes. An Irish poet, bless his Irish soul, falls into an alcoholic sleep right there on the podium in front of his microphone. A humorous Englishman makes sense for a few minutes, jolting everyone into upright incredulity. A young French philosopher speaks more incomprehensibly than anyone else.

The setting, however, is worth the price of admission. The conference is taking place in the Waldstein Palace, which now houses the Ministry of Education, but which was the first of Prague's Baroque residences (the building of it began in 1624), and is reputedly still the grandest. The room in which the puerile proceedings natter on is so luxurious that it takes a while to begin assimilating it visually. The sumptuous paintings covering every inch of wall and ceiling, the rich red hues, the gold mirror frames and crystal chandeliers, the sparkling reflections and coloristic heat achieve an effect of almost orgiastic abundance. The doors leading into the room are about ten feet tall, and the handles are placed unnaturally high—because, I'm told, the palace's original owner liked to ride into this salon on a horse and open the doors from the saddle. Nothing succeeds like excess was the Baroque idea, and in this interior, I can be convinced that nothing does.

I let my eyes wander over this splendor until the reception is announced. "We're here for the beer," the Englishman keeps announcing merrily. I chat for a while with Ivan Klíma, one of Czechoslovakia's best-known writers both here and abroad, though his home renown was spread exclusively through *samizdat*. His face is simultaneously boyish and very ripe, and as gentle as if he'd never known or seen human meanness or cruelty—or has seen infinite amounts of it. He is gently fed up with the insistence that literature has a God-given duty to be "political," or that Eastern European literature was especially significant because it was written in special political circumstances—that last affectation of Western intellectuals, perhaps, who were so eager to see a special heroism in their captive brethren. "To ask what a writer thinks about politics is the same as asking what a carpenter thinks about politics," Klíma says with consummate good sense—and perhaps also with a writer's reflex against being straitjacketed in easy categories.

I note that Czech literature of the Socialist period seemed

less obsessively spellbound by issues of politics and national identity than Polish literature; that it had more room for describing daily life and personal relationships; and that its style was less consistently Aesopian. Well, that is because of the "aristocratic tradition" in Poland, Klíma says; Czech literature is more plebeian. "You discuss politics differently in the manor than in the pub," and though there are certainly plenty of pubs in Poland, it is the manor there that sets the norm. Besides, the relations between the writer and the censor were different in the two countries, Klíma explains. In Poland, writers could get away with fairly subversive messages if they were willing to play the games of allusion, metaphor, coding; in Czechoslovakia, there was no such leeway. Writers who were in any way antiofficial had to go entirely underground—where, in paradoxical effect, they gained a literary, if not a personal, freedom; they wrote without hope of getting published, but therefore, without censorship. That may be why Czech literature of those decades was more transportable than writing from other parts of Eastern Europe and why it may have to undergo less of a shift now, as it comes up into open air.

But apparently it has to get through this convalescent phase of pulse taking, congratulation, commiseration, and having its eyes and throat examined before it's quite let out to lead its ordinary life. "This is a somewhat strange conference, isn't it?" Klíma says tentatively, in his extremely gentle voice. I nod, and allow myself the discreetest raise of an eyebrow.

❚ make an expedition with Wendy to Milovice, about forty kilometers north of Prague. The innocuous rural town—more a village, really—climbs up the side of a small hill, which is bisected by a horizontal road. But this is not quite an ordinary village. Below this dividing line, Milovice is Czech; above, Russian is the first language.

Empires aren't built in a day, nor can they be dismantled in an instant. At this late moment, there are still traces of the Soviet presence here, the once-dangerous dragon that continues to live a sort of ghostly afterlife. The remainders of the Soviet army are scheduled to leave Czechoslovakia in a few weeks, but in towns like Milovice, military bases are still functioning as they have been for the last several decades.

The visual clarity of the division is almost willful. The village clinging to the lower part of the hill is old and quite charming: stone cottages, winding paths, a church spire. The top part is built on a grid of streets, in the flat postwar style. It, in turn, has its own heirarchy. There is the good part for the officers, with pleasant single houses and gardens in front. Then there are several streets of uniform apartment buildings housing the lower ranks. Above the entrance of each one, is a stone bas-relief of a soldier or a worker, carved in the stolid Soviet style: an almost pleasingly clichéd touch. The buildings are in a state of advanced deterioration and disrepair, with broken windows, and shabby-looking laundry on clotheslines. Wendy says that the Czechs have resented the Russian intruders, among other things, for wreaking havoc on their surroundings.

In the grocery store, a saleswoman adds her sums on an abacus—the timeless Russian method. The goods in the window are Czech, but Wendy, who has been in the Soviet Union, says their arrangement—the diagonal lines of cans used as decoration—is recognizably Russian.

The apex and the center of gravity of the town is the military installation. In front of a long barracks, several tanks displayed as monuments project their long noses aggressively toward the street; just now, some children are playing on them as on jungle gyms. Next to the tanks a row of large metal shields with proud slogans lettered in Russian. "Let us praise the great Soviet army," they say, or "In honor of heroic Soviet tankists." At the end of the barracks, a rather inconspicuous sign warns unequivocally, "Stop. If you walk beyond this point, they'll shoot." I encourage Wendy to turn back briskly. On the lawn in front of the barracks, a young father pushes a pram, looking like happy young fathers elsewhere, except for his Soviet uniform; in the officers' part of town, another uniformed man is mowing the lawn in front of his house.

A group of planes in very low formation fly with explosive noise about our heads. Maneuvers, at this late date? Well, Wendy points out, the soldiers stationed here still have to have something to do; and what else can they do but this? On the street, I approach two young soldiers, hoping to ask them a few questions, but they look at me suspiciously and, muttering, "What does she want?" walk quickly away.

It is a bit surreal, this conjunction of ominous symbolism and flat, uninteresting normalcy. It must have created a peculiar psychological effect, a constant reminder to the Czechs that Czechoslovakia existed in an "as if" state, that its supposed status as a regular autonomous country was a sheer masquerade. I think it's not a sophistical exaggeration to say that one of the worst aspects of life in the "satellite countries" was their reduction to this kind of ontological absurdity. It might have been better if it had been stated outright that they were occupied—for this would have been an understandable condition. As it was, they had no real political existence; they were a nether realm, an acknowledged charade, a bracket between the great powers. In one of the most famous essays of his dissident days, Havel asked his countrymen to live "as if" they were free—that is, to act in the spirit of internal freedom, despite their external constraints. But the regime practiced a grotesque inversion of this injunction: the citizens of Czechoslovakia were required to believe and pretend they were free, when they were effectively enslaved; that is, they were supposed to live a lie—and an imperative to live a lie sucks sense out of all activity. This is an abstract statement of Czechoslovakia's situation, and yet I believe that if many wanted to flee from Eastern Europe, it was not only for economic or "purely" ideological reasons, but because of this—because even if their situation happened to be comfortable, it was always, to some extent, absurd.

Czechoslovakia is a small country, and towns such as Milovice were many, and they were a constant reminder to the inhabitants of this country that they could neither acknowledge their condition nor try to change it. This is why most people here hate the soldiers with a gut hate: for not maintaining their houses well, for polluting the local air and soil with military wastes—but most of all, for what their presence meant.

Wendy, though, says that right now she can find it in herself to feel sorry for the Russians. Most of them have no desire to go back to their mother country, where there are no jobs or housing or food—where there is only the dubious interest of turbulence and upheaval. By comparison, they've lived a peaceful existence here, and they've gotten used to Czechoslovakia's relatively abundant food and higher standard of living. Some of them want to stay so badly that they have resorted to a device well known to immigrants in America: they've married local women in order to obtain citizenship papers.

I leave Milovice with a quite palpable feeling of oppression. A few days later, in Prague, I happen to be talking to an aide in the foreign minister's office in the gorgeous Černín Palace. While he gives me a tour of the resplendent rooms, we run into a cluster of men with briefcases engaged in a tense hallway conference. The aide whisks me away discreetly, for he's still new at his job and unsure about protocol—whether it's all right to be seen with a person such as me in the corridors of power. "Those were the Soviets talking with our people," he whispers, clearly a bit impressed by finding himself in such proximity to important events. "They're talking about reparations."

"Reparations?" I ask.

"Yes, we're demanding payments for all the damage they did to our environment," he whispers. "But they're resisting. They want us to pay them for all the buildings they've built and are leaving behind."

"But that's outrageous!" I whisper back, for there are some historical injustices that are fuzzy, and some that are crystal clear. "Surely that's only a strategic ploy."

"Of course it is," he says. "They won't be able to get a thing out of us." And then he laughs, because the Soviet colossus is now a broken Humpty Dumpty, its representatives negotiating nervously with their former subjects, and in a poor position to demand anything from those whom they had so carelessly crushed.

I've taken off, with an American friend who is stationed as a journalist here, for a short excursion to some of the historic towns of Bohemia, one of the three parts into which Czechoslovakia is divided; the other two are Moravia and Slovakia. Outside Peter's Toyota, mild, rolling countryside; peaceful villages; temperate sun; no traffic. Quiet. Until, that is, he puts on a tape of rap music. The contrast between the strutting, aggressive sounds and our surroundings is so startling that I laugh. Another world.

My friend complains about the blandness of the landscape, the small size of the country, the lack of drama. But I find the temperateness restful, and the small size a blessing to the traveler—and perhaps even to the inhabitant. Smallness has made Eastern European countries easy prey for the neighboring empires; but it may also help explain that attachment to landscape and place and local customs that people here still feel so strongly. Homeland is more of a home when it comes in these friendly dimensions, when its every corner can be easily reached and known, and begins to occupy a palpable place in one's psyche.

Our goal for the day is Český Krumlov, which boasts the supposed distinction of being a Baroque town preserved in its entirety, and having what might be the oldest theater in Europe. The town is indeed pretty, with whole streets of elegant, though rundown, historic houses. Picturesque sights picturesquely crumbling. The central square is surrounded by almost miniature buildings restored in pastel colors. Around the graceful fountain in the center of the square is a group of young people who, with their smooth, dark-complexioned faces and sparkling, velvety black eyes, look as if they had stepped out of India just yesterday. They're dressed in ordinary modern dress, and it takes us a while to realize they're Gypsies; but once we do, Peter commences a restless search for a place where Gypsy music can be heard. At first, our inquiries fail to lead anywhere; people either don't know, or don't want to tell us, whether such a place exists; but eventually we're led by the sounds emanating from a low, undoubtedly Baroque interior, to just the place we want. Mind you, if we're seeking complete authenticity, this is not quite it. The music throbs out from instruments plugged into a large electronic console. Still, the lilt is the old Gypsy lilt and the musicians play with enthusiastic abandon. Aside from the performers, the only customers in the tiny, whitewashed "club"—it's the size of somebody's living room—are several burly, black-eyed men, getting seriously drunk.

This, however, doesn't prevent them from keeping perfect balance as they dance—for as we come in, they all decide to exercise their right of gallantry, or proprietorship, I'm not sure which, and take turns squiring me around the stone floor. Though their eyes are cloudy with beer, they move with a courtly dignity and make low, stately bows as they return me to the long bench at the one common table.

When I was growing up in Poland, the Gypsies would appear occasionally like messengers from another world. They drove through the streets of Cracow in covered wagons, and wore clothes of almost indecent colorfulness and raggedness. I remember staring once at a Gypsy girl of about my age, wearing a dress that was half falling off her body, and wondering if it was all right to talk to her; wondering, really, whether she was a child like me. In villages where we spent summers, they came to read our palms and tell our fortunes in a thick accent. The Gypsies of Český Krumlov seem much more modern than that; and we chat with several people who seem more sober than the others, especially with a serious-looking younger man, who seems to be the historian and spokesman of the group. We talk to him in a mix of my Polonized Czech and my friend's German, and he tells us that, despite the Gypsies' nomadic reputation, the community here is a settled one. Most of them came in the 1950s from Slovakia, where, he says, they were treated very badly; and they've found more courtesy and less prejudice here. The changes have mostly changed things for the better, though now that thuggery is less repressed, they've been attacked by bands of *punkovce*. This club, for example, is a child of the Velvet Revolution. They couldn't get a permit for one before, and now even some Czechs come in occasionally; so two cheers for Vašek, he concludes.

No Czechs are in evidence today, but as the evening goes on, the little space heats up with pulsing music and more people. A woman comes out from behind a tiny bar, carrying a tray of single-shot vodka glasses. She weaves her way among the musicians and pours the liquid directly into their throats; they bend their heads way back to receive it, without breaking the rhythm of the music. A group of women come in, late in the evening, and the stone floor fills up with people dancing, men with women, men with men, women with women, it doesn't seem to matter. . . . They dance without coyness, or self-consciousness; they dance seemingly for the sake of the dance, with their bodies held strong and straight, with a kind of gravity.

In the midst of these revels, my friend causes a minor disruption when he jokingly tells somebody that I'm a musical impresario and can take the band to Broadway. Instantly, I'm surrounded by the musicians, whose eyes glint as if I represented genuine hope. *"Bro-advai,"* they keep saying, and though I try to explain that this is a misunderstanding, one of them insists on writing his name and address in my notebook. Černý Milan, he's called—Black Milan.

The next morning, a small Gypsy girl approaches us on the street—she is prodded toward us by an older man—and plays a plaintive song for us on her guitar and sings in an oddly grown-up, sensual way. Then she asks for money. Later, we pass Černý Milan on the street, with another man to whom we had talked at some length, and they look right through us as if they'd never seen us before; they were apparently even more drunk than we knew.

Back in Prague, I visit Milan Knížák, an artist who has just been appointed the rector of the Art Institute in Prague. The art scene in Prague is fairly dormant, though there are a few "mavericks," and Knížák is regularly mentioned as one, as if "maverick" were a recognized professional category. His apartment is an astonishing place, especially after all the drab and monotonous homes I've been frequenting. The interior itself, in the heart of Prague, is beautifully old-fashioned, with parquet floors, French doors, and immaculately white walls. But the furnishings compete, for funkiness and idiosyncrasy, with any Lower Manhattan bohemian loft. In one corner of the living room, there's a whole zoo of small, squat, eerie creatures, part animals, part fairy-tale monsters, coated with an odd muddy gold color and emitting a dull, synthetic Naugahyde shine. On the walls, there are paintings that combine a great delicacy of line with postmodern thickness of encrustation: there are sculptures that use parts of bicycles and other *objets trouvés,* and sculptural pieces of furniture with surrealistic touches.

The maker of this eclectic profusion is big, portly, with a broad, well-lined face, a tight blondish pony tail and several earrings twinkling out of both earlobes. We sit at an oddly-angled table from whose middle rises a snaky, gravity-defying line of metal, topped by a playful, Miró-like shape. Somehow, I expect from his "environment" that Knížák would cultivate a fey, provocative manner; but nothing could be further from his style. Though some of his ideas resonate with New Age echoes, he's serious, even earnest. He means business.

These are some of his thoughts: First of all, people in Czechoslovakia should become more businesslike. He spent some time in the United States, in the late 1960s, and he stopped being an artist during those years. Art didn't make sense in America. The interest was elsewhere—in the streets, in the landscape, and in learning how to do business. He started a house-painting company in New York, and one of the important things he learned from it was how to make price estimates. Price estimates in his view imply a whole system of human relations. They require forthright statements and forthright disagreements. In Czechoslovakia, nobody has learned how to talk directly with each

other; everybody fudges and looks at the floor during any transaction. It's this habit of hiding and fear that simple business con-
tracts could help overcome.

Also. Art is a crutch, the goal is to get to the point where you
can do without it. You can do a lot in your mind. He was forbidden to exhibit his work in Czechoslovakia for twenty years, and
was isolated from his fellow artists as well. The authorities declared him a public enemy and jailed him repeatedly, and the artists, who at first wanted him to be "king of the underground,"
started being afraid to be seen with him. During that time, he
practiced "processes of the mind," which were exercises in concentration, and in a sort of self-invented "imaging." He would
arrange a stone garden in his mind, for example, and meditate
on it. He knew he could live without art.

Also: Art in Czechoslovakia is boring, literature is boring,
music is boring. As the new rector of the Art Institute, he finds
that the students are boring. This is because, after such a long
time, people become different. They think they want freedom,
but their minds are very conservative. He tries to tell them that
art is to disturb, to interrupt society. He tells them they have to
think, define themselves. He gives them exercises—for example,
how to combine a thought and a chair. But they're timid.

Artists are boring, too. Now you can finally express yourself
freely, but after all this time, the first thing that comes out is
junk. You have to get rid of that junk before anything interesting
happens. For now, artists are only interested in making money.
And, of course, you have to respect that. They could never make
money before, they couldn't be successful that way. Anyway, art
is not necessary. It's secondary.

He shows me a catalogue of his work, made for a show in
Berlin, which led to one of his jailings here. There are canvases
and sculptures, but there are also fantastic fashions, and earrings
that extend several inches back of the head in spiky leaves,
which would be a considerable danger at a cocktail party. The
insouciant eclecticism seems to hark back to interwar Czech art.
There are wit and playfulness in it, a disregard for the distinc-

tions between high and low—characteristic, perhaps, of small countries, where artists don't mind being artisans, and don't have to aspire to the greatest grandeur all the time.

On the way out, I ask about the price of a "Malevich" coffee table I like, whose surface is painted with a constructivist design; Knížák's price estimate shows perfect awareness of what the market—the Western market—can bear. I try to sound very forthright and look him straight in the eye as I say I can't afford it; then we shake hands and say good-bye.

"I am one of the people who have no difficulty in adjusting to society," Zdeněk Sofar says. "Like now, I'm adjusting to my new situation. I adjusted after 1968, too. I'm like most people—I was looking for the easy way."

Sofar doesn't seem to feel that he is revealing anything untoward about himself by saying this. He is a tall man, lean and ruddy-faced, and he looks much younger than his fifty-odd years, like someone who spends a lot of time outdoors, or who maybe plays soccer a lot. He looks as friendly and sympathetic as most people do when you first meet them, and there's no reason yet not to be pleasant to each other.

Until recently, Sofar was a professor of philosophy in that target of dread and mockery, the Marxist-Leninist Institute. But the institute was closed down one month after the changes, and he is the more or less proud owner of a restaurant he bought shortly after that. It has taken me a while to find it, since it's way out on the outskirts of Prague, in a very prole sports center, where the city gives way to weedy lots. Once I do locate it, it hardly looks like a place of glamorous promise. It consists of a bar, several tables with red, rather wilted tablecloths, some flies idly buzzing in a shaft of dust, two very large pinups of bare-breasted women, and several disaffected-looking adolescents in leather jackets. If this is the kind of place in which the former *nomenklatura* are sinking their fortunes, the fortunes can't be all that impressive.

Still, the restaurant represents Sofar's bid for security at a time when he feels quite insecure. As a matter of fact, as a Communist, or an ex-Communist—it's difficult to know which it is, or was—he feels positively nervous. "You see, I'm afraid that it'll happen again," he says, "the same thing that has happened so often. They'll want to blame the Communists, the Jews, the Gypsies."

Sofar doesn't bother to hide his bitterness about the folding of his institute. "It was a great injustice for us," he says unequivocally. "We were fired by the Minister of Education. Well, we were much more liberal than the Minister of Education. But they wanted some credit for the new era.

"I bought this place right away, after I was fired, with two pals. I got six months' salary, and this is what I used it for. We're not making any profit, but maybe we can make enough money so I can be independent. I never want to be dependent anymore. You see," he continues, in a galled tone, "I was in the same situation in '68—the same situation. I was competent, but I became so"—he brings his thumb and forefinger together—"small. For five years I was in big troubles. I don't want to belong to anything anymore."

Sofar came to the party naturally—"I came from such a working-class, Communist family"—and, in the early 1960s, he veered toward its reform wing. He was part of a team of sociologists who wrote a book about Czechoslovak society that was incendiary enough to be banned after the crushing of Prague Spring. Most of the authors included in the collection were persecuted; somehow—he turns his head this way and that—Sofar evaded reprisals.

"I could have emigrated then," he says. "I had been in the West." (As a party person he had received a scholarship for a year abroad.) "But I had a wife who doesn't know languages, a child . . . so I stayed, and I climbed again. Many of my colleagues who got out believed the new regime after 1968 would last five years at most. And I thought, You'll lose the five best years of your life. Nobody expected it would last twenty years."

He had reentered the ranks of the party at the time when it

had become an arena for building comfortable careers, when the early, deadly fervor was replaced by the softer vices of corruption and endemic mendaciousness. Because of the book with which he was associated, it was politic for him to leave the field of sociology and enter philosophy instead. "It's not what I wanted," he says, again without any self-judgment, "but sometimes it's better to bend."

I ask him what his attitude to the party was during the period of "normalization." "Oh, I never supported the regime in the 1970s," he says, as if there were no contradiction between his various postures. "You see, when I read Milton Friedman, I went from the left to the extreme right."

Milton Friedman? But party people had better access to enemy literature; and after hearing his name mentioned as a lodestar by aspirants to capitalism on all sides of the political spectrum, I'm beginning to think that this representative of capitalism red in tooth and claw has been the true secret agent in Eastern Europe. But just what appealed to Sofar about him? "Well, the worst thing about this Communist system was economic deadlock. In theory, I supported Marxist economics—and after a while, deadlock. People were used to just sitting somewhere. Didn't bother to pretend to work. I saw this degradation of the system. And on questions of unemployment or social equality, nobody could put it better than Friedman."

It was probably from such utter internal disenchantment that Communism in Eastern Europe expired, as much as from external opposition. Not that Sofar abandoned his early training completely. "Some Marxist ideas—economic determinism, the influence of life experience—I fully accept them. If I would be in the university again," he says, clutching his sweater in a gesture of uncharacteristic passion, and lapsing into some passionately contorted English, "they couldn't take it away from me. It's a basement concept, it's in me. Phenomenology is very popular right now, but it's too fuzzy, irrationalistic for me. And religion for me is nothing. I'm very close to positivismus."

Still, as a positivist, Sofar has come to certain conclusions that have more to do with Friedman than with Marx; and with that ruthlessness I've noticed in his fellow ex-apparatchiks, he would like to see those conclusions enacted without compromise. No half measures for him. "If you subsidize health or education," he says, "it'll conserve the old system. But I want to break the old system and create something else. The conservatism is inside people. Most people didn't accept 1989 in their daily behavior—just like in East Germany. It's like after a revolution—anomie, alienation. Very big alienation. This place—" he gestures around the restaurant—"we had four robberies here last year. This didn't happen when we were the government. This is what worries me."

Sofar says that after 1968 many of his former friends went on to become dissidents. What did he think of them? I ask. His answer is frank to a fault. "I underestimated this movement completely," he says. "In the early eighties, I was in the United States, and when I talked to people, I saw that Charter 77 had no credit. We thought the changes would come from within the party. Nobody expected what happened."

So if he had been more prescient, he would have bet on a better horse. Again, I seem to find this more revealing—more disconcerting—than he. But this, probably, was the crux of the incompatibility between the two sides, unevenly matched though they seemed to be: that while the dissidents were making a Pascalian gamble of formidable dimension and consequence, Sofar was trying to place his safest bet in a very different currency—of position and job promotion and a little power.

Given his consistent pragmatism, it is not surprising that once the handwriting was on the wall for the Communists Sofar was eager to affix his signature on the side of the new winners. He joined the demonstrations in Wenceslas Square. "For me, it was the problem solved," he says succinctly. "I knew the Marxism-Leninism was finished. I put all that behind me."

And what does he think of "all that" now, from the perspective of a little time? "Well," he says, "I had a good life. When I got a scholarship to the West, that was a reward. I had a good salary. I did well for myself. I am a person who adjusts."

And there it is, his theme, his *modus vivendi*. He is, quite un-abashedly, a self-declared opportunist—a genre of late Commu-nist just a touch different from such self-declared cynics I have encountered as Michał Malicki, a Polish ex-censor. The cynics tended to have a sharper notion of an ideal from which they di-verged; the opportunists seem to have forgone an ideal even as a point of reference. The cynics seem to have bent the rules more to their own purposes; the opportunists bent more them-selves.

Acting on the basis of expediency is the most ordinary of impulses, and yet there's something disturbing about hearing it professed so blithely as a guiding principle, and I find myself shrinking slightly from Sofar—sitting back a bit more stiffly as he tells me how inconvenienced he was by his son, who signed Charter 77, thereby creating some trouble for Sofar with his bosses. "After that, I had to blame him," he says, as if that, too, were self-evident. But I also feel oddly tired as I talk to him—tired by the call to judgment, I think, by the demand to frame a moral attitude toward Zdenek Sofar and others like him. It's a demand felt palpably in Eastern Europe these days. Just how guilty is this one, and of what, just how much damage did that one do to her friends? Was he a collaborator, an accommoda-tionist, a silent oppositionist? Was she responsible or just complicit? It seems impossible to avoid such questions, as if they had to be settled before the oppression of the last era can lift en-tirely. But the stifling weight of that time was precisely in this: that nothing could escape the moral net; that going along with the system—that most common of choices—involved participa-tion in such uncommon unpleasantness. And it is perhaps this disproportion between the ordinary, individual decisions and the systemic guilt in which they became implicated that creates the muddle in Eastern Europe right now, the ambivalence about how to view the past. How to reckon with a perfectly unexcep-tional person like Zdeněk Sofar? He represented a kind of nor-malcy, after all—several decades of it. Everyone here has known a Zdeněk Sofar and has said hello to him in a local pub, and many know how close they came to being Zdeněk themselves. That makes it harder to judge, and harder not to judge. I feel the great, dull fatigue of this; the desire to declare the whole, tedious case closed; to declare it null, void, canceled, revoked. I suppose I feel my own pull to forgetfulness, to denial.

What's happening here? A sort of haunting by the past, for one thing. This summer a year and a half after the Velvet Revolution, Czechoslovakia is in the throes, not of forgetfulness, but of something like obsessive remembering, a fixation on the injuries and injustices of the past. Almost every conversation I have in Prague eventually hits upon the shoals of "the list"—a roster of purported secret police informers, containing as many as 200,000 names. The majority favors the publication of the list, with the argument that "Those people are still with us, and some of them are getting promoted in their jobs. It's not fair; we need to know who they are." Others—these are in the minority—point out that informers' files were, after all, compiled by the secret police, whom no one has trusted until now on anything else; that the files of the most prominent informers may have been destroyed during the changeover; that the list undoubtedly contains names of real swine, but also of people who may have buckled under interrogation or torture, and signed a piece of paper that might now condemn them for life.

Still, despite these objections, there is widespread support for "lustration" laws, which would remove people on the list from their jobs. "Lustration" means purification, and the word, with its echoes of Nazi terminology, sits awkwardly in this new time, as if the language itself were issuing a warning about the wrongness of this process. In the meantime, names of ten MPs, whose secret police files implicate them as informers, have been made public; and though members of Parliament cannot be legally forced to resign, these politicians are under intense pressure to do so.

I have spent some time talking to one of these MPs, a man

whose situation is full of fateful ironies. His name is Ján Kavan, and it is the most immediate irony in what has befallen him that he has just returned to Czechoslovakia recently, after twenty years of working abroad on behalf of the dissident underground.

The day I first meet him, he has made a speech in Parliament in his own defense; thirty people walked out as he began to speak. This gives him an intricately layered sense of déjà vu, he says, summoning memories of his days as an ostracized student dissident—but also evoking shadows of the further past, and of his father.

Love and Freedom, one of the great memoirs to come out of the Slánský trials, was written by Ján's mother, Rosemary Kavan. Rosemary was a spirited, charming, and very witty English-woman who had the interesting misfortune of falling in love with a Czech Jew and coming to live in Prague at the wrongest of times. Within a short time of their arrival, the Slánský trials began, and Rosemary's husband, Pavel, an ardent Communist who had served in the Foreign Service, disappeared one fine morning into the maws of the Czech prisons.

Kavan was a supporting character in these stagings, one of the so-called "witnesses" whose "confessions" were meant to bolster the evidence of the main participants' guilt. Because of this, he escaped execution and was released from prison after more than four years. He died shortly afterward, of a heart attack.

Like Anna's mother, Rosemary went through hell during the years of his imprisonment, the hell of poverty and isolation and bitterly hard physical labor. Nevertheless, she stayed in her adopted country, which, despite everything, she had come to love. She finally felt forced to leave after Prague Spring was squashed; she had become involved with the youthful opposition and was in danger of being imprisoned herself. Her two sons left at about the same time.

Ján wasn't all that close to his father, who was taken away early in his childhood and died soon after his reemergence, and who, in Rosemary's testimony, was a very difficult man. But the son later became interested enough in the father's world to write his university dissertation on the prewar International Student Union, which his father had led. "Surprisingly, I already felt a great sense of déjà vu even then," Ján says, for during that time he was involved in student politics himself. He was becoming a radical, in his period's style, which meant that for a while he considered himself a reform Communist, who hoped that the party could be changed from within. Then he became involved with a group of students known as the Prague Radicals, who were instrumental in leading up to the Prague Spring.

On first acquaintance, Kavan doesn't cut a heroic figure; he's a shortish man who tends to awkward movements; his hair is thinning and his complexion pale. He has just suffered his second heart attack. He speaks very carefully, without overexcitement or overstatement—perhaps like a man who doesn't want to fall into the trap of justifying himself. I believe that he gives quick checks to see whether I trust him; he's very accustomed, after all, to being mistrusted.

I talk with Kavan in the offices of the Helsinki Citizens' Watch, which monitors human-rights abuses and for which he does some work. The office is in a building that houses no fewer than three other organizations dedicated to human rights and peaceable intentions, including the John Lennon Peace Club. The Helsinki Watch is staffed by bright-eyed multilingual young people in chic narrow pants and oversized T-shirts, who have come here from various countries to participate in their generation's revolution and who are fortunate enough to have these pleasant surroundings, complete with computers and international phone lines for their trenches and barricades.

Kavan's story seems out of place in these surroundings, an anachronism. His current trouble emanates from a secret service file from which it could be inferred that Kavan was an informer for the service during his years in England. The allegation is based on a report describing several meetings between Kavan and a party functionary that took place when Kavan was in his early twenties. Kavan has readily admitted that, when he first

went to England after Prague Spring and still had hopes of returning to Czechoslovakia, he met with an education official
from the Foreign Ministry, who presented himself as sympathetic
and wanting to help. Kavan says he talked to this man politely,
but never gave him any meaningful information.

That was shortly after the Soviet invasion; for the next
twenty years, Ján worked tirelessly as the Czech Cassandra
abroad. From England, he wrote about his country's situation,
smuggled out interviews and manuscripts, and started a journal
that came to be greatly respected among Eastern European spe-
cialists, *The East European Reporter.* He founded the Palach
Press, which placed manuscripts with Western publishers—
among them Havel's essays. There were eighteen-hour days, illicit meetings, illegal trips to Czechoslovakia. The fact that he
came into the country during very restrictive times is thought to
be evidence of his collaboration. But Kavan has shown me British passports that enabled him to come into Czechoslovakia, with
photographs of himself changed unrecognizably by beards and
other paraphernalia of disguise, and with a series of aliases;
under English laws, name changes are easy.

This went on until November 1989, when history did another somersault, and Ján decided to return to his homeland. After twenty years in England, he says, the decision took all of five
minutes. Shortly after his return, Kavan went to work for the
newly formed Civic Forum; and a few months later, he ran for
Parliament as a Civic Forum candidate, though on a platform
that may have been too progressive (in the Western sense of the
term) even for his ex-dissident colleagues. He thinks that his politics may have once again become uncomfortable for just about
everybody, and that this may be part of the trouble right now.

"I don't mind being in the minority," he says, "but to be
branded this way, to be accused of collaborating with people
who were lifelong enemies . . . well, it's terrible." In the corridors
of the Parliament, he says, carefully avoiding the tone of grudge
or bitterness, people look the other way when they pass him, or
conversely, they make a point of talking to him with excessive so-

licitousness or joviality—just as when he was a fledgling student oppositionist.

Kavan is well known enough internationally so that his case has become a cause célèbre abroad. British and American newspapers have expressed chagrin at the handling of his case; but in Czechoslovakia he is almost entirely isolated. Rumors about him proliferate; rumors about how he was responsible for the trapping of several dissidents after one of his visits here, how he informed on his own father—though the newspaper that printed this placed the date of the supposed incident ten years after his father's death. Although no one can be absolutely sure at this point what Kavan did or didn't do twenty years ago, the will to condemn him seems to be enormous. No one I've talked to about him—and the "Kavan affair" comes up all the time— seems willing to give him the benefit of the doubt. There was something there, people say stubbornly; there must have been something.

Rumors about the list proliferate as well; who's on it, who should be on it, who did what and to whom. . . . Of course, informing on fellow citizens was a profoundly disturbing phenomenon in Czechoslovakia; and perhaps the acuteness of the need to exorcise it is proportional to how widespread it had been. But it is precisely the pervasiveness of collaboration, or accommodation, that makes real redress, real catharsis, so difficult to achieve. Who is going to be singled out for prosecution, who will be accidentally left out? What degree of complicity constitutes guilt? And what was ordinary citizenship in a socialist republic? How can you "cleanse" the many without scapegoating a few?

Kavan's story is intricate, its details difficult to disentangle; but because of the turns of his family history, he seems an almost allegorical example of how the intention to "purify" might only lead—as in a frightening morality tale in which you get just the opposite of what you supposedly desire, the dark side of your intention—to perpetuating the cycle of suspicion and punishment in which Czechoslovakia has for so long been locked.

In one version of the myth of transmigration, a person cross-

ing to the next world has to drink from the waters of forgetfulness and the waters of memory; enough from one to slough off
the burden of the past and be able to return with some hope and
innocence to the mortal world, and enough from the other to return with some wisdom and knowledge. Such balances are beyond most mortals to achieve; but I keep thinking of this myth
and how at this moment of crossing to a "new time," Eastern
Europeans may be learning the hazards of too much remembering after having learned so well the dangers of too much forgetting.

"We take notes, we make journeys. Emptiness, emptiness."
Thus Flaubert, writing from exotic Egypt. Thus I, in Bratislava.

A small-town train station; I stagger with my suitcases to a
taxi, standing idly on the other side of a square. On the way to
the hotel, the lull of early dusk; nothing. A group of young men
in leather jackets laughing rowdily in front of an ice-cream place.
Then more lull. From my conversation with the taxi driver, I discover Slovak is so close to Polish that I understand it quite well.
He extolls the beauties of the countryside outside of Bratislava.

This is the capital of Slovakia, the site, these days, of sim-
mering discontent and separatist sentiments; I've read reports of
crowds and rallies and incipient violence; a large movement has
been burgeoning here, under the leadership of Vladimír Mečiar,
a Communist-turned-nationalist, to make Slovakia, which has
been part of Czechoslovakia for the last seventy years, an independent country. I've come here partly out of curiosity about
these phenomena. But I've come on the weekend, and on the
weekend even the most urgent political passions are put on hold.

The Kiev, where I'm staying, has a dimly lit *moderne* style,
which passed for high elegance among the *apparatchiks,* and unusually surly clerks. I brave the inquisitive glances of tourist
groups in the dining room and the screechy shouts of frolicking
Scandinavian adolescents, for I must have dinner. In another
mood, it might strike me that I've entered the set of an operetta:
the waiters look proud and manly in white, billowy shirts under

black camisoles, and the waitresses wear skin-hugging, tightly laced-up white boots. A pianist, dressed in a long gown, plays a cocktail medley that moves from "Somewhere Over the Rainbow" to the Beatles and the theme song from "Fiddler on the Roof," ubiquitous this summer throughout Eastern Europe. But my morale is low, and even the food fails to cheer me up, though in all fairness it must be recorded that the dinner is tastier than anything I've eaten in the Czech lands part of the country.

In my room, I dial a few phone numbers of people I've been given. Nobody home. I don't want to go out into the empty streets. I don't want to go out into the lobby and subject myself to more curious glances. There's nothing but this sterile hotel room and me. I nurse an iceless vodka and wonder dismally what I'm doing in this corner of the planet. When a friend in Prague asked me how I like being on the road, I told him that the great discovery I've made is that the world is round, and that no matter how afraid I become that I'm about to fall off its edge, it turns out that there's always the next place ahead. "Ah, but the great question," he responded, quoting a Polish writer, "is whether the world ends in barbed wire or a picket fence." Now I feel I've come to a place where the world has always ended in both, and where it dwindles down into this trite, touristic vacuity.

Bratislava looks friendlier in the morning light, though hardly charming at first glance. The Kiev is in a section whose epidermis comes from the socialist era. Many old buildings were willfully destroyed here, and the replacements have the special tackiness of a provincial city, probably built on the cheap, with the talent for ugliness that They specialized in. Nevertheless, as I walk around on a breezy, sunny morning, I begin to find something pleasant about Bratislava's unstrained, small size; about the utter lack of affectation. Near a department store, groups of men with sturdy, country faces, dressed in baggy, threadbare jackets, stand about talking animatedly. The women are dressed à la 1955, and look very pleased with themselves as they click down the street in their spiked heels. All of this—the outmoded dress, the idle pace—brings back echoes of another Central European city, the Cracow of my childhood; and I feel a seminostalgic satisfaction one sometimes finds in places that are "behind the times," a mix of nostalgia and mastery. We've been through this; we've left it behind and it poses no challenge to what we might be.

In an enormous, nearly empty store featuring folk crafts, there's some of the most beautiful pottery I've seen outside of Provence—blue and red interweaving fruits and leaves, and delicately glazed, elegant peasant figures on large plates. I've spoken to Czechs who have said that the Slovak esthetic sense convinces them of a special Slovak genius—in the sense of spirit or identity. There's probably a touch of condescension in such observations—the condescension of which Slovaks complain, and which fuels their sense of beleaguered nationalism; but the native esthetic does seem strong and vivid, evident in the crafts, and in the wonderful folk music that composers from Janáček to Bartók have studied. Even an edifying mural I see on the wall of a library is drawn with an elegant stylishness.

The question of just what Slovak "identity" consists of is a highly charged one, since Slovakia's very existence at this point represents a minor historical mystery—the mystery of very small nations, in which this region of Europe so prolifically specializes. There are four million people in Slovakia, and they speak a language that so closely abuts Polish on one side and Czech on the other that it might have easily, over the centuries, blended with one of them altogether. Moreover, except for a brief and sorry interval during World War II, Slovakia has never been an independent country in modern times. Its brief moment of grandeur came in the ninth century, when the Slovaks were united with the Moravians for the first time. But the Great Moravian Empire was short-lived, and by the tenth century the Slovak part of it had been conquered by Hungarians, who reigned here for almost one thousand years, under the Hapsburgs' aegis in the later stages. After World War I, Slovakia was united with the Czechs in a supposedly equal federation—though Slovaks never got over the sense that they were treated like second-class citizens.

Small countries being auctioned, traded, appropriated, and betrayed by bigger countries—so much of this region's history consists of such transactions. It must have taken a special pertinacity to maintain a distinctly Slovak identity, and perhaps the current militant nationalism, which seems to come from another era, is the other side of that pertinacity, and of the insularity that has been the means and the price of self-preservation.

Bratislava's Old Town also has the charm of modest ambitions. On this very hot day, with the intense sun refracting into narrow cobblestoned streets, I have the sense I might well be in a small Italian town. The houses, with their whitewashed walls and the geraniums in the windows, the noises of uninhibited conversation coming from behind the shutters, the men's voices emanating from the corner bar give a delicious sense of contained but dense life.

In a house where the composer J. N. Hummel once lived, there is one of the most unpretentious museums I've ever seen—a room with a clavichord and a few graceful pieces of furniture, opening out into a garden in the back—all visible from the street through a store-front window. I think how pleasant it must have been to compose well-wrought music within the quiet frame of this room and of this town.

In a modest wine bar—one of the ways in which the Slovaks consider themselves distinct from the Czechs is that they're wine rather than beer drinkers—I meet Jozef, a writer and translator who somehow neglected to leave for the weekend at his usual time. He is about to take off for his country cottage, and declares resolutely that he has time only for a drink. Once we settle in, however, he seems to have all the leisure in the world and the willingness to drink and talk without cease. He's a roly-poly, middle-aged man with merry eyes and the olive Slovak complexion. Everything in his demeanor proclaims a zestful love of pleasure, a good-humored enjoyment. This weekend, he'll be making preserves out of the fruits of his little orchard; he's going to his cottage by bus, because he's never learned to drive. "Machines are alien to me," he proclaims, "and besides, if I had to drive, I wouldn't be able to have my afternoon drink. One must have one's relaxations, don't you think?" And he laughs merrily.

He's translating a book of philosophy and doing some writing of his own. I wonder if it's frustrating for Slovak writers to work in what's considered a very minor language, with small chances of being translated or known abroad. "It doesn't matter whether the world pays attention," he avers. "Each culture is a self-contained organism. It has all the elements it needs."

I find this an unexpected and somehow cheering notion, for it implies a vision of sufficiency and plentitude, of a manageable, local world that isn't yet provincial. But then comes the other side of the coin. When I ask Jozef what he thinks of the separatist movement—I pose this question in a rather obligatory manner, fully expecting a good, progressive answer—he suddenly becomes evasive. Complicated questions of national identity are involved, he says. The Slovaks have always been treated as inferior by the Czechs. Even Father Tiso has to be understood as the person who stood up for Slovak independence. . . . Then he looks uneasy, and decides not to finish the sentence.

A small gulf opens up. During World War II Father Tiso was the Slovak premier, whose cult has been revived recently by the nationalists. He presided over the only period of national "independence" that Slovakia enjoyed in modern times—and it was gained as a result of having allied itself with Germany. Tiso was a puppet of the Nazis. The story of Slovak fascism and anti-Semitic atrocities in that time is almost unbearably awful.

So I experience something like a suspension of belief when I understand that Jozef is ready to defend Tiso. I expect to hear such opinions professed by people who can be safely dismissed as extremists; but I'm baffled to hear them come from this nice, genial "intelligent" who has nothing of a fanatic about him. This implies a different kind of nationalism from what I've sensed elsewhere: a burning, nineteenth-century kind of nationalism, which overcomes other scruples because it involves basic questions of selfhood. Another revenge of the repressed past, perhaps: an insistence on "national identity," which had been so long stifled, unlived, unmoderated by time.

Later, I have a meeting that conforms more closely to my expectations—though perhaps not to the local realities—with the editor of the oldest Slovak literary journal. He's a serious-looking man who chain-smokes throughout the conversation, and who dismisses the separatist movement as a minority phenomenon; it has managed to make a really big noise, but when push comes to shove, he thinks, sanity will prevail. After all, Slovakia would have a very hard time economically without the Czech lands of Bohemia and Moravia. And, if the delicate stability of borders in Eastern Europe started to be upset, who knows where it would end? Slovakia still has a large Hungarian minority, left over from the centuries of Hungarian rule, which the Slovaks now in turn try resolutely to control. He expresses proper liberal chagrin about Slovakia's treatment of the Hungarian population. There were demonstrations here, recently, *against* granting full linguistic rights to the Hungarians, and so far, not even wedding ceremonies can be performed in Hungarian—a state of affairs at which the editor shakes his head and takes a long, reflective draw on his cigarette.

He leaves me a copy of his journal, which has pieces of Elias Canetti, Czesław Miłosz, Jan Patočka: the Central European crowd. There are also Slovak writers whose names I've never heard of, but when I make my way through one of the poems—I can understand Slovak enough to make it out slowly—I find I'm in familiar territory. The poem is a fierce, meditative examination of loneliness and female pain, and stumbling upon it so unexpectedly, I feel stupidly startled. Why is it always a surprise to find a genuine life of feeling and mind thriving elsewhere—or what is elsewhere to us? Poland is to me always a here, a fully real place. Slovakia, only a stone's throw away, is a remote corner in my imagination; and while we allow the inhabitants of imaginary remote corners the authenticity of savages or sufferers, we rarely suppose them to possess the authenticity of complex, sophisticated perceptions. Perhaps it is simply impossible to encompass the whole globe pulsating with authentic complexity; or perhaps the desire for simpler worlds is nearly ineradicable. The vision of an entire world becoming just like us is at least as discomfiting as the thought that most of it won't.

The next day, I take a taxi to the Devín Castle, which was the seat of the Moravian Empire in the ninth century. It's several miles from the center of town, and on the way, the taxi driver points to a group of people walking down a country road. "Vietnamese," he says. "A problem." The Vietnamese? I ask in some perplexity, for their presence here is incongruous the way it would not be in any Western countries. "Oh, yes. They came to study during the war and they stayed. They're a problem." Ah yes, the Vietnam war; these are the North Vietnamese, of course, who have wandered here and stayed, undoubtedly because it's easier here than at home—though it seems hard to think of Eastern Europe as anybody's haven.

Devín Castle is a majestic, hoary ruin of crumbling tower and worn fortification walls emerging from, and subsiding into, a rocky promontory. It overlooks the Danube, which rounds a grand, serene bend here, joining with the Morava River. Cyril and Methodius, Byzantine monks who were brothers, traveled to these remote parts in the ninth century, often at considerable danger to themselves; they came here on their Moravian mission, to bring Christianity and the Cyrillic alphabet to these still-pagan regions. These early multiculturalists had to put up considerable argument to defend the Cyrillic script, since most of the Church powers at the time thought that only three languages—Greek, Hebrew, and Latin—were fit for the writing of holy texts.

From this strategic lookout, the Moravian princes could see the movements of Germanic tribes on one side and Bohemian ones on the other. Now, across the Danube, there are the farmlands of Austria, their compulsively regular plots as clearly delineated as blocks and squares in a drawing; shiny cars drive along perfectly smooth roads. The contrast with the grassy, disheveled hills on this side is like a show-and-tell demonstration. Until recently, Austria was this close, and yet so far; now, one can go there and see for oneself, and it's an aggravatingly proximate presence, a reminder that some people have it easier and better.

Somewhere near the Devín Castle, a cock crows; good-looking couples saunter about. It's a warm, lazy Sunday. As I walk down the ancient, worn steps, I look at the castle again, and think about generations passing like grass. And about the perennial nastiness of what we know as "history," and how it is bearable only from an enormous distance, when it has changed into well-smoothed stories and a few crumbling stones.

At dusk, the light turns eerily magical; near the ground, under the trees of a small park, it's entirely dark; the sky, however, is a brilliant indigo blue. It's an effect worthy of Magritte, this simultaneous luminosity and darkness. A chorus of crows rasps its loud, croaking song. On a small street, five policemen, hefty and tall, face a picket fence and proceed to piss in concert with unhurried dignity. A group of drunken adolescents, dressed à la Western punk, carom down the street, shouting. I try to find a taxi, can't, and board a bus; my inquiry about whether this will take me to Bratislava is answered with loud rudeness.

Fatigue; a post-post-world. How can you go through the paces with any enthusiasm when you know how it all ends, that it never ends, and that it always ends badly?

Before I leave Czechoslovakia for good, I throw my first classic traveler's temper tantrum. It takes place at the Čedok Travel Agency, where I go with the simplest of requests: I want to buy a train ticket to Budapest, which lies less than three hours away from here, on what must be one of the most frequented routes. The woman behind the glass barrier looks at me as though I've given her an utterly unreasonable task. Schedules? She gives a contemptuous shoulder shrug. She has no idea. Could she find out? With utmost reluctance, she takes down a thick, dusty old volume and consults it as if she'd never seen it before. I congratulate myself on maintaining icy calm. Finally, she comes up with some information. Could I then have a ticket? I get a foul look, as if I were putting her to extraordinary trouble, but she sits down and makes one out. Then, in a voice gravelly with grudginess, she informs me that to get a seat assignment I have to go to the train station. At this I rebel. No way, I inform her; I want my seat assignment now. The woman ostentatiously turns away and begins chatting with her colleague. I ostentatiously plant myself in front of the glass barrier in a pose that indicates that not ten horses will budge me from the spot. We're at an impasse. A few minutes go by. In the queue behind me, mutterings of impatience and sympathy. Finally, without the slightest nod or gesture to indicate that she has yielded, the clerk picks up the telephone, makes out a slip of paper and wordlessly hands it to me; it has a seat number on it.

Throughout my travels, I've looked disapprovingly at Western tourists who, in restaurants, hotels, travel offices, and airports have expressed their rage at Eastern European officialdom by hurling at them the greatest insults of all, such as "This is still a Communist country!" or "You deserve socialism!" Now, as if the phrases were emerging from an atavistic capitalist-imperialist unconscious, I shout—though in my unimperial Polish— "Nothing has really changed here! You deserve everything you've had!" The clerk registers this, too, with impassive contempt. Then I walk out, shaking with rage and vindication.

On the train, I share a compartment with a blond girl of about ten, wearing jeans and a Mickey Mouse belt, and her grandmother, whose face and fresh blue eyes would be youthful were it not for a fine net of wrinkles covering her weathered skin. They speak Czech, and throughout the trip, they play games of cat's cradle and rhythmic hand slaps, with a sort of puppy playfulness. There's some good-humored, sensual affection between them, something that must be passed on from generation to generation in just this way, through such gestures and smiles. They get off somewhere before the border, and I'm pleased to have this image to carry with me as the last memory spot of Czechoslovakia.

F O U R

← ← ← ←

H U N G A R Y

The Nyugati train station in Budapest feels further south. It was designed by the same architect who built the Eiffel Tower, and under its beautiful glass roofing, resembling the fin-de-siècle railway palaces in Paris, the smells are more pungent, the complexions more olive than in Warsaw or Prague. There are barefoot Gypsies in flowing, colorful clothes and Transylvanian peasants in stiff layers of skirts, and somebody holding a naked child over a small, graceful fountain; and everywhere, there are the smells and runny juices of fruits and tomatoes.

I contemplate the enormous length of the station rather nervously. Which way for a taxi, how am I going to lug my suitcases across it? I know there's no hope of understanding a word of Hungarian. But as I pick up my suitcases, a man approaches me, asking "German? French? English?" and, once we settle on a language, escorts me out to a taxi very politely, and then returns to the station. He's a kind of station cicerone, apparently, employed to guide the lost traveler. The Hungarians have been at the tourist business longer than the others and they're better prepared.

The street on which I'm staying is dark with that Eastern European darkness—no neon lights, no street lamps; but no fear, either. An almost village darkness. "Madame Hoffman?" a voice from a window calls out, in the melodious Hungarian inflection. Someone is waiting, as promised. The name of the street on which I'm going to be staying—Rumbach Sebastyén—has about the same connotation, I've been told, as Delancey Street does in New York. It used to be at the very heart of the old Jewish ghetto, in what is now a neglected, forgotten corner of Budapest. And, indeed, the flat I've rented is supervised by a perfect Hungarian version of a little old Jewish lady, bewigged, tiny, and soft, but with the decisive voice and manners of a domestic martinet. She has bought a few breakfast items for me, and she writes out the prices on a piece of paper, totting them up resolutely in German. I don't know any German, but this doesn't deter her from talking to me all the while. She shows me the tiny flat, which thankfully has a few amenities: a private bathroom, phone and a large TV, to which my landlady points proudly, trying to explain something in louder tones, as if she were determined to cut through my stupidity.

After she leaves, I flip through the channels and see what her satisfaction was about. There's a Hungarian channel, of course, but also Czech, Russian, and German ones, the latter of which is just now showing some soft porn; also, some sort of Eurotrash station which, to Muzak-like sounds, is filling empty time by running schedules of upcoming rock concerts all over the continent. If Budapest is further south than Poland or Czechoslovakia, it's also further west.

Outside the window of my room, the darkness of a deep, narrow courtyard is interrupted by a few lit-up apartments. There are noises of TV, of cooking, of conversation. As I fall off into sleep, angelic sounds of a Schubert sonata emerge from somewhere with a startling clarity; they're followed by lunar, yearning Magyar tunes, as if to signal that mix of cultivation and wildness, of East and West that is somehow, still, Mitteleuropa. If Hungary is further south and west, it is also, as I should have remembered, smack dab in the center.

▌make many phone calls that come to naught in Budapest. The telephones here are even worse than those in Warsaw, and three times out of four there is no dial tone, or a false busy signal, or the wan click of disconnection. And then, more often than in Warsaw, nobody is at home, or somebody advises me to call back before 8 A.M. Budapest is an early-rising, hard-working, busy city. Hungarians are accustomed to holding two jobs at once, or moonlighting heavily, and now that the prices are climbing fast and wages less so, and a few people are getting rich and everyone is getting more competitive, they are working harder than ever.

The signs of hustle and bustle are everywhere. Budapest has the pulse, the tempo, and the traffic of any other big European city, plus the impressive, Eastern European pollution. Getting stuck in traffic on a hot day is a daunting experience for the respiratory system, and even the wiliest taxi drivers have to accept long standstills, though the tactics they're willing to employ to get out of them can be quite amazing even by New York standards.

Sitting down for coffee at the Hyatt Hotel, I meet two Englishwomen, who complain that Budapest has no magic, that it's just like the West and getting more so all the time. One of them remembers it from a pre-*glasnost* tour, when it was gray and gloomy and much more gratifying to the other-seeking eye. I remember the gloom of Budapest from a brief student visit more than twenty years ago. People walked with their heads bent and a sense of burden that seemed to have settled permanently into their shoulders. But in the meantime, there have been two decades of János Kádár and his "goulash Communism," which mixed a party monopoly on power with some economic freedom, and which made Hungary the best-developed country in the Eastern Bloc. Now men in suits and women with briefcases rush around with the trancelike look that comes from being hellbent and in a hurry. Much as I would like to resist the temptations of exoticizing, it's true that the exterior Budapest spectacle feels so "normal," that is, so Western, that it induces in me a twinge of paradoxical disorientation. Where is Eastern Europe in all this? What am I looking at, or for? We need the tint of difference, of contrast, for perception to arise. But the center of Budapest exhibits all the conditions of life in a modern metropolis—fumes and crowds and a quantity of shops, and restaurants in every part of town. Most of it is still muted and utilitarian, but in the glitzier neighborhoods, the boutiques might almost be Parisian or Viennese, and so might the prices.

But one commodity that is getting scarcer everywhere in Eastern Europe as others become more available is time. Time used to be different here, more plentiful and slow. There were long summer vacations and conversations stretching into the night, and people staring out the window to see what was happening that afternoon in their street. . . . There was no reason to hurry, no promises of great careers or fortunes to be made. And now, all over Eastern Europe, time is picking up speed because maybe there's something to rush toward, calendars are acquiring a scribbled-over look, and people are learning to say, "Yes, I can meet you for a quick quarter hour." This seems to me as fundamental a change as the shift to the multiparty system, for the shape of our time affects our deepest relations to other people and our own experience. There'll be fewer coffee klatsches from now on, at which people can gossip and observe each other at leisure; fewer moments of pure gazing and slow reflection; fewer spontaneous visits without an appointment beforehand—for the business of getting a living and reconstructing the world is taking over. But perhaps there'll be less time for stewing in slow, acrid observations of the awful neighbors, for turning over the bitterness of unjust lives; fewer dull, profitless hours, empty of purpose and the dynamism of hope.

All Hungarians complain that Hungarians complain too much. Indeed, it's impossible to get anyone to admit that anything good has come of the changes. "Nothing has changed at all," people assure me with zestful gloom. "Absolutely nothing."

Since a dark-hued irony seems to be as much a matter of honor here as in Poland, I know that I'm supposed to take such statements with a large pinch of salt. But perhaps there's also a dash of reality to this attenuated sense of change. "The revolution" came upon Hungary at a very different point of evolution than in either Poland or Czechoslovakia, and the distance Hungary has to travel to become a "normal" country is visibly shorter. After twenty years of Kádár's reign, Hungary already had a well-established infrastructure of private enterprise by the time 1989 came around, and Communists who had practically admitted that they had given up the ideological ghost. New political structures were beginning to crystallize before the *ancien regime* fell, and by the mid-1980s, the dissidents had already divided into two hostile groups, which formed the embryos of the two major parties. As a result, Hungary is also further along in the sequence of various post-Communist symptoms and syndromes. The stage of embracing solidarity and consensus was almost entirely skipped. There are several clearly defined parties by now, and a conservative party—the MDF (Magyar Democratic Front), which grew out of one dissident branch—is in power, something that, by the seemingly unavoidable logic of post-Communism, seems to be the next step everywhere after the progressive dissidents have had their brief shining moment.

And now, moving through the subsequent phases with precipitate speed, Hungary has even attained a Western level of political apathy; in the last local elections I've been hearing about, something like 8 percent of the population bothered to turn out.

People tend to talk about the government as a sort of operetta that unfortunately has its serious and worrisome side. They roll their eyes at interminable discussions of symbolic matters— for example, whether the coat of arms in the Hungarian flag should feature a Hapsburg crown dating to the days of the Dual Monarchy. I've been told about histrionic parliamentary battles, though some people attribute the heated level of rhetoric to the Hungarian language itself, which apparently carries within it a tendency to flourish and dramatic exaggeration.

I myself am tempted to believe that it is the Parliament

building that might be responsible for these inflationary tendencies. If language can contribute to political style, so surely can the setting where politics is enacted—and the architecture and decor of the Hungarian Parliament are an invitation to excessive self-esteem. The Parliament was built at the end of the nineteenth century, the age of Hungary's near-imperial glory, and it bespeaks a sense of stately grandeur. Its neo-Gothic exterior extends over a tremendous length of arches, cupolas, campaniles, and highly wrought entrances. The main assembly chamber is compact, but orgiastic with gold ornament and glittering chandeliers and neo-Gothic woodwork. It's an interior that would encourage all but the most modest of politicians to fall into Oscar Wilde's dictum that "The first duty in life is to be as artificial as possible. What the second duty is, no one has as yet discovered." The MDF, I've been told by its critics, has been encouraged by its ascent to power to fall into postures that certainly could be construed as imperious. Shortly after the changes, it instituted religion classes in schools by a ministerial fiat—though this ruling was retracted later; on another front, a prominent government spokesman declared, in effect, that "since we won the election, the press now belongs to us." This business of democracy—of restraining your own power and politely sharing it with others—must seem rather unnatural at first; and aside from questions of their actions, Eastern European politicians haven't yet consistently mastered the reflex of the egalitarian, power-sharing statement.

György Konrad is probably Hungary's best-known writer, and he possesses my idea of a classic Central European face—with an expression of skepticism so deep that it seems like a kind of sadness, and eyes that are almost disturbingly serious and alert. "Things have changed very dramatically and not at all," he says, as if impatient with either side of the reduction.

"I'm interested in the dramatically," I say, "since everyone has told me about the not at all."

"The language has changed," he says. "This rigid language

is gone. Now people can try out their own language. But originality is hard to come by. Already, there's a whole new set of clichés."

"What kinds of clichés?"

"The clichés of democracy."

Of course; I've heard them all through Eastern Europe—the rhetoric of tolerance and pluralism and individual rights and human rights—noble ideas, all of them, but quickly beginning to sound as banal as anything does once it is turned into official slogans. Repetition creates its own credibility gap, since it suggests automatic speech.

But the conditions of people's lives, are they any different now?

He shrugs slightly. "People can think about fundamental questions in a different way," he says quickly, as if not to give this statement too much weight. "But it's a mistake to think that under Jaruzelski they were unhappy and under Mazowiecki they can be happy. Whatever 'ski' comes along, there'll still be fortune and misfortune, hope and hopelessness."

Yes. That, finally, seems to me the true note to sound on what has happened after the changes: a note large enough to take in both the astonishment of the recent events and the strange quiescence that has descended upon Eastern Europe. We've come to know too much about revolutions and cycles of history and progress followed by regress to be easily inspired by utopian hopes; we've come to know about too many political systems and their limitations, and the limits of politics itself. It can make for more or less tolerable conditions, but it's powerless against the human condition—against envy, age, the struggle for power, disappointment in love, or the common cold. It is hard to be naïvely enthusiastic about the entry into the "normal" world when the shortcomings of that world are so clear, too.

"But let me tell you a story of something rather dramatic," Konrad says, just as I am ready to sink comfortably into the fatalistic view. "A few months ago, a man from the secret police came—yes, still the old secret police—a very nice man, very polite. And he said very politely that they would like to remove the bug in my house. In most cases, they've removed the bugs without the owner's knowledge, but in about seventeen cases, they wanted to do it openly, so that everyone would know that a debugging operation was taking place. He was very concerned about my wife, and about whether she might faint when she found out that this device was in our house." Konrad looks quietly amused. "I told him she would be able to take it."

I must confess that I'm surprised by this. Hungary was relatively so "liberal" in the last years of the Kádár era that I would have thought bugging would have gone out of style some time ago. But while there are outer limits on what any political system can accomplish, the internal limits in even the softest totalitarian regimes were apparently tight and narrow indeed.

Martin, my recently repatriated Czech friend, arrives on a few days' visit and instantly begins to complain about everything. The Danube is too broad in Budapest, not perfectly proportioned, like the Vltava. The city is too gray and the Buda Hills too sprawling, unlike the gratifyingly compressed hills of Prague.

Indeed, the Danube is enormous here, and it rushes forward in a powerful current, gray, filled with debris, and hardly lyrical. On one side, the older Buda climbs up several layers of hills; on the other, the flat Pest bustles with commerce. The beautifully designed bridges, all rebuilt after they were gratuitously destroyed by the retreating Nazi armies, stretch for impressive lengths, obscured by smog and traffic. And there is a grandiosity to Budapest's architectural dimensions. Given its geopolitical situation, almost as disadvantageous as Poland's, Hungary won for itself a better fate in the age of rapacious empires. The Historic Compromise of 1867, which established the dual Austro-Hungarian monarchy, made Hungary the imperial overseer of several Slavic nations. Toward the end of the nineteenth century, Hungarians could seriously talk about "Hungarian supremacy," and dreams of "Greater Hungary in the Heavens," a hypothetical entity consisting of all the lands that had ever belonged to it throughout its history, and that would eventually be consolidated right on this earth. Much of Budapest's design and architecture dates from this period of national ascendancy, and reflects Hungary's sense of its own glory. The central avenues are as wide as the Haussmann boulevards in Paris; and many older apartment buildings are stolidly outsize.

But Budapest is an Eastern European city after all, and the majestic dimensions coexist with soot and grime and unkempt façades. I come to like this combination, and Budapest's solid seriousness, and the way the city shows the ravages of its history without embarrassment or self-consciousness. There are noble-looking edifices that look as if they haven't been touched by a restoring hand for centuries; and the stone exteriors of many ordinary buildings bear the heavy pockmarks of bullets, which date from the defense of the city against the Nazis in 1944–45, or from the 1956 uprising against the Stalinist regime of Mátyás Rákosi. Budapest has been many times besieged, and gallantly defended.

All in all, Budapest feels like Florence to Prague's Venice, a no-nonsense city rather than a magical one, in which beauty is framed in everyday business. But there is of course Váci Utca, where both the standards and the scale are different. This charming stretch of narrow street has been turned into the main tourist strip, and spiffed up to a glisten. Váci Utca is one of the Budapest spots where Mitteleuropa reached its apotheosis, and part of the charm comes from a former age. The street was already fashionable at the end of the eighteenth century, and some of the coffeehouses and antiquarian bookstores have been here for a long time. In one of the small squares the street gives onto, an enchanting statue of a girl carrying baskets of fish spouts a delicate stream of water. These small statues and water fountains are a lovely Budapest specialty, a form somewhere between domestic and public art, mediating between broad urban vistas and the intimate gaze.

Budapestians are very proud of Váci Utca, of the modern hotel with covered walk-through arcades in the middle of it—"like something in Milan," a friend says. In the more expensive stores, there's the shine of good leather and the sparkle of jewelry and the bright colors of Hungarian embroidery; there are places where you can get your photos developed in a few hours, an incessant queue in front of the Adidas shop, and a McDonald's, looking particularly garish and ugly in contrast to its surroundings, though my Hungarian friends seem to be proud of it as well, and keep trying, unsuccessfully, to drag me there.

And then the mill of tourists, Austrian and German and Dutch, eying the prices with a speculative look in their eyes; the money changers, mostly Arab, tugging at your sleeve and whispering exchange rates in your ear; a black man carrying a placard advertising a striptease nightclub. Eastern Europe après Communism.

At any time of day, one can see rows of Transylvanian peasants standing on Váci Utca. They have come here from their much poorer part of the world to peddle a few wares. Their faces and demeanor speak of something nearly forgotten in urban settings, of some basic health, or dignity, or perhaps just simplicity. They're ruddy-skinned, robust, with direct, clear eyes and frank, cheerful smiles. In the way of peasant cultures, they are all dressed in exactly the same fashion—the women in starched white blouses and very wide skirts covered with the same, delicate flower patterns, and kerchiefs on their heads; the men in gleaming white shirts with embroidered vests over them. Their wares are also done in a few repeated styles and patterns: tablecloths of rather thick linen with large, somewhat crudely embroidered flowers, pottery with a lovely green glaze, and religious pictures painted on glass. Although much must depend on making a few sales, they never solicit or plead. They simply stand, straight and upright, holding a tablecloth or a camisole in front of them, and looking at passersby with an impassive forthrightness.

The one time I approach them to look at something more

closely, our transaction is interrupted by the approach of several policemen. The Transylvanians, together with their wares, vanish into the crowd as swiftly and deftly as if they were made of smoke. I am left standing in my all-too-solid flesh, looking at the disappearing rustle with some amazement. I wonder by what rules the police are playing; after all, the Transylvanians stand on the street for hours on end in plain view, and undisturbed. This must be yet another one of those games of we-pretend-to-hide-and-you-pretend-to-seek to which the Eastern Europeans have been so accustomed, and which they may be playing still, if only out of habit.

At night, even the shabbiness turns charmed, and grandiosity turns to serene grandeur, as the strings of jewel lights over the Danube throw deep reflections into the water, and the crests of the Buda Hills trace a long, inky line, its blackness punctuated by illuminated monuments. From the Pest side, the Castle complex holds the center of attention, with the Gothic thrust of the Mattias Church nearby. From the Buda side, looking toward Pest, the gaze focuses on the splendidly lit Parliament and its ethereal double in the water; and from there, the eye travels along the Danube to the succession of flickering bridges and their liquid reflections.

My Czech friend and I sit in one of the open-air restaurants that line the Danube on the Pest side. He complains about the food, which he finds far inferior to his native variety. In my view, they are close competitors for awfulness, but it's true that Hungarian cooking could well take the prize. What's happened to the famed Hungarian cuisine of yesteryear? Everything comes swimming in grease and a colorless version of paprika sauce. Fresh vegetables seem to be banned from restaurant menus no less than in Prague, probably on the same grounds of excessive healthfulness. A dessert arrives with too much whipped cream on it, and a Gypsy band lets fly at full volume with its overrich melodies: pure *Schlag* for the soul. All around are the enchanting and utterly perplexing sounds of Hungarian language, with its Bartókian syncopations and sensuousness. Even when they speak

English, Hungarians manage to transport some of the off-rhythms and softness of their own language into that flatter tongue, and to give it strange, lunar resonances.

An evening gathering of the Budapest intelligentsia at first glance might be mistaken for something teleported from the Upper West Side, except maybe for the somewhat better dress and manners prevailing here; the Hungarian new class hasn't yet acquired the full affectations of laconic cool, or conspicuous inconspicuousness. In the funky little sitting room—a space off the kitchen, with old plush chairs and sofa—the mood is high, the conversation flows smartly and sharply; there's an openly homosexual couple, several people in the room have had professional stints in the West, and almost everybody has been divorced. There's talk of new journals and real-estate prices, which, for commercial spaces at least, are outdoing Amsterdam's. Everyone speaks impeccable English and most people have several other languages at their disposal as well, though they're oddly cavalier about the use of "he" and "she." Hungarian has no genders, I am told, though I can hardly imagine such a state of linguistic affairs, and even in other languages, the difference between feminine and masculine apparently seems to Hungarians a minor distinction.

But no, I am in Eastern Europe and not in Manhattan, after all. I remember this as soon as the anecdotes begin. An activist economist tells me how difficult it is to get factory employees to drop their old socialist union and join a new one, for the very simple reason that the old union still has the lock on hotels and vacation spas—and between ideology and vacations, most people will inevitably choose the latter. Someone else tells a joke about Hungary's efforts to sidle up to Austria economically. "Have you heard who lost the Austro-Hungarian soccer match?" the joke goes. "No, who?" "The Italians."

"Ah, that joke used to be told during the Hapsburgs," someone points out.

And then the characteristic Eastern European note is

sounded clearly when Zsuzsa, the hostess, launches with great zest into the second bugging story I've heard within the space of a few days; there was *this* much bugging in Kádár's Hungary!

The hosts' fortunes have just undergone a full turn for the better; Péter, a very energetic, very clever man with a perpetual sparkle of sharp amusement in his eyes, has been named to a high academic post; but until recently, he had the distinction of being one of the more seriously persecuted dissidents in Hungary, jobless and hounded for many years.

During those years, Zsuzsa and Péter knew very well that their upstairs neighbors informed on them—that is, they had a listening device in their apartment on which they recorded whatever went on in the apartment below, and which they later turned over to the police. Not surprisingly, the two couples never spoke to each other. The softer Péter couldn't refrain from nodding at the neighbors in the elevator; the tougher Zsuzsa stood her ground and ignored them completely. Then, one day, the man upstairs emerged from his silence and pleaded with Péter to meet with him for a talk. In a pub, the man got moodily drunk and confessed that he'd been informing on Péter for many years. But now he couldn't bear to do this filthy work anymore; he liked Péter, he felt horrible pangs of conscience, and all in all he wanted Péter to know that he was going to disconnect the bugging device.

Péter, who really is a kind as well as a reasonable man, advised the neighbor against doing anything so drastic. Someone else would be asked to do the informing anyway, he pointed out, and in the meantime, his neighbor would get into trouble and maybe lose his job. Nevertheless, for several weeks, whenever they ran into each other, the man from upstairs was unusually cheerful and friendly to Péter and Zsuzsa, as if a burden had been lifted from him. Then, gloomy silence descended once again. Péter and Zsuzsa assumed that the device had been reconnected.

About two years after these episodes came the larger events, and with them, a complete reversal in the two couples' positions.

Péter was suddenly vindicated, famous, interviewed. For the up-stairs neighbors, the game was suddenly up.

"And this is where the story changes from Dostoevsky to Balzac," Zsuzsa comments wryly. One day, when she was walking her dog in front of her apartment, Zsuzsa was approached by the woman upstairs. This time, the woman said hello and awkwardly tried to start a conversation. There was much patting of the dog, to disguise the years of what had gone on between them. The woman said how happy she was to see Péter on a television pro-gram recently. ("I'll bet she was," somebody throws in. "She was probably proud. After all, Péter is somebody she knows very well.")

"Now, the next part probably bears some analysis," Zsuzsa continues. "Because I really don't know what got into me—but I invited her to come up for a cup of tea."

Once in the apartment, the woman proceeded to look around eagerly, and exclaim with wonder at how modern and wonderful everything was. "Oh, I've always wanted to see how it came out," she said, not realizing how much this revealed; she had apparently closely followed the course of the apartment ren-ovations on the listening device.

And then the story turns into something that doesn't yet have a literary precedent, for it's pure post-Communist Eastern Eu-rope. The woman turned to Zsuzsa passionately. "Please," she said, "maybe you can use your influence to help us. You see, we used to have some property on Lake Balaton, and the bas-tards took it away in 1948. We've been trying to get it back, but we're having problems. Those bastards, they took every-thing from us. But you, you have connections, you could do something for us."

Zsuzsa says that she listened to this speech in astonishment and managed to mutter that she didn't think she had it in her power to do anything. And that's the end of it, at least for now, though somebody suggests there's material here for a TV series called *Neighbors,* in which the vicissitudes of the two couples might be followed into the new era. Neighbors, Eastern European style, with that peculiar intimacy that inflected into either solidarity or swinishness. It's an intimacy that made for the close, steamy moral goulash the Eastern Europeans learned to live with simply because they had to, because they literally didn't have the space or the luxury for the moral purism we occasionally idealize, though so rarely live up to, in the richer and freer countries.

The brutal intimacy of power: there is a sort of voyeuristic bond between the spy and the object of spying, and a sadistic bond between the torturer and the tortured, which must make a face-to-face encounter horribly compelling to both. A few days after I hear Zsuzsa's story, someone tells me of an encounter from an earlier time—a time in which the banality of "neighborly" meetings had a more grotesque aspect. The incident was recounted by a woman who was tortured during the Rajk show trials in 1949. A few years later, she was approached by two men in the foyer of a theater. "Do you recognize me?" one of them asked. "No," she said at first. At which point he covered most of his face with his hands, making openings for his eyes with his fingers—the way she would have seen him when he tortured her.

"Now do you recognize me?" he asked again.

"Ah, yes, now I do," she said.

"And me?" the other man asked. "Do you know who I am?"

She looked at him more closely. "You. You're the one who used to beat me," she said.

"Well, what do you want?" he asked amiably. "I was under orders."

"Yes," she said. "But you didn't have to beat me so hard."

And then they all walked into the theater to see the performance.

Fragrant Buda Hills. A steep street surrounded by parklike lushness of old trees; overgrown gardens, tall yellow weeds; enormous villas, faded, crumbling, pastel. A set for a Tarkovsky movie. I'm visiting Katalin, whom I just met recently. In her apartment, faded rugs are elegantly draped over sofas and desks;

on the walls, some old paintings of rustic scenes, a peasant boy represented as Pan. From the porch, a spectacular view of the Buda Hills winding down to the Danube and the grand urban vistas. We sit there, sipping drinks. Katalin is tall and lithe, with dark hair coiled at her neck, and a permanent pensiveness, a wistfulness in her manner.

She tells me softly about how she grew up, and how she's only now beginning to excavate her Jewishness in psychoanalysis. For some reason, Jewishness became a more deeply camouflaged subject here than in Poland after the war, and in her family it was never mentioned. She knew that there was something hidden in her background; but half knowledge can be more troubling than complete amnesia. She has an early memory of being taken to a synagogue by a grandfather, some allusions to wartime traumas in family gatherings, and a sense of a veil covering *something.* "And this is the story of my generation," she says, "that we didn't know who we were. And what are we supposed to do with this new knowledge? Do you know how troubling it can be?" So now, as if to exorcise the secret, or at least bring it to light, she has become passionately interested in Judaism. She's a schoolteacher, and she thinks she might want to teach at the new Anne Frank school that has opened in Budapest.

There's something like a revival of Jewish consciousness in Hungary nowadays, and worries about the revival of anti-Semitism as well. Hungary has the largest Jewish population in Eastern Europe, estimated between 80,000 and 100,000, most of them concentrated in Budapest. At the outset of the changes, there were fears that there would be a putsch in the professions where Jews hold important positions, most markedly in the media. The governing party, wheeling out a stale, prewar distinction between "populists," supposedly truly patriotic Hungarians attached to countryside and land, and "urbanists," who stand for cosmopolitan intellectuals, made statements suggesting that Jews aren't *echt* Hungarians. But although much unpleasant noise has been made, no actual actions have followed from these rumblings, and there are signs to suggest that anti-Semitism isn't really taking in Hungary. Nobody has been fired so far; and SDS (Free Democrats Union), the major opposition party, many of whose leading figures are Jewish and progressive intellectuals, gained votes *after* a not-so-subtle anti-Semitic campaign was directed against it by the other parties. Perhaps—I allow myself to hope—the repellent rhetoric of anti-Semitism is losing some of its effectiveness, its hold on the public imagination, after all.

The word "schizophrenia" keeps coming up in Hungarian conversations. People talk about how schizophrenic they felt in the past, and about the sense of self-division, of doubleness, that afflicts them even now, or especially now, since the system—ah, they admit it after all!—has changed.

Perhaps it's another word for the melancholy that is a prized quality of the Hungarian character, as it is of the Polish; it is part of the soul's lyricism and the obverse side of the heroic impulse, of the penchant for risking all in a grand, fiery gesture. The Hungarian melancholics I've known tend to be brilliant, charming, with a mercurial streak of high spirits. One could do worse in the realm of neurosis.

But no, "schizophrenia" seems to strike a different note from anything I've heard in Poland or Czechoslovakia, and it recurs again as I talk with Gabor, a sociologist, one afternoon. As far as I can make out, Gabor did honest, if unprovocative, work, and he would seem to have no particular reason to feel this— whatever "this" is, for I find its exact nature elusive. "Is it that people—you—have to change so much to accommodate to the new conditions?" I ask, when he says that he feels strangely "schizophrenic" these days.

"No, it's not that," he answers. "It's that twenty years of our past are acquiring a different coloring. I have to rethink everything I did, and I'm not sure ... well, I'm not sure where I stood, or where I should have stood. You see, we all lied to ourselves so much."

"But is there anything with which you reproach yourself? Is there anything you think you shouldn't have done?"

"No, it's not that exactly," he says, and a look of distress passes over his mobile, sensitive face. "It's just that there were hundreds of small ways to be in bad faith if you didn't think about it, and of course you didn't think about it, you can't think about your fundamental motivations every day, you'd never get to the office. But now I keep lying awake in the night trying to figure out if that article on the ethnic minorities in Hungary was fully honest, or did I stop short of what I could have said . . . ? Well, you see, I simply don't know. Because I think I stopped myself from knowing certain things before I even knew them."

"But isn't that being overscrupulous?" I ask. "After all, if you decided to stay here, you had to act somehow, and you weren't required to do anything really compromising."

"Ah, that's exactly the problem," he says. "We lost track of what was compromising and what wasn't."

"I see," I say, but I don't, completely. Is this an example of the much-vaunted subtlety of the Hungarian race?

Sometime after this conversation I come across a short story by Péter Nádas who, I'm told, is one of the great writers of the postwar generation, though very little of his work has been translated into English. The story, called "A Tale About Fire and Knowledge," is written in a style that both parodies and approximates a very complex and arcane philosophical essay. The convoluted and subtle argument concerns the doubleness of language in which people of a certain country speak and how the public language infiltrates and becomes the private, internal language, so that only a certain mental discomfort remains as a memory trace of the disparity between them. One night, fires erupt all over this unnamed country, and the crisis is announced on TV. In the excitement of the moment, the announcer slips out of the double-speak, and, for the duration of a phrase, she conveys a sense of real crisis. All over the country, forks are suspended in midair, as people pause in astonished recognition of this almost forgotten tone of truth. Then the alarm passes, the announcer resumes her business-as-usual mask, and so, with an unacknowledged relief, does everyone else.

The story begins to give me a clue to "schizophrenia." If a similar story were written in Poland, the audiences listening to the announcer would have been busily analyzing the "real" meaning behind the announcer's charades; in a Czechoslovak version, the intrusion of reality into the announcer's speech would probably never have taken place, and if it did, it would have provoked fear, for everyone would have expected her to meet with punishment for her slip. But in Nadas's story, the charade has been internalized by everyone, so that the people listening to the announcer no longer know what they know, or what they have forgotten. This more complicated doubleness must have corresponded to the complicated climate of Kádár's Hungary, where it was almost possible to believe that the near-truths and near-freedom the government offered were the real thing; and it was therefore possible to play along, almost forgetting one's doubts.

Almost, but not quite; for it must have been nearly impossible to quell the doubts entirely. There were too many people who remembered that the Kádár regime began in terror and betrayal, even if it ended in goulash Communism. Kádár's early career is quite gripping in its exemplary awfulness. After the war, he was an inner-circle member of Mátyás Rákosi's ruthless Stalinist government; and when the time came for the first purges, in 1948, Kádár was the man designated to arrest and supervise the trial of László Rajk, Rákosi's chief target. Rajk had been Kádár's superior in the party hierarchy, a committed Stalinist himself, who had his share of atrocities to his credit; he was, among other things, the founder of the Communist secret police. Kádár promised Rajk that his life would be spared if he "confessed" to being an American spy; Rajk agreed and, of course, was subsequently executed. In 1951, in the second wave of purges, it was Kádár's turn to be the imprisoned and tortured; he was released, by another fiat of Communist justice, in 1955. In the tragic uprising of 1956, he again showed his skills of survival by the stab in the back. At first, Kádár joined a revolutionary group gathered around Imre Nagy; but within days he defected to the Soviet Un-

ion, and he was next heard on a radio broadcast—after the uprising was defeated by the second Soviet invasion—announcing
the formation of a new pro-Soviet government, with himself at
the head. He next proceeded to betray Nagy—who had briefly
been at the country's helm—by promising him security, and instead arresting him and his allies; two years later, Nagy and several others were executed, after secret trials. (Some of this
material has been gleaned from *The Captive Nations,* an excellent
history of postwar Europe by Patrick Brogan.)

Kádár began his reign by instituting his own purges, nearly
total collectivization, and a widespread terror; it was only later
that he was forced, by the desperate state of the country, into his
experiment of increasing liberalization. Eventually, the great majority of Hungarians came to approve the Kádár regime, which
offered more goods and mobility and leniency on private enterprise than any other Eastern European country. Foreign observers coming to Hungary in the latter decades of Communism
often had trouble figuring out how Hungary was *not* like a Western country; the Hungarians themselves said that it was "the
pleasantest barracks in the camp," though funnily enough, the
Poles said exactly the same thing about themselves. The beginnings of the Kádár regime were nearly erased from public consciousness, and didn't resurface again till the very end—till the
symbolic reburial of Imre Nagy in 1989, which was the Hungarian gong sounding the end of Communism. But still, it wasn't
possible to extract the origins of the barracks from memory completely, or to forget entirely that what their keepers were offering
was a sort of deal, in which the barracks might be made more
and more comfortable, but the enclosing walls could never be removed, even if they were covered by discreet and rather pretty
Swedish ivy.

I imagine that it was in this blurriness, this close "as-if" ap-
proximation of normalcy, that the "schizophrenia" inhered. It
must have been harder here to know what one really thought
and believed than in the clearer Polish or Czech circumstances—
almost as hard as in the West. It must have been easier to tell

fibs to oneself about the terms of the system, or not quite tell oneself the truth to the end—to believe two things simultaneously. And if one was honestly lying to oneself a little all this time, it must be harder, now, to come to terms with this ambiguous past; to accept it or reject it, to approve of one's former posture wholeheartedly, or to feel honest pangs of self-reproach for what, after all, resembled so closely a perfectly normal life.

It fascinates me, in all of this, how the refined Hungarian scruples turn out to reflect the complex circumstances in which people lived—how the structures of the macro situation become inscribed and repeated in the microcosm of the psyche, as, in a fractal series, the whorls of the leaf repeat the leaf.

Budapest is a city of museums. I have walked through galleries upon galleries filled with artifacts of an old, richly articulated culture; I've ambled through enormous rooms of paintings—a world of art unknown in the West though closely related to Western painting. So much a part of Europe, and yet so excised from the European consciousness: as always, when contemplating this, I feel a certain sense of loss—from the part of me that has become Western—and perhaps even a touch of anger from the other side.

The Castle complex up in the hills of Buda houses several museums, as well as being a museum exhibit in its own right. The Royal Palace and its surroundings were built, reduced to rubble and rebuilt again with devastating regularity. Citizens of Budapest first started taking refuge in the inaccessible Buda Hills during a terrifying Tatar attack in the middle of the thirteenth century, and in the subsequent centuries, Buda became a thriving, cosmopolitan city. Its golden age, however, came to an end with the beginnings of Turkish rule in 1541; and the liberation from that dominion in 1686 was marked by a siege that lasted seventy-five days and left the city in ruins. The Baroque city that grew here thereafter met its untimely end in a siege of 1849, as the Hapsburgs marked the local end of the 1848 Spring of Nations by crushing a stubborn revolt. The most recent assault came, heartbreakingly, from Hungarian and Soviet armies in January 1945, as they tried to dislodge the German forces who refused to yield this last ground. But these are only the highlights, for historians have counted no fewer than thirty-one sieges of the strategic Castle fortifications.

In one of the museums within the restored Castle complex—the socialistically named Museum of the Hungarian Working Class—there is now a show on the period in which Hungary went into a forced quarantine from contemporary Europe. The recent past has all of a sudden become visible as the past—and, like any past, it is quickly becoming the object of curators' and historians' attention. There have been shows on Socialist Realist art in Warsaw, and on the last days of Communism in Prague. The one in Buda is on the Stalin-Rákosi years, those worst years of the Hungarians' lives.

And what a strange, aberrant interval it was, I think as I walk through the exhibit's rooms—half European after all, but part Byzantine; part twentieth century, part some earlier, darker age. Like the Byzantine Empire, the dominions of the Soviets were an empire of signs, as is vividly shown in the restricted and repetitious iconography of these exhibits. Every object, gesture, utterance had an assigned and strictly defined meaning within a symbolic system, and it's hard not to wonder whether this highly formal, hieratic sense of the world wasn't indeed descended, by some deep thread of continuity, from the Byzantine Empire itself—an empire in which control of icons and signs was a fundamental form of power.

But there's another analogy that presses itself irresistibly on the mind as I walk into the first galleries of the show. The enormous posters and monumental statues of the great leaders, the photographs of massed crowds marching with their arms raised, the cult of good physique and the heroic New Man and clean, happy "working class"—in all of this, the resemblance to Fascist iconography is inescapable.

And the art! In a room devoted to the painting of the period, I feel a pang of sympathy for the artists who submitted to the esthetic reign of terror. Some tried to resist, of course, by indirect as well as open means. In the contests for the ubiquitous statues of Stalin that had to be erected in every major city, there were sculptors who tried to do their worst, so that they wouldn't have the disgrace of winning. The poignant thing about the paintings is that clearly some of their makers tried to retain a measure of workmanly self-respect. Several of the paintings are an odd combination of competent, restrained style and the peculiar mawkishness of ideological correctness. There's a moody, neo-Impressionist genre scene of a girl looking wistfully out the window, while she's embroidering the hammer and sickle on a red flag; and one of a little boy looking adoringly at a fully uniformed woman soldier. The cake for shamelessness goes to a large canvas depicting a young boy soldier reading what's obviously an inspiring manifesto, while his family, gathered in a shabby little room, listen in rapt silence with faces upturned at the young hero, and the grandmother peels potatoes in a pose of submissive attention.

I try to look at this as one might look at Victorian kitsch, to find it quaint or amusing. But the analogy doesn't work. In Victorian art, we may not like the artist's sensibility, but the art reflects the artist. In this, there's camouflage, or violation, of the artist. The paintings are simply too lifeless to have even the vitality of vulgarity. This is, in a sense, academic art—except what are codified here are not the conventions of high art but the formulas of philistine taste.

After the art, the documentary exhibits are more affecting by far. There are photographs from the 1949 show trials, including an unforgettable one of László Rajk—a tall man with a beautiful face, looking upon the courtroom with simultaneous contempt and an utter understanding of his fate. It adds to the *frisson* of this image that he understood so well because he had been, so recently, on the persecuting side.

The exhibit continues with reconstructions of modest "bourgeois" interiors, which were destroyed because they were the lairs of the enemy; and, on enlarged photos, desolate lengths of prison barracks and fields framed by barbed wire—the barracks before they got to be more pleasant. The terror of the early 1950s was, in Hungary, particularly awful, and claimed up to forty thousand victims, who were either executed or tortured and imprisoned. As the exhibit's finale, an actual, felled statue of Stalin, with crumbling nostrils and an enormous, metal paw chopped off from the body and lying on the ground in rusted impotence. The beginning of the 1956 Revolution, and the next turn of the grinding wheel.

People contemplate these dark documents in a mood of hushed gravity, and in a book provided at the end some have written long statements. Even though in Hungary, as in Poland, pretty much everyone could have known, if they wished, what had gone on, there must be a certain somber catharsis in bridging the cognitive gap publicly at last, in possessing this knowledge fully and in common. It may be the beginning of unconstrained discussion, of mourning and of mastery.

In the window of a chic gallery near Váci Utca, glossy photos of naked men embracing each other. In an underground street passage, magazines with photography à la *Penthouse,* and sometimes harder core as well. Eastern Europe is being deluged with pornography. One area of life that Communism never succeeded in repressing was sexuality, and the popularity of pornography can't really be explained as a reaction against actual puritanism. It is, however, probably a reaction against the visual puritanism, and the long prohibition on pornography and erotic images; still a reaction against Them.

One day, I notice an enormous red balloon placed in front of the Parliament, with a banner bearing a Levi's sign floating above it. The juxtaposition is iconically perfect: from the red star to this red balloon advertising blue jeans. But this is probably the last moment when an object, an image, can be charged with such symbolic meaning. The empire of signs has fallen apart, and pretty soon a red balloon will be just a red balloon, pornography no more than pornographic.

Back in my Rumbach Sebastyén apartment, I turn on the TV and happen on an American movie—something made for TV, with all the requisite silliness—about the single life in San Francisco. This is followed by an old Elvis Presley film. Though in New York I probably wouldn't last through either, I remain glued to the set. I'm a bit homesick, I guess, but also, after several months in Eastern Europe, it's the sheer *Americanness* of what's on the screen that keeps me riveted. Why are these people grinning so much, and showing their very white teeth? Why do they move with such bouncy cheerfulness? Why are they so coy when boy and girl (for everyone in these movies seems adolescent, whatever their supposed age) come together? From this distance, the movements, the gestures, the notion of personality conveyed through these characters seem to come from another world—a world whose kooky, madcap energy suggests a lesser gravity and an entire absence of threat. From here, that seems very odd.

I come to Budapest by plane the second time, and examine the taxi meter before getting in; the tariffs, in these unregulated times, vary wildly. The taxi driver has a humorous, long face that combines a Pinocchio nose with a delicately pursed mouth, and he speaks a perfectly intelligible English, though with an inordinate emphasis on the apologetic phrase.

"Your English is good," I compliment him.

"No, not very good, not at all. Sorry!"

"Where did you learn it?" I inquire.

"Of course, my teacher thirty years ago told me I should learn a useful language. Not Russian. But after all, I got married, I had children. Sorry! But eight years ago, I took a course at the Postal Planning Institute. That's where I worked."

"And why did you leave your job?"

"I thought the taxi was a good business. And, after all, I have no big boss. That's good."

"And is the cab a good business?"

"Sorry, it's not a business at all. There are too many cabs, the government didn't stop them. There are ten thousand cabs in Budapest. Too many. Maybe you'll find another cab. Maybe!"

"What has the government been doing during the last year?" I inquire.

"I do not know. Sorry! Nobody knows. They say they're working hard, and they raise the prices. Not the wages. Sorry!"

I have permitted myself an interval of self-indulgence, and I check into the elegant Gellért Hotel. Ah, the luxury of a truly fluffy towel! The Gellért is a bit of rather odd architectural folly, completed in 1918, and its white stone exterior, elaborate with arches and curves, seems to grow directly out of the white limestone of Gellért Hill. At the same time, the building has a kind of broad, gravity-bound squatness that I've noticed elsewhere in Hungarian architecture. "Earthy vigor" is what a Hungarian friend called this tendency, and indeed there's a peculiar energy expressed through the bursting, bulging pressure of these forms. Inside, though, all is calm elegance, thick carpets, French doors. On the main floor, a cornucopia of restaurants and coffeehouses; outside, spacious terraces, their effect somewhat spoiled by the redoubtable Budapest pollution.

I meet friends there, for drinks and coffees and tall ice-cream concoctions, and, of course, everyone tells me what has happened on the political scene in the last year. Post-Communist logic is unfolding in its specific Hungarian variant: the progressive SDS has lost some support; the conservative MDF is trying to consolidate its control over the important institutions and establish a "monopoly majority" in a way that apparently repeats an old Hungarian pattern. A temporary scandal erupted when the very conservative, nationalist Freeholders' Party defiantly requested to have all its members' secret police files examined, implying that no unpatriotic stool pigeons sullied its ranks. Naturally, it turned out that a major figure among them was a major informer. Among the people I know, this has raised zestful speculations about how the Freeholders would handle this embarrassment—but the matter was in effect quickly dropped, with not much more than a shoulder shrug amidst the absorbing demands of more current business. The popular Hungarian appetite for vettings and verifications and vendettas seems, at the moment, limited.

Altogether, politics—for all its potential consequences—seems less centrally defining here than in other Eastern European countries. Of course, this is still the time of beginnings, when the shape of the new world is being formed, and each step in its making is closely watched; but the pulse taking seems less urgent, the business of governing just one business among others; ordinary life has taken over, with its multiple tracks and concerns.

Best of all, the Gellért Hotel has the famous Gellért Baths. The culture of baths in Budapest is as variegated and refined as the culture of cooking in France. It is one of the legacies of the Ottoman Empire that has lasted. Hungary was under Ottoman domination for almost 150 years, in the sixteenth and seventeenth centuries, and though the rule of the Turkish overlords and the Greek *phanariots* who collected extortionary taxes was, for the most part, bitterly fought and resented, no relationship that lasted that long, as a wise Hungarian friend points out, could have consisted of unmitigated anger. Anyway, the difference between the Turks and the Soviets, she says, is that at least the Turks didn't make their subjects observe their holidays. They were, in fact, religiously and ideologically permissive, if highly exploitative in other ways.

And the Turks left these aquatic customs, which have survived all bad times, one of those interstitial institutions that made life bearable. There are some authentic Turkish baths still functioning in Budapest; but there are also outdoor complexes of pools built long after the Turks left, inexpensive populist baths and beautiful, elaborate baths for the bourgeoisie.

The Gellért Baths are among the most luxurious, and after I spend a morning there I decide baths are an institution of some metaphysical, as well as hedonistic, interest. The foyer entrance is enormous, echoing, filled with marble pillars and a carved central dome—architecture usually reserved for the weighty affairs of money or of state, rather than something as evanescent as the rituals of bathing. Inside the women's section, the scene turns Felliniesque. Among the lockers, on the marble floors, women come and go, either entirely naked or with apronlike white cloths covering the front lower halves of their bodies. The place is whitish with delicate steam, and quite silent. The attendants wear white uniforms. After some gestured negotiations and a few *forints* passing hands, one of the cicerones reluctantly agrees to help me and leads me up marble stairs to a changing room. Everything is immaculately clean; no wetness mars the floors. After I've undressed, my brusque and glum guide takes me to a misty massage room. There, I am unceremoniously doused with water from a hose, placed on a table, and soaped thoroughly. Then, my masseuse, a broad, athletic personage dressed in a squarish bra and shorts, applies her ruthless fingers to my body, punctuating her ministrations with loud slaps, and talking to one of her coworkers all the while. I might as well be a slab of inanimate matter on the kitchen table or the conveyor belt.

Then, into the baths themselves. Two half-moon pools of different temperature are separated by an aisle in a marbled, dome-ceilinged space, the shower room forming a niche built of rich green malachite. And in this grand, harmonious interior, the women bathe, shower, and walk about, some wrapped in long white sheets like Roman togas, without the slightest self-consciousness. Mostly, this morning, they are old women, and their flesh comes in all varieties of decline: pendulous breasts, wrinkled arms, skin hanging over stomachs in complicated folds. It is distressing at first, this living instruction in the ravages our flesh is heir to. But the women sit on the pool's stairs and ledges, gossiping as if they were at the hairdresser's. They are used to their own and each other's bodies, and the baths are for some of them a regular part of their day, and a very practical solace for aching muscles and bones.

And gradually I get used to them, too. There's a dignity in their ease; and there's also the redeeming dignity of the surrounding space—its beauty containing the frailty of the bodies, the permanence of the civilized construction acting as a consolation for the human impermanence. It's as if the domed stone interior trapped time in a permanent stasis, to make up for its terrible passage in our lives.

I spend a moment in a very hot, rosemary-scented sauna, and then proceed, in swimsuit, into the main, common swimming pool, brilliant with the sun filtering through the glass roof. This space is designed with playfulness as well as grandeur, with yellow spiraled pillars surrounding the pool, lions' heads spouting water off the edges, and a lovely sculpture of a farm girl feeding a flock of geese acting as a fountain at one end.

As the last act of the ceremony, I emerge onto one of the sun-flooded terrace restaurants. Here Hungarian Lotharios used to carry on their flirtations and sometimes challenge each other to duels over matters of sentiment or honor. They kept up this bravado custom well into our century. Now groups of tourists and businessmen spoon up their elaborate ice creams and duel over deals.

I feel both vigorous and calm after all the ablutions, as if some essential balance were for a moment righted; such harmony, honoring the body with the tribute of esthetic splendor, seems to me a subtle, and high, achievement of civilization.

There's an old saying in Polish that roughly translates to "Poles and Magyars are two cousins," and that expresses a sense of temperamental kinship between the two countries. The affinity has to do with the propensity for melancholy and grand gestures, and also with both countries' penchant for revolutions, uprisings, and other, usually doomed, acts of protest against foreign masters. Like Poland, Hungary has its roster of romantic revolutionary heroes, who had a flair for burning brightly and dying young. Leopold I, Hungary's first Hapsburg master, thought that "Hungarian blood, which was inclined to revolution and restlessness," could only be subdued by particularly stringent measures. His reign, like all subsequent ones, bred its dissidents; and the archetypal Eastern European pattern of rebellion, secret societies, conspiracy trials, and uncompromising suppression recurs at every important historical juncture. The revolutionary movements of 1848 gave forth a trio of great leaders—Lajos Kossuth, Ferencz Deák, and Sándor Petőfi—all of them men of letters as well as action. Petőfi, who had the most Byronic career of them all, was also one of Hungary's great romantic poets; he was killed in battle at the age of twenty-six. There was also a prominent Polish participant, General József Bem, who, in an act of revolutionary kinship, led a temporarily successful campaign in Transylvania. The bids for independence ended in the usual way when the Hapsburgs invited "the gendarme of Europe," that is, the Russian army, to help them suppress the popular movement. In 1849, the Russian commanding general reported to Tsar Nicholas I, not without a touch of braggadocio, that "Hungary lies at the feet of Your Majesty."

For all its enormous discontinuities, history never snaps the threads of continuity entirely in two, and there is surely a line of descent leading from the earlier series of insurrectionary movements to that spontaneous and ultimately tragic outburst of outrage that became known as the 1956 revolution. Ironically enough, the more recent oppositional tradition leads, as in Poland, through the early Communists to postwar dissidents, who were their figurative, and often literal, children. As in Poland, there have been several distinct generations of dissidents in Hungary since the war—generations derived from each other, educated by each other, and now sitting in the "wedding cake," as the Parliament is called, in more or less uneasy proximity. I have met with three of them—a study in the movement of postwar Hungarian history, and the different intensities of its burden.

Miklós Vásárhelyi belongs to the generation of the 1956 revolutionaries, remote enough by now to loom in a heroic light. I meet him one day in his apartment deep within the flowering Buda Hills—a small, compact man in his early seventies, dressed in rather baggy jeans and a threadbare sweater, slow-moving, with a mild face and tired, all-seeing eyes. He speaks slowly and with a laconic understatement—not out of reluctance, I sense, but as if the turbulent events through which he has lived had simplified themselves into a perfectly clear shape, a sequence of scenes, and a few crucial yeses and nos.

He had been in the eye of the storm and at the center point of some of the most disillusioning events of remembered history; and he seems to have emerged with a kind of distilled calm. In his youth, he was one of the idealistic Communists from bourgeois families, for whom it was natural, after the war, to join the group of internal party reformers clustered around Imre Nagy. Vásárhelyi had known Nagy from college days, and later, they were expelled from the Party together. It was their group that, in 1955, began opposing Mátyás Rákosi, and in 1956, became central in the confused and tragic sequence of events that came to be known as the revolution. The students' manifesto, which precipitated the uprising on October 23, 1956, demanded, among other things, the formation of a government led by Imre Nagy.

In its first stage, the revolution was a spontaneous act of defiance against all odds. In fights between the populace and segments of the army that had joined it on one side, and the secret police and Soviet tanks sent to help prop up the regime on the other, thousands of people were killed and injured; but the Stalinist government, led at that point by Ernö Gero, was brought to its knees.

On October 24, four hundred Soviet tanks rolled into Budapest—but later in the day, the Soviets, in an attempt to control the situation, acceded to having Nagy direct the government. His victory lasted less than two weeks, during which the group around Nagy was, as Vásárhelyi says with some pride, "the legitimate government of Hungary."

During subsequent days, the fighting went on; some two hundred tanks were destroyed; and on October 28, amazingly enough, the Soviets started pulling out.

On November 1, they were back, with three thousand tanks and several army divisions. The Nagy group appealed to the

United Nations and waited for a gesture of support from the West.

It never came. At this point in the narrative, I find myself in my customary and highly uncomfortable position, in which my divided East-West allegiances eye each other suspiciously across the Atlantic. All of the American propaganda about rolling back Communism and liberating slave nations led the Nagy group to believe that when one of the slave nations made a heroic effort to liberate itself the United States would come to its defense. As it was, the State Department didn't even put the Hungarian situation on the agenda of the Security Council; the Suez crisis was happening simultaneously, and it seemed the more important of the two world events.

Once the Soviet army reached Budapest, the Nagy group knew that they had to run for their lives. They went to the one safe haven available—the Yugoslav embassy, where Tito had offered them refuge. The group consisted of several families, forty people in all, including children and grandchildren.

Then, on November 23—exactly a month after the beginning of the revolution—they were approached by representatives of the newly formed Kádár government, who told them that they should go to their homes, that no reprisals would be taken against them. Instead, once they boarded the buses the government had sent for them, they were taken to a place in Romania that Vásárhelyi describes as a concentration camp.

It was there that Vásárhelyi's time of extremity began. One day in 1957, some officials from Hungary arrived at their place of exile. This time, they loaded only the men into a bus, leaving the women and children behind. Their destination turned out to be prison and a succession of secret trials that were a fittingly horrible sequel to the Rajk trials of the previous regime. I ask Vásárhelyi whether he tried to defend himself on the stand. Not very much, he says mildly. He and the others knew it was no use. Of the ten defendants, the four central ones were executed; one died in prison; five got varying prison sentences. Vásárhelyi was sentenced to five years, of which he served four. For one and a half of those years, he was in solitary, with no visits or contacts with other prisoners or the outside world.

By now, I've heard many accounts of a time in prison, but I continue to be intensely fascinated by them—by just what enables some people to survive in such circumstances, and survive without being broken or bitter. Prison has been so much a part of Eastern European history as to be a normative, indeed formative, experience—but even in the seeming monotone of suffering, there are gradations. A Polish friend of mine has said quite seriously that "there was a time when people liked going to prison"—because it was a badge of moral honor, and a confirmation of one's beliefs, and because the company tended to be first rate. But Vàsàrhelyi's imprisonment was not of that period, or kind. It came as a result of morally crushing betrayals; and it was no longer leavened by a faith in the victory of the cause. How did he manage to retain his sanity, I ask, during such an unbearably long period of utter solitude? He smiles quizzically. "I hoped," is his answer. "I am of an optimistic temperament; I'd say I'm a rather gentle person. I had already read Arthur Koestler earlier and I knew that the only question was whether they'd leave me alive or kill me. If they left me alive, then there might be a time when I was free." Optimistic and gentle: how curious that such qualities would have made a mode of strength, and how rarely we think of them this way. And yet I can see how they might have helped him to endure, better than the bitter interior struggles of rage and hate.

After a year and a half, Vàsàrhelyi was transferred to a cell with other political prisoners and was allowed access to books and newspapers. He developed a great taste for Flaubert and read through the whole Pléiade edition of French literature that one prisoner received from his private library. The inmates included people of all political persuasions, and in the gruesomely overcrowded cell, there were constant discussions. It was then that Vàsàrhelyi came to the conclusion that his belief in reforming the Communist system was wrongheaded; the system, he decided, was irredeemable.

It must have been, again, the resilience that comes from hope that allowed Vàsàrhelyi to resume life after prison without rancor or retreat. It helped that his wife and children supported him throughout his ordeals. For twelve years after prison, he was forbidden to do intellectual work, and was employed on a farming cooperative as a combination clerk and worker. Then, in 1972, the Kádár regime loosened the reins, and Vàsàrhelyi was allowed to go back to the kind of work that interested him. And once again he started taking part in oppositional activities. He was harassed, spied on—and undeterred.

His last great effort—a touch of pride enters his voice as he mentions it—was organizing the funeral of Imre Nagy in June 1989. There's a tradition of grand, symbolically and ceremonially charged burials in Hungary—the funeral of Lajos Kossuth, the 1848 revolutionary, conducted in Budapest after his many years in exile, was one of them. Nagy's belated funeral, held in Heroes' Square, with its dramatic, dynamic statues of the founding Árpád dynasty, drew one of those enormous, testimonial crowds that signaled 1989 as a revolutionary turning point. It was a moment of great emotion and vindication for Vàsàrhelyi. Three of the men who had been executed in the Nagy trials were his college friends, he says simply.

After the changes, Vàsàrhelyi became one of the founders of SDS, the progressive opposition party. He's an MP, although he says that he has become too old and tired for practical, daily politics. Nevertheless, he serves as the chairman of the Committee for Historical Justice, which fights for moral, and in some cases material, compensation for the victims and prisoners of those years.

There have been junctures in his life when he has felt bitter, he says quietly, but now is not one of them. He doesn't want a vendetta against the former Communists, or "trials against seventy-year-olds, thirty years after the fact." He doesn't think that people responsible for serious misdeeds should hold the highest positions, but he recognizes the need for the Communist expertise in the new Hungarian era; after all, the managers within the Communist society were, at least formally, Communist. "I feel no personal resentment against anybody," he says. "It happened this way, and I can't help it. I try to live my last years in peace."

This is the opposite of a revanchist mentality, and perhaps it comes from Vàsàrhelyi's knowledge that he has done everything he could; from a self-acceptance. Perhaps the peace is possible also because the truth about what happened to him and his friends has been brought to light and recognized—since the need for that recognition seems as basic and powerful as any instinct, and the drive for its fulfillment and resolution as urgent.

"One way to look at it is that you've had a very interesting life," I hazard, inadequately; I have no way of expressing the full awe I feel at his story, or the larger history that spawned it.

"Ah, yes, very interesting indeed," he answers with the mildest of smiles. "But perhaps in this case less would have been more."

To come into Miklós Haraszti's apartment after Vàsàrhelyi's is to know that one has jumped periods and esthetics—into a style that, in America, would be instantly identifiable as belonging to the sixties and that, lo and behold, is identified in just those terms here. Haraszti lives in an old building in the shabby, somnolent, charming inner heart of Budapest; but the apartment itself has been converted into a loftlike space—open, airy, full of light. There are white cabinets and blond wood furniture and a somewhat earthy clutter. On a door there's a poster with the motto *"Igen, Igen, Igen, Igen"* printed on it boldly. *Igen* means "yes," and the four yeses were a slogan used in a referendum that brought the Communists down, and in which Haraszti's dissident group was instrumental.

It was a feature of his formative time, and of Hungary's somewhat more relaxed situation in that period, that Haraszti could be both a dissident and a sort of counterculture romantic; that he could experiment and play with various personae. At one point in our conversation, he shows me, with bemusement, a photograph of himself from the 1960s, which, he says, "will tell you everything." Indeed, it does. It is the standard male youth-revolt photo of that period—the military uniform, in this case of Soviet derivation, the Chè Guevara hair and beard transforming Haraszti's delicate face into a cookie-cutter revolutionary.

Haraszti is neatly dressed and clean-shaven now, and there's no way of not noticing his striking handsomeness. His friend György Konrad has described him as "a slim, boyish man with dark eyes and black hair, a face both beautiful and sad." It's also a face lighted up by wit, the openness of an alert mind, and sheer niceness. There's a lightness of being in him that perhaps corresponds—I don't think this is too fanciful—to the lightening up of circumstances in his Hungarian generation. He has had his share of harassments, police surveillance, and censorship—but these were no longer life and death matters. He spent a month in prison at some point, but the threat of solitary, torture, or show trials didn't loom over him. More important, such threats didn't loom over his generation. The wand of dissidence was passed on to him after Kádár's government had relaxed its worst repressions, and it no longer threatened to explode in his face.

He came by his oppositional ideas the way many of his generation did: simply because it was so obvious to him that, in the name of a putative idealism, his elders lied. Yet, unlike many of his peers, he had to come to this conclusion pretty much by himself. He was the son of Communists whose brand of ideological commitment was fervent; and so Haraszti, as he puts it, didn't have "the benefit of a double education" from which most Eastern Europeans profited—official ideology in school, and utter skepticism at home.

Haraszti is a great aphorist, even in English, and he has enough self-consciousness to know how much he derived from "the Marxist culture" against which he so sharply rebelled. The strongest feature he retained from his early, Marxist education, he says, is an inclination to idealism and principles, a basic impulse to look for what is true. The other tendency, which propelled him toward various forms of engagement, was something he calls, with an easy self-mockery, "this stupid activism." "A deep unconscious notion in all Marxist culture," he says, and he smiles at his own formulation, "is that society is something the intellectual has to change. Indeed, society is *defined* as the thing you have to change."

Aside from the extreme geniality of his manner, Haraszti has the flair, the self-confidence, that must come partly from being known as one of his generation's best and brightest. It's entirely apt that after mocking his own voluntarism he should recount an anecdote about meeting one of the Kennedys, and his surprise at being told that "at their home, at their dinner table, they spoke in that language, too—what to do about the poor, how to help reform society, etc. It was funny to hear that." Funny, but comprehensible; for while Haraszti's background hardly resembled the Kennedys' in its particulars, he did belong to a caste that, as he is the first to admit, was given a great deal of power under socialism, and with it, sometimes, a sense of responsibility, or noblesse oblige: the intellectuals.

During the sixties, the deep political unconscious of the young Eastern European intelligentsia expressed itself in forms that would be very recognizable to their contemporaries in the West. For a while, it was hard to tell whether he was a hippie, a rocker, or a mad poet. He wrote poetry and translated Bob Dylan songs into Hungarian; he also read voraciously, whatever he could get his hands on in Hungarian, or in the three other languages he knows well. Haraszti couldn't travel out of Hungary until 1977; but, he says, "our face was turned to the West." For a while, he even became a Western-style Maoist—no Chinese dissident of his generation would have been one—but soon he was denounced by his Maoist group for being too insubordinate.

His circle of friends had lively discussions with people coming to Budapest from the West—that cultish mélange of students, academics, and other Eastern Europe aficionados, who usually sympathized with the Other Europe from the left—with all the attendant misunderstandings. "We often thought," Haraszti says casually, "that the observed knew more than the observers." For while the Western new left was experimenting with all kinds of ideologies and ideals, the Eastern Europeans were the subjects of ideological experiments *in vivo*—and that made for a different knowledge indeed.

Paradoxically, it was a knowledge that made them less dogmatic. Or perhaps not so paradoxically, for pure dogma is better sustained in the empty space of pure theory, and Haraszti's peers had to grapple with theory incarnated into actual conditions, and with actual actions that might change those conditions. By the seventies, Haraszti had left Marxism and Maoism behind; the oppositional movement in Hungary had become a human-rights, rather than an ideological, movement. "The main impact of Communism," Haraszti says, "was to kill the concepts of left and right." The same kinds of conclusions were being reached all over Eastern Europe. Haraszti's contemporaries had a strong sense of being part of an Eastern European generation. In the 1970s, they learned *samizdat* printing techniques from the Poles; they started exchanges with their counterparts in Poland and in Czechoslovakia; there were famous secret meetings in the Tatra Mountains, right on the border between Poland and Czechoslovakia.

Haraszti remembers the period of his young dissident adulthood as his heyday, the way Vásárhelyi never could. Haraszti's circle established a journal, *Beszélö,* in which "real political language" could be used. There were warm friendships, literature, the pleasures of meaningful action. They even managed, Haraszti says wryly, to be "self-ironic," that rarest of qualities in any group of politicized intelligentsia.

Moreover, they were exempt from some of the conflicts that began to dog their Western counterparts with a sort of iron inevitability, as soon as the latter entered adulthood: conflicts between the attractions of protest and the pull of money and career. There was no big money to be made in Hungary, and official careers came loaded with opprobrium: the Eastern European young Turks had no fears of being metamorphosed into that dread beast, the "bourgeois," no incentive to turn corporate, or officious, or workaholic.

Haraszti spent his one year in regular employment as a worker in a factory—though even that was partly in the nature of research. Out of his experiences there came a book, *Worker in a Workers' State,* which was never published in Hungary, but which became the subject of a widely publicized trial after the police confiscated typed manuscripts of it. Haraszti was sentenced to eight months in prison, though he served only one of them, after public opinion in the West rallied on his behalf. Aside from this episode of routine employment, Haraszti supported himself by illicit "black jobs," writing for pay under pseudonyms, and even some smuggling. His second book, *The Velvet Prison,* is a complex, incisive analysis of intellectuals who grew up under state socialism, and the tricky, subliminal modes of self-censorship and self-deception they engaged in. That special Hungarian split in the psyche never had a subtler exegesis.

Nowadays, Haraszti is a leading member of the SDS party, and he smiles bemusedly when I ask him whether the change from dissidence to official opposition is a big leap. "The challenges and joys of professionalism are quite interesting," he says with a deliberate evasiveness. "We're all fully aware that it's too late for us to learn how to be professional politicians. But I try to approach it very realistically—I don't think I'll be guilty of a mistake classical for Hungarian politicians—not knowing the moment when to go." But what, exactly, is so difficult about being official? Well, there's the business of being an administrator, though he doesn't mind working with secretaries, doesn't mind it at all. But there's also the need to be—oh, irony of ironies!—more careful than he's ever had to be in the past. Still, in this, he will only go so far. "I'd quit my job," he says, "the moment the mixture of diplomacy and telling the truth shifted in favor of diplomacy—the moment telling the truth became impossible."

For now, though, he thinks that the presence of his generation in politics is crucial, that its antiauthoritarian, antistatist impulses may be the saving grace in an atmosphere that, for his taste, is becoming too centralized again. But the Eastern European version of this new leftism grown-up is different from the

Western one. "There is a special consciousness of people born under socialism," Haraszti says—"an anti-ideological consciousness." The politics of his peers is neither left nor right, nor concerned with such labels anymore, but combines, in Haraszti's formulation, "some mixture of American and European liberalism."

European to some extent. Haraszti says he agrees with Milan Kundera that if anything good came out of the former Central Europe, it was because of this region's aspiration to be more European than Europe. But in some ways, he says, Hungary right now is closer to America—an earlier, pioneering America. Communism had tried to crush all traditions, after all, with the incidentally beneficial side effect of crushing feudalism as well. To some extent, by confiscating wealth it succeeded in making Hungary into a classless society. And so now, Haraszti says, "we are ready to jump into self-creation—we are arriving in a quasi–New World."

A New World with the Old World's burdens, it's true—but also with its experience. Once again, Haraszti's contemporaries are in an interesting situation; and as I think of the many lively, intelligent people I've talked to—people who combine their generation's particular openness with some hard-earned historical lessons—it seems to me not impossible that they could bring something original, some mix of consciousness and just possibly conscience, to the ever trite and tired world of official politics.

Zsolt Németh is something else—and something newer still. One could write an entertaining guide—though it would have to be updated more frequently than the Michelin—to the parties, associations, forums, councils, and assorted other political bodies proliferating in lush and unchecked profusion in the Wild East of Eastern Europe. In this guide, the Fidesz Party, (an acronym that stands for "Young Democrats Union" but that plays on suggestions of "faith" or "loyalty") to which Zsolt Németh belongs, would be listed as a characteristic feature of the Hungarian landscape, a specific and unique outgrowth of the local scene. Fidesz is an organization predicated on youth, and its upper age limit is thirty-five. Of course, three years into its existence, some of its elder members are beginning to find this low ceiling somewhat discomfiting and are thinking of raising it before their moment in the sun runs out.

Despite the risible aspects of its generational premise, Fidesz is a perfectly serious party taken perfectly seriously by many people, including certain circles of the intelligentsia. It's one of the standard wistful observations in Eastern Europe these days that the only solution to the mess of the past is to put the very young in charge, and this is undoubtedly part of the attraction of Fidesz. It comes untainted and untarred. Don't trust anyone over—well, thirty-five—has an entirely new meaning here. The trio of adjectives invariably used to describe the young party is "energetic, professional, pragmatic"—the very values that many people wish for the new era.

It must be admitted that Zsolt Németh seems the embodiment of all these adjectives. His broad, seemingly stolid face can flash with a lively, intelligent smile. He sits back in a pose of assured relaxation belonging to somebody accustomed to power and control, puffs on a light cigarillo, and talks with a mature, measured self-confidence confounding for someone who's all of twenty-seven years old. Of course, this is twenty-seven Eastern European years; but still, I feel a bit out of my depth here. Just who, what, is this newest political species?

The very last chapter in the Marxist saga, for one thing, the characters who entered the plot when it was already winding down to its dénouement, and who, therefore, could get a jumpstart on something truly new. Zsolt Németh graduated in economics from the quaintly named Karl Marx University. But his real education took place in a special college, which had nothing to do with Marxism, organized by the students themselves, with the grudging permission of the authorities. In the eighties, there were several such colleges in Hungary, where students set their own curriculum and brought in teachers of their choice. Németh describes these structures as neither underground nor official; they were barely tolerated, but they weren't threatened, either. This was the Hungarian difference—and it's now the Hungarian leg up and advantage.

The Fidesz people were among the budding young elite of these colleges, and in the summers, they went to special camps on Lake Balaton, where they held marathon discussions and seminars on de Tocqueville and John Stuart Mill and Locke, on contemporary Americans like Robert Nozick and John Rawls, on the meaning of liberalism and democracy. "All our discussions centered around the philosophical categories of truth, justice, and freedom," Németh says—those old categories, which were given new life by the Eastern European circumstances. But the future politicians combined these high-minded concerns with a self-confidence that usually belongs to the young in the West. Part of their self-assurance, and a large portion of their intellectual formation, came from their personal contacts with the West. In the waning days of goulash Communism, many of them spent some time studying at Oxford and Cambridge. They had Xerox machines—whose role in the Eastern European upheavals has yet to be fully appreciated—and on these they copied entire books. They knew they weren't alone.

Perhaps the most revealing moment in my conversation with Németh comes when I ask him whether the future Fideszians— still students at the time—considered the older dissidents their mentors. The earlier rebels—people like Vásárhelyi or Haraszti, or others who are now running the two main Hungarian parties—were often invited to the special colleges and the Lake Balaton chautauquas. "What do you mean?" he asks in genuine surprise. "We were *their* mentors. We had the legal framework. We could play the role of a mediator between them—by the mid-eighties, they had begun to quarrel already."

Whether this is retrospective hubris or the voice of a new politician speaking, it certainly betokens the kind of seriousness with which these young people took themselves, and perhaps also the sense of entitlement in which they grew up—and which was probably impossible even among the most confident of

Haraszti's generation. They knew that to a large extent they could buck the system with impunity; they must have intuited that, no matter how rebellious they were, they would eventually come into their own.

And they didn't have certain burdens of the past. Were there any traces of Marxism in their thinking? I ask. "We were fed up with it, honestly," he says. Perhaps the only residue of its influence was that Németh's intellectual contemporaries were, as he puts it, "strongly, emotionally anti-Marxist. We couldn't think of it as just another set of nineteenth-century ideas." But in effect, the long chapter of intellectual infatuation, conflict, and disenchantment with Marxism was utterly over by the time they came round—finished in plain indifference.

The Fideszians describe themselves, unapologetically and cleverly, as "liberals without adjectives," and they stand for all kinds of good, right-minded things—helping disadvantaged children and young people among them. But the values that really permeate Németh's rhetoric are those of a professional politician. He talks a lot about strategy and being "effective," and "the political process," as if that were itself a concrete entity, or an idol to which one must bow. He talks about opinion surveys and gaining local support. Fidesz has conducted some of the smartest campaigns in Hungary, complete with inventive posters and media consultants.

The exercise of power has broken up some of the old camaraderie among his Fidesz friends. Sometimes that's painful, but "we understand it as part of the political process" he says—the way neither Vásárhelyi nor Haraszti probably ever would. Of course, the older men knew of friendships broken over politics, but such ruptures were a matter of tragedy, and sometimes of life and death, because politics still, in their time, held the elements of both the demonic and the sacred.

But politics now is being smartly demystified. In Németh's generation, it is becoming, above all, pragmatic, requiring, in lieu of sacralized ideas, a degree of earnestness about the "process," and about yourself—your very own cult of personality. Certainly

I can't find in Németh any of that self-deprecation or self-irony that I've come almost to expect from Eastern Europeans, even if they're politicians. He comports himself with intelligence and some charm, but also with all the seriousness befitting a full-fledged representative of a normal country in the normal, serious, and very pragmatic world.

It may be that just as tonality recurs in music and realism in painting, so the idea of liberalism recurs in politics—though each time in a different vein. Eastern European liberalism seems not so much born again as refined in the crucible of successive skepticisms. It has seen the dangers of fanaticism, dogmatism, and cynicism; the dangers of too much belief and none at all. It's not so much a credo as a balancing act, an attempt to combine the energy of hope with the modesty of reasonable expectations.

About an hour out of Budapest, as you travel in a southwesterly direction, all of Hungary seems to become vacation land. Looking out the train window, I suspect I'm in Italy, so crowded is the landscape with the signs and accouterments of summery pleasure: terraces with red umbrellas, outdoor cafés, swimming pools, and glistening gardens. Hardly an underdeveloped area. This is the approach to Lake Balaton, Hungary's answer to the Hamptons. The Balaton is advertised as the largest lake in Europe, and since Hungary is one of the continent's smaller countries, this "inland sea," with its beaches and resort towns covers a goodly part of Hungary's surface. Like the Hamptons, it has its towns where artists congregate, its snobberies and mystiques.

In the resort town where I've disembarked, the main drag is lined with the usual tacky chachka stores and places where they wrap delicate *palacsinta* pancakes around four kinds of sweet fillings to a most delectable result. Everybody walks around in a very brief bathing suit, with no coyness or self-consciousness; some different sense of the body seems to prevail here, less insistently eroticized, and—perhaps precisely for that reason—more erotically easygoing. The town is filled with Austrians, still profiting from the advantage of their Western currency, and with Hungarians, who take their vacations seriously and do them with zest. Fruit stands with lush peaches and plums are everywhere; houses crowded close together; a cluster of small, uniform four-square cottages—the vacation settlement for the workers of some institute, one of the perks of the passing system.

And the lake—the lake is worthy of many myths. Its surface is an unruffled, opalescent silvery celadon that seems to have absorbed a permanent, delicate fog into its surface; the archipelagos of reeds extending far into the water reinforce the dreaminess of the effect. Even the plant life nearby grows wispy and romantic; some of it, like a white wool-soft flower beautifully named "orphan's hair," seems to have emerged from the muted colors of the lake.

The house where I stay with friends is shared by several families, and during the day the garden is occupied by people engaged in their different activities: a grandmother knitting, a father playing ball with his son, people eating picnic lunches, and my three friends working on their various manuscripts in the sun. Somehow, no one disturbs anyone else, and the mornings pass in companionable quietness. In "civilized" circles, the culture of coexistence seems highly developed here, and people seem to have learned the trick of being neither unduly reserved nor getting in each other's way: the better lessons of living in close proximity.

Iván Berend, my host, has been close to the centers of Hungarian power, and was one of the people who engineered Hungary's economic reform; these days, he thinks quite a bit about why the reform failed. We talk about this a little in the sunny garden, and he tells me that, in a sense, the failure was built into the very idea of reform. The reformers thought they could tinker with the system, introduce a bit of free enterprise here, a dash of decentralization there. But systems, Berend says, are very consistent; that's, after all, why they are systems. A system centralized to the Sovietoid degree is simply incompatible with the free market, because the restrictions it imposes on initiative and enterprise are too stiff.

Supper is in a crowded restaurant overlooking a meadow, and it includes another kind of *palacsinta,* suffused in dark, liquid chocolate. Why aren't there more overweight Hungarians? Perhaps a thousand years of the national cuisine has produced special antibodies to catalyze chocolate and whipped cream with extra efficiency.

Later, Berend talks ruefully—if there's any resentment, it's been thoroughly reined in through self-control or a civilized sense of how the game is played—about the difficulties for people with his kind of history in the new climate. In the Hungarian situation, the borders between the internal party reformists and the outside dissidents were hardly very sharp, and certainly could be crossed socially and—almost—ideologically. It's just that it was the dissidents who were on the margins before; now the former reformists are. Berend's resolution of the dilemma is to teach in the West, but I imagine that there must be a measure of loss in a decision to leave behind what was, after all, a life-long work—even though it was a work that ultimately didn't succeed.

The next morning, we take a long swim out in the lake. A group of swans, looking like an *haute-bourgeois* family on a Sunday outing, makes its stately progress near us. The water is that enchanting color. A wonderful wistfulness mingles with the vigor of the swim. A moment in which ambiguities, and almost wrongs and almost rights, dissolve evanescently into the sense of just right, just as it should be.

Poles talk about "men of money"; Hungarians talk about yuppies. Perhaps this is because the Hungarians are more *au courant* about America, or because for some reason—my analytic powers come to a halt here—the Hungarian nouveaux riches tend to be younger than the Polish ones. But it's also a matter of attitude; the serious "man of money" suggests an unironic respect for such solid and accomplished personages. Hungarians, further ahead in this, as in other matters, introduce a tinge of scorn to dilute whatever respect or envy they may feel for those

who are succeeding on the free-market fast track. Perhaps a
tinge of chagrin as well: the business entrepreneurs are the ones
who are really running the country, everyone says, and they have
no social consciousness; they've dropped out of the moral polity.

Eva Jeles, whom I meet through a friend, isn't exactly a
yuppie, but then maybe nobody is when you see them up close.
She is, however, by any standards, a hugely successful entrepreneur. The apartment in which she lives with her husband and
daughter is one of the grandest I've seen anywhere, upper Park
Avenue not excepted. Its prewar proportions reflect the Budapest penchant for immensity, the parquet floors gleam, the ceilings suggest empyrean heights. The owners have attractiveness to
match. Eva is a large-boned woman in her mid-thirties, with a
pretty, creamy-skinned face and a mass of chestnut-colored curly
hair. She's dressed just the way a hip American woman of her
generation might be, with a tongue-in-cheek eclecticism, complete with funny pink shoes and saucy socks whose design playfully doesn't match her skirt's. Her husband, András Török,
looks handsomely *echt* Hungarian, with very black, straight hair,
very black eyes, and high cheekbones—a cross between a Tatar
horseman and a twenties matinee idol, neither of which he remotely wishes to suggest. On the jacket of his very good *Critical
Guide to Budapest* he's described as "a thinking dandy with a
family"; he's one of the editors of a new literary journal called
2000. He translates for us, because, though Eva understands English quite well, she prefers to speak in Hungarian.

The apartment is still sparsely furnished, because they just
moved into it a few weeks ago. It's clear that it's Eva's money
that brought them here, and Eva's money was made with more
than Horatio Alger speed. One of the peculiar conditions of
postwar Eastern Europe has been the confiscation of inherited
wealth, which meant that everybody was starting virtually even,
and wealth, at this early point of raw capitalism, is still perceived
as a bonus over the natural condition, which is shared impover-
ishment.

Eva Jeles certainly started from nowhere, from scratch. She

grew up on a farm in the eastern part of Hungary, and had visited in Budapest only once before she came there to the university. She studied economics, in which she wasn't at all interested, attended underground seminars, and lived from hand to mouth in youth hostels and rented rooms in family apartments. After finishing at the university in 1982, she was offered a research position at the Institute for the Economy, which came with high prestige and a very low salary. She always assumed she would be an intellectual of some sort, a scholar, because that's what a smart person of her generation assumed. But she didn't feel happy at the institute. "There I was, revising and revising the same paper. I was twenty-five, I had no flat, no roots in Budapest, no money. And I was feeling more and more that I didn't have this cannibalistic ambition to do research."

When she talks, the look of unapologetic seriousness and concentration transforms Eva's face into something more interesting than just prettiness. And when she talks about business, she's utterly serious. She discovered her calling for entrepreneurship the way some people discover a calling for art. In 1985, she got a job that quintupled her institute salary. Fotex, the photo minilab for which she was hired, was revolutionary both for its activity and because it was one of the first joint ventures in Hungary, though that simply meant that somebody's American friend had invested a bit of money in it. Technically, under the Kádár rules it was easier to begin a joint venture than just a regular private firm; socialism or not, Western currency was always held in high regard here. Fotex, having a virtual monopoly on quick photo development, grew like a hurricane, and Eva rose quickly to a high position within it.

Still, when it was proposed to her that she join an upstart group that had the notion of beginning a wholesale video company, she jumped at the chance. "I joined an idea," she says, and it's that—having a business vision and then creating a reality to execute it—that she finds so compelling. What fascinates her is not so much making money as "venturing"—a word her husband translates after a careful pause. She has the classic entrepreneurial temperament, which thrives on start-ups, risk, and strategy. She likes figuring out how to make something work, and then she likes to move on to something else.

The idea, or the company, came to be called VICO, and it was daring and simple: buy video films from the United States, dub them into Hungarian, and then sell them to people with rental video shops. By that time, most Hungarians had TVs, and sufficient numbers of them could buy VCRs—but the trick was to induce people to open the shops. Eva masterminded the whole operation. "My task was to persuade people who had some money and some dreams of starting a business—people who had been housewives, or waiters, or shop assistants—to take their money from under the pillow and put it in this."

Within two years, there were eight hundred video rental stores in Hungary. Eva taught the new owners how to do it. She understood what their fears and uncertainties were—she was no stranger to their circumstances. She learned something about running such businesses from information on comparable Western European enterprises, but the conditions in Hungary were so different that mostly she had to trust her own instincts. She says she's good at that; good at imagining where the problems might lie, and good at putting herself in somebody else's shoes.

The company became an enormous success, which was all well and good, except that meant that it was time to move on. "Video didn't need revolutionary ideas anymore," she says. So, on New Year's Eve 1990, she sealed her decision to start her very own company. This time, she would be the top boss.

I've visited her office, which is white and gleaming and decorated with beautiful botanical posters—and which, in a gray, crumbling building in an old, rundown section of Budapest, manages to convey a look of hip California stylishness. Her new business has to do with book distribution, which, to a less strategizing eye, might look highly unpromising. The state book-distribution giants are disintegrating and book publishing itself is shattered. But for a classical entrepreneur like her, that's just what makes it appealing. Book distribution, she says, is in the same "phase of development" as video was when VICO started, which means that she's the first to leap in. She talks with an intense absorption—I've seen writers talk about their fictional characters with this kind of inward gaze—about the marketing studies she's started, and about what sort of success she expects for her fledgling creation.

I keep wondering, while she sketches plans that will undoubtedly translate into millions of *forints,* where this woman, who grew up in the Hungarian countryside in the time of socialism, found the nerve, not to speak of the inventiveness, to think of herself as a business adventuress. But I suppose that's the wrong question. The gamut of human temperament may run everywhere the same; but temperament needs certain conditions to encourage it.

Still, I ask her whether her own career is a surprise to her. "The biggest surprise," she answers after mulling it over for a while, "is that it works." That what works? I ask. "That business works," she says. "That things work at all."

Ah, yes. That must be one of the Eurekas people are shouting all over Eastern Europe, at least those who have stumbled upon this unlikely principle. It's a discovery antithetical to the assumption—or rather, knowledge—that prevailed until now, that nothing works, least of all plans in a person's head. Undoing this assumption, discovering that there might be mechanisms for transforming purely personal aspiration into action, must require a shift of mind as fundamental and difficult as anything Eastern Europeans are undergoing right now. Indeed, the division between those who believe that initiative, plans, enterprises, gleams in one's eye have a chance of working and those who don't is probably more basic right now than divisions between conservative democrats and democratic conservatives. Where will the influence of the entrepreneurs lead? I can't make it out; in the double-ledger historical accounting, the costs and benefits of enlightened self-interest, as opposed to enforced enlightenment, seem to me impossible to calculate. Eva and András are careful to tell me that they don't behave like standard nouveaux riche: they didn't buy their apartment in the more fashionable hills of

Buda, and their interests and circles extend well beyond the moneyed spheres. I can't make it out. But I must confess that, though entrepreneurial business is not the activity for which I have most empathy, I find the spectacle of someone like Eva, making something out of nothing by sheer power of intention and intelligence, as interesting as watching a very good athlete or a precocious violinist giving a performance through which one can intuit unusual human energy and will and skill.

Later, I run into András, Eva's husband, in his natural habitat, the New York Café. Even more than Cracow or Prague, Budapest used to be a city of cafés, many of which were known for their particular social sets and dominant personalities—a sort of cross between semipublic salons for artistic eminences and refuges for those down on their luck or royalties. New York Café was a highly literary place, where writers were given paper and ink, newspapers, and stretchable credit. Some received their mail here. After the war, the café came in for puritan disapproval as a symbol of bourgeois decadence, and was turned into a sports shop. The word "decadent" doesn't begin to describe the restored interior, which hovers somewhere between fabulous and monstrous, with three endlessly long floors, a balconied gallery, and an overkill of crystal and glitter and gilded decor that puts Fontainebleau to shame. András describes the café lovingly in his Budapest guide, and, in a revival of a prewar tradition, the editors of his magazine meet here once a week to discuss house matters and receive visitors. I happen to come in one afternoon when the meeting is just disbanding, and we have coffee in the main gallery—thus disconcerting a waiter, who approaches András with apologies, explaining that he has just missed a phone call because he couldn't be found in his regular place. Old rituals, old politesse: they seem no less charming or convenient to me for being willfully revived.

Anna and Gábor are a literary couple in their sixties who, in my mind, correspond to some archetype of the Central European I cherish and occasionally even find. That they are Jewish doesn't modify the matter—after all, many of the archetypal Central Europeans were. Between them, they've lived through every up and down of their lifetime's history and they've adapted with a sort of mobility that strikes me as coming out of that history's perennial turbulence. They're erudite, multilingual, vivaciously youthful. They've thought about everything and they're frank about everything, with that civilized frankness of Eastern Europeans, who seem to know fewer taboos than we do, except perhaps for their relations with the Communist Party, though Anna and Gábor seem to be frank even about that.

I visit them this time, as I did a year ago. Their apartment is hardly posh, but it's comfortable and pleasant and has a wonderful collection of Hungarian paintings, including lovely watercolors of a village where Gábor grew up and where his father was the glamorous Jewish aristocrat. The study is filled with books they've both written, mostly about theater and literature and, on Anna's part of the shelf, about women. Anna has worked for many years as an editor at a women's magazine, Gábor at a literary journal.

Gábor looks like a robust Kafka clone, with large, prominent brown eyes and equally prominent ears. He's so quick and casual in his responses that I sometimes have the impression he's missed something I've said. But he misses nothing—on the contrary, he takes everything in instantly and makes his judgments and conclusions before I have noticed. The conversation in their house moves with ease from topic to topic, and never dries up. While Gábor makes his darting leaps, Anna moves forward vigorously with great good sense. She doesn't insist on any marked style of personality and chooses a rather ordinary, amiably respectable look; but the forceful edge of her intelligence sharpens everything it touches.

This time, however, I'm surprised to find them wary and maybe even a little worried. At the beginning, Gábor and Anna were great enthusiasts of the changes, and they're surprised too, they tell me, by how difficult last year has been for them. They dislike the conservative, Christian nationalist tenor of the government; they are troubled by the abandonment of cultural values; they find it difficult to accept the exigencies of a more commercial culture. Gábor is unsettled by the decline of his literary magazine, which may go out of business, and by the requirements of running his new venture—a Hungarian edition of a Paris-based magazine, *Lettres Internationales*—on a commercial basis.

Anna is the first woman I've talked to in Hungary to mention the "woman problem," and to be distressed by a certain retrogression on this front as well. She doesn't consider herself a feminist, exactly, and she knows that the concept of feminism was corrupted by the former regime, by the "shop-window women" of Communism, who were exhibited much like Potemkin villages to the unwary foreigners. Nevertheless, she's troubled by a reversion to the *Kinder, Küche, Kirche* ethos among younger women.

How odd, I reflect, to find these energetic and congenial views in an older woman, when the younger ones are rendering them unfashionable. But then, Gábor and Anna were formed by a sort of cosmopolitan modernist prewar liberalism that underwent such strange vicissitudes in Eastern Europe after the war. They're the kinds of intellectuals for whom Communism initially seemed like a progressivism with teeth, and whose romance with it never turned to fanaticism. The portraits of Gábor's mother and father hang in the living room, their beautiful faces painted in an elegant early modernist style. Gábor remembers an idyllic childhood in his village in northern Hungary, in which the only automated vehicle was his toy car, and where weekends were often spent at friends' houses, in the company of artists and writers. Anna's memories reach back to her mother's stories of her own father, a printer who read Heine's poetry to his daughters while they were doing embroidery. Her paternal grandfather, like many Hungarian Jews, served in the Austro-Hungarian army in the First World War, and—in the noble Eastern European lineage—spent six years in Siberia after being taken prisoner of war.

Neither Gábor nor Anna was much aware of their Jewishness—not until the war, that is. Hungary had entered the war on the German side; and already before that the regime of Admiral Horthy had started reversing decades of Jewish assimilation. But "the great caesura," as she puts it, came in 1944, when Hitler ordered the occupation of Hungary, and installed a pro-German government, with Horthy as regent. Until then, there had been no Germans in Budapest, and Anna's family and their circle felt immune to bad luck.

In 1944, the quarantining and the deportations of the Jews began. Anna's father was sent to a labor camp. Anna, with her mother, had to move to a Jewish quarter. Then came the familiar sequence: the closing of the school, the yellow star, the crowded quarters. But they still thought it would soon be over. One of Anna's aunts, who had been deported to the countryside, wrote a postcard with a single sentence: "We're being taken to Auschwitz." Nobody knew what it meant.

In October 1944, Horthy made a speech on the radio asking for a special peace with the allies. Anna's father briefly came back from the labor camp; once again, the family thought they had gotten over the worst. But it was exactly then—as Horthy pulled back from the Axis alliance completely—that the actions against the Jews intensified. Anna's mother was taken away; a resourceful cousin came to Anna's aid, and together they hid for a while in a friendly artists' studio, in an "Anne Frank situation." The Germans came to the building once and didn't get past the courtyard; the second time they did.

That night, Anna was taken to the shore of the Danube. ("Have you been to the Lukacs pool?" she asks. "It's near there." I have. It's one of Budapest's lovelier bath complexes, with tiers of terraces and open-air pools of different temperatures.) The first four people in the groups rounded up that night were shot and thrown into the Danube. Anna and her cousin were in the next cluster of four; they were asked to step forward; this, they knew, was the end.

But once again they were mistaken. The Hungarians who were performing this job said that it was not in their interest to kill innocent women and children. They'd go away for five minutes, they said; and they gave each of the four some money.

Anna and her cousin ran for the nearest hiding space, which turned out to be the pool toilets. Standing there through the night, Anna thought, "Is it possible that I'll live through this, and that sometime in my life I'll once again be afraid of a mathematics test?" And indeed, she did; she lived through hunger and more hiding and the siege of Budapest; and she convinced herself afterward that, even after such experiences, the concerns of normal life take over and one can still be nervous about school exams.

Anna was reunited with her father after it was all over; and shortly afterward, they found out that her mother didn't survive. And then she went on to the next chapters, as impossible to envision in advance as the previous ones had been.

We know so much less about Jews who stayed in Eastern Europe after the war than about those who left. They were usually the more assimilated ones, and anyway under Communism there were supposed to be no ethnic distinctions. That was part of Communism's promise and appeal to many Jews who joined the party—and there's no denying that in the Hungarian party, as in the Polish one, there were large numbers of prominent Jewish figures. Anna joined in 1947, partly for idealistic, partly for practical reasons; a woman from the party hinted to her that they could help her go to the university, which otherwise she could ill afford.

But the formative experience of the war also made her think that the world could use some reforming. "I was enthusiastic until the world changed," Anna says in her even manner. "And the world changed rather quickly." First of all, Anna herself became suspect soon because she was from a "bourgeois" background, because she knew English, because she once wrote the word "curriculum," which proved she was a snob.

Then she met Gábor, which caused even greater complications, because at that time Gábor's stepfather was in prison.

"Our illusions were shattered in 1953," Anna says, for in the history of all ex-Communists there are these dates that mark the transformation of consciousness as clearly as if a snap of the fingers announced the end of a hypnosis. For Anna and Gábor, the shock followed not from Stalin's death but from a visit Gábor's mother was finally allowed to pay her imprisoned husband. What she learned was that her husband had been imprisoned for nothing. Until then, like many relatives of such prisoners, she thought that maybe there had been something, a minor transgression, to explain what happened. It's a natural impulse to look for some rationality in our world, and too terrifying to suppose that it had turned into pure, dark unreason. But there was nothing.

After that discovery—and similar ones were being made by many others—Anna joined a circle of internal, oppositional reformers, and became associated with a literary magazine that prepared the thinking for the 1956 revolution. She remembers this period fondly—the literary friendships and scandals, the liveliness of conversation, and particularly the sense of common aim. The magazine's editors were fired regularly for disobeying central policies, only to be supplanted by others, no more obedient and no less heretical. At one point, the former police chief was appointed editor-in-chief—and, to his superiors' chagrin, continued the reformist line. Then came the two extraordinary weeks of the 1956 revolution and its unceremonious crushing. It was the peculiar character of the uprising in its first days that while intense, violent fighting went on in some parts of the city other sections remained untouched and quiet. At first, Anna felt a sort of holiday mood; then events turned tragic.

When it was all over, the conclusions, to Anna, were inescapable. She left the party. She was in danger of not getting a job as a consequence, but she didn't feel much choice about her decision. "I knew too much," she simply says. For her, there was never a question of rejoining; the question, rather, was on the order of whether she would ever use the word "counterrevolution"—the official double-speak for the 1956 revolution—in her writing and thereby indicate her compliance with the distortion of the truth. "And this I never did," she says. "I never used this word."

Leaving the ideological house of Communism was harder. Anna remembers a phrase that a friend used shortly after 1956. "You know, when I was a Communist . . ." was what he said, and Anna was very startled. "But I'm still a Communist," she thought. "It's the party that isn't."

When I ask her what caused her ultimate disillusionment, she compares it, without any sense of melodramatic incongruity, to the death of her mother. "I lost her the day she was taken away. But I didn't know it then; I kept waiting; maybe there would be news, maybe we would find her. The loss of political faith also didn't happen in a day."

For Anna, as for so many Communists, it took the double shock of the 1956 uprising and the invasion of Czechoslovakia of 1968 to come to full consciousness of what she half knew, as if to give reverse credence to Freud's idea that it takes a repetition of a trauma in order for it to register on the unconscious.

Gábor stayed in the Party until the end, perhaps out of some sense that the fates governing their lives were not very rational anyway, or perhaps out of a sort of temperamental insouciance that made him reluctant to reckon with the grimmest facts head on. He says he's a person who never wanted to leave his childhood, and he's so full of zestful playfulness that he talks even about the more dangerous moments of the war as a kind of high-flying, absurdist adventure. He joined the party before the war, and continued with it even as people began to be arrested around him, even as his own stepfather was taken away. "I didn't understand a word from the whole thing," he says. "I knew that those were people not in line with the official point of view. Then I knew that the whole thing works like the Inquisition—that they decided who was guilty and then set out to prove it. But the trouble was that I accepted this. It was a sort of self-defense. There was always some sort of schizophrenia in this whole Communism."

The one time Gábor found himself in an irreconcilable conflict with the party was when he was asked to take an eight-to-five job. For a self-respecting Central European intellectual, this was an indignity that could not be brooked, and Gábor flatly said no. Anyway, his motives for staying in the party were becoming increasingly pragmatic, though in the later stages he says he found membership in it "amusing." The discussions were often lively, and one could learn and do some things from within that one could not accomplish from without. "Not bring down the walls, you understand—but perhaps push at them."

But basically both he and Anna went on to become the kinds of generalist literateurs who could still thrive in Eastern Europe after the war, and whose conditions, for highly paradoxical reasons, put them rather closer to intellectuals in interwar Paris, say, than to the intelligentsia in postwar New York. They had plenty of time, minimal worries about money, and an intense sense of the importance, the mission, of culture. Gábor became a theater critic with a particular interest in the avant-garde, worked on a literary magazine, and wrote many books on the theater. Anna did eventually find a job at a women's magazine, which gave her a chance to travel and to write her books as well. Her one regret is that she remained, somehow, marginal as a literary figure. But when I ask her—since I know that she's alert to such matters—whether she thinks her career was partly hampered because she was a woman, she says no, not really. "There were so many other discriminations," she says. "At the end of the war, we used to joke that, if the Germans conquered us, we'd be Jews; if the English, we'd be Hungarians; if Russians, we were bourgeois. You didn't need to be a woman to be discriminated against."

It's Gábor who says that the current changes have been as difficult for them as anything they've been through. And while that may seem strange after such drama-filled lives, these changes, too, involve a profound shift in the deep structure of their world. The level of uncertainty, Gábor says, is greater now than for decades before; during the Kádár era, you knew the rules of the game, and you knew that the wall was there. You could push against it, but the wall stayed in place. And while the metaphorical disappearance of the wall may seem a benign form of change, it must create its own sense of chaos and disorientation. How do you position yourself without it? What do you push against?

Anna is particularly disconcerted by the abandonment of cultural values—now, of all times, when culture could at last be truly free! After staking much of her life on avoiding self-falsification, she's being asked to adjust to entirely new compromises. She bridles angrily when she talks about how her magazine is trying to accommodate to "public" taste. "I will not write about actresses and their dogs. I will not write promotions of books instead of critiques. This I will not do." Once, in the bad old days, she was asked to take out a chapter on György Konrad from her book of interviews with Hungarian writers. She refused; there were some discussions, she took out a few sentences, but the chapter stood. Now, she says with some incredulity, her regular publisher cannot bring out her new book because it isn't commercial enough.

"To tell you the truth," she says, "we're still in the opposition. We're surprised by how hard it has been for us." Throughout the vicissitudes of their lives, they've tried to cleave to the values of enlightened, modernist culture—and this is a sensibility that is once again, and not only in Eastern Europe, endangered.

"We're too old for this," Gábor says, and then ruefully adds, "The next thing to think about is death, and that's not very pleasant." And though they hardly seem old to me, that, too, may be the effect of the changes: they're a kind of marker indicating the passage of time, and of personal eras, calling for the summarizing of lives and for gauging of strength to begin anew—like all ruptures and beginnings, a kind of memento mori.

When I was here last year, I briefly visited Köröm, a small village in the northeast of Hungary, which quickly won my heart, and I decide to visit it again this time. I drive there with Tomàs, a young literature instructor and translator, and his mother,

Ilona, who is an archeologist at the National Museum. The village is near Miszkolc, a horrid-looking industrial town that boasts Hungary's highest "skyscraper" (about sixteen stories, to the naked eye), but as we near Köröm, we pass through some lovely, gently uncombed landscape, dotted with small lakes and ponds. Then we cross the lazy, shaded river Szajo by means of a ferry, big enough for one car, and ingeniously powered by navigating against the current. Near a big weeping willow overhanging the river, cows water themselves calmly. Tomàs has been coming here since his childhood, and for Ilona it's a second home. I can see that there is an evocative appeal for them—as there is for me—in the pastoral, loose-haired mildness of this scene.

Our accommodations in Köröm are in a Baroque parish house, presided over by a Catholic priest whom everyone simply calls Tony. As we arrive, we find Tony in the act of varnishing a delicate Louis XVI table he found in a nearby farmhouse, and which was used for butchering pigs; the knife marks are still visible. Among other things, Tony is an esthete and a dandy, and the venerable, sturdily constructed building in which he lives is full of clutter and art and antique pieces of furniture he had discovered.

Tony is also a man of seemingly endless energy, and in this remote village, he has created a veritable fiefdom of good works. He ships vast amounts of books and clothing to the beleaguered Hungarians in Transylvania; he runs an educational vacation camp for retarded children and teaches in the local school; last summer, there was a phalanx of Dutch adolescents here helping him with his projects.

Köröm itself is a perfectly picturesque village of small cottages and sparkling air and dew-covered flowers. The houses are brightly painted, in contrast to the mostly earth colors of Poland and Czechoslovakia—this *is* further south—and most of them have side porches lined with square white columns. Tony has a theory—or rather, as far as he's concerned, data—about these columns, which he avers are derived from no less a source than the Acropolis, via Renaissance and Baroque architecture, which the villagers, on their modest scale, tried to imitate. Tony has a theory for just about every subject under the sun.

Of course, there's a story behind Tony's being here at all, a historical story. But as we sit down to dinner, at the big table in an enormous, old-fashioned kitchen, he discourses with great vivacity on matters close at hand. He's a tall, vigorous man with white hair, a ruddy complexion, and direct, youthful blue eyes. He says that when he travels, he's often mistaken for a "Yankee," perhaps because of a certain innocence or frankness of expression. The dinner was cooked by his housekeeper, Ilonka, a thickset, clumsily moving woman with the flummoxed air of a very shy, plain person. There's nothing clumsy or retiring about her cooking, though, which verges on artistic greatness. This evening, she has made an interestingly bitter salad composed of twelve green ingredients, including several local grasses, which Tony encourages her to use; he's a believer in using local resources. This is followed by a bouillon soup with goose liver that is the most delicately flavored I've ever tasted; a dish of pasta squares with cabbage, in which Ilonka has managed to endow these unpromising ingredients with a true subtlety; and a dessert resembling sponge cake rolled around an apricot filling, with a texture so light and airy that it's hard to know how it's held together. I rave quite sincerely about each dish, causing Ilonka to look down defensively behind her thick glasses, as if she suspected that I'm mocking her. Tony, however, picks up the subject of food happily, and gives a quick history of the fall and the impending rise of gastronomic culture as related to Communism and whatever comes after, and also an encomium to Tokay wine, whose pleasures are eternal.

Then he goes on to explain that the local flora and fauna have a particular strength and robustness because of the extremely changeable weather in the Carpathian basin, to which living things have to keep adapting. This elides into a lecture on the Hungarian character, which, according to Tony, also has a special vigor formed through a balance of resistance and adaptation. The Magyar tribes, he says, originated deep within Asia, and differentiated themselves from the surrounding Mongolian tribes some three thousand years ago. For about two thousand years—so he continues the tale—they proceeded to wend their way westward, before settling down in their present territory. The strength of this people—all the time according to Tony—lay in its ability to incorporate certain qualities and customs from the surrounding cultures, while resisting complete assimilation and swamping of identity. And so the Magyars developed a delicate balance between Asian and European qualities, and a fluidity that enables them to adapt to various influences without losing their core character. "The French, you see, are stuck on their *gloire*," he says. "They're burdened by their *gloire*. With the Hungarians, there are fewer absolutes."

I fall asleep immediately after our long dinner in a big room with arched, cross-vectored ceiling and with windows set in deep niches within the thick walls. The next day, I walk around the village, whose life reveals itself as simply as an oyster shell being opened.

Köröm is divided, with great geographical explicitness, into two parts—Hungarian and Gypsy. We walk through the Gypsy part, with Ilonka distributing clothing to all comers. A gaggle of kids, with beautiful, large-eyed faces, follows us everywhere, instantly mimicking our movements and English words they hear. The Gypsy Köröm has its own, quite evident, hierarchy. In the "good" part, the houses are stuccoed and some of them are of decent size, if bare of any external adornment; the poor part is a shantytown of shacks, some of them not much more than large cartons stuck together with mud and straw and other chaotic-looking items. In the summer, with naked babies and people lounging about, and straggling dogs, this has a somewhat carnavelesque look, but in the winter it must be terrible to live here. I'm told that each season somebody freezes to death, though to tell the truth, it's often someone who is drunk and falls asleep on the way home.

Harsh opinions about Gypsies are voiced quite openly in

Hungary, but to Tony their very presence in large numbers is evidence of Hungarian flexibility. "With the Hungarians," he says, "borders are less hard. That's why the Gypsies are here and not in Western Europe. By a certain time, all land in Western Europe was divided into private property. Here, in each village, there are some common lands that don't belong to anybody. And in every village, there's a dirt road through the middle, which made it easy for them to travel in their wagons. Hungary is the only country left where you can travel hundreds of miles on dirt roads."

For centuries, the Gypsies were the other Other in Europe. Like the Jews, they have been the object of fear and scorn, but otherwise, they are the Jews' counterpart and antithesis. While the Jews have survived by books and the Book, the Gypsies have persisted without a written culture or an elaborated system of belief. Often, they take on the religion of the neighborhood, and in Köröm they come to Tony's church, though they introduce traces of their customs into the ritual. They leave such items as cigarettes and bottles of vodka, and once a violin, on the coffins of the dead, to ease their passage to the next world, and they often feel haunted by the ghosts of those who are in the midst of that passage. Altogether, the Gypsies seem to me a strange and unique experiment in living a life outside laws or the Law—a fluid, nomadic, temporal existence in which there's little evidence of social rules or desire to be anything beyond what they are. What's amazing is how tenacious this way of being has proved, how unassimilable the Gypsies have been—as if living without systems is as strong a proposition about human existence as living firmly within them.

All this has been changing gradually, and might be about to change even more, and I am torn between a morally correct approval of progress and a tinge of esthetic regret. Another bit of colorful difference will be lost; but needless to say, I know that the world is not a Cinerama arranged to produce interesting pictures for my benefit. Anyway, the hazards of the Gypsies' way of life are immediately apparent as I walk around the village. I pause to talk to a young family next to a truly woebegone dwelling, in a yard strewn with bits of wire, car tires, weeds. The father is soaking his feet in a bowl of muddy water. He tells us proudly that he watches news programs on television and knows the names of various Hungarian parties. But as for the larger changes . . . no, he doesn't see that they've done much for the Gypsies. "It's like with the street names," he says. "The names have been changed, but the streets are the same." He looks pleased with his analogy. The mother is holding an infant son and I ask her whether she dreams that he might go to high school, or even a university some day. "Why should he do anything I didn't do?" she retorts.

But the young man who is the local representative of a new Gypsy party, Phralipa, declares right off that one of his people's new aims is to educate themselves. Ronto Attila is a quiet, shy man who folds his arms around his stomach as if to protect himself from harm. Our conversation takes place in one of the more prosperous concrete houses, in a room decorated with a medley of cheap fabrics, rows of liquor bottles, and the kitschiest of plaster figurines. Pinned up to the wall is an old Marlboro-man ad, which has traveled here by heaven knows what route. There is a human medley in the room as well—people of all ages, just standing around, coming in and out of open doors to observe what's going on.

The scene and the conversation with Ronto Attila suggests the very beginnings of something like a political self-consciousness—though a political understanding of life must seem a far cry from that concrete, almost heretically unideological existence the Gypsies have led. To most of my questions, the young party rep gives canny and, to some extent, canned answers, just like any politician. The sameness of answers all over the world! But the problems he outlines are severe. In the last two years, 50 percent of the Gypsies, who mostly work in the factories of Miszkolc, have lost their jobs. Without jobs, they can't build new houses, and sometimes, they live twenty to twenty-five to a house. Ronto Attila is applying for funding to start their own construction company. He spends a lot of time filling out forms, as a matter of fact—the Gypsies' hygienic conditions are not of the best, and they get sick a lot, and have to apply for disability payments. He shows us some forms, to demonstrate that he's telling the truth, or maybe just out of pride—he's one of the few here who knows how to do it. He wants to do everything for his people, he assures us in his soft, dutiful tone; he is, after all, their representative.

Are there any other Gypsy parties in the village, it occurs to me to ask, innocently enough. But at this the new democrat gives way to something more primal. "I wouldn't let anybody else get in here! I wouldn't allow it!" he declares, his eyes flashing. Well, these are just beginnings, and by next year, Ronto Attila will undoubtedly have this answer, too, if not his feelings, perfected. We stop near another hopeless shack, and a thin, nervous woman smoking a cigarette invites us in. A mud floor, a very old picture of Rita Hayworth, cut out of a magazine. "I am all alone," she tells Tomás, looking terribly unhappy. Her husband died last winter, and her children have left. "I have nobody." "It must be difficult to live here," I say, looking round. "No," she says, shaking her head miserably. "That's not it. It's that I am alone." The sameness of the human condition everywhere.

We wend our way out of the Gypsy town followed by our mimic children's entourage, and Tomás leads me to the office of the local cooperative, in which much of the Hungarian population of the village is employed. Here we talk to the cooperative's treasurer, a blond, stocky woman in her forties who speaks with great energy and eloquence. The changes have brought to the coop a very ironical reversal, for while in 1960 the village underwent forced and hated collectivization, they are right now facing enforced and unwanted privatization. Yes, people balked terribly at first at having to enter the cooperative, the accountant tells us; for many, it was a kind of tragedy. But then they got used to it, the cooperative became very successful and increasingly profitable, and shared farming became easier and more efficient. So now, everyone is facing the approaching privatization deadline with dread.

The treasurer's brow furrows with genuine worry as she talks about the practical difficulties of dismantling so much common property. The staff is somehow supposed to distribute 100 million worth of *forints* to two hundred people through giving away vouchers. But how do you value a piece of land against a truck? What can somebody do with a square of land too small for a self-sufficient farm—especially since most people have lost the knack of independent farming by now? She sees no solutions on the horizon, and in the meantime, the coop is running into trouble already, the sort of vicious-circle trouble currently plaguing many large enterprises in Eastern Europe. As state subsidies have dried up, the coop's clients—some of the factories in Miszkolc, for example, which buy milk from Köröm—are beginning to forfeit payments. How are they supposed to pay for fodder for the cows in the meantime? Pretty soon, the employees' salaries might be in danger, though she hasn't told them yet, not wanting to make them nervous—a bit of paternalism, or maternalism, which I'm quite ready to excuse in my mind when I see how personally she takes the coop's problems.

I ask her whether she finds any of the new political parties helpful in her quandary—but this provokes an expression of rather impassioned disgust. None of them are any help at all; they all have their postures, while she has her two hundred employees and her practical problems to solve. They worry about who can support their ideas—"that's how they're political"—and none of them is concerned with actual, daily difficulties.

Next, however, I meet a politician who seems ready to take on all problems and comers. He's Köröm's mayor, another person bursting with energy and an unstoppable stream of speech. I am beginning to believe in Tony's theory of the robustness of all species born and grown in the Carpathian basin. The mayor is small, flamboyantly red-haired and freckled, and effusively hospitable. He comes to greet us in his garden, treats us to a Tokay wine from his family's vineyards (it really does have a uniquely delicate taste, hovering somewhere between a light retsina and a sweetish Bordeaux), and while we sip, he gesticulates broadly and talks. He tells us that "the people" are finding it hard to get used to their new self-sufficiency, and are still waiting for directives from "above." He, however, is taking some action without waiting for anybody. He has started an independent elementary school, for example, and has plans for many other projects. He's a teacher himself and a soccer player, and he likes novelty, activity; that's why he decided to run for this post in the first place.

And what about the coop? I ask him. Here he heaves a long sigh. Yes, that's terribly difficult. But there's a solution, he thinks, and it comes from a hot spring, which fortunately exists right outside the village. His own idea is that the coop should reconstitute itself as a new coop just as soon as it is dissolved, and build a holiday resort around this spring. A fancy, first-class resort.

Tony is amused when I mention this to him. "Ah, yes, the spring," he says. "It's been Köröm's *idée fixe* for years." The spring, lying so provokingly close and unused, has been the village's dream of a goose that should surely lay a golden egg, if only they knew how to encourage it. With this, I feel I've come full circle around the village life, with its dream spring and its cottages, built on the same plan for the last hundred years, its Gypsies who've been here for centuries, its modern problems and its return to that tantalizing spring, which could magically solve everything.

But there is, of course, another kind of history cutting through this slow, long arc. I spend some time talking to Tony, in his room, about his time of persecutions. Tony, too, has spent his years in prison—eight of them. He had been one of the activist priests led by Cardinal Mindszenty, and during "the little time," as he calls the 1956 Revolution, he was among a group of clerics designated for special reprisals.

Tony says it was easier for priests to survive in prison, because they didn't have wives or children to worry about, and because seminary prepared them both for shared living quarters and for the larger isolation. "Each cell was a small monastery with four priests. We could strengthen each other." In this "monastery," they taught each other languages, scratching out vocabulary in soap; they wrote prayers on toilet paper. Sometimes, they administered secret mass to each other, using prison bread and a grape seed his mother sent him in a cake, and over which they poured water. "One drop was enough," Tony says; and I think of *The Power and the Glory*, and the mystical, transformative power of the mass for the fallen priest of Graham Greene's novel.

Later, the priests were transferred to cells with other prisoners. The company in his cell, Tony says, was excellent. There was a minister of the prewar regime, a Marxist philosopher, a gendarme. Some very interesting conversations resulted, and from their own microcosm, the prisoners tried to put together a picture of "the mentality of the system." The friendship that developed in this common predicament "went very, very deep"—even though at times people fought and "hated each other terribly."

Eventually, Tony was recruited to be part of a prison team that translated for the secret police documents that otherwise never saw the light of day: articles from American foreign-policy magazines, Churchill's memoirs, books on how the Soviet spy system worked, and manuals on dog training and medicine. Undoubtedly, this was reading that reinforced Tony's penchant for somewhat fantastical speculations: for example, he thinks that the whole Kádár era was a careful experiment conducted by the Soviets on the Hungarians. But then, you can see how, given his experience, he would assume that when it comes to the world of power suspicion is the mother of truth.

Did anyone fall into despair? This is my standard question, as I try to fathom this other antiworld. Tony's answer is the same as everyone's. He doesn't talk about faith—perhaps it's too delicate a matter—but says that psychological survival depended very much on temperament. Tony remembers a sportsman who refused to do any physical exercise, because he found the air in the cell too foul. "For me, sport was a great help," Tony smiles, "and also yoga. But for him it was unendurable to think of physical activity in such conditions. So he said the air was terrible."

But what has really stayed with him from that time, he says, is the knowledge that you can always, in any circumstances, find a little opening, a hole, a grain of something just for yourself; that a man can work to make "a reasonable life" in any situation. It's a piece of knowledge that is slowly beginning to make its way into my mind as well, through the steady trickle of stories against the usually hard matter of perception. These are the narratives with which Eastern Europeans have lived, part of their common repertory; and I imagine that they possess in common the kind of knowledge that proceeds from them—a simultaneous recognition of power and injustice, and an understanding that one never need give in completely. There is always something that can be done from within.

For a while after prison, Tony was forbidden to preach, and worked in factories and a parish library. He used the time to study art and the cello and to organize church exhibits and concerts, which began attracting wide attention. The Budapest Bureau of Church Affairs eventually came to the conclusion that he was causing more trouble than three active priests, and decided to let him preach, on the condition that he accept virtual exile in provincial Köröm.

He did, and for the last twenty years he has in effect been nose-thumbing the authorities' verdict by turning his provincial periphery into a small center for artists, students, and international cadres of Catholic youth. With his great vitality, he seems to me like a man who has lost the inhibitions on his energy because he has lost his fear. In Tony's room, where we're talking, there's a grand piano he's just learning to play, a pleasant clutter of books, and some modern religious paintings. He shows me a book he's written, "out of a private passion," about János Pilinszky, a poet whom he describes as a Hungarian T. S. Eliot. The incongruously secular notion that living well is the best revenge seems apt for this thoughtful version of the *via activa*. It's not surprising that Tony is full of optimism about the changes, and has great confidence in his countrymen's ability to adjust to them, as they have adjusted to so much else. "The Hungarian people are very talented," he says. "And they want the good. They want the best." Then he puts on his cassock and goes off to give an evening sermon.

I walk about Köröm after our conversation at a quiet hour. The cows are making calm progress down the main path, and with their noses nudge open the gates into their yards, like the five-o'clock crowd after the office. The village looks sparklingly clean; neighbors chat with each other across their tiny porches, and in a bit of no-man's meadow, a Gypsy boy is singing. Time moves lazily, sensuously, and, so it seems, does the sun.

There's another highly energetic personage who emerges from this mellow landscape before I leave Köröm. She's introduced to me as Margit néni, which means something like "Auntie Margit," auntie being a word often applied here to elderly women. Margit néni has very large blue eyes, a scarf on her head, and exactly one tooth in her mouth. She smiles perpetually and talks a blue streak, addressing herself to me as well as to her friends, even though she's talking in Hungarian. In her seventies, Margit néni became an artist. It all started with a tapestry bee in the local church, led by a famous artist from Budapest, during which Margit néni discovered that she had a calling. After that, she started making tapestried pictures of her own. She shows us her work, which mostly consists of miniature scenes woven on pieces of canvas a few inches in height and width. There are pictures of her children's weddings and somebody's funeral, and portraits of saints. Out of an old chest of drawers she brings carefully folded tablecloths and doilies embroidered by her mother and grandmother. All through her childhold, she saw women doing these bright red embroideries which hadn't changed in centuries, and she says they were her initial inspiration. When I tell her she's following in the footsteps of Grandma Moses, she clasps her hands in delight; then, as we're about to leave, she brings out a tiny tapestried St. Anthony, and she puts her hand on her heart and transfers it to mine, pressing with surprising strength, to show that her little work should go from heart to heart.

This is somebody who changed her life, I think, politics or no politics. Not everything fits into preordained patterns, thank heavens, and the unquantifiable factors of vitality, or optimism, or a melancholy disposition perpetually surmount, or subvert, the more systemic facts of life.

Back in Budapest, I attend two very different events. One is an international psychoanalytic conference organized by the Sándor Ferenczi Society and entitled in slightly skewed English translation "Toward the End of Millenary: Political Changes and Psychoanalysis."

The conference is not the first of this kind to be held in Budapest, but still, in the new circumstances, it's something of a watershed. Hungary is the only Eastern European country where the psychoanalytic tradition survived the ice age; but even here, for about two decades, it was practiced in the catacombs, and preserved its continuity only by a thin thread. But in the early years of the century, Budapest was second only to Vienna as the city where the strange new cultic knowledge grafted and took. Ferenczi was one of Freud's closet disciples; and several other founding psychoanalytic figures, including Michael Balint and Margaret Mahler were Hungarian as well.

The general subject of the meeting could be summarized as the relationship of political oppression to individual repression. The lectures bear such titles as "Memory and Responsibility: The Political Unconscious," "A Three-Generation Neurosis Model," "Character and the Change of the Political Regime." As far as I can tell from the simplified English translations of the lectures, the problems preoccupying these analysts of the internal life replicate almost exactly the preoccupations "outside": they talk about the "cumulative traumatization" of history, and "the strategies of survival," of which the most important was forgetting. "It was *demanded* not to remember," somebody says, and someone else talks about splitting and fragmentation, which came from experience being kept apart from knowledge. "The great problem for Hungarians," somebody tells me during intermission, "is that they were taught to have two faces, one public, one private, and that eventually they couldn't distinguish the lie from the truth in themselves; you can imagine that a certain amount of splitting followed."

In the succession of Hungarian traumas, "history never allowed us to sit back and reflect, to work through the previous stage," someone explains, and now the question, on the deepest psychological level—no less than on the national one—is how far back one should go in an attempt at reconstructing a coherent narrative of a life, or of history. Someone else suggests "the script concept" for psychoanalysis, in which external and internal reality would be examined simultaneously.

These are very different problems from the neuroses of loneliness and individualism, which psychoanalysts would be more apt to discuss elsewhere; but then, psychoanalysis, like everything else, is to some extent unavoidably part of the culture within which it is practiced. I talk for a while to György Hidasz, the president of the Ferenczi Society, under whose auspices the conference is organized, and the man largely responsible for the perpetuation of psychoanalysis in Hungary, and our conversation turns to the taboos encountered within psychoanalysis. The subject of money—in the West, a highly mystified matter—is apparently discussed with ease by Hungarian patients and analysts. On the other hand, Hidasz says, he knows of entire analyses in which the patient's Jewishness was never mentioned at all. I am a bit shocked and fascinated by this, but perhaps I shouldn't be; culture really is reflected in the psyche. In the case of psychoanalysis, East and West are heirs to the same tradition, but their very divergent historical experiences have created different problems, perhaps even a different construction of the human creature. Now the great preoccupations of the psychoanalysts gathered here is the great preoccupation of Eastern Europe in this moment of transition—the return of the common past from its long darkness, and coming to terms with its discomfiting truths.

I can't think of a more fitting finale for the Hungarian part of my journey than an evening at the operetta. The operetta is one of the Hungarian traditions that has survived regimes, revolutions, and counterrevolutions—perhaps because it was too frivolous to receive the compliment of suppression. It is performed in a special theater, a perfect setting for its excesses, with wine-colored plush banisters and gilding everywhere. The audience is garishly dressed, jolly and plebeian. The operetta I happen to see is something called *Victoria,* by one Abrahàm Pàl, and, as far as I can make out without the aid of an English program, it concerns a sentimental conflict suffered by the eponymous heroine, as she tries to make up her heart between a dashing American diplomat and a smashing Hungarian hussar. Drums of war—First World War, I think—come into it somehow. On this slender thread of a plot is hung a mayhem of music, movement, costumes, and spirited high-jinks. The evening moves smartly and stylishly through a truly multicultural medley, ranging from Hollywood numbers à la Busby Berkeley to Cossack acrobatics, Viennese waltzes, Romanian and Polish folklore and Japanese god-knows-what. In the middle of it all, there's a wonderfully bittersweet number, in which a Yiddish tune, played more and more rousingly, is used as a mocking comment and counterpoint to a military parade. The whole thing reminds me how much Hollywood movies and Broadway musicals were a progeny of Central Europe, and how much American popular culture was influenced by this high-kicking spirit of sophisticated hilarity. There's lots of applause and laughter and rhythmical hand clapping, fully justified by the carryings on.

The idea of *Victoria* could be repeated in post-Communist Hungary today, with an updated version of an international musical mélange, and with an American businessman to substitute for the diplomat—though the hussar would probably have to be replaced by a less romantic figure, perhaps something like a yuppie. On one level, *plus ça change, plus ça la même chose*—though I hardly know anymore whether that's a pessimistic axiom or a very optimistic one.

FIVE

← ← ← ←

ROMANIA

There's probably in every traveler's fantasy a Bermuda Triangle of the mind, a place that concentrates all one's anxieties about unnamable dangers and the darkness of the unknown. In my imagination, which proves itself rather platitudinous in its choice, it's Romania that stands for such dangers; and within that country, the word that activates all my vague fears in the middle of hotel nights is Transylvania.

It's not only the associations with blood-feeding aristocrats that lend themselves to these anxieties, though reading about the real model for the mythical Dracula is blood-curdling enough. He was the son of Vlad Dracul, himself named Vlad Țepeș, or Vlad the Impaler, and though he isn't recorded to have drunk blood from the necks of maidens, his actual exploits were quite as monstrous. Vlad Țepeș was a mid-fifteenth-century *voivod,* or prince, of a Transylvanian principality, whose method of rule was unmitigated cruelty, and who specialized, as his sobriquet indicates, in impalings. At one point, hundreds of feudal overlords were expiring by this means in the courtyard of his castle. Given the less-developed technology of his day, he surely qualifies as one of the precursors—though only one of many—of the mass murderers of our day.

But my mental image of Transylvania is darkened by closer traces of violence as well. Romania is the only country of the ones I visit in which the changes were accompanied by armed fighting, and some of the worst bloodshed took place in the Transylvanian city of Timişoara, where the Romanian "revolution" first erupted. Then there are stories I keep hearing as I move through Eastern Europe, of train piracy in the night and tourists disappearing in the dark Transylvanian woods. Hungarian friends warn me that I shouldn't go into Transylvania in a car with Hungarian license plates—the tensions between the Romanian majority and the large Hungarian minority are high. They themselves routinely make a jog to Vienna to rent cars before making forays across the Romanian border.

Nevertheless, I make my first entry into Romania through Transylvania, in a car with the telltale Hungarian numbers. But as insurance against my own trepidations, if not the more external dangers, I have an American friend, Peter, accompanying me on this part of my expedition. Intimations of Romania begin even before we cross the border. Peter has knocked about some of the more remote parts of the world, and has gotten into the habit of picking up hitchhikers; halfway between Budapest and Debrecen, we stop for two passengers, who accompany us all the way into Transylvania.

They are young men, very black-haired and black-eyed, and they're desperate to get food supplies before we leave Hungary. "There's nothing to eat in Romania," they keep saying nervously. "It's utter chaos. You can't get anything." Both of them are from Bukovina, the region east of Transylvania, and both are electricians returning home after a futile attempt to get working passes in Austria. They were turned back at the border, an event they seem to accept with a certain fatalism; perhaps the sight of the great crowds they describe, trying to press their way into the magical West, was chastening. One of them speaks passable English and French, and we communicate in a laborious but intelligible pastiche of the two. Things are awful in Romania, he keeps repeating ritually. President Iliescu has promised much and done nothing, and the Securitate—the dread secret police— are still everywhere. It is true that Iliescu's party—the National Salvation Front—got a large majority in the elections; but, the electrician thinks, that's because it had all the advantages of controlling television and radio. *"Intérêt porte un fez,"* he says, a phrase that must be inherited from the times of the Turkish occupation; and I take it to mean that self-interest is shrewd and ruthless, like the fez-wearing Turks.

As it happens, we can't find any open food stores on the Hungarian side, and after an al fresco lunch made up of ingredients we've brought and eaten in a stubbly field of wheat, we leave this land of plenty with nothing more than a few pieces of watermelon. On the border, a long line of cars, and some perplexing signs in English: BUILT-UM CITIES, STOP THE ENGINE DURING THE FEEDING, a third sign detailing different speed limits for different-sized engines. For some reason, our passports are taken away for an inspection, and we're waved to the side of the road while we wait. Fortunately, I've brought some English books of poetry from the Budapest bookstore, and we read some poems by Joseph Brodsky—not at all incongruous in this setting—to pass the time and slake our slight unease. But after two hours or so, our passports are returned to us politely, though with no explanations.

The moment we find ourselves on the Romanian side, our passengers begin apologizing. They apologize for the road, the landscape, the poverty. Neither Peter nor I see anything so out of the ordinary, but the habit of national self-deprecation is something I've encountered all through these travels. It's as if the citizens of these countries, in addition to the real humiliation they may feel from having been reduced to second-class conditions, wanted to ward off the immediate humiliation of a foreigner's judgment. At least, they want to indicate, they're not so provincial as not to understand that their country is a poor province.

It's true, though, that as we drive on the countryside gets visibly poorer, the roads less asphalted. And the traffic on those roads! Gaggles of geese cross in front of our car as nonchalantly as if we were perhaps just another goose, carts drawn by broad oxen share our narrow lane, cows walk in rotund groups as if they owned the place. In each village, people stand about in clusters in this dusky time, and children shout and laugh at us, as if the sight of a car—for long intervals, we pass no others—gave them unqualified happiness.

Our goal for the evening is Oradea, a town that, according to my trusty Fodor's, offers the hope of a hotel. But we're still far from it, when it gets dark and late—our progress has been very slow—and we settle for the first shelter we see, in a hilly hamlet whose name we never ascertain. This turns out to be a hotel from hell. The rooms shown to us are unlit and dank, and smell of something foul that has permeated the fabric of things—a combination of rancid oil and layered sweat, I'd diagnose. We have no choice, however, but to stay. Our passengers decide to pursue their clearly hopeless project of hitchhiking and we leave them on the untraveled road with twinges of guilt.

The thick darkness outside the *soi-disant* hotel is disrupted by one flickering light, emanating from a structure that looks like a house for a very tall troll, or, alternatively, a narrow, wooden kiosk on stilts. Sounds of music emerge from it. We make our way toward these signs of human activity, climb a rickety exterior staircase, and enter the night life of wherever it is we are. In a room the size of two walk-in closets, there are a bar, three tables, and about six people dressed in international youth style: leather jackets, narrow pants, long earrings. The sound pulsing out of the stereo is American disco. I'm both bemused and a bit deflated. There are no remote corners of the world anymore. But the liquor we order is local, a plum brandy called *rachia,* with a deceptively smooth, light taste, which conceals the most fiery liquid I've ever consumed. After one shot, Peter and I easily give in to an offer of exchanging some dollars for *lei* with one of the leather-jacketed youths. After the second shot, my vision becomes eerily clear, while negotiating the exterior stairs is oddly difficult. Given the quarters I'm facing, I'm grateful for these unexpected effects and I refrain from examining the bed or anything else in my surroundings before falling soundly asleep.

With the onset of day, my imaginary heart of darkness turns out to be the heart of light. The sun is brilliant, the hamlet nestles in a green valley. The *rachia* has left no hangover—that's one of the qualities it's prized for. To our considerable surprise, we get breakfast—sort of. It's served on a concrete terrace next to the hotel, on a table of very dubious cleanliness: edible eggs, a piece of dry bread, but alas, no coffee. A request for something cold to drink produces a thick, yellowish liquid that the taste buds definitely reject. We decide against drinking the water. On the BBC there've been reports of cholera outbreaks in Romania—much further south, it's true, but too close for comfort.

Still, the day is serenely sunny, the landscape beautiful. What was I so afraid of? For the moment, I can't imagine anything awful happening here, though that's clearly a failure of the imagination, too. We head off in a leisurely way, toward the town of Cluj-Napoca, where Peter has an appointment. At times, the landscape seems subtropical, somehow Asian. In the intense sun, the green of the sensuous large hills vibrates and refracts; oxen drink from a languid pond; people ride by on bicycles, wearing wide, cone-shaped straw hats.

In the villages we pass, cottages are painted with washes of brilliant sunflower yellows, lime green, indigo blue; only this intensity of light could absorb these colors and render them less than garish. There are low stone churches that, despite their small dimensions, contain the complexity and detail of Gothic cathedrals. Then there are extremely simple white wooden churches with elegant, elongated silver spires that seem to shimmer and nearly dissolve into the sun.

Mircea Eliade, a Romanian philosopher who probably traveled in these parts a lot, thought that in everyone's mind there's an image of an archetypal village; and I find that the hamlets we pass satisfy some such pastoral ideal in my imagination. On a more practical level, I can see why this beautiful and fertile region would have been desired and fought over as much as it has been. Transylvania could be said to be Central Europe's Central Europe, the heart of turmoil, if not of darkness. After enjoying a period of autonomy during the fourteenth and fifteenth centuries, Transylvania changed hands and masters with an exemplary frequency. Its first union with other parts of Romania came about in 1600—a state of affairs that lasted less than a year and that wasn't to be repeated until the end of World War I. After nearly a century of servitude to the Turks, Transylvania came within the Hapsburg aegis, and in 1867, as part of the "historic compromise" between Austria and Hungary, it was annexed by Hungary. In 1918, however, it was given back to Romania, as the latter's reward for entering the war on the Allied side. During the second World War, a large chunk of Transylvania was in turn reclaimed by Hungary, only to be awarded back to Romania in 1944, largely as compensation for parts of Bessarabia and Bukovina, to which the Soviets felt entitled to help themselves. It's no wonder that tensions between the Hungarian and the Romanian parts of the population have never had a chance to simmer down or be resolved.

Near Oradea, we pick up another hitchhiker, a stocky, energetic woman who also speaks passable English and French. She says she's an engineer, though in Eastern Europe that term covers a multitude of sins. When we refuse to take the *lei* she presses on us for the ride, she invites us into her home, in a block situated in a weedy no-man's-land. It's the first Romanian apartment I've seen, so I am curious. It is small and poor even by Eastern European standards, but pretty much in the same mold. In the tiny living room, a Gypsyish-looking daughter is watching an American rock group on television. But on the bookshelf, Romanian titles stand alongside *Faust* and *The Possessed*. Our hostess tells us she had wanted to teach literature, but *"on fait ça qu'on peut, pas ça qu'on veut,"* she says elegantly, giving a shoulder shrug suggesting lessons in resignation.

She looks a bit distressed when I ask for the bathroom. "Our construction is good in Romania, but we have no *finissage,"* she explains, veering between national loyalty and embarrassment. I see what she means. The floor is exposed concrete, there are loose wires sticking out of the ceiling and walls, and in the bathtub, filled with dirty water, something that looks like a fragment of a car tire. Whatever *finissage* means exactly, it's very poor here indeed.

My silent supplications for food go unanswered, but our hostess serves us thick Turkish coffee in demitasse cups and tells us she's extremely glad to be able to invite us into her home like this; until recently, meeting with foreigners was a punishable crime. In her factory, for example, an employee who befriended a Polish coworker was threatened by the Securitate *apparatchiks*—every workplace had them—with unnamed punishment. The men avoided each other from then on. And this was a fellow worker from a "fraternal" country! The anecdote betokens a level of recent repression, a control of private behavior, beyond what I've encountered in the other countries.

"Are those Securitate men still around?" I ask.

Another meaningful shrug of the shoulders, saying, "What do you expect?"

Then she speaks very energetically: "But I don't blame Iliescu," she says. "That's a childish approach. We can't have democracy in a day. We have everything to learn. We have no democratic traditions. We're practically Oriental."

My hunger becomes more preoccupying after we leave. The only eatery we saw during our day's journey is a dim, echoing "restaurant," where the only dish was something that looked like tripe soup, with a greasily indeterminate taste. I couldn't touch it, and despite my growing thirst, couldn't swallow the treacly yellow beverage.

All of which means that, by the time we get to Cluj-Napoca, I'm utterly unresponsive to its charms, and we head straight for a hotel restaurant recommended as the de luxe joint in town. There's something odd about the place—perhaps the vague, pervasive sense of decay, juxtaposed with the overlarge proportions that are supposed to herald luxury. In the terrace restaurant, people sit in groups at long, wooden plank tables, and we take the unoccupied places next to a young couple. He's another "engineer," though he's training to be a mime, and he speaks French, which is fortunate, because we need somebody to help us negotiate our way to supper. This is a process that apparently requires patient diplomatic skills. First, we exercise our patience by waiting. Eventually, a waiter arrives and we convey our seemingly minimal request for something—anything—to eat. I hardly dare mention my desire to drink something cold and nonyellow. A long exchange with the mime ensues. The waiter departs. I nervously ask what we can expect. Our intermediary makes a this way, that way gesture. "He'll talk to someone," he says. "He'll see what he can do." Another long interval, followed by the return of the waiter and another animated powwow. "He'll bring you some meat!" the mime announces triumphantly. But a cold drink! I must have something cold to drink! The mime gets up and engages in earnest conversation with a whole cluster of waiters standing in the doorway. Some ten minutes later— *mirabile dictu!*—a bottle of sparkling mineral water is brought to the table. Eventually, an edible dinner appears as well.

"What's happened to the food?" we ask our beneficent translator. "Where has it gone?"

"The mafia," he says. "The middlemen. They buy everything from stores and sell it to a few people for high prices." He looks heartily disgusted. "It's chaos, absolute chaos. Before, you knew you could get beer—oh, not every day, but once a week, on Tuesday—but now there's nothing, nothing. We're a third-world country! We're practically Oriental!"

In the course of a strolling after-dinner inspection, however, Cluj-Napoca proves to be a lovely town and unmistakably European in a way that surprises me—recognizable, beautiful Europe, in this far region of the world! The "Napoca" comes from its ancient Roman name, and the Hungarians, who constitute a sizable minority, still call the city Kolosvàr. The city was built up by the Renaissance Hungarian king, Matthias Corvinus, and in its center there's a respectable Gothic cathedral; along the pleasant central square, the façades are painted in the creamy yellows and whites that are the preferred Baroque color scheme in these parts.

But while the architecture is European, the atmosphere is somehow . . . well, Balkan. *"Bizhnitze? Bizhnitze?"* men whisper to us confidentially, approaching on the street, though what kind of business they have in mind isn't at all clear. *"Cigaretten? Chocolaten?* Soap?" a group of urchins inquire, and they look not so much disappointed as disgusted when we show them we're empty-handed. As we near our car, we see that two men are inspecting the locks intently. They walk away nonchalantly only when we come right up and indicate that we actually have the keys to the car. Later in the evening, we see a brigade of street workers, mostly women in wide skirts and scarves, sweeping a street with enormous brooms in almost utter darkness. Who has sent them out to sweep in the dark? There's an absurdist pathos about the scene worthy of Ionesco—or perhaps of Ceauşescu, who also specialized in a certain grotesque whimsicality.

The next morning, we set off for Maramureş, a section of Transylvania abutting the Soviet border. Heading northeast, we soon find ourselves in mountainous landscapes of great wildness and beauty. The villages we pass are assuredly not wealthy, but they show evidence of a rich esthetic sense that pours out over everything we see. The houses are painted in those extravagant bright colors, and their balconies are decorated with elaborately wrought borders. The roofs often contain an ebullient complexity of turrets, gables, and spires, all constructed on a miniature, fairy-tale scale. In front of most cottages, there are gorgeously carved, free-standing wooden gateways; they signify the passage from life to death, someone has told me—a journey that the people here imagine as serene rather than frightening. Then there are stone wells, with a sort of baldaquin roof over them, in the shape of an umbrella.

On the village roads, women in the same dress I saw on Váci Utca in Budapest, hold fluffy spools of white wool in front of them as they walk, combing through it smoothly all the while. In the waning afternoon, they sit at outdoor looms, under trees by the roadside, and weave the same wool into thick, knobbly rugs. We pause to watch them at their work, and they smile at us cheerfully, encouraging us to look more closely, without interrupting the rhythm of their task. Although the particulars are different, this is close to the kind of age-old rusticity I remember from the Polish villages of my childhood, and something in me is deeply gratified that it still exists—this familiar exoticism, this powerful taproot culture from which Europe grew up.

In the late afternoon, we reach Borsa, a town high up in the part of the Transylvanian Mountains called Muntii Maramureşu- lui. Its main square is filled with people, mostly men, just standing around. It's odd but not unpleasant to see such guiltless idleness, with no pretense, even, of busyness or aim. Our arrival, however, provokes a flurry of activity. People approach us offering incomprehensible services. A taxi driver standing next to his battered vehicle suggests through a rigmarole of gestures that he can sell us gasoline; since we haven't seen a gas station for two days, this is a welcome offer. "How much?" we ask, and the man conveys to us that for a tankful he wants $15. Peter is about to accept, but some atavistic instinct in me, undoubtedly springing from the depths of Eastern Europe, prompts me to say "Ten" in a bluff-decisive voice. The man pretends to think hard. Twelve, he finally says, in a tone of making a big concession. O.K., I say, and he immediately slaps my hand across the palm in a "Yes, brother," gesture, while others make approving noises, because I know the rules of the game.

The deal clinched, everything goes back to normal. Our man props himself up against his taxi and continues to chat with his buddies. In answer to my inquisitive rise of eyebrows, he puts up his hand in a steadying gesture. I shrug. Since there are no signs of anything happening anytime soon, Peter and I walk down Borsa's main street and into the one store we find along its length. Inside, there are odious-looking vinyl jackets, but also some brightly colored, handwoven rugs of local make that catch Peter's interest. Another bargaining transaction takes place. "How much?" he inquires of a young woman who speaks a little English. She giggles a little and consults with an older sales-person.

"Maybe $30," she finally brings out. "Maybe $50." This is no way to dupe the unwary foreigner!

Back at the square, our man is still kibitzing. He's unper-turbed by our return. We stand around. "Hotel?" we ask, point-ing to a woebegone structure across the street. "No," everyone agrees, waving in an eastward direction. *"Moderne* hotel. Com-plex. Over there."

At long last, moved by some invisible impulse, the taxi driver gets into his car and beckons us to follow him down a country path. We stop outside his house, near a brisk mountain stream, and there he brings out some canisters of gasoline, which he pours with exquisite care into our car.

At the "complex," which looks mercifully comfortable and clean, a ruddy-faced clerk with carrot-red hair looks at us tensely and assures us that he'll do everything in his power to persuade the waiters to serve us dinner. Behind-the-scenes negotiations, followed by adequate food. I keep wondering whether the wait-ers sometimes actually refuse, and on what grounds. It all seems nerve-rackingly personal.

My room is surprisingly decent, except for piped-in sounds emanating from the walls with Muzak insistence. When I ask the woman who has shown me in to turn it off, she complies, but not without shooting a look of amazement and disapproval in my direction. I clearly don't know what elegant or *moderne* is. For the last few days, I've dreamt of a genuine hot shower, and now I think I may attain my wish. Alas, the water coming out of the *moderne* faucets is as cold as everywhere else. "At eight, we turn on hot," the red-haired clerk assures me energetically. But when

I get back to the room at nine o'clock, the water is ice cold again. "Between eight and eight-thirty we have hot water!" I am informed. So much for fantasies of luxurious ablutions; but the indefinite postponement of such pleasures—they cease to seem absolute necessities—is one of the things you learn in Eastern Europe.

In compensation—the standard Eastern European compensation—we have a drink on the terrace, and our vigorous clerk entertains us with tales from the "revolution." He was in Bucharest, he says, when it all happened. He drove a car into the interior of a government building and got out just as it began to go up in flames. He describes this with expressive hand waving and an air of braggadocio. It's hard to tell whether there's any truth to it at all.

The next morning, we walk up into the mountains, which are covered with grassy meadows and alive with brooks and breezes. From time to time, we hear the transparent tinkling of cowbells. At the top of a hill, we come to a storybook scene—I suppose this is where the storybooks got them from. Near a long wooden hut, a few cows are grazing, overseen by an old man and a small boy. The old cowherd has one of those compact, bony, leathery faces about which the word "weathered" comes irresistibly to mind. The boy is dressed in a white shirt and heavy green woolen pants, a black, silver-studded vest, and a wide embossed belt. His complexion is olive, his large eyes are filled with intelligence, and his face has one of the clearest, sweetest expressions I've ever seen on a child.

The cowherd invites us into the hut, so low that we can barely stand up in it and filled with bitter, thick smoke. He gives us spoonfuls of a sweetish, milky curd cheese precipitating in a wooden vat; but the smoke so stings the eyes that Peter and I can't stand to be inside for long. The old man indicates that he wants to try on my sunglasses, and nods his head appreciatively; he could use them against the sun and the smoke, and if they weren't prescription lenses, I'd give them to him. As it is, we leave some of the smoked sausage we've brought along from the hotel, and walk on, wondering how long this excruciatingly slow means of production can survive in our speeded-up times. (Later, though, I learn that such shepherds and cowherds are among the few people in Romania who are making money, because their cheeses are exported. One nouveau-riche shepherd, according to local lore, has bought a helicopter to take him from hill to hill.)

On the way down, we meet a group of picnickers, who invite us to join them. Pieces of meat are roasting on a spit, and a bottle of some fiery drink is passed around. So there is food somewhere—probably passed along by these personal channels to which people resort when official life fails. We contribute the rest of our sausage. Out of sheer excess of good spirits, a man bursts into song, which he accompanies by vigorous slaps of his thighs.

"Iliescu, *da!*" a woman shouts, giving a thumbs-up sign. "National Salvation Front, *da!*" This is a degree of enthusiasm I find strange about a man who had just recently summoned helmeted miners to Bucharest to disrupt a demonstration violently, and, it seems, lawlessly.

"What do you like about him?" we ask.

"He's like a good father," the woman says in French, looking reverent. "He'll take care of us. He's for us."

Another woman, who has been watching this quietly, speaks to us in English. "You see, this is how we are," she says. "We have no democratic traditions. We still need a strong leader."

She introduces herself as Cornelia, and invites us to visit her the next day. While she prepares coffee for us in a boxlike room, she talks to us with a hungry and generous eagerness. She's a lovely-looking person, olive-skinned and almond-eyed, dressed with an easy elegance, in loose silk slacks and a long khaki jacket. She has somehow achieved a cosmopolitan look—perhaps the same way she learned English—from watching television and the movies. French is considered a kindred language and was often taught in school, or passed on privately; Romania has been a highly Francophile culture, and prides itself on having a Romance language—though with strong Slavic elements. But she's never been abroad, and she's curious about everything. She's a schoolteacher here, and her husband is in the army—though she quickly assures us that "we know nothing about what happened. We're in the dark. We're confused." She's talking about the gnawing uncertainty about how the "revolution" took place in Romania, or whether it was a revolution at all. Iliescu was, after all, a party insider and Ceauşescu's ally in the early years of his career—though more recently he belonged to a "liberal" splinter group. Despite this, despite the suspicions that the Securitate is still intact, and despite those murderous miners, Iliescu enjoys widespread support among the Romanian population. Cornelia can't enlighten me about the reasons for this; she seems almost painfully confused herself. "No, I don't like him, exactly," she says, "but maybe we should give him time. I don't know, I just don't know." She looks distressed. Then, as if she found the right way to talk about it, she says with more energy, "You see, that's how we are, a very emotional people, and not very rational. We're part Greek, part Dacian, part Latin. We're a Mediterranean people. We're practically Oriental."

That isn't very consistent, but I'm beginning to recognize it, the Romanian formula for the time of transition. In every country, there are such formulas, repeated like protective mantras, or like straws of understanding to hold on to amidst confusion. "We must get through this somehow," the Poles keep saying. "Nothing has changed at all," the Hungarians aver in unison. And now these Romanian tropes, reiterated with impressive consistency. "It's chaos," people say. "We're not ready for this. We don't understand democracy. We're practically Oriental." A formula, of course, is not an explanation, but it is a clue to how people experience their situation, their world. The Romanian phrases are usually uttered with a sort of accepting resignation—as if the muddle were nobody's fault but an inevitable condition, a fate.

But Cornelia says she's a "patriot," and she loves her poor country, particularly Maramureş, whose history and culture she's studied closely. "What you probably don't know," she tells us, apparently deciding from our names that we're both Jewish, "is that this was a place where many Jewish people lived. Now there are none left. I think about them a lot. Sometimes I go to look at their houses, their cemeteries. Some of the most beautiful, big houses you see around here belonged to Jewish people. Sometimes I think I can feel their presence."

No, I didn't know, I didn't expect, in this tucked away corner of Transylvania, to hear about a once-thriving Jewish community that disappeared with the war. But the Jews, it seems, are the specter haunting Eastern Europe these days, the inescapable absence, an absence that is itself felt as a presence, a wrongness. On the whole, I'm consoled that traces of their memory live on in the minds of people like Cornelia, who speaks about her desire to know more about the former Jewish inhabitants of her town with such credible emotion. Perhaps, if we don't always have a conscious conscience, we have a subliminal one, from which the memory of past wrongs is not so easily erased.

Throughout our conversation, two of Cornelia's friends have been watching *Smiles of a Summer Night* on television, never turning away from it, though we're sitting close together in a cramped space. They wave to us languidly as we leave. Cornelia escorts us to our car and parts with us with a nearly Latin emotionality.

Whoever suspected the existence of a village named Sapinţa? But now, we're headed for Sapinţa, to find out about the "revolution." In the last few days, we've been hearing that something important just happened in Sapinţa—something involving a highway blockade and army helicopters from Bucharest. "It was a real revolution," people underline in excited voices; perhaps the revolution, the real article, has finally come to Romania after all.

Sapinţa lies a few hours west of Borsa; in the late afternoon, when we get there, it seems to have been deserted. Not a soul is to be seen on its dusty roads, not an animal sound to be heard.

Nothing but curtained windows, and the impenetrable silence. I keep in mind, however, the injunction of a Hungarian friend. "Find the priests," he advised. "They know everybody and everything." The spire of the Orthodox church is well visible above the low cottages, but the church is deserted, too. Near it, though, there is a cemetery so curious that—though this is not what we came for—we linger for a while. The cemetery is a copse of crosses, all of uniform size and shape, but bursting with vigorous primary colors. Each cross is covered with a scene depicting the grave's inhabitant at his or her profession, painted in a primitive, miniaturist style: there's a woman at a loom, a shepherd, a cobbler; even a taxi driver. It's not for nothing that this is called the "Merry Cemetery," as I find out by consulting my Fodor's, for the whole exudes an almost disturbing gaiety. Initially, the cemetery was the creation of one man, Stan Pĕtraş, who must have had an intimate and antic relation to death. But he died in the late 1970s, and now his portrait, which must have been painted by an ambivalent disciple, scowls thickly from one of the crosses. In the back of the cemetery, we notice a man working on yet another picture, for merry death seems to have become the standard in Sapinţa. He directs us to the house of the priest, just a few steps down the road.

The house is large and quiet, and we walk in through the open garden gate. Within, a woman inspects us wordlessly and motions us to follow. We're taken into a large room with a desk in the middle. The priest is seated behind it in his cassock. He's young, very tall, and boyishly handsome. He, too, examines us unhurriedly, and asks a question in Romanian. We shake our heads to let him know we don't understand, and try all the languages at our disposal; nothing works. For a long moment, we stare at each other silently. Then the priest makes a decision and ushers us into another room, pleasantly dim and even larger than the first. This one is furnished in the style of a Turkish seraglio, with a profusion of red-hued rugs and large pillows strewn all over the place. The priest courteously indicates that we should sit down. We do. We wait in silence. Eventually, a young boy comes in and respectfully stands behind his father's chair, waiting to do his bidding. A low exchange between them—everything is happening in this odd, unrattled way—is followed by the boy's attempt to speak to us in English. His vocabulary, however, consists of about ten words, and we come to the end of our communications quickly. Another exchange between father and son, and the boy makes a slight bow and leaves the room.

Now again we wait, facing each other silently. Balkan time. We sit, the way Zen masters sit. There's no awkwardness in it, no frantic noddings of the head or reassuring smiles. I'm beginning to find it strangely relaxing. I'm shifting to another sense of events, in which you don't insist on fulfilling a plan, but wait for what happens next. Something always does.

What happens next is that we're taken out into the garden, and seated at a long wooden table under a cool canopy of vines. The strong sun flickers in through the leaves; beyond our enclosure, in the garden, women in peasant dress are scything the grass, with smooth, steady movements. This is just fine, I feel, though I have no idea what it's leading to. Another one of the priest's sons—younger and less retrained—comes out and, in lieu of making conversation, throws out talismanic words. "Patagonia," he says, and looks at us inquiringly. "Arizona, Argentina, Minnesota. Bogotá." He wants to know if we've been there, and with every nod, his eyes glisten with wonder. The world, to him, is all suggestive names, virginally full of mystery.

The priest's wife comes out, with a tray of food and drink. The priest downs several shots of the local brew and encourages us to do the same. After another day of undernourishment, we wolf down the eggs and the spicy sausages. We sit some more. I begin to lose faith and fidget.

But no, a hidden purpose works its way in things. The older son reappears, followed by a short, bouncily stepping man, who introduces himself as a journalist from Bucharest; he's been here for several days, covering the "revolution." He speaks French and he's in a state of tremendous excitement. He'll tell us all about it. Things liven up as the priest and the journalist vie to talk about the recent events. They both speak with great emotion, though with perhaps more heat than light.

This is the tale as it emerges from their eager account: Under the "post-Communist" dispensation, a new mayor was elected by the five thousand inhabitants of Sapinţa. He was a man of enormous integrity, the priest says, his eyes shining, a good man, a moral example. And the people of Sapinţa loved him, because he wanted to give the land back to private owners. Enter—or rather, reenter—the old Communist mayor, as hated as the new one is loved. "The Communists here did monstrous things, monstrous," the journalist passionately declares. Just several days ago, the deposed Communist chieftain, accompanied by an armed entourage, burst into the mayoral office, threw out its lawful occupant by sheer force, and proceeded to install himself and his buddies in the seat of power. And that's when the good people of Sapinţa rose up and sat down on the main highway, blocking traffic from all over Romania for two days.

As the recounting of these events unfolds, excitement mounts. The priest practically dances in his cassock, pouring more liquor into our glasses, and, out of an excess of good feeling, showing us his new baby and asking me to photograph it. Everyone tries to impress on us that the people around here are very special, with great integrity and attachment to the land. They work very hard, not like people in Bucharest, and it's terribly wrong to deprive them of the land they love.

At some point, a stubble-bearded peasant is brought in, in his *bleu-de-travail* jacket and a wide-brimmed black hat, as a firsthand witness and participant in these events. For the next hour or so, he stands stock-still under the canopy, occasionally downing a glass of liquor. But his eyes, too, begin to well up with emotion as he talks about what happened. People held hands and sang together during those two days; grown men and women cried. "It was a real revolution," they all keep repeating. They're terribly proud of having taken their own action, as if they've discovered its possibility for the first time.

The narrative, however, doesn't work up to a satisfactory resolution. After two days of the highway blockade, state troops swooped in on Sapinţa in helicopters. The soldiers, unbelievably enough, arrested the elected mayor on trumped-up charges; he's now awaiting trial in the regional prison. The villainous Communist mayor is holding office, though he's so afraid of the ill feelings he's stirred that he spends the nights away from the village, in the town of Satu-Mare.

Nobody seems to know what to do next, or what the legalities of the situation are, or what their rights consist of. Excited as they are about their rebellion, they still seem to accept the stark ways of power. This is an essential difference from what I've found elsewhere in Eastern Europe. Some bridge hasn't been crossed here, a step hasn't been taken.

Night has fallen very gradually and gently while we've been sitting in our grove, and when the tale is over, we take a stroll around Sapinţa's darkened roads. It's utterly silent, except for the neighing of a horse coming out of a barn, and so dark that the white pebbles seem to emanate a low light. The younger son murmurs softly the names of American basketball players. Peter, in a journalistic mode, tries to talk to the bad mayor's wife, but she, of course, will have none of it. When we get back, the priest's wife shows me into the seraglio, where she's prepared a bed with many pillows. I stumble my way through the dark to the outhouse, and then search the house for water. There's a promising spigot in the kitchen, but nothing comes out. In the morning, I'm given a metal cup filled with cold water for my ablutions and try to leave some dollars—I don't have more graceful gifts with me—but am decisively refused.

On the way back to Budapest, where we drive to return the car, it's so hot that the road begins to do a flickering dance. There's a curious item on the BBC, about Iraq marching into Kuwait. Peter and I look at each other in perplexity. The world is full of strange tremors. The priest, counting perhaps by Balkan time, said that the trip would take five hours; it takes twelve. I am supposed to catch a plane into Bucharest in the afternoon; by the time we get in, it is long gone.

It's because I've missed my plane that I decide to double back to Romania on the Orient Express. Peter has gone to Prague; once more I am on my own. The wait for the fabled conveyance begins in an endless, sweaty ticket queue, and continues later in the evening at the station, where I've been directed to come early, if I wanted to get a berth. I do, I badly want a berth, and so I've come an hour ahead of time. Stupid of me, really. For the next three hours, the board announcing arrival times keeps updating the lateness of the Orient Express. I'm very tired, hungry and immobile; even if the bar near the entrance looked more appetizing, I couldn't face dragging my suitcases across the vast lengths of the station again. I stand and mope and feel the sapping sensations of self-pity. No wonder travel books are written mostly by men, I think, not for the first time in this journey. Whatever possessed me to do this in the first place?

I'm just about at the end of my rope—though the length of the rope, I'm learning, is elastically extendable—when the Balt-Orient Express pulls into the station. It's a battered thing. There's a great rush of people, materialized out of nowhere, toward the front; I follow the herd. A slight-looking man walking near me offers to take one of my bags. I quickly appraise him—no time for reflection, only for reflex—and hand over a suitcase. He propels me toward the sleeping car and wishes me luck. I try to convey to the conductor that I want a bunk. He pushes me impatiently into the train, which begins to move almost immediately.

This is a low moment. I feel utterly exhausted, nervous, and unprotected. I can't face the prospect of a fifteen-hour journey standing in the corridor. I make a wordless plea at the conductor as he walks by, trying to compress authority and desperation into one look, but he's now turned into a slow-moving dignitary, and he makes a gesture indicating that patience is required.

The end of the rope threatens to dangle in front of me again. And then everything changes. The conductor comes out of his cubicle and opens a sleeping car for me. It's true that as soon as I sit on the bunk it caves in and falls on to the floor. But that's no problem; the conductor shakes his head wryly, and lets me into another cabin. I make so bold as to ask him about a dining car. I haven't eaten since the morning. But I must be thinking about the Orient Express from the movies. Of course, there is no dining car. But the conductor, my new friend, raises his index finger as if to say, "Wait!" In a few minutes, he returns with a plate on which there must be half his supper: some goat cheese, tomatoes, and a few slices of very dry bread. There's also a Swiss Army knife and a bottle of mineral water. I'm touched; somehow, rescue always comes. And so I eat my supper, for which I've paid with some dollars and a pack of the highly desirable Kent cigarettes, and suddenly, my mood makes a strange roundabout turn. Simply, and without fuss, I stop being scared. I have to admit that something akin to fear has accompanied me on large portions of these travels. Not of anything extreme, for the most part; not of robbery or violent attack. There isn't all that much to steal from me, and violence moves one into another dimension that I don't care to imagine at all. No, mostly it's been a low-level, discomfiting anxiety that this business of trekking on the Eastern European road will get to be too much: that I can't manage my luggage, can't find food or drink, that I'll get lost on dark roads in a godforsaken town, with no language to explain myself in to unfriendly strangers. Perhaps the unease has been that this Gypsy wandering is no business for a nice, middle-class woman; that it's defeminizing to put oneself in such rough, ill-decorated conditions.

But now, for some reason—the anxiety simply lifts. I don't know how many hours I'll have to spend on this seedy train, and I don't know whether the very new friends who have promised to meet me in Bucharest will be waiting for me, but suddenly that's all right. I can cope with the next thing when it comes. Something always happens next: the principle I've been slowly soaking in. The world doesn't run out, and neither do human beings, who for the most part are a source of help rather than threat.

A passenger in the next compartment knocks on my door

and whisperingly asks if I'd exchange some dollars for *lei*. He's going on vacation in Turkey, and how can he have a good time without real money? Of course, I say. Why shouldn't he have a good time in Turkey? For a while, I contemplate the fat, fat stars moving outside the train window. Then I fall soundly asleep, only to be awakened by customs officials at the border. They're two burly, uniformed Romanians, who sit on my bunk for about half an hour filling out forms in laborious handwriting. In my new mood, this seems perfectly natural and companionable. Then I fall asleep again and wake up just as we emerge from the Transylvanian Alps onto the parched plain below. At about one in the afternoon, we pull into Bucharest.

It's a good thing that I've just managed to achieve my new serenity, since the train station in Bucharest calls for strong nerves. It's huge, chaotic, and very hot. The milling, pressing humanity within it looks shabby in the extreme; variously disheveled men approach me with offers to carry my suitcases. I'm extremely glad when Pavel and Stefana arrive as they promised they would. I met them only once in New York, where Pavel was teaching at the New School and felt a rapport with both, in which the age difference—they are some twenty years older than I—didn't seem to matter at all; and they, on an instantly generous impulse, offered to put me up in Bucharest. I'd need someone to look after me, they implied.

We greet each other as if we know each other quite well, and they take me to a car resembling a beaten-up, ancient London taxi, driven by a thick-necked personage to whom Stefana refers as "the family chauffeur." I report on my trip, and the train conductor's acts of largess. "Was he Romanian or Hungarian?" Stefana and Pavel begin to ask almost simultaneously, and then laugh with recognition that for international sophisticates like themselves this is an oddly patriotic reflex.

Stefana's apartment—she and Pavel live separately, though they're long-time companions, and I'll be staying with her—is small and very modest, but it has a lovely Turkish feel. In the little living room, there are tapestried chairs, and in a larger room, which Stefana uses as her bedroom and study, there's a carmine velvet quilt on the bed and a deep-hued rug hanging above it on the wall. The shutters on the tall windows are closed against the heat and sun, giving the interior a pleasant dimness. A home softened by some taste and charm, in the absence of any other resources. Our meal is served to us by Domna Florica, who has been "with the family" forever and who bustles in the tiny, very primitive kitchen with authoritative decisiveness. She's old, squat, and rumpled, but there's a look of sharp intelligence in her eyes. She's made a delicious meal of baba ghanouj and various vegetable salads—in the next few days, I'll come to appreciate better how hard it is to put together such a feast—and I collapse into sleep early in the evening, registering the fact that Stefana and Pavel are being hospitable to me beyond all obligation or expectation. Early in the morning, I'm awakened by the cock-a-doodling of a rooster, emerging from a courtyard somewhere outside the window.

In the morning, Stefana takes me for an introductory walk to the local food market. The streets, on this first walk, emanate a sort of absolute dismalness, a dismalness so beyond the ordinary that it's almost ineffable. The heat, even in these early hours, is close and heavy. The air is filmed with dust. Forbiddingly broad avenues are torpid with emptiness. For a while, we walk along nicer streets—trees, low villas, a pretty church. Then the market announces its proximity by the acrid smell of vegetal rot. Within a small square, there's a roofed-over area with stalls selling a few vegetables, seeds, goat cheeses. Outside, people have set out their goods on newspapers, right on the ground; there's lots of eggplant, some mangy apples and pears. Rivulets of mingled waste add to the pungent odor.

Stefana looks on the market as a sign of improvement, of relative plenty. But for public food supplies, this seems to be about it. Surrounding the square are "food stores" of a grotesque character. The windows are encrusted with filth, the interiors are perversely large, cavernous, dank; the paint has long ago peeled off, the floors are exposed concrete. On the shelves, nothing: the great Eastern European *nada,* the Balkan *nada.* In one, a display of boxes with corn flour; in another, a row of cans of preserved fruit on a shelf and a large milk canister outside. But Stefana says she wouldn't touch the milk, which is often spoilt by the time it has arrived here from the countryside. There's a queue in front of one store: that means, Stefana says, that there's fresh bread. Despite the heat, I feel a cold touch of something like devolution, deathliness; why is this acceptable, this slide into chaos? Why isn't everyone shouting in protest? Instead, women walk into those ghastly interiors; in the street, groups of open-shirted men hang about. There's little movement, and almost no noise, as if there were no energy to expend even on talk.

After buying a few vegetables, Stefana takes me down Calea Victoriei, the main "boulevard," to show me some of the memorial spots of the "revolution"—whatever its accurate name might be. Stefana looks and acts much younger than her years, and her face has a fragile loveliness. She grew up in Cluj-Napoca before the war, and became a Communist after. She stayed in the party in a pro forma way, as one of its low-rung members, though for many years now she's participated in Pavel's subversive activities. She's a sociologist with a special expertise in the media, but she's as much in the dark about what really happened during the "revolution" as everyone else. Like everyone else, she probes the unsolved questions with the obsessiveness that comes from knowing that something is resisting your efforts at clarity.

Where Calea Victoriei enlarges into the Piaţa Gh. Gheorghiu-Dej, signs of recent violence become depressingly visible. The Athenée Palace, a hotel whose interior still shows signs of faded glory, is heavily pockmarked with bullets. The National Library, which lost thousands of books, looks severely damaged behind its scaffolding, as does the Palais Royal, which housed the Foreign Ministry. Not so the party headquarters, which got off scot-free, though it's close to the other buildings. Why this was so is one of the questions people worry obsessively. Does it mean that the party was involved in the coup against Ceauşescu? That

a deal was struck about who would take over after his dethrone-
ment? Nine months after the changes, Bucharest air is still full of
rumors, interpretations, conjectures, and no certainties.

A short distance from these landmarks is the Piaţa Universitate, which commemorates the next watershed events, the next
bout of violence. Here, in June 1990, a months-long student
sit-in was brutally ended by miners summoned by Iliescu from
the north. Since then, a sort of organic shrine has been growing
in this spot. On the façades of the Law and Architecture faculty
buildings, cloth banners have been stretched out, proclaiming, A
ZONE FREE OF NEO-COMMUNISM, and HERE MURDER WAS COM-
MITTED—WALK WITH RESPECT." In the niche of one façade, a portrait of Marian Munteanu, the student leader who was badly
beaten by the miners, is framed by dried flowers and a black
banner. On the street, there are black covered metal braziers
with glowing coals and candles. A small crowd is milling around,
as it does each evening.

Throughout Eastern Europe, new sacred spots have been
erected, honoring the revolution's protagonists and martyrs. But
this improvised shrine is more dramatic than any of them and
more live, the way volcanoes are live; its strength doesn't seem
quite spent, the possibility of another eruption implicit in the
still-glowing embers.

The Group for Social Dialogue was founded by a constellation
of intellectuals and artists shortly after the "events" to provide a
forum for independent discussion of social and political issues.
At the outset, there were high hopes for the group, which might
have brought a genuine critical voice in a country where, for all
intents and purposes, there are no significant political organizations aside from the government. The two "historical" parties,
springing from the old Peasant and Liberal parties, have hardly
any voice or popular support. And, in contrast to the three
northern countries in Eastern Europe, such seeds of dissidence
as existed here were completely dispersed and quashed during
the Ceauşescus' reign; as a result, there are no structures to pro-

vide a springboard for oppositional politics. But for all the hopes invested in it, I'm told that the Group for Social Dialogue has spent most of its time bickering, and has so far accomplished very little.

Its headquarters, however, serve as a casual center of information for the few interested foreigners—a valuable role in Romania, where anything resembling information is hard to come by. The building in which the group is housed, a nice turn-of-the-century residence, belonged, under the pharaonic order of the Ceausescu regime, to one of the Ceauşescus' sons; now there's a decent office, and a few academic types milling around.

In the marble-floored foyer, a man who's referred to as "the artist" says he'll show me some video documentaries on the miners. Then he says he can't do it, maybe later. This goes on for some days, in a disconcertingly muddled way. Eventually, though, I catch him at the right moment. He sets up the equipment, and a young woman appears from somewhere to watch with me, and to translate the spoken part into very broken English. But the images, raw and unedited though they are, are mostly self-explanatory. There are shots of the students sitting in the Piaţa Universitate, well-known figures making impassioned speeches, everyone singing instantly composed songs. They sat in the square for many weeks, demanding that the government cleanse itself of "neo-Communism." One song asserts, "I'm a hooligan," which transmutes this insult into an honorific. "The only contribution of Iliescu is to make this word noble," a speaker says. To my surprise, though, the young woman who's translating says the students didn't behave as well as they should have, that they irritated people by singing and playing late into the night. That's why so many people were happy when the miners came in. It's obvious that she was on the students' side, but she seems unwilling to rise to sharp anger or a definite position.

Then the miners. Their arrival on the outskirts of Bucharest is recorded in eerie quiet; they wear large helmets, they wield leather sticks, they have young, eager faces. Shift to downtown

Bucharest. The miners are running seemingly at will, chasing people, closing in on a man, beating a woman. "I was there," the girl next to me says. "They beat you for nothing. If you wore jeans, that meant you had dollars and were a traitor. If you wore a short skirt, you were a slut." The miners are going at it with zest, with glee. An elderly gentleman shouts at them, "This is not a revolution, it's a victory of the state. Shoot me if I don't say the truth." Others, however, make a victory sign at the miners and point at people, as if to say, "Beat this one." Then the miners are boarding the trains to go back home. They swing their sticks nonchalantly against their leather boots; they have flowers on their helmets; anyone can appropriate symbols of innocence and sweetness. They look pleased, satisfied with a job well done. One says happily, "For liberty!" Some women run up, handing them more flowers.

I walk back to Stefana's in a gloomy mood. There's something I don't *get*. I don't understand how Iliescu, who hopes to be a credible figure of the new age, could have chosen a tactic so redolent of fascism; I don't understand how he retains his popular support. This implies not only particular aberrations, but different norms; and like all encounters with a deeply different sense of reality, this one is disturbing. In the evening, while we sit in the single pool of light over the table, Stefana goes over the litany of questions surrounding those strange and surreal events. Why did Iliescu have to summon the miners in the first place? Is it because the police and the army wouldn't follow his orders? And who instigated the atmosphere of unrest that made the restoration of order ostensibly necessary? Among people who landed in jail afterward, there were many who were simply "riff-raff," who looked as if they had been taken out of other jails or madhouses. Certainly they were not the kind of people who would have been capable of organizing anything. Stefana is distressed by these quandaries. She knows where she stands better than most people in Romania; but even her style is too gentle for outright outrage.

But then, nobody I've talked to has sounded shocked about

what has happened; nobody has spoken in the tones of unequivocal condemnation I keep expecting, even waiting for. Yes, what happened was terrible, people say, but Iliescu isn't ill intentioned after all, just not all that competent; anyway, he's the best we have for now. Somehow, through this ambivalence or fatalism, the miners' violent advent, seemingly so straightforwardly unacceptable from a "normal" point of view, is accepted, incorporated into the muddle and murk of conjectures, interpretations, rumors.

I brave a walk through downtown Bucharest on my own. More esthetic torment, of the kind that's nearly indistinguishable from moral torment. Aside from its man-made catastrophes, Bucharest was visited by the natural disaster of an earthquake in 1977, and most buildings in the central downtown area have been constructed since then. But they already have that look of dilapidation, as if their natural state were regression into decay. The heat is laden, movements lethargic. Some "stores," with windows clotted by dirt. The few woebegone items visible behind them—some toys, crates of orangeade, cans of shaving cream—add to the sense of absurdity, of an antiworld.

I feel my own steps slowing down. It's the heat and the physical surroundings, and also the people around me. On first impression, I find the anonymous Bucharest crowd as disturbing as those eerie buildings. I know that one of the things that Ceauşescu managed to ruin, through lack of medicines and awful living conditions, was the health of Romania's citizens—and the ravages of the regime seem to show on people's bodies. The Bucharest faces are pasty, pale, prematurely worn; bodies often contorted in odd ways, sometimes deformed. But there's something else that troubles me—a sort of amorphousness of feature, a lack of sharpness, of expressive definition. It's something that Olivia Manning noticed in her *Balkan Trilogy* as well. Can it be that the long confusions of history—and no country has had a more muddled past than Romania—can show on people's faces as well? And everywhere clusters of aimless men. The only spots of vivid color are provided by a few women dressed in cheap, overbright fabrics and made up with a garishness that may be meant to compensate for everything around them. On the way back to Stefana's, I stop at an open-air "café," which has been pointed out as a new, hip place; but there's no coffee, and the only cold drink it offers is that yellowish liquid I remember all too well from Transylvania.

Elsewhere in Eastern Europe people debate how much they're a part of the "real" Europe; but Bucharest seems barely to cling to the edge of the continent, threatening to fall off into some other space, some other idea entirely.

Stefana takes me to visit a friend of hers, a woman whose career as a journalist has been revived under Iliescu. We climb a dark staircase and come into a tiny, dusty apartment. Stefana's friend, Anna, is tall, very dark, with highly pronounced features. She wears a long, very décolleté dress, and to me she looks somewhat Turkish.

Anna worked for many years at the national radio station, until that institution came to the tender attentions of Elena Ceauşescu. All Romanian culture was Elena's imperial province, and to come to her attention was never propitious. For no discernible reason, Madame Ceauşescu executed a purge at the station and fired about eighty people. In the lexicon of Communist caprices, these mass, arbitrary firings were a Romanian specialty, adding to that sense of monstrous whimsicality, of absurdity, that people have tried to convey to me when they describe the atmosphere of those years.

I ask Anna if her colleagues at the station protested, got together. "Are you kidding?" she says, emitting a great, hoarse laugh. "It was against the law to send a memo signed by more than one person. So you can imagine what the laws were about getting together."

But did people at least commiserate privately, or talk about what might be done? I persist. I'm transposing the Polish experience onto this situation; but things were different here. Anna shrugs expressively. "With informers everywhere? We were scared. We were cold. We had enough problems getting through the winter. We stayed at home."

For several years after being fired, Anna worked as a ticket seller in a movie theater; then, "somebody" who was highly positioned intervened with "somebody" else, and she was allowed to work inside the theater, as an assistant to the manager. After the "events," a friend of hers, who had been barred from practicing journalism for twenty years, was asked to run the formerly Communist newspaper and invited Anna to work for him.

In Romania, as elsewhere in Eastern Europe, hundreds of newspapers and journals have sprung up practically overnight; but most of them, I've been told, are not much more than rumor mills, churning out misinformation from different points of view. Anna certainly doesn't believe in distorting facts, but neither does she believe in anything like journalistic "objectivity." In her view, a journalist is somebody who has interesting thoughts and opinions. She writes about the government and about politics, but when I ask her where she gathers her material, she tells me she gets it from television—itself government-controlled—and from her own head. The more investigative, or reportorial, mode of journalism, she says, is here practiced only by scandalmongers who intrude on people and reveal gossipy details of their lives. She is hardly troubled by any of this—as if the entities known as "facts," or "impartiality," or "the truth," unattainable though they all undoubtedly are, didn't even constitute an important standard. But then the ideal of "objective" journalism hasn't arrived fully anywhere in Eastern Europe—it's another one of those notions that may be less natural than we suppose.

And what is her opinion of the government about which she writes, I ask her? Does she approve of what Iliescu has been doing? Well, not exactly, she says; though she doesn't exactly disapprove. . . . That curious amorphousness again. Anna is a person of obvious vitality and intelligence, and, as so often here, I'm puzzled by her reluctance to form a conclusion, to say "yes" or "no," to rise to anger, or to a definite point of view.

Stefana and I walk back in midevening, through streets that are entirely dark, dark the way country woods get dark, but never city streets. In this fairly central part of Bucharest, there are no street lamps or lights from the surrounding buildings. A heavy fog thickens the air, and it takes me a while to make out the pavement beneath my feet. Stefana reminisces about long, ice-cold winters, when Ceauşescu cut off the heating in his citizens' houses and in most public spaces—another one of his monstrous measures, meant to save money and keep Romania debt-free. Debt-free and miserable. Old people sometimes froze in their homes; children died. Stefana suffered terribly. There was no relief from the cold: actors shivered through performances in icy theaters, as did their audiences. Often, the electricity went out not only on the streets but in people's houses as well; and then Bucharest subsided into huddling, preindustrial darkness.

Stepping gingerly over the cobblestones, we're startled by a man who is suddenly standing right next to us, like a materialized specter. In the pitch black, we didn't see him walking toward us. He wants to know the time. We answer his innocuous request and walk on, stumbling a bit. I imagine years of this darkness, and months of vicious cold, and I think it's no wonder that people lost the energy to fight, to resist, perhaps even to hope.

But when I ask Stefana how she felt about coming back to this after a year in New York, she says, "Oh, I was so happy to be home I almost cried." This is what cannot be fathomed from the outside: the million tendrils that attach us to home ground, even when the ground is harsh; sometimes, perhaps, especially because it is harsh.

Among all the shortages in Romania, perhaps the most serious is the shortage of a usable past. The recent past represents a kind of negative capital, an almost pure deficit. And, if the new goal is something like a pluralist democracy, the longer past has few precedents for it, few points of reference around which new ideas might coalesce. Romania's history is marked by discontinuities more than continuities, by oppression more than by independence, by various forms of authoritarianism more than by liberalism.

Why, or how, a collective past should matter in the present has always been a puzzlement to me, and I don't believe that the mere act of remembrance is a guarantee of learning, of profiting from experience. And yet today's Eastern Europe is a living lesson in how much it does matter. It matters if you had a grandmother who, in your childhood, told you tales of a time in which heroes fought for everyone's freedom; or if, in your high school days, you read about visions of a good society; or if, for that matter, the family lore included the memory of an energetic uncle who started a little store with his two friends, which then developed into quite a business and began exporting hat pins to America. It matters, because such stories point you toward certain standards and actions; they humanize ideas; they make it plausible that you might fight for freedom, too, or take a risk of opening a store all your own.

One day, I talk to Daian Daianu, an economist who believes that even economic reform is very much dependent on certain social legacies. "Nobody knows how to do the transition in Romania," he says, "because there's no social base, no traditions from which to start."

Daian himself is a rarity in Romania, a young man wearing a neat T-shirt tucked into neat pants, with an American-inflected manner and the confidence of technocratic expertise. In the recent old days, he tried to analyze how the economic system of socialism was "flawed in its genetic code." Needless to say, he didn't get much help in this project from his teachers, and one of the reasons he could publish at all was that his studies were too sophisticated for most of his colleagues to understand. He's just started an institute for economic research financed, he tells me with great pride, by Western money.

But despite his self-assurance, Daian admits to being entirely stymied by his country's current situation. "The problem is a lack of a lived collective experience," he says. "In Poland, there was a decade of Solidarity. People learned how to get together, how to act on their own. That's why their reform got off the ground so quickly. "Here, we don't know how to trust each other. We have this habit of waiting for the authorities to solve everything. Or we keep waiting for the West to come to the rescue. Well, we've waited, and the West isn't coming. We have to learn how to do things ourselves."

But how does a country get a jump-start from a state of muddled paralysis? The question, in Romania, is not so much what comes first, the chicken or the egg, as whether there *is* a chicken or an egg; and without a past in which they already existed, how are they supposed to spring into being?

In the dark post office, I request postcards, and am given yellowish pieces of paper with nearly erased images of Bucharest at its ugliest. "Garbage," comes a succinct comment from a teenage boy, dressed in an oversize Hawaiian shirt with black smudges on his face. Then this scampish-looking personage follows Stefana and me resolutely into the street. "America is not so expensive," he declares defiantly. "No?" I say, surprised. "No," he says. "See? You can get an apartment there for $200." And he shows me a crumbling piece of paper, which, on closer inspection, turns out to be an ad page from a Los Angeles newspaper. It looks as though he's hoarded it for years. I don't think he's likely to find apartments at this price nowadays, I tell him. But he looks skeptical, trails after us, and keeps grilling us with questions. "How much does it cost to buy food each month? How much for the subway?" I try to satisfy him with some figures, which he writes on the palm of his hand. "What do you plan to do in America?" I ask him. "There are many rich people in America, I'll work for them." "And what about going to school? How are you going to do that?" "I think many great businessmen didn't go to school. I think Andrew Carnegie didn't go to school." Then he runs off.

Ah yes, the American dream in its pure form, undisturbed by any information. Who knows, though, perhaps he has the right entrepreneurial spirit, I say to Stefana. But she looks upset. She's heard stories of exactly such urchins making their way to the land of myth, and promptly being recruited into drug or prostitution rings. Of course, that's the more likely outcome.

⬤nce again, stereotypes prove to be archetypes. General Culda, with whom I have arranged an interview, fits my preconception of a certain kind of military man perfectly. He could come out of a group photograph of a Latin American junta, or a Philippine one. He's short, compact, stocky, and he holds himself very straight. He's wearing a short-sleeved military jacket; his eyes are pale blue. He has brought a bit of an entourage to our meeting, and there are two other men in uniform in the room as well, one of whom translates our conversation.

The general, who is highly positioned in the Romanian army, is the first person I've talked to here who enjoys the luxury of unambiguous views, and a rhetoric to go with them. He refers unhesitatingly to "the values of the nation" and "the supreme patriotic values," which the army is supposed to protect. He talks frequently about certain "elements" within society that don't sufficiently respect those values, and about the necessity of "playing by the rules," a phrase he seems to relish. I am fascinated by the predictability of his persona, the repetitiousness of his language; does he believe what he says? When language becomes formulaic, it loses the sound of personal conviction; and yet it occurs to me that taking on the formulas of one's faith is one of the symptoms, or expressions, of belief.

In the general's view, it was, of course, the elements that refused to play by the rules that were the cause of all the recent troubles. But was it really necessary, I ask, to summon the miners?

He gives me a sideways glance. "Were you in the country then?"

I admit that I wasn't.

"Then let me provide you with some details," he offers politely.

This is his version of the events I've heard so endlessly, and fruitlessly, analyzed: For many weeks, forces that didn't respect the rules of the game occupied Piaţa Universitate. Traffic was blocked. There was a tendency to "disorientation of the people"—i.e., people were getting the wrong ideas—which the elements tried to augment in illegal ways. They made unfounded affirmations—especially that some persons shouldn't have power. They said the majority of Romanians couldn't understand the situation and the minority had a right to impose a solution. They weren't democratic.

Nevertheless, the authorities restrained themselves from the use of force. "I was many times asked by correspondents from Rome and Paris," the general says, invoking, like everyone else, the opinions of the West, "how long we would tolerate this."

Finally, on June 13, as the election was approaching, an intervention was called for. In the morning, "the forces of order" liberated Piaţa Universitate, and "Bucharest sighed with relief." But the unruly elements attacked again; they burned police cars and attacked the remaining policemen so violently that the latter practically ran away.

Fortunately, at just about that moment, the representatives of the true will of the people were rising up in spontaneous outrage in the north. "We now know," the general asserts, "that even before the appeal of the president, thousands of people, and not only miners, started to move toward Bucharest. You must understand that people living outside of Bucharest thought that the population of the capital is corrupted."

This climate of opinion, the general adds, explains why the miners went directly to the headquarters of the opposition parties, where they found such illegal objects as bottles with gas for Molotov cocktails. Another interesting aspect of the atmosphere was that sometimes people gave the miners wrong information about innocent people whom they wanted attacked out of personal revenge. This accounts for some excesses committed by the miners, which were unfortunate. But the main problem was the forces that refused to play by the rules of the game.

And there it is, a perfectly consistent counter-story, with its counter-version of the bad and the good. Later, in conversations with friends, the interpretations, the conjectures, the exegeses begin again. Why did the general concoct that nonexplanation about the miners' attacks on the opposition parties? And how did the miners know their addresses in advance? There are so many details that don't fit. The powerful have the advantage of coherence, among others. Like the author of a whodunit, they know what happened and the picture they want to convey, while their "readers"—who are unfortunately also the objects of their actions—have only fragments and clues and a sense that something is rotten somewhere in the state. And in Romania, there is still no belief that the sources of that rottenness can be discovered, questioned, called into account. Power—which has become so much more transparent elsewhere in Eastern Europe—is here still opaque and mystified, unreadable.

But curiously enough, the general, too, has his mystifications, his belief in a force that lurks ominously within events: for him, this force is embodied in the Hungarians. Throughout our conversation, he returns to the Hungarians as to an *idée fixe,* no matter what my question, or the subject at hand. The Hungarians, to him, seem to be the explanation behind the explanation for most of Romania's woes, the "elements" behind the other elements. The general believes that the Hungarians in Transylvania are fomenting unrest in the country; that the ultra right-wing organization Vatra Romanesca is only responding to their provocations; that Romania's poor reputation in the world is the work of Hungarian disinformation. "I wouldn't say that Hungary is preparing a war," he says, "but this is a nonclassical way of fighting, involving the manipulation of public opinion and information. That's what a modern army has to be prepared for and we're trying to develop methods for this kind of warfare."

The general speaks about the Hungarians obliquely, and with sideways, foxy glances; he's giving me to understand that there's more to it than he's willing to say, and much more than meets the eye. Even those at the center of power, apparently, seek a power somewhere else—a dark hidden cause, the secret agent that makes the exercise of absolute will impossible after all.

"A Hungarian," "a Romanian," "a Pole," "a Czech": after they've been invoked again and again, as if they were concrete entities, they begin, on the contrary, to seem like figures of allegory, hobbling across an abstract, worn landscape of the mind. What can such designations mean in a world in which it takes less time to go from Poland to Hungary than to sit through a Woody Allen movie, and in which most computers in Slovakia are IBM compatible? But the problem is that these essences have so much history behind or within them. One day in Bucharest, I talk to Zoia, a mild, thoughtful woman with good liberal convictions. I expect to hear from her a benign view of the Hungarian-Romanian relations. Instead, she speaks passionately about the cruelty of the Hungarians when they were the overlords in Transylvania; she remembers stories of mistreatment and injustice from her parents. "I'm not a prejudiced sort of person," she says, "but the Hungarians are arrogant. They think we're lower. They treated us like slaves. We've been a slave nation for a long time, and we're still people who walk with our heads bent."

I ask whether it changes matters that there are only two million Hungarians in Transylvania now, to eight million Romanians, a ratio that surely isn't conducive to Hungarian arrogance. But the whole question clearly strikes a chord not easily recomposed just because the reality has changed. The centuries of injuries and inequities have now been distilled into abstract entities— "Romanian," "Hungarian"—that continue to wreak their own damage. Many times throughout my travels, I've thought of *Huckleberry Finn,* and the feud he describes in the remote American South—that absurd, violent quarrel whose causes have long been forgotten, and of which the only thing that remains is the obligation, the duty, to revenge.

In Bucharest itself, I keep thinking of Olivia Manning's *Balkan Trilogy,* that awkwardly written trio of novels, which nevertheless conveys something about Romanian atmosphere that's still palpably recognizable today. The first volume is set on the eve of and during World War II, but Manning's descriptions convey exactly the same murkiness on the political scene, the gossip, the rumors, the corruption and official ruthlessness. It's true that in her Bucharest—Manning spent several years here—there was an abundance of food, and of sleazy, wealthy aristocrats, as well as impoverished peasants. But otherwise she saw the same apathy and disarray, and sudden seizures of power. Manning's narrating Englishwoman is both repelled and fascinated by the scene around her, and full of sharp observations and judgments, which are not so much wrong as insufficient to the vague and amoral depths of what's going on around her.

But then I remember Paul Goma, a Romanian writer who suffered his share of persecution, but who, in his memoir, writes about his country with sensuous lyricism. He grew up in a village near the Russian border, and he remembers the nearly subhuman conditions of the peasants huddled in their huts, the whimsical political injustices, and the discomfiting proximity of Bolsheviks and of war. But his pages are also filled with memories of animated landscapes, precocious sexual initiations, interesting local eccentrics, and the excitement and interest of close, uninhibited human contact. That perhaps is one of the clues to the strong attachment that people in Eastern, and Central, and Central-Southern Europe so often feel for their countries, and the nostalgia they unaccountably express when they leave: that human behavior in this part of the world has been less encumbered than in the West by puritanism, or individualism, or an excessive sense of self-importance requiring a commensurate dignity and distance. From my Polish childhood, I can intuit this much: that what Goma describes is a more intimate proximity between people, with all the excesses of love and hatred that follow—and with the binding power of both.

The sense of place received from the outside is always incommensurate with the view from the inside, and perhaps nowhere more so than in Romania. As long as I maintain my usual points of reference, my "standards," my sharp observer's distance, life here seems practically impossible. But after a few days—perhaps because I have no choice—I yield to a sort of negative capability. I begin to relax into the ambiguity and lassitude of my surroundings as into a bath. Once I do, an interesting transformation occurs: all the conditions that seemed unbearable begin to seem quite tolerable. I fall into an oddly carefree humor. It's as if the usual strain of being on good behavior, of internal *trying,* even if it's unclear what the aim of that trying is, has gone by the wayside. There's no point in any sort of effort, pretension, affectation, keeping a stiff upper lip or putting on a brave front in Bucharest. One might as well relax. Temporarily, I lose the sense of how to judge anything at all; but I begin to understand how people got through.

On my tenth day in Bucharest, I see meat displayed in a store window. It comes in the form of quartered cow carcasses hanging from ceiling hooks, still dripping blood. Some people are sitting inside the store, right under the unsightly slabs. For some reason, no crowds are pressing to buy. I spend a few long seconds staring at the shop window; the sight of meat is very startling. But why aren't there long queues in front of the store? Does everybody know it's bad? I never find out; the scene remains an unintelligible snapshot, another piece of Romanian surrealism.

Casa Scînteii, where I go to visit Nicolae Manolescu, the editor of the journal *Romania Literara,* literally means *House of the Spark,* but its informal name until recently was *The House of Lies,* and currently it's been renamed *The House of the Free Press.* The House is one of those wedding-cake structures that the Soviets in their largess either donated to the fraternal countries or demanded to be built as a sign of allegiance. This one, in addition to the campy architecture, has that special Romanian *je ne sais quoi,* the look and feel of far-gone disintegration. Mainly, the effect comes from the unlit halls through which people bustle as if they were on the Champs-Élysées, and from the dubious smells emanating from the walls and floors.

The *Romania Literara* office, however, combines disintegration with faded elegance. The glass covering Mr. Manolescu's desk is cracked, and there are also yawning cracks in the walls, which date from the 1977 earthquake. But there's a long, thick wood conference table and chairs with worn plush seats.

Romania Literara has for many years been acknowledged as Romania's premier literary journal, and Nicolae Manolescu himself has credentials as one of the most impeccably uncompromised public figures in the country. He exudes an ebullient energy, and his face is enlivened by a look of perpetual mischief. He comments wryly on the poor state of Romania ("If we had had capitalism in Romania, we would have destroyed that too; we're masters in this destruction"), yet expresses surprising optimism about the future. The staff of *Romania Literara* gathers in the office; they make me feel immediately at home. They are like staffs of literary journals everywhere—sharp, nervous, ironic, amiable. They show me some issues of *Romania Literara* that appeared during the week of August 23 in years past. Until now, August 23, which marked the anniversary of Romania's liberation by the Soviet army, was celebrated as the national independence day, and during Ceauşescu's time, it turned into an occasion of collective obeisance to the ruling family. The first pages of *Romania Literara* from recent August 23 issues are covered with gigantic photographs of the Ceauşescus and headlines in praise of the great leaders. It makes a shocking impression—especially since the Ceauşescus so completely lack anything like dignity or charisma. They look, rather, like small-time parvenus, on whose faces shrewd suspicion and self-satisfaction sit together in an unpleasant mix. "The real *Romania Literara* starts on page five," one of the editors explains, "and from there, it's untouched. That was the trade-off." A better trade-off than for most publications, which were permeated by genuflections through and through.

A young writer, smoking nervously, tells me that they were pressured to write pro-Ceauşescu articles frequently, but that it was possible to resist, even though just about everyone assumed you couldn't. It was probably this assumption that decimated organized intellectual resistance as much as anything else. Very few dared test the actual powers of the Securitate, which purveyed the impression that its tentacles spread everywhere. Then there was the capriciousness, the sheer unpredictability of the Ceauşescus, who ruled by personal whim more than by any discernible rules.

"And the Ceauşescus were just the latest in a line of farcical figures who have held power in Romania," one of the editors tells me, dragging on his cigarette. "It's no accident, you know, that Ionesco emerged from here. To him, theater of the absurd was merely theater of the real."

Nor have the pressures under which the writers in this room work been lifted entirely. Several of them have been the targets of slanderous articles and threatening phone calls from the "official" journalists—the very same ones who used to harass them in the past even though their power is supposed to have waned. What are they doing now, exactly? I ask. In other post-Communist countries, the former "official" writers have mostly kept a low profile. "They're riding the strong horses," Mr. Manolescu answers—that is, betting on the new politicians—and apparently allowing themselves a little personal intimidation still.

In the evening, Mr. Manolescu invites me, and several writers, to dinner at Capsa, which used to be the prewar hangout of Bucharest's glitterati, and which is always mentioned as the one "good" restaurant in town. Indeed, with its white tablecloths and discreet lamps affixed to wooden wainscoting, in the local context Capsa looks positively opulent, though the effect is somewhat undermined by the sweltering, stuffy heat of this summer evening, and by the two-hour wait for dinner.

While we nurture our hopes for food, we console ourselves with tepid beer, which is the butt of jokes between the guests and the waiters. The conversation, however, flows more flavorfully, even though some of it is conducted in halting or translated English. "I know about three thousand words in English," one of the writers says mournfully, "but they happen not to be the words Ms. Hoffman is using tonight." Usually, the communication gap is filled by Magda, a vivacious woman who is Mr.

Manolescu's assistant, and a writer herself. Everyone is in excellent humor, even though the writers—perverse breed that they are everywhere—confess that they are nervous about their new literary freedoms. "There are no more alibis," Constantin Țoiu, one of Romania's best-known older novelists, says ruefully. He means that they can no longer hide behind the veils of symbolism and coding to which the writers in Eastern Europe have become so accustomed. The Aesopian style has suddenly been rendered as old-fashioned as medieval allegory, and for similar reasons. The ancient allegories derived their existence from a common, Biblical system of reference. The games of allusive hide-and-seek that Eastern European writers played made sense only by reference to an all-encompassing system at which everybody could wink together, or against which writers and readers colluded in a mutually understood conspiracy. Now writers have to find ways to say what they mean straight out—perhaps the hardest trick of all. "I don't know if I can do it at my age," Mr. Țoiu, white-haired and charming in an old-world manner, confesses. "Perhaps it'll turn out that I have very little to say."

Mr. Manolescu teases another writer, Augustin Buzura, by saying, "He is—that is, was—the best writer in Romania. Until now."

"You mean he has to prove himself all over again?" I ask.

"I do, it's true," Mr. Buzura says, assuming a hangdog look. "And then I'll have to wait for Manolescu to tell me if I've managed to do it."

A whole transvaluation of literary values is taking place in Eastern Europe, and, like all transvaluations, it's affecting the past as well as the future. Books that were significant as coded *cris de liberté* may—many of them undoubtedly will—turn out to be perfectly uninteresting, now that freedom can be taken for granted.

This, however, doesn't mean that the writers caught in the middle of this theoretical twist can't eat, drink, and be merry. After dinner—adequate enough, once it arrives—Buzura suggests that we all go to Piața Universitate, where "something" is sup-

posed to be happening. Before dinner, we saw a crowd gathering
there, larger and more restless than usual.

Now, as we approach through the dark streets, we make out
an eerie sight. Several dozen policemen are unhurriedly arrang-
ing themselves into a neat rectangular formation. In the darkness, their shadowy silhouettes are offset by rows of long, white
shields, held in front as by medieval knights. On the other side
of an invisible dividing line, a crowd huddles into a tighter mass.
Once they've readied themselves into perfect symmetry, the policemen advance upon the crowd in concert. Simultaneously, the
crowd moves forward in an almost ceremonial surge and then re-
cedes like a wave. The policemen step back. Then they move forward again, as in a dance, a Kabuki representation of "threat," a
shadow play.

"Happenings," Manolescu says merrily. Buzura watches and
watches. Manolescu watches him watch. "Ah, the writer," he
says. "A scene in his next novel."

Undoubtedly. Eastern European writers have their subjects
still. At the moment, though, nobody understands the meaning
of the event we're looking at so intently. Is it a protest? Is it organized? By whom? The next day, there are a few arrests; then
the rumors, interpretations, conjectures. For now, this is a minor
episode in the theater of Romanian politics. But this is theater
that has a way of turning real. Nobody knows whether this is a
gathering tragedy or a farce; nobody knows what comes next.

What is it that marks the atmosphere as Romanian as soon as I
disembark at the airport a year later? There's always, in a new
place, as in meeting a new person, that moment of whole perception, of sure intuition. Then the certainty dissolves into a hundred pieces, and subtleties begin to pile upon ambiguities. It
takes many reformulations of understanding to put the fragments
together again into something like a whole picture. But for a few
moments, as I arrive in Bucharest the second time, it seems to
me that I see a piece of Romania before my eyes. Perhaps it's the
hopeless, starved-looking mutt following passengers pleadingly

on its crooked legs; perhaps the crumpled, faded faces with that oddly despoiled look. Two men, their shirts hanging out of their pants, circle around the small waiting space and then huddle, exchanging some confidences; God knows what *bizhnitze* they're engaged in. Another man attaches himself to me as soon as I come through passport control, muttering "Taxi" in a voice that is both obsequious and insistent. "No," I keep saying, since I'm waiting for Stefana. It doesn't help. He trails after me to the telephone and to the bench, now joined by a buddy of his, and keeps whispering "Taxi" until I snap "No!" so abruptly that they both jump back a little and leave me alone, though they keep eying me from a safe distance, in case I change my mind.

Stefana appears, followed by thick-necked Mr. Gradici, who drives us into town in his funereal vehicle with ceremonial slowness. In her apartment, there are hot water, vodka, Domna Florica's ingenious salads, Pavel, and good conversation.

There's even something like pleasure in seeing Bucharest again—perhaps the sheer pleasure of familiarity, or of subsiding into those slower, lazier rhythms. But the main parts of the city look unchanged since my last visit here. There are no signs of new commerce on the dusty streets, except for a dusty store selling shampoo, Scotch, and cigarettes. The store, I'm soon informed, belongs to a former Securitate man.

Among the emblematic horrors of the Ceauşescu era were his infamous projects of razing whole towns and villages, in order to give way to his own constructions, such as dams and "modern" housing projects. Fortunately, Ceauşescu didn't live long enough to carry this undertaking as far as he wanted, though something like forty habitations, including many historic buildings, fell victim to this particular caprice. Several of them are near Bucharest, and one very hot morning I set out with Stefana in Mr. Gradici's car to look at them; emblematic horrors exercise an odd fascination.

Given Mr. Gradici's stately progress, it takes us an hour to traverse the fifteen or so miles from Bucharest to the first of the villages, Vladicescu. What greets us, though, is not a village but a gaping absence. For a long stretch, after we turn off the empty main highway, there's only a bleak, flat expanse of land, stretching treelessly toward the horizon. Nothing. After several kilometers, we come upon something, a lone mark on the flatness. In the middle of the empty plain, three bare-chested men are toiling on a half-built house. When we approach, we see that they're working with straw, clay, bits of carton, planks of plywood. This will be rudimentary, but this is where two of them—a very old man and his son—lived before their village was destroyed.

When Ceauşescu decided to raze their village, they tell us, they had to leave the place where they'd always lived on two weeks' notice. They went to stay with relatives in Bucharest and got menial jobs there; they had no other choice. It was not part of Ceauşescu's plan to provide them with alternative housing or livelihood. "Fortunately," one of them says, "Ceauşescu died before he could put up anything here." So now they're reconstructing their home on exactly the same spot where it stood before. "But you know how it is," the son tells me, "there is no money. There are no materials. We just wanted to do this because father is old. He wants his home back."

Across the street, a very old woman bends painfully over buckets she's filling from a roadside well. She's taciturn when we approach; she has earned her right not to talk to intruding strangers. But as we're walking away, she calls after us, almost angrily, "I'm coming back here to die. I want to die where I was born."

Vladicescu is a site of purely wanton destruction; the next village we come to, Ghermanest, is a place of greater ambiguity. There Ceauşescu had time to execute at least part of his intention. On one side of the road, Ghermanest is a traditional village made up of colorfully painted cottages and small yards with flowers and chickens. Facing this rustic cluster from across the road is a complex of three-story buildings, hard and towering by contrast. The awful truth is, though, that the buildings are not so awful. Since they're Ceauşescu's creation, I want to hate them unequivocally; but I've seen enough such structures in Eastern

Europe to know that these are not the worst. They're painted a mellow yellow, and there are bits of vegetable gardens between the buildings. A woman is looking out the window, her big arms spread on the windowsill, observing us with interest. But when Stefana says I'm an American visitor and asks her if we could come in, she snaps, "I want to have nothing to do with the U.S.A.," and slams the window shut. Is this an old habit of fearing foreigners? Genuine antipathy?

Another young woman, though, invites us into her apartment gladly, and on entering it, Stefana and I are again ambiguously surprised. The rooms are good-sized and the kitchen has a feature almost unknown in Romania—a washing machine. Stefana and I look at each other in bafflement. The young woman tells us she prefers this to her old house, where she had to live with her husband's parents. Here she has running water, hot and cold; she doesn't have to draw it from the well. This is "modern," good for young people; only the old prefer the old houses.

When we get back into the car, Stefana admits that this doesn't correspond to her notion of what these places were. Perhaps even monsters have their ambitions—or even something like ideals. Particularly in his early phase, Ceauşescu had aspirations to become an enlightened despot, a sort of Romanian shah, who would lead his country to greatness and the modern age— even if the modernization was accomplished at the cost of terror and with an iron hand. Most Western leaders fell for Ceauşescu's line, and his defiance of the Soviet Union in foreign policy, and greeted him gladly in their capitals.

Back in Bucharest, I visit the famous Piaţa Naţiunile Unite, a plaza built by Ceauşescu as the final tribute to his own glory. It's a monument to a maddened megalomania. The promenade leading up to the square is monotonous with bigness. The sidewalks are three times as broad as normal sidewalks, the windows of the apartment buildings larger than any windows need to be. Even here, though, there are signs of an ambition to stylishness: the buildings are made of clean white stone, and their roofs, topped with fantastical statuettes, gables, and other miniature structures, seem to echo both the village esthetic of Translyvania and the oddly postmodern concoctions I've seen on a few older Bucharest buildings. Mere façadism, Stefana tells me; behind these exteriors, many apartments don't have heating or indoor plumbing; and just behind these front-line buildings there are skeletons of half-finished structures, probably destined never to be completed. For this Ceauşescu razed some of the most charming neighborhoods of Bucharest and many ancient buildings.

As we approach the centerpiece of this architectural extravaganza, the proportions get, if possible, even more bloated. In the office buildings, behind enormous windows, oversized spaces gape, dusty and empty, except for stacks of boxes rudely strewn about. And then the apex—Ceauşescu's palace itself, a gloomy monstrosity reputed to have four thousand rooms, and surrounded by a weedy field. The style is impossible to describe; there is, in effect, no style, except the campiness of failed grandeur. Here, the Communist-pharaonic disease of gigantism reached its apogee, and here Ceauşescu met his fall, when he came out on the balcony to speak to the people and the people jeered. Perhaps the fall could have been forecast from the setting, in which the logic of grandiosity without substance reached its limit and burst like an overinflated balloon. From there, it was only a few days to the Ceauşescus' absurdist escape attempts and their unceremonious execution—an event over which few shed any tears, but which nevertheless was a bizzare originating event for a new, supposedly democratic era.

Augustin Buzura, who last year was worried about maintaining his standing as Romania's best writer, is now the head of something called the Cultural Foundation, where I have some *bizhnitze* of my own to transact. The publishing house attached to the foundation would like to publish my first book, which is partly about growing up in postwar Poland, and I've been invited to talk over the terms.

I make my way there with Magda, Mr. Manolescu's assistant, who is also the book's translator; on the way, we stroll a bit through the area nearby. Here, I discover another face of Bucharest, a neighborhood of tree-lined streets and single-story houses designed with a fanciful eclecticism. Oriental coiled pillars coexist with tiled roofs, Spanish patios, and modernist symmetries. It makes me think of California's syncretic architectural fantasies, though in California the mix is a function of newness, in which all styles and significances can randomly coexist. Here the juxtapositions are a function of history and the long intermingling of many cultures. In this neighborhood, Bucharest glides off the edge of Europe not so much into the third world as into the old Orient. The rich are always with us, I think—even in Bucharest; the houses, Magda says, mostly belonged to the *nomenklatura,* and mostly still do.

There's an Oriental sense of space, too, about the room into which we're invited by the chief accountant of the publishing house—a spacious chamber, empty except for rows of tapestried chairs placed against the walls. The chief accountant and Magda try to make out phrases like "flat sum" and "royalties," which have been insouciantly mentioned in a letter from my agent. Throughout our conversation, the accountant grins an unchanging, gold-toothed grin. I grin back, in reflex mimicry. Magda keeps smiling, too. In this strained state of static politeness, we conduct our negotiations. I'm not about to bargain in Romania; but I think that Magda is being offered much too little, even by the meager local standards. When I suggest to her afterward that she might have tried to negotiate for a higher fee, she says pensively, "Yes, that's a good idea. I should become more resourceful." But I can see that the notion is novel to her, and will be hard to learn.

The accountant tells me that the number of copies printed will be decided by a central office that will gauge what the needs of the Romanian public for my book are. Centralism isn't dead; on the other hand, he mentions that in the last year something like three hundred new publishing houses and over six hundred journals and newspapers have been started—data that I find nothing short of nightmarish. I console myself, however, with the thought that most of the publications will probably disappear without a trace even before they've been registered in whatever central office takes cognizance of their ephemeral existence.

Our business completed, we bow, widen our blank smiles, and are ushered into the foyer, where Magda and I wait to see Mr. Buzura. This is not my first waiting room in Romania, and I gird myself for a long, patient stint. The people around us also wait stolidly, resignedly; they wait like people accustomed to waiting. An aged man ascertains that I'm from America, and looks at me reproachfully. "You betrayed us at Yalta!" he throws at me, in a tone that suggests that this is still a freshly rankling injury. "You abandoned us!" This is not the first time I've had this accusation hurled at me, as if from a slingshot, and for some reason, it often happens in just such waiting rooms. It's as if, for this old man, the last forty-five years were but a long interval of waiting between the moment of injustice that had paralyzed his life, and this moment, when he can finally speak of it, to whatever representative of "America" happens to appear before him. "Well, we're back," I say jokingly. He bows with a flourish.

The last time we spoke, Mr. Buzura was among those hoping for the advent of some Western prince or magnate to fund his publishing dreams. A year later, he's utterly disillusioned with such personages. "They come here, they express their interest—but when it comes to something concrete, nothing happens. Nothing," he says with gusto, his fleshy face taking on a certain firmness of anger. "I'm fed up with Western-style lies. I'm fed up with the primitive Occidental style."

I laugh. So from where he sits it's we who seem primitive! But just what does he mean?

"Well, you see, they come here, and they think in these stupid categories. Just because I run this foundation, because I'm trying to do something, they think I must be the new *nomenklatura*. They prefer to listen to somebody on the street who's shouting, 'Down with Iliescu,' because they think that's the opposition."

I am, of course, flattered to be implicitly exempt from Buzura's charges of Occidental primitivism, though I'm not sure

I should be. How am I to know what's what or who's who in this infernal Romanian muddle?

"They only understand black and white," Buzura continues. "It's primitive. It's Ceauşescu-style thinking. There's hardly any difference."

"But, you know, the Romanian scene is sometimes very confusing to foreigners," I hazard. "Full of ambiguities."

"I thought civilized people understood ambiguity," he avers with vigorous disgust. "But actually they're not interested in the first place. It's just that they wrap their refusals in such elegant packaging."

In any case, Buzura says, he's doing this job out of a sense of public duty; really, he'd much prefer to go back to his own writing pad and the secure complications of fiction. And I think I sense in him just a touch of defensiveness about holding a position with political implications. In the other Eastern European countries, this is a rare, exceptional moment when it's perfectly acceptable for the intelligentsia to collude with power—and the intelligentsia have leaped on this opportunity with an almost unseemly haste. In Romania, power is still far too suspect for such luxury of clear conscience, and the choice for the politicized intellectual is the tediously familiar one—between impure effectiveness and pure marginality.

Still, in the year between my visits, something *has* shifted, moved, crystallized in the political air—if not the chicken or the egg, then at least a Petri dish for the production of one or the other seems to have appeared. The USHR, or the Romanian-Hungarian Party, whose very right to exist was questioned a year ago, has marshaled a greater following than any of the existing opposition parties—thus repeating a pattern evident throughout Eastern Europe, in which vocal expression of ethnic prejudice seems to be belied by actual preferences and acts. Then there's been the creation of an organization—not yet a party—called the Civic Alliance, which emerged out of the Group for Social Dialogue, and which in many people's minds holds out some hope of presenting a real challenge to Iliescu's National Salvation

Front. As it happens, Mr. Manolescu is one of the alliance's leading players and its probable presidential candidate, and he invites me to come to its meeting.

So, one afternoon, I climb a wide and dusty staircase of some
official building, accompanied by the ever-vivacious Magda, and
we knock on the door of the Civic Alliance office. A young individual with a lean and hungry look opens up and immediately
tries to push us out; after Magda's protest, he questions us
sharply and closely about who we are and what we want. Finally,
he lets us in and locks the door carefully behind us. Once we're
in, however, he places himself before us and begins right off to
recount his recent political exploits. He was a crane operator, he
tells us proudly, and he was the one who destroyed, on his own
initiative, the statue of Petru Groza, Romania's first Communist
president. When I'm properly impressed, he's emboldened to tell
us that he also brought down the statue of Stalin in Braşov.
"Since childhood I've fought Communism!" he declares and
smiles a mostly toothless smile. Magda and I decide to dub him
the statue smasher.

Another man enters the large, dimly lit room, and replaces
the statue smasher beside us. He's pudgy, very soft-faced and
soft-voiced—a sort of antidote to our previous raconteur—but
he, too, launches into what's in his heart, without introduction or
ado. He's a union leader in Constanţa, a shipbuilding town on
the Black Sea, and he's preparing for a general strike, which is
supposed to start in a few days. But he doesn't know who'll join
the strike, whom he can count on. The accursed middle-level
nomenklatura is still with them, intimidating the workers and
splitting them among several unions. Some of these unions are
creatures of the government, of course, and they're claiming that
there's no need for a strike at all. His very presence here is
significant—a representative of the working class being drawn
into the political process—and he's very happy to be associated
with the Civic Alliance, where he can meet "the greatest people
in Romania," and where no one ever points out to him that he's
not a *professore*.

While he's been talking, people have been coming into the room, and now the meeting proper begins. The Civic Alliance may be the seed of the most important opposition force in Romania, but at the moment it consists of several men in shirtsleeves in this unlit, unimposing room, feeling their way forward from bare beginnings. Their budget, as far as I can make out from their discussions, comes to the equivalent of about $185. They think they need to raise more money. They also think they need a newspaper, though they can't figure out how they could subsidize it. But here my deepening horror at the proliferation of useless publications prompts me to make my only intervention in another country's political life. Perhaps they don't need a newspaper, I suggest; perhaps a bulletin would do just as well. The proposal is first greeted doubtfully, but Mr. Manolescu makes a similar one almost simultaneously, and it is adopted. I'm pleased as punch.

They discuss who to invite to their big launch meeting, at which they'll formally announce themselves as a party. Does one invite one's political enemies? This unnatural business of democracy . . .

In the meantime there's the general strike to think of. Mr. Manolescu hopes it'll happen, though it's unclear what would follow if the government were brought down. Would the Civic Alliance be ready to jump into the fray? Would he be ready to be nominated for the presidency? In a crunch, they think they could marshal their forces; but for high-level politics this seems a pretty improvised business.

Afterward, Mr. Manolescu, Magda, and I go to Capsa for another spirited conversation. Mr. Manolescu tells me he's just been accused of receiving, and pocketing, no less than one million dollars from an American organization. This bit of fiction was reported pretty much as fact on the government-controlled television. Subsequently, a journalist called him to ask what he'd done with the money. "I drank it away," he responded, but the humor was apparently lost on the interlocutor.

Like most of the new politicians emerging in Eastern Europe,

Mr. Manolescu is—in Western terms, at least—a social liberal and an economic conservative. There is, however, a purely Romanian twist to his views: he is also a royalist. If he became president, he says, he would try to bring back King Michael—the last of Romania's royals—to set up a constitutional monarchy, on the Spanish model.

I'm less astonished at this than I might be, because I've heard enough talk of the new royalism in Romania to know by now that it is a perfectly serious political posture, probably more indicative of desperation than *opéra bouffe* histrionics. King Michael, who was on the throne briefly during the war after his father was forced to abdicate, played a not-ignoble role in the anti-Fascist putsch of 1944 before abdicating himself in 1947, after the Communist "liberation." He was in his early twenties then, and for the last few decades he's been living quietly in Switzerland, one of the forgotten figures of history. But now history, in its unending turns, may make him important again. Many Romanians think that, precisely because he hasn't been implicated in the country's life since the war, he could accomplish the cut in the Gordian knot of Romanian impossibilities. "The king would be *not* Iliescu," Magda explains succinctly. "He would be something definitely different from what we have, from what we have had. The king and Iliescu?" She laughs. "No, incompatible."

Mr. Manolescu agrees that the king would be a unifying figure, who could rise above the hatreds of Romanian politics, and above general suspicion. He could play a role similar to that of the Spanish king after the fall of Franco—of a democratic arbiter whom everyone could respect without abandoning partisan loyalties. Moreover, Mr. Manolescu says, the king is an extremely nice and dignified gentleman; then he can't refrain from telling us a funny anecdote about meeting him and his wife in the United States, and we're off and running with serious joking once again. Mr. Manolescu has weighty things on his mind, but he's irrepressibly humorous and I tell him that he could become the first president of a country to introduce the ironic style into office.

"That's my dream!" he exclaims, though I wonder if any country in the world is quite ready for that.

The Intercontinental is Bucharest's "in" hotel and the approved *auberge* for foreign businessmen and journalists. It's in fact an odious place, with a graceless lobby crowded with dubious-looking characters and a bar worthy of a bus station terminal in a provincial part of Arkansas. The Interconti, as it's popularly called, does, however, have two restaurants with tablecloths and air-conditioning, and it's to one of those that I invite Ion Manolescu, a remote relation of Nicolae, and an up-and-coming young writer. My suggestion is greeted by a strained silence.

What is it, I ask? Well, you see, he says nervously, they don't always like to let Romanians in there, especially young Romanians who aren't accompanied by foreign businessmen.

Well, that's not right and we won't allow them to get away with it, I say high-mindedly, half disbelieving what he tells me anyway. I shouldn't. As Ion approaches the waiter—he's too proud to let me do it—he's greeted with a rude scowl and told that there are no tables. This is a plain lie, in view of the nearly empty room. At this point, I step into the fray, and am told that for tourists, by all means, we have another restaurant—one that charges about five times as much. We retire there, Ion looking humiliated.

After he finishes apologizing for his country, Ion tells me about his literary ambitions. He's twenty-three years old, with dark, intent eyes, and he talks a blue, but very intelligent, streak. I've heard it said often that the younger generation, not tainted or twisted by the extreme compromises of their elders, is Romania's real, perhaps its only, hope. Certainly, Ion has the impassioned, fully awake intelligence that is perhaps available only to a young man in a time when his work is more than a profession or a career—when it's charged with a sense of mission. He belongs to a group of very young writers who became besotted with the idea of literature when literature was forbidden fruit. During the dark times, they read every piece of contemporary

writing they could get their hands on: copies of novels by
Pynchon, Barth, Barthelme, left by the odd foreigner and circu-
lated till their pages crumbled, books of poetry copied by hand.

The group's most earnest desire is to make a clean break
from the recent Romanian tradition. The whole older generation
of writers is, in their eyes, if not compromised, then at least insufficient as models. "In a way, they always wrote for the censor,"
Ion says. "There's always a sort of veil, a curtain, covering everything they write." There was so much Romanian reality that has
been untouchable in print, even more than in speech. For example, Ion says, the character of a man beaten up by the Securitate
doesn't exist in Romanian literature. So one of his group's first
credos and promises was, "No allusions. No camouflage." They
want to write books in which the man beaten up by the
Securitate will exist. Indeed, there's such a character in Ion's first
novel, which he's about to publish. He and his group are confident of the book's merits, he says, as if the novel were everybody's property; and he's confident that his friends have told him
the truth. That's another thing they promised each other early
on: nothing less than the truth, no matter how uncomfortable it
may be. "Our whole society was accustomed to lies," he says.
"So we wanted a place where we could be really honest, sincere."

They've decided that the literary forte of this part of the
world will be the political novel. But not in its traditional form,
heaven forfend; he and his friends are postmodernists to the
core. "You can't write like Solzhenitsyn now," Ion says. Orwell is
more like it, though they want to be more "novelistic" than he
was. Politics, yes, but also imagination and style. And thought,
definitely thought. They're all philo-American, Ion says, partly as
a reaction to their elders' Francophilia, and they want to write
"in the American style—straight on, directly, sharply." But they
read as much French critical theory as they can get their hands
on, because they believe that you can't be a good, a great, writer
without being completely self-conscious about what you do.

I'm quite overwhelmed by this fierce seriousness, by the energy of intention, resolve, surprising knowledge. Aside from his fictional endeavors, Ion also writes political essays, not because he likes doing it, he quickly assures me, but because "in such times, one must." I doubt that such a sentence would be uttered by a twenty-three-year-old in the West; but then, Ion and his Western counterparts live in different sorts of epochs. Much as Ion aspires to be a sort of postmodernist dandy, he cannot free himself from the pressure of roiling, disturbing, hard reality.

The earnestness and the voraciousness with which Ion speaks of what he needs to read, know, do, puts me in mind of another Romanian intellectual, Mircea Eliade, in his youth—at least before he developed the dubious political convictions that took him much too close to the Fascist right for comfort. From his little eyrie in Bucharest, Eliade wanted to devour the world with an insatiable, polymathic hunger characteristic perhaps of "provincial" intellectuals for whom the great world is a remote object of desire and who don't have the anxieties, or the arrogance, of their own "major tradition" to screen them from the multiplicity of other cultures. Such marginality has often been a source of strength in the past; it may well become so again for people like Ion and his friends.

Pavel looks so much younger than his seventy years that I find it hard to reconcile his person with his age. He dresses in jeans and open-collared shirts, and his movements have the springiness and elasticity of youth. His face habitually arranges itself into an expression of skeptical bemusement, as if a flicker had settled into something more permanent. He speaks in precise, eloquent English, though he's occasionally stumped by the mysteries of the article, and he has a penchant for sharp aphorisms that whip sentences around to something unexpected but clearly just. In him, the muddle I often feel in the Romanian air has refined itself into a lucid and delicate perception of paradox, contradiction, complexity.

Odd sentences he's dropped in our conversations begin to give me clues to his history. He's somebody I've come to know quite well—and he's a species I hardly know at all: he's been one of Them, and he's been it fully and committedly. He reminds me of my father a bit, perhaps because they come from not dissimilar backgrounds; and I think, as I so often have in these travels, how easy it would have been to have a completely other fate—how much our fate chooses us, rather than the other way around. For all its terrible aspects, Pavel's could almost be my alternate family history.

Pavel doesn't talk easily about his past—not so much out of secretiveness, I sense, as out of a deeper complex of feeling. When he does, finally, decide to tell me about it, it turns out to be archetypal: a classic life of an Eastern European Communist in our time—except perhaps for its dénouement. Eastern Europe has bred such patterns, such more-than-individual lives.

There were the beginnings, at a time in which, as he puts it, "there was a great danger of evil." In Romania especially, Fascism in the interwars years was becoming a palpable, popular force. For a person like Pavel—a young Jew growing up in a desperately poor, semiliterate family—the alternatives to this force weren't many; and through a combination of chance and proclivity, Pavel was drawn into the Communist Party. He was inducted into the small, highly conspiratorial movement when he was still in his teens; but he didn't immediately become the fully obedient soldier that the movement preferred. In 1936, during the show trials in Moscow, he informed his cell liaison that he disagreed with what was going on. This youthful gesture was duly recorded and remained "a black page" in Pavel's party files for the rest of his life.

But gradually his commitment, and his capacity for obedience, deepened. Though he's one of the more erudite people I know, he never finished high school. The financial burden of sending him to school became too heavy for his mother, who was the family breadwinner; and then war and prison intervened. He continued to read voraciously, developed literary passions, and later, in prison, began to teach himself languages. But his most intense education was received from two sources: the party and prison life itself.

His first arrest came in 1940, and he stayed in jail for half a year. The second time, he was arrested by the Fascist police and that "difficult moment" brought home to him the strange contra-dictoriness of Romanian behavior. He was arraigned by the Fascists; nevertheless, a man whom he knew from the neighborhood—a member of the Iron Guard, the virulent, semi-legal Fascist organization—visited Pavel, in order to give him some useful advice on how to behave during his interrogation. On that occasion, Pavel was sent home after three days' deten-tion. A few days later, he learned that his helpful neighbor had participated in a notorious killing of fifty members of the pre-Fascist Romanian government, which included the flower of Ro-mania's political aristocracy.

"I really think the Romanians have a kind of feeling of the transitory character of everything," Pavel says, reflecting on these incidents. "Romanian Fascism was finally not very serious, and Romanian Communism wasn't all that serious, either."

Perhaps this—this sense of transitoriness, the insubstantiality of all phenomena and beliefs—may account for that amorphous-ness I've sensed in so many Romanian conversations. Why take hard positions on something that is ephemeral, that will pass anyway in the eternal flux? But that fatalism may itself spring from an irrationality of circumstances that cannot be fought, from being ruled by a succession of capricious powers imposed upon one without choice or preference.

Pavel's third arrest came in May 1941, just before Romania's formal entry into the war, and on this occasion, he was sent to a labor camp where he remained for three years. This was the formative rite of passage, the initiation shared with so many fu-ture cadres—and Pavel speaks about it as the best and the worst of times. The best thing was the company. The prison and labor camp had been built especially for Communists, and Pavel came into a group of people who would soon become the new leader-ship of the country. In their shared predicament, they achieved what he describes as a combination of solidarity and "natural hi-erarchy" that constituted a sort of microcosm of an ideal society. "It was a special experience of socialization," he says, "a small community in common danger and with a very precise distribution of roles. It was the only period in my life when I felt the *pleasure* of being a subordinate. Some of the older leaders had been in prison for ten years; some of them were extremely charismatic persons. I believed in their virtue, in their natural leadership."

Then, with an echo of the pain this discovery must have initially caused him, he adds, "But this—this pleasure in hierarchy—is exactly the condition for being a fanatical dogmatist, a Stalinist."

At the time, though, Pavel didn't understand the moral hazards of his ideal society. The esprit de corps was so strong that when Pavel's group arrived in prison they decided immediately to stage an anniversary celebration of the Russian Revolution, which consisted of a reading and interpretation of Gogol's *Inspector General.*

One of Pavel's fellow prisoners was none other than Nicolae Ceauşescu, who had also been arrested as an active young Communist. As far as Pavel was concerned, it was hate almost at first sight. For two months they shared a small cell, which included other prisoners as well, but Ceauşescu was a sullen exception to the general spirit of friendship. "We lived in conditions of intimacy, we weren't even allowed a walk in the prison yard. We were two young Communists in prison. What would have been more natural than to establish a feeling of camaraderie, to get to know each other? But no. His fundamental way of relating to others was to despise them. Psychologically, he made me think of an old Asian institution—eunuchs. The eunuchs were castrated to provide the real proof that the emperor was superior. Ceauşescu's contempt worked by the same mechanism—he was superior by denying the virtues of others. I felt in him the instinct of hatred."

Pavel remembers one incident that sealed his hostility to Ceauşescu for good. At one point, the prisoners organized a chess championship, played with pieces molded out of bread. Pavel won. "I wasn't all that great," he says, "but in this poor cell, I was the best. Ceauşescu was a beginner. But after I won, he challenged me to a match. I said it wouldn't be a pleasure for either of us. He insisted. We played. The end was predictable. But there was a post-end, which was not: he never spoke to me again."

When Ceauşescu became general secretary, Pavel expected him to become even more monstrous than he did become. "He wasn't cold, he was hot in hate. I expected him to become a kind of Stalin, to order executions. Perhaps external circumstances weren't favorable for him to act on all his wishes." To see Ceauşescu as relatively restrained surely derives from an Eastern European sense of possible extremes. Just the opposite, however, happened with Elena Ceauşescu, whom Pavel first knew as a poor, quiet young woman without any ambition, but who went on to become a gargoyle of grandiosity. It was she who forbade public birthday celebrations for anybody except herself and her husband and who prevented new admissions to the Academy of Science, because she was supposed to be a sufficient avatar of all learning. "For a while," Pavel said, chuckling, "we had quite a shortage of academicians."

But such hostile encounters were rare in prison. The real hardships were physical, and the worst of those was hunger. "Those of us who were very young had a very natural need to eat," Pavel says, as if even this bit of frailty needed to be justified. "From that point of view, prison was really horrible. The strategy—the only way to survive—was to work. I was in charge of cutting wood. I worked so hard that in the winter the upper part of my body was hot, while my feet were frozen. But the hunger was real torture, because it puts you in this internal prison. For a while, even my nightmares were about food. But at a certain moment, I accommodated, and after that, I had the advantage of losing my appetite. Even now, though I enjoy good food in good company, I feel no more need, no more necessity, to eat." I look at him questioningly and he nods; he means this literally.

Pavel emerged from prison "not only a convinced Communist, but ready for action." After the consolidation of Communist power in Romania, his prison mates in effect became the Central Committee. He was in his twenties; for a while, he worked with the youth cadres, and then was placed in the Department of Foreign Relations, where he was "in charge of the Greek civil war, and of the Yugoslav defection"—that is, of organizing the opposition to Tito. The latter task was a preparation for show trials and widespread purges; Pavel's work must have implicated him in these awful events. And both his jobs were, to put it mildly, risky; in the game of Communist politics, you never knew when loyalty would be reinterpreted as betrayal.

From his inside observation post, Pavel could witness exactly such turns, and the deadly skulduggery in which his friends were beginning to specialize. He knew about the murders that Gheorghiu-Dej, the first postwar general secretary, managed to engineer even while he was in prison. He could see how the show trials against Anna Pauker (who was herself ruthless enough to have her own husband shot) and other "right-wing deviationists" were cooked up. He saw how people who had fought in the Spanish War became targets of special, deadly reprisals, because they were needed as illustrations of a conspiracy supposedly perpetrated by Tito, who had fought in Spain as well.

In this period, what was perhaps most disturbing to Pavel was watching the people he had so much admired turning into dangerous flunkies. "It was very disappointing," he says with a dry understatement, "the transition from genuine heroism to cowardice, which I saw and which I lived. One of the most awful accomplishments of Stalinism was this combination of material, moral, and political corruption." Perhaps the worst blow came when his mentor, a man he had particularly esteemed in prison, was transferred to a new, at first mysterious, job: his task was to establish the Securitate.

What had this man been like before? I wonder. Pavel looks as if the question still causes him pain. "He was the most human of them all," he finally brings out. "He retained his humanity even after jail." It was this friend's last service to Pavel not to take him along on his new assignment. If he had entered the Securitate, Pavel thinks, he too would have become "a monster." I start to protest, but he stops me; he would have, he says with great certainty. It is precisely the fault of some systems that they are capable of transforming people this way; and the party was becoming—had long been, in fact—an infernal machine capable of making monsters of us all. "What you cannot imagine," Pavel says, as if he wanted to impress on me the horror of this, "is the interior dislocation in such a process, the desperate defeat."

And yet, despite all this, the separation from the party was as wrenching for Pavel as an act of betrayal would have been, or the loss of any deep attachment. "This is a painful process," he says, "the transition from a happy phase of life, which is life in fanaticism, to a critical approach in which you understand the discrepancy between ideals and reality. This is a process in which you hesitate repeatedly. Many times, you have either the coward-ice to agree, the humiliating heroism of keeping silent, or the risky heroism of making ambiguous statements. There were mo-ments when I was absolutely unhappy, not knowing what my duty was as a disciplined soldier of the revolution, and what it was as a human being."

I ask him whether his Jewishness played a part in his break with the party; but Pavel thinks of himself as a Romanian first. The time of Pavel's youth was probably a more secular age than ours, an age whose dreams of universalism and rational enlight-enment coursed even through the humblest citizens; his parents were nonobservant. "I'm a citizen of the world," Pavel says half-jokingly, using a phrase that comes from that earlier time. But then he corrects himself. "No, actually I belong to Romania. This is not always a happy condition"—and he smiles at his own un-derstatement. "Rationally, it's much more interesting to be a Jew than to be a Romanian, but it's not really a choice. Some people tried to impose on me the quality of being a foreigner. This is one form of anti-Semitic coercion—forcing a person to take on a Jewish identity that he may not have. I've never submitted to this coercion."

It was his temperamental resistance to any coercion that eventually enabled him to pull away from his real faith. His doubts—which he calls the first taste of freedom—grew stronger. It was becoming harder and harder for him to mask his dissatisfaction, or to accept the orders he was given. "In the fanatic period, I was happy to execute orders," he says. "Later, I was offended to get orders. I was becoming an individual, which was, from the party's point of view . . ." here he pauses to find the right word . . . "let's say 'dubious.' " By the time he decided to leave his position, he says, the apparatus wanted him to disappear as much as he wanted to leave it behind; in effect, they agreed to part ways.

In 1956, at age thirty-five, he entered the Academy of Science as a student of history and sociology. Partly, he wanted to make up for his lack of formal education, for being "an autodidact." Emotionally, the new phase of his life began with a period of something like despair—the despair of losing his faith, which was accompanied by a "deep feeling of culpability—something almost religious—a feeling of sin."

The road out of despair involved, paradoxically, going back to the sources. Like many militants, Pavel had become a Marxist without reading Marx. Now, he read him. He studied Lenin. "To have a critical approach to Lenin—that was an act of intimate heresy. In emotional terms, I couldn't separate. I needed a theoretical approach. Developing a critical approach was a way to fight against my feelings."

Part of Pavel's political psychoanalysis was to write, to explain to himself his involvement with Stalinism. He wrote obsessively; and when he had covered more than two thousand pages, he decided to burn them; they were too dangerous to have in his possession. In a society of total surveillance, however, even this act of destroying one's own writing roused suspicions. The paper was heavy, and there was a lot of smoke, and some worried neighbors came to Pavel asking him to stop the bonfire, because they thought the Securitate—the omnipresent Securitate—would recognize the smell of burning paper and would come to investigate.

After finishing his studies, Pavel began to work for the Rumanian radio; and in 1967, he obtained the surprising permission to start an institute for sociological research. From then on, his position was, if not dissident—for there was no context for that in Romania—then at least critical. The institute did surveys and polls of public opinion; and for some years, Pavel says, he "had the pleasure of publishing results the powers didn't want to hear." He wrote speeches and articles which, by the standards of the time, could be judged subversive; he could get away with all this, he thinks, because the middle-level *apparatchiks* supervising his activities were afraid that he was protected by his former friends in the higher echelons; the mechanisms of paranoia created by the system had a way of turning in on themselves.

But the feeling of sin, which first pursued him because he was leaving the party, now began to haunt him because he had been in it. In 1980, he returned to a project that he thought of as a "a settling of accounts"—an analysis of Stalinism and the sources of its distortions and failures.

The writing of such a manuscript was, of course, extremely dangerous, and neither Pavel nor Stefana got away without a brush with danger. One hot day in June 1982, Pavel came to Stefana's apartment to find it turned upside down; Stefana had disappeared. The manuscript itself, miraculously enough, was still lying on a sort of shelf under the table, where it had been hidden on the principle of Poe's purloined letter, practically in full sight. The trick had worked.

Now Pavel ran with the manuscript to somebody he thought was an old, reliable friend. About thirty years before, this man had himself been in trouble. He was one of the people who had fallen out of favor because he had fought in the Spanish Civil War, and he was beginning to be shunned by his fellow Communists. Pavel continued to see him, not, he says, as an act of courage, but because he was simply unable to take another approach; and he remembers being shocked by his friend's gratitude at this decision. So when, thirty years later, Pavel asked him to keep the manuscript for a while, he didn't expect a refusal. But that was what he got. Pavel never forgave his friend for this; they never saw each other again.

In the meantime, Stefana was being interrogated by the Securitate. She adopted the stonewalling method; she talked to them politely and pretended to know nothing. It turned out that, in a crisis, she was quite fearless and the Securitate finally let her go without being able to extract anything from her. Pavel's daughter was interrogated as well, also with no results.

The manuscript was eventually published in the United States, to Pavel's great satisfaction. It is a highly compressed, almost aphoristic study of the centralization of power and property, which, in Pavel's view, were the underlying mechanisms that made the economic decline and increasing repressiveness of Stalinism inevitable.

I ask him whether, aside from Stefana, he had any intellectual companions during the writing of the book. No, he says, he "didn't want to make a conspiracy of it." But undoubtedly the isolation was also built into the logic of Romanian life, into the atmosphere of pervasive fear and mutual suspicion.

The sense of isolation remains with him now. Pavel is no less of an anomaly since the changes than before them—a lapsed Communist who still likes to think of himself as "a man of the left," and who, with that double burden, doesn't fit comfortably anywhere in the new Romanian puzzle. "To the old ones," he says, "I'm a traitor. To the new ones, I'm not a person of confidence, because I've been a Stalinist. So I'm vulnerable." And, with a sort of stoicism that perhaps comes from his deep sense of guilt, he adds, "The best way for me to help the left is not to be directly involved. The left I tried once to produce was *that* one."

Did he eventually accomplish the emotional separation from the party completely? "It was slow; very slow," Pavel answers wistfully. "But well—I presume that the faster you can move away from this dogma, the less deep the move."

Pavel's "move" seems to have been very deep; it seems to have entailed nothing less than a reconstruction of his internal world, as well as his convictions. But there was maybe, after all, something to return to, as he made his break with dogma. "The sad truth is," he says, "that I'm not a fanatic by temperament. I became a fanatic because of my youth and circumstances. And then I lost both incentives—the circumstances and the youth."

In this, he's hardly exceptional. What is so rare about him is his admission of responsibility, of something like guilt. His complicity in a terrible history has never ceased to disturb him. At a recent conference, Pavel met a well-known Hungarian ex-Communist, who told him that she feels "absolutely no culpability" for her past, because she was a true believer and therefore acted in good faith; and because, once she stopped believing, her actions followed accordingly. Pavel considers such self-forgiveness, "a comfortable form of innocence. The other form are men and women of steel who will be real believers until the end—and who believe that real nobility lies in this immobility.

"Why I bring this up," he continues, "is to tell you that I don't consider myself an innocent person—not only because I participated in the first steps but because I participated in the next steps. I don't know if you can imagine," he continues, traces of torment still visible in his expression, "how difficult it is to say that the thing you've been devoted to—the essence and core of your life—has been a mistake."

I can, of course, imagine the distress of making mistakes; but this is a far more searing anguish. There's no way for anyone to say to Pavel, "It's all right"; the circumstances in which he was involved were too awful for that, his complicity too deep. And yet, as I listen to him, it seems to me that he has also achieved something large. Through wrestling with his angels and demons, he has converted the terrible events of his life into the stuff of consciousness and conscience—that is, a form of experience that might prove instructive in thinking about the future—into a fragment of a usable past.

It's perhaps out of some sense of duty that I decide to see one of the orphanages that have become so unhappily associated with

Romania and its latter-day horrors. I've seen distressing photographs of places where babies with AIDS—all contracted
through blood transfusions—are kept; of children, dirty and bru-
talized, looking out of pens that resembled cages. I don't relish
the thought of confronting such sights; but I don't think it's right
for me to shirk them. Magda offers to accompany me, and,
chauffeured by Mr. Gradici, we set out for Ţuican, a town where
we've received permission to visit one such orphanage. As we
near it, directions become harder to get, the landscape more uncharted. Stretches of mud, where the road nearly disappears. An
oil-drilling site, through which we weave among the machinery;
in a grim little swimming pool, set right next to a drill and glistening oil puddles, children splash. More muddy hills, in which
Mr. Gradici's ancient vehicle is almost bogged down. We manage
to push it out.

We find the orphanage, finally, up on a hill away from the
main village. At the gate, children of various ages clutch at the
metal grid fence. The sight of them, I must confess, frightens me.
There are faces distorted by mental illness and retardation,
bodies whose movements are barely coordinated, a boy with awful white blotches on his shaved head. There are also children
who look normally alert, and I'm frightened not of them but for
them.

A woman in a nurse's uniform comes to escort us and fend
off the children, who surround us tightly as soon as we enter;
they recede with a chillingly quick obedience. Inside the main
building, an unattended, filthy-looking baby is crawling up a
dark staircase. We're ushered into a small, dubious-smelling
kitchen, where the matron, also in a nurse's uniform, is listening
to classical music on the radio. She consents to talk to us, though
she can't show us the rest of the orphanage. There are rules
against visitors' walking around on Sunday; that's probably why
we've been invited for that day.

But I feel I've seen almost enough. By the time I sit down in
this odd "office," a sense of sickness descends upon me. The matron, a stocky, inexpressive woman, has been here more than

thirty years and she tells us about the phases the orphanage has gone through. The orphanage takes the hardest cases; many of the children have been abandoned by their parents; many are disabled. In the early sixties, a period of relative well-being for Romania, it had some amenities, an adequate staff, toys, and crafts for the children. Then, in the late seventies and early eighties, as Ceauşescu's ravages set in, money was withdrawn, and so were staff, water, electricity. One untrained worker had to suffice to oversee sixty children. Often, there was no water with which to wash them or their clothes. Many of the children are disturbed or anxious; the main method of coping with them was sedation. These days, conditions are much improved, largely because a team of Swiss workers has become interested in the orphanage and has come in with money, medicine, and expertise. The Swiss personnel have discovered that many of the children who were considered hopelessly retarded only had motor problems, and could be easily rehabilitated with proper training. Now some of them are attending school.

The matron speaks of all this in a calm monotone, smiling blandly as if she were giving us a report of a company's quarterly earnings. There's a convoluted story about a girl who left the orphanage and then ungratefully told terrible stories about it—of being beaten and kept in chains. Several times, children peek in curiously during our conversation, and recede at the matron's glance; at one moment, an overwhelming stench of defecation fills the room without rattling the matron's imperturbable manner. This is as close to hell as it gets, I think, in this room where this indifferent woman has been listening to Beethoven.

Magda and I have brought boxes of cookies for the kids, and before we leave, the matron tells us, "You may be sure that they'll be distributed." Since I had no thought they might not be, this is a glimpse of an unexpected venality. On the way out, the children surround us again. "When will my mother come? Whose mother are you?" they keep asking. One of them puts his arm through mine, and walks with me toward the gate with the look of the purest sadness and supplication I've ever seen in human eyes.

On the way back to Bucharest, Magda has an uncharacteristic headache. "You know, the Securitate took a lot of people from such places," she tells me. "People who grew up in these conditions were said to be very obedient and cruel. You can see that if somebody gave them food and some attention, even if it was brutal attention, they'd be loyal as a dog." I can see it. But mostly, instead of a sense of duty fulfilled, I feel a strange guilt for having seen what I did, the guilt of an uninvolved witness at a tragedy.

The Bucâloiu family—Lena, Gheorghe, and their sixteen-year-old son, Ionuţ—are intensely patriotic, and it is out of some combination of pride in their country, a large-hearted generosity, and, perhaps, a sense that it doesn't hurt to have an American friend, that they've offered to show me various parts of Romania. Lena is a psychiatrist, her husband has a managerial job at a factory, and Ionuţ is a thoughtful teenager, endowed with an impressive English vocabulary, a wide range of literary references, and an unquenchable curiosity about all things American.

In their Dacia—a car that looks as if it's been put together out of a cardboard by a not very dexterous adolescent—we've driven to look at villages and ancient ruins near Bucharest. Now Lena, Ionuţ, and I are setting out by plane for Bukovina, in the northeast corner of Moldavia—one of the three main regions of Romania. Our main goal is the famous painted monasteries, which I have long wanted to see.

At the Suceava airport, where we disembark from a small propeller plane, there're signs of that perplexing Romanian disarray—strange smells, mysterious puddles, right in the middle of the lobby. Outside, we meet Lena's friends, Coca and Mihai, with whom we'll be staying. In another makeshift Dacia, we drive through countryside that, by comparison with the landscapes further south, is richly lush. The grass *is* greener here; the foliage thicker; the play of light and shadow over fields livelier, the breezes more animated. Bukovina is the eccentric realm depicted in *Memoirs of an Anti-Semite* by Gregor Von Rezzori, a fertile province in which decaying aristocrats and illiterate peasants, erudite Jews and ambivalent anti-Semites coexisted in ideological disagreement and daily intimacy. And even now one can see a mix of the modern and the preindustrial. On the roads, cars jostle with carts, peasants with Gypsies. The horses have red pompoms and fringes on their manes, which bob up and down in bright spots of color. The houses are less elaborately decorated than the ones I saw in the nearby Maramureș, but they too have beautifully wrought wooden gateways; they look decently prosperous.

"Didn't Ceaușescu's hand reach this far?" I ask, marveling at all this. "Or did people in this region resist him?" Ionuț translates Coca's answer. "We didn't hear him," she says, laughing. "We didn't listen, and we didn't hear."

This is the advantage of being far away from the center; when the emperor is wicked, his messages take much longer to reach the periphery, and usually get lost along the way. One of the salient divisions in our world, I'm beginning to think, is not between North and South or East and West, but between the capital and the provinces; and in turbulent times, the provinces have it all over the hub. "Cultivate your own garden," I observe, half to myself. "Yes, Voltaire always gives good advice," Ionuț picks up.

Our destination is Cîmpulung, a small timbering town close to the Soviet border. On the other side is the part of Moldavia that had been separated from Romania in the last carving up of territory, and that is now burning with secessionist fervors.

Coca and Mihai live on the outskirts of Cîmpulung, where the town gives out onto the foothills of the Carpathians. They are farmers who have also done city jobs: she's been a nurse, he an auto mechanic. Right next to their low, plain farmhouse, a new concrete house is being erected, in a fashion I've seen throughout Eastern Europe. The villages begin to look like accordions, with the ungainly new structures pushing out jaggedly between the lovely old houses. Mihai and Coca are exceedingly proud of their modern dwelling. They've been working on it for twelve years, and can't wait to move in. In the back, there's about an acre of well-tended vegetable garden, a field of corn, and a lovely fruit orchard.

It's from here that some of the ingredients for our drop-dead meal come. Dinner, served in a pleasant garden alcove, is introduced by big mugs of bitter coffee, which we're supposed to alternate with sips of another fiery local liquor, *palinka*. "Drink up," Coca goads me on, since I'm slower than the others. "I want you to see Bukovina through the eyes of *palinka*." This heart-attack combination is followed by a delicate veal broth with vegetables and sour cream, and veal steak garnished with spoonfuls of minced garlic.

"Ah, *dolce vita*," I say, hoping that Romanian is close enough to Italian so that this will be understood.

"La Dolce Vita," Mihai says. "Fellini."

"You've seen it?" I ask, surprised.

"Twice," Mihai says. "Good movie."

So much for my preconceptions of rural provincialism. But why isn't some of the *dolce,* the gustatory overload, getting down to Bucharest?

"What's the point?" Mihai shrugs. "They don't pay us enough. They only wanted to take, and they'd still take everything if they could." And Mihai tells us a story of a peasant who was brought to court because he'd slaughtered his cows rather than give them away to a collective. Even this is an act with a tradition behind it. I've read about Romanian peasants within the Austro-Hungarian empire who sometimes resorted to killing their livestock to avoid excessive taxes imposed by their foreign overlords.

If you listen to Mihai and Coca, the changes have hardly made a ripple in their lives. "In Cîmpulung, the same people are running things," Mihai says. "But they don't bother me, and we don't bother them. We just want to be left alone."

It's the Gypsies who catch the brunt of my hosts' resentment. They're the ones really profiting from the new situation, says

Coca. They have good heads for *bizhnitze,* and they're used to moving around, so now they go from country to country trading their wares. Coca speaks with undisguised scorn and anger. I've heard others talk this way; Gypsies are considered fair game for prejudice, and even young Ionuţ, who's soul-searching about his opinions, is not exempt from such attitudes—though he says he has great respect for any Gypsy who "makes something of himself." Gypsies live so much by "the law of the jungle," Ionuţ thinks, that such a person must be really strong, "a real man." And then he proceeds to recite some relevant verses by Kipling.

Though everybody else seems undaunted by the meal we've just eaten, I find it suddenly difficult to move, and decide to take a brief siesta. Coca takes me to a large room filled with quilts, pillows and treacly embroideries, and she turns the television on for my benefit; this is considered a sign of genteel hospitality, the way background music used to be in suburban American homes.

Afterward, Mihai takes us on a walk up the high hill that rises steeply practically out of his backyard. The climb takes about two hours, and most of it goes through a dense, dark forest of powerful evergreens; but for the last stretch, we emerge onto a grassy hill bathed in light. A peasant is scything down a steep slope; a small boy sits curled up in the tall grass, looking like a small creature nearly blended into his surroundings; an eagle hovers in the air, spectacularly still, surveying the territory for prey. Sheep bells gently clink from somewhere on the other side of the hill. There's something enchanted about the purity of the air, the cool breezes that sweep over the ridge, the sharply cold water from a spring, the golden green colors of the grasses. Mihai pulls up a fern root that, he says, has the invigorating properties of ginseng, and he encourages us to chew on it. I don't know whether it's the root or the magic of the scene, but I do indeed start feeling lighter and less tired.

Even this idyllic scene, though, isn't innocent of history. The peasant who has been working his pastures comes to greet Mihai, and together they show me small dips and hillocks in the grass, from behind which the Germans, during World War II, gunned down the Russians who were trying to storm up the hill. What were the loyalties of the locals? I ask. "Oh, we were all for the Germans," the peasant says proudly, and Mihai confirms. Romania entered the war on the German side, and shifted loyalties only at the last moment; but to these men, it's the Russians who are the real enemy, still.

On the way down, Ionuţ tells me about the concept of "Mioritic space," often mentioned as essential to Romanian mythology and mentality. The "Mioriţa," from which this notion comes, is an ancient poem that has been transmitted orally in many versions. In its written form, it is a brief narrative of three mountain shepherds hailing from the three parts of Romania— Moldavia, Wallachia, and Transylvania—two of whom connive to assassinate the other. The Wallachian, who is the target of this plot, is warned by a ewe of what's coming and prepares to give himself peacefully to the starry sky and his wedding with death. Since it is a story of a prototypical betrayal and division, the "Mioriţa" strikes me as an unlikely national myth—but Romanians stress not the murder but the poem's easeful acceptance of transience and death. "Mioritic space" is a space of transit, of mountainous wandering, of fluctuation. In his patriotic way, Ionuţ loves the poem; and he points out that its opening lines— "Near a low foothill/ At heaven's doorsill,/ Where the trail's descending/ to the plain and ending . . ."—could well describe the place where we're walking now. I reflect that the contradictions in this compressed legend—the gentle fatalism on the one hand, the violence on the other—are something I've sensed in the Romanian air even today.

Back at the homestead, Coca has prepared plump potato pancakes topped with cream and sugar, plums glazed in sugar, and of course, *palinka* and coffee. She seems quite drunk, clutches me effusively to her large bosom, and asks me to tell "everybody in America" about her vacation spot. In the meantime, Mihai should go to America to make lots of money, and I should find him "a second wife" so that he won't be too unhappy. Mihai protests that he doesn't want a new wife, he only wants to come back with a big car. A Cadillac, perhaps. The American dream is alive and well in Cîmpulung.

I make my way through the dark, past the chained, snarling dog, to the outdoor facilities, stumble back, and fall exhausted into the soft bed, swathed in layers of quilts. "I'm going to put you to sleep between two straws," Coca said earlier, meaning, I think, that I'll fall asleep in a wink. She's kept her promise.

The next day, Lena, Ionuţ and I set out to visit the monasteries. At first sight, they are brilliant bits of color in the clean air. The Voroneţ monastery, where we go first, is tiny and compactly designed, except for the wooden roof, which extends out and down over the stone body like a protective bird wing. Over the tower, the roof furls up in the Chinese umbrella shape I've seen on peasant houses and wells—a sort of signature form, repeated in simple cottage and spiritual dwelling. Inside, the small space expands and presses upon one with an almost unbearable richness, for every inch of the stone interior—the high circular rotunda and the niches and walls—is covered with frescoes representing Biblical and historic narratives. There is perhaps an almost Oriental sense of spirituality here, in which transcendence is achieved by a sensuousness that—through sheer excess—leaps beyond itself. Outside, the famous external frescoes are a spillover of beauty. The scenes they depict are often gruesome—angels spearing little devils, and the dead rising out of graves—but the vivacity of the style, perfectly poised between folk and high art, and the sheer plenitude of the panels and the details make for exuberance rather than gloom. The Voroneţ blue, which is the predominant color of the exterior, has something uncanny about it. The secret of achieving this exact color has apparently been lost; but it's a blue that has the sort of absoluteness, the rightness, of Fra Angelico's blue—though this is a tone darker and more muted.

The monastery of Humor, not far from Voroneţ, repeats approximately the same experience of beauty in red. In front of the church, though, there's a very different sort of sight—a beggar

whose skin is covered with white, leprous-looking scales. I drop
something into his basket and then turn my eyes away, finding
his extended arms unbearable to look at. But Lena, to my surprise, gives a little laugh; she has looked at the beggar with
her doctor's eye, and says that he has created this hideous effect for our benefit; he may not be ill at all. "I like this kind
of thing," she says merrily. "It's spectacle, theater." This is
hard for me to fathom; the fakery doesn't make the figure
any less upsetting. But I see that she derives genuine amusement from the flamboyant grisliness; the show, the passing human show.

Lena has a psychiatrist friend in Cîmpulung, and together we go
to visit him in the local mental hospital. I brace myself for more
Romanian horrors; but the hospital building, at least, doesn't
conform to expectations. It's left over from Austro-Hungarian
times, and though the façade is crumbling in places, there are
tiled mosaic floors inside and nice watercolors on the walls. Dr.
Petrescu, Lena's friend, tells us that he deliberately keeps the exterior in disrepair—so that They don't set their sights on the
building for their own purposes.

Petrescu is a man with a diffident, sad manner, and that
somehow nebulous appearance often found in Romanian faces—
soft features, blue eyes dimmed by a kind of uncertainty, and a
very quiet voice. He gives us doctors' robes, in which we'll be
less disturbing to the patients, and takes us on a tour of the hospital, of which he is very proud—particularly the hygienic conditions prevailing in the bathrooms.

As we come into the men's ward, all the patients get off their
beds and stand at attention beside their beds in a show of respect. Despite this authoritarian touch, Petrescu treats them with
a sort of familial kindness, putting his hand on their shoulders
and foreheads, and giving them words of encouragement in his
soft voice. One of the men begs the doctor for some alcohol;
Petrescu softly refuses. Later, he tells us that the patient is a
priest whose alcoholism seems resistant to all treatment; once, he
interrupted a funeral procession he was leading so that he could

go into his house to get a drink. By the time his parishioners followed him inside, he was fast asleep. But Orthodox congregations seem to tolerate a large range of foibles in their spiritual leaders, the priest has been in this hospital several times, and has gone back to his religious duties each time.

In the hallway, a man who looks like the personification of despair, unshaven, wearing an open robe over his pajamas, walks back and forth, stopping sometimes to stare into space. "Polish," Dr. Petrescu says, "melancholia," as if these two words explained everything.

In the women's ward, the same muttered kindness and more diagnoses: "neurasthenia," "inversion," "schizophrenia with stupidity," Petrescu summarizes, in categories so quaint that they seem to place us instantly at some earlier stage of history; I wonder whether the patients have more old-fashioned symptoms to go with the terminology.

Back in his office, Petrescu tells us that he is the only psychiatrist for the seventy patients in the hospital, and for the region. In one of his cabinets, there's a stack of medicines from France, Italy, England, America—the fruits of the recent medical relief that followed the revelations of Romania's scandalous health conditions. Given the lack of staff and time, the main method of treatment in the hospital is medication, though often Petrescu doesn't know the precise purpose or dosage for the foreign medicines; he plays it by ear. But the most important form of therapy, he keeps repeating, is "an affective relationship" between him and his patients. "We know each other, we understand each other," he says. "We're members of the same society. I know their troubles. It's a relation of mutual respect." He spends maybe half an hour a week with each patient; and after ten weeks, most patients are sent home, where the family is expected to take over. The aim is not so much to analyze the patients' souls, he says, as to reintegrate them into society.

The real problem at the hospital, the doctor says as we leave the building, is that the Securitate is still around. That's why he invited us in the evening, and didn't turn on any lights outside. And, as he locks up, he looks round him nervously.

"But what are they doing these days?" I ask, by now genuinely baffled by this shadowy brotherhood's role.

"Warming their seats and playing checkers," the doctor replies ambiguously. Lena thinks that although the secret police don't have a clear function right now, they are biding their time, waiting for their next dispensation. It's very hard to know whether this is true, or whether Securitate's ubiquity is a projection of the old, very justified, paranoia; whichever it is, the atmosphere of shadowy fear still prevails.

After our tour, Petrescu invites us to his house, where, he says, we can talk more freely. By Romanian standards, his home shows signs of considerable wealth: large rooms, nice wood details, a vegetable garden, some fruit trees. One of the rooms is filled with a collection of Russian and Romanian icons dating from the fourteenth to the nineteenth century, dozens of them stacked up against the walls. The doctor smiles evasively when I ask him where one might collect such things. More *bizhnitze* of some kind, probably from money collected through patients' tips. Doctors have been among the lowest-paid professionals in Romania, if one looks at their government salaries; but every patient knew that *bakshish* in some form—money, or food, or gifts—is an expected part of the medical fee. In my travels with Lena, we've stopped at houses of her former patients, who have received us with great hospitality; she can always count on them, Lena has told me. In turn, in the course of such visits, she has often taken the patient aside for a little informal therapy—with no one regarding either part of this bargain as unusual.

During dinner, Petrescu and Lena tell me how cut off they have been from contemporary developments in their field. They were forbidden to have contacts with colleagues in the West and they had so little access to literature or medical information, that they can't even gauge how far behind they are. And now their insulation continues for economic reasons: travel to the West is completely beyond their means, and they can't afford books or journals either.

Were psychiatric hospitals used for political purposes in Romania? I ask them. At first, this is met with blank denial; then, the hesitant admission that maybe, somewhere, such methods might have been practiced. But, they hasten to assure me, the government would have used special personnel for these purposes; most doctors were honest people and weren't even aware that such things went on. The telephone rings several times during our evening; the patients want Petrescu's attention, and he seems to give it to them readily, talking to them in vague, worried voice. Both he and Lena work very hard, they say, harder than most people. "It's a sacrifice," Lena says. "I just have the bad luck to burn in that fire." Adjusting for the Romanian penchant for dramatic exaggeration, I take this as an expression of real dedication. As is so often true in Romanian conversations, I have a sense, this evening, that the vagueness covers some impenetrable miasma of half-truths, or lies, or conditions I can't fathom or suspect. And yet, I'm also pretty sure that despite all this—despite the obstacles, the corruptions, the strangeness of professional relations—the desire to help and do some good exists here as well, in its peculiar and, to us, alien forms.

During a walk around Cîmpulung, Ionuţ comes out with something that surprises me. He says, "I envy you. You act like a free person."

"Don't you feel you are a free person?" I ask.

"You see, we're still afraid," he answers. "We still look over our shoulders. We have this habit, which I hate and which I try to fight. But it'll take time."

"But what about your generation? Are you hopeful that you'll grow up differently? That you'll be growing up in a different country?"

"Of course, we're hopeful. We're teenagers. If we're not hopeful, who will be? But we're entering university in this period when everything is changing. . . . It's confusing. There are so few teachers we can trust. You see," he continues, "I'm disoriented because I want to read everything, know everything, but I don't have a system. I don't know where to start."

"But you're so young," I interject. "You can do it step by step."

"Yes, I know I have many years," he admits. "But it's funny, I'm in a sort of time crisis. . . . Everything happens in time, that's the problem. I read Mircea Eliade's early novels, and they're very symbolical, and I don't know the symbols, but everything leads to everything else, like in a dictionary." And he makes a braiding gesture with his hands, to show me how everything is intertwined.

"Perhaps I'm not strong enough," he adds despondently.

"Strong enough for what?"

"To have an aim. I don't want you to think I'm vulgar, but I don't want this intellectual masturbation. To know, know, know . . . There must be something to know for."

Ionuţ thinks he would like to become a psychiatrist, like his mother, because psychiatry combines "gnosis" and practice. He thought he would like to go to America to medical school, but he worries about his parents. "I see them as so . . . confused, tired by this period. And not only confused—marked. My father is grayer now than he was a year ago. He could lose his job. My mother works harder than before, because they're taking staff away. If I stayed away for a few years . . . well, so much can happen.

"But on the other hand, I love them very much, but I don't want to be too linked. . . . I don't think children should fight their parents' wars. That's not freedom.

"You know," he continues, "I'm thinking of a Romanian folktale that begins this way: An old couple has no children, and they pray very much for a child. And a child is given to them. And, of course, it's a marvelous child—it grows in three months as much as others do in a year. But then, quite quickly—it is taken away. And I think it means two things: that life follows its own destiny, and that everything has its freedom."

Indeed, freedom is not only a political concept, and as I listen to Ionuţ, I'm struck by the freedom inherent in the mystery of personality; his curiosity, his very need for more expansive horizons, can't be explained by the circumstances that formed him. Occasionally, human individuality can surmount almost any conditions, to pursue its own aims and paths of expression; and perhaps the basic hope for the changes is that they'll create a sufficient space to leave those paths open.

Time to leave Cîmpulung. We're going back to Bucharest by train and we're worried about being late, but Mihai, who drives us to the station, proclaims that "one should never rush after trains or women." Apparently, I'm just missing a peasant wedding this evening, with lots of authentic local dancing; but I'm beginning to think such stories are made up especially to tantalize me.

We've paid for a sleeping car, but someone—that ubiquitous someone—has cheated us, and we're shown to a compartment with ordinary seats. Lena launches into intense diplomatic negotiations with the conductor, who eventually produces one berth. Everyone insists I take it; Lena and Ionuţ try their luck elsewhere. In the berth above me, there's a young doctor who speaks little English, but who manages to tell me that the Securitate still controls everything. I fall asleep to the lulling sound of that by now familiar idea.

On returning to Bucharest, I have a more personal brush with the idea of the Securitate, if not the thing itself. To say good-bye, Magda, her friend Mircea, and I meet for dinner at the Interconti. Mircea, a big, jovial man, is a doctor who happened to be on ambulance duty that fateful dawn of June 13, when the miners came, and he still has a vivid sense of drama about what he saw in the Piaţa Universitate, in the dawn hours of that day. The dramatic point is that there was so little happening. On one side of the square, there amassed about three thousand soldiers; on the other, a crowd of stragglers and riffraff. Objects were thrown desultorily at the soldiers. It looked like a show, Mircea keeps saying. The soldiers approached the crowd in concert, the crowd retreated—and then the soldiers retreated like a wave.

This is exactly what I saw in Piaţa Universitate during my last visit here. "It was theater," Mircea says. "If they had wanted to disperse the crowd, they could have done it in fifteen minutes, with no trouble." The Romanian Political Theater. But on that occasion, of course, the staging—by whomever it was produced—was meant to trigger action in the sphere of reality.

Magda follows this with an anecdote of the "they're still here" variety. Today, as she was walking near the passport office, she glimpsed a man whom she remembered all too well. She had applied for a passport sometime in the 1970s. While she waited for this document, the clerk in charge of her case tormented her elaborately. The wait for the passport took ten years; and during that time the man insinuated, threatened, made her come on useless errands, frightened her with sexual innuendo. "Have you really been waiting that long?" he would say in feigned surprise after they had met regularly for many years. The doorkeeper in Kafka's *The Trial* comes irresistibly to mind; but then, Kafka perhaps comes to mind too easily in this part of the world.

Our bit of live drama comes at the end of dinner. It happens because I change my mind on the method of payment. I begin to pay with my American Express card, then, at Magda's and Mircea's persuasion, I decide to use Romanian *lei* after all. This throws the waiter into unrestrained fury. "You cannot! You cannot!" he screams, trying to grab the American Express card from my hand, while his face gets very red. To demonstrate that, indeed, I can, I tear up the American Express bill he has brought me. This causes him to escalate all the way to the Great Threat. "You cannot!" he shouts again. "I'll bring the Securitate!"

"Please do," I say, making a nonchalant gesture of invitation. Blatant unfairness causes me to find my sang-froid—though, of course, I can afford the luxury of this behavior because I'm a foreigner. The waiter storms off, and I check with Magda and Mircea to see just how unpleasant this is for them. "You're doing the right thing," they say, but I see that they're quite nervous.

The waiter comes back and wordlessly throws down a new bill. He's been told, I suppose, that foreigners have to be humored. But not Romanians. "You'll never set foot in this hotel again!" he screams at Magda and Mircea. He looks for a moment as though he might start hitting Mircea. On the way out, a strange man follows us and mutters to Mircea, "It will be a pleasure to come to your funeral."

We're all rattled as we leave the hotel, and I can't stop myself from looking over my shoulder to see if we're being followed. Suddenly, the atmosphere on the streets seems charged to me, and I don't like the sight of soldiers strolling around with their automatic guns exposed. I'm probably experiencing a faint echo, a small drop, of the fear with which Romanians have lived for decades, as with constant weather. "You know, it would have been easy for them to call the Securitate—the hotel is run by them," Mircea says. Still, there was no real danger; what happened was no more than a silly irritation. But the incident gives me a glimpse of how nasty it is to be frightened of someone's stupid whim, and how defeating, over countless such encounters, to suppress one's exasperation and fury; how embittering, finally, to have to keep one's natural sense of justice curbed and leashed, until it gets squashed into a miasma of frustration and bitterness.

A few days before I'm scheduled to leave, a general strike is announced. Nobody knows whether it will come off, but the day before the announced date, the Bucharest atmosphere heats up. I'm supposed to visit a factory that day, but in the morning, two gentlemen who are managers there appear at Stefana's to dissuade me from going. The workers are restless; I may not be let in; why ask for trouble?

Could I try to go anyway? I ask. Well, if you insist, the gentlemen say, and fall quite silent. Stefana informs me that this is their polite way of saying they really don't want to take me. Since I have no other way of getting into the factory, I yield, and everyone looks relieved.

On the way to the travel agency, where I go to check if the trains will run as usual, the taxi driver, maneuvering his mutilated machine, points out rows of men who stand on the street bearing banners. They are workers from the very factory I was about to visit.

At the travel agency, there are endless, immovable lines. But how well I now wait! I wait as if my role in life is to wait. I wait in a state of mystic acceptance. A placid, bovine patience has replaced my usual restlessness. My sense of time and comfort have been utterly altered on this journey. When I finally reach the counter, I am told to listen to the radio for further developments.

The next afternoon, a motley crowd marches down Calea Victoriei, bearing flags each with the dramatic hole in the middle where the Communist symbol had been. There's an air of tension, excitement. People scurry fast through the streets.

And then, nothing; fizzle. Handsome Petre Român, the prime minister, went to visit the workers, and explained to them that there isn't enough money to raise their wages. They apparently understood. And that's it—another nonstarter, another unfinished gesture; another bit of muddle-as-usual.

On my last evening, I go to a production of *A Midsummer Night's Dream,* which is the talk of *le tout* Bucharest. To begin with, the show has the imprimatur of two glamorous émigrés, who have returned for this occasion. The translation, which I'm told is brilliant, is by Nina Cassian, a poet who has lived in New York and can now freely visit after many years of exile. The director is Liviu Ciulei, who has gained authentic recognition in the United States.

The production, held in a small, stuffy theater—nothing like air-conditioning here, and in June Bucharest gets very hot—is first rate, and subtly fitted to the Romanian context. In Ciulei's interpretation, *A Midsummer Night's Dream* becomes a play about violation, and the malleability of human beings. On the way home, Stefana, Pavel, and I have one of these conversations, endlessly replicated throughout Eastern Europe in the last four decades, in which we try to match the symbolism of the play to the Romanian situation. "I'm afraid we still have to have these interpretations," Pavel says. "It's still always about us, us, us."

I keep thinking of a brilliant play by Tom Stoppard called *Dogg's Hamlet, Cahoot's Macbeth,* which dramatizes the very different weights that language, and art, can assume in different contexts. In the first act of Stoppard's play, language is not much more than colorful blocks to throw about and play with; in the second, a clandestine production of *Macbeth* in a Czech writer's apartment carries the freight of risk, danger, protest, a defiant desire for freedom. A beautifully staged production of *A Midsummer Night's Dream* in New York can be art for its own sweet sake; in Romania, where neither freedom nor normalcy can yet be taken for granted, art still can't help but be more than itself.

In the night, I have a dream that synthesizes my impressions of Romania in a condensed scenario. In it, I'm among a group of Italian men—Romanians always talk of themselves as Latins— with vaguely disturbing faces. One of the men keels over—he's having a heart attack. The others don't do anything to help him, though they're doctors. I try, with great difficulty, to cover him with a blanket. He grows paler and paler, though strangely he isn't quite dying. Then, the door opens, and another ambiguous-looking person enters and informs me, "This was all an experimentation. A show." Stefana and I agree that the Romanian atmosphere has penetrated my consciousness.

It's time to leave. In the evening, Stefana takes me to the train station. The train, unbelievably enough, is on time, and the conductor shows me to a private sleeping compartment without any special fuss. I'm so grateful I'd gladly give him my whole hoard of Kent cigarettes, but Stefana resolutely stays my hand. Bakshish has to be distributed with wisdom and moderation. Then we say good-bye, and I soon fall asleep. I next wake to a stopped train, and to the sound of birds singing in full-throated ease in the middle of absolutely nowhere. It's about five in the morning, and I believe I'm in Bulgaria.

SIX

BULGARIA

In coming to Bulgaria, I've traveled beyond my preconceptions and prejudices. A few exotic echoes reverberate from the name; Bulgaria, after all, is the real site of Shakespeare's Illyria, and also of ancient Thrace, the county of Orpheus; it's the crossroads of Byzantine and Ottoman and Slav influences and of old trade routes. But as for modern Bulgaria, it exists outside my imaginative ken; even in my Polish upbringing, it was a country beyond the periphery; a remote place.

But it's a thoroughly up-to-date mood I find when I first set foot in Sofia, one of restlessness and transition, of something brewing, seething, roiling. In the summer of 1990, the exit from Communism hasn't been completed, the tectonic plates still haven't stopped shifting. I left Bucharest to images of milling crowds, policemen in formation. In Sofia, driving in from the airport, I discover that the central part of town is cordoned off, with policemen guarding the perimeter; in a square, another milling crowd.

"There are problems, many problems," the taxi driver immediately informs me, after we ascertain that we can communicate

346

in basic Russian. Last night, he explains, the Communist Party building was attacked; then somebody threatened to burn himself because he wanted the party out.

"But perhaps it's not wise to do it like that?" I hazard. My Russian is not subtle. "Yes, it is!" he responds vehemently. "Everyone in the whole world knows that Communism is no good except us." Bulgaria is the only country in the bloc in which the Communists—even if they're renamed Socialists—won a majority of votes in the recent free elections; this makes them the first Communist Party ever to achieve this feat nationally, in unrigged voting.

The next taxi driver, though, thinks the attack on the party headquarters wasn't very wise at all. "Vandalistvo," he practically spits with disgust. "Hooliganstvo."

Since telephone communications from Romania verge on utter impossibility, I haven't made any hotel arrangements in Sofia, and I choose the Grand Hotel Sofia rather at random, with the help of the taxi driver's enthusiastic recommendation. It's in the middle of town, very large and the last word in tawdriness. The interior decor comes mostly in plastic, in muddy oranges, beiges, and purples. The hallways smell of onions and prolific sweat. The lights are half down everywhere, perhaps as part of an austerity regimen. Piped-in cocktail-lounge music, circa 1955, further deflates my mood. In an immense, unclean restaurant, there are groups of Russian and Vietnamese men who sport that telltale, foursquare party look; the Sofia is a *nomenklatura* hotel.

Since I can't face the restaurant for dinner, I order a meal in my room; it includes a beef fillet that tastes distinctly on the rotten side. "I'm not sure it was fresh," I tell the waiter when he comes to retrieve the dishes. "I'm not so sure also," he responds gravely, giving me my first taste of Bulgarian frankness. The next morning, I change my quarters for something better and less expensive.

After my unfortunate introduction, there's something about Sofia's ramshackle, neutral tenor that I find immediately pleasant. Perhaps it's the undemanding, modest size and scale or the teasing combination of Eastern European elements and strong, southern heat and light that transports everything into a different modality. On first perusal, Sofia looks like a cross between a rather dilapidated provincial town in Eastern Europe and an equally dilapidated provincial town in Italy or Greece. Most of modern Sofia began to be constructed at the end of the nineteenth century, and grew up, not very rich, in the twentieth, which accounts for its characteristic characterlessness. It's a low-built city—there aren't many buildings more than three stories high. Neighborhoods of nondescript gray stone buildings remind me of peripheries of Cracow; but the outdoor "cafés," consisting of rickety plastic tables and orange chairs, bespeak a greater southernness. In the streets and the small, unfussy parks, there's a constant, low cooing of pigeons.

And then there are the faces, with their wonderful variety: the tall, lean woman with distinctly Slavic features and a bony stylishness; men with very dark eyes and beards who look like models for Byzantine icons or covers of Harlequin romances; Orthodox priests in black, capacious robes; and Pomaks, or Bulgarian Muslims, in cowl-like headdresses.

The human brew seems thicker, more pungent here, as if created by a long-brewing history. Bulgaria is one of those minor cultures that make up for their small size by the great, vertical density of their past. The density seems to me enchanting, as if I'd come upon a small hidden pool among mountain rocks and discovered that its depths reach nearly to the middle of the earth. In the National History Museum, I look at gold artifacts of impeccable and intricate workmanship, which may be the oldest in the world. There are ceremonial bowls with delicately wrought rims and filigreed necklaces dating from 3600 B.C., about a thousand years earlier than anything comparable found elsewhere. There are later Thracian vessels that look like elegant sauce bowls, whose spouts elongate into gorgeous horses or griffins. The Thracian stone friezes show graceful human figures with the ease of body you can still discern in people on Sofia's streets. Then there are tiny goddess figurines that predate all these artifacts; you could easily hold one of them in the palm of your hand, and yet they manage to give an impression of great power and size because of the fertile breadth of their hips.

Even in terms of national identity, Bulgaria boasts a great longevity. The First Bulgarian Kingdom consolidated its power in the seventh century, long before England was England, or France France. The second kingdom lasted through the thirteenth and fourteenth centuries. The monks Cyril and Methodius, who created the Cyrillic alphabet and disseminated it throughout the region, came from here, and the first Slav literature was written in Bulgarian; the early Russian literature drew on Bulgaria's flourishing monastic tradition.

But despite these long continuities, Bulgaria, being small and an important trading crossroads, was vulnerable to all manner of invasion, pillage, and rapacious designs. Sofia itself has been leveled and rebuilt many times. It was first inhabited by a Thracian tribe of Serdi, and later by the Romans, who built it up into a rather splendid provincial capital. In Byzantine times, it became known as Triadica, which means "between the mountains," and Constantine the Great fancied its high mountain plain location. The Slavs, arriving around A.D. 400, renamed it Sredec, or "center." One of the city's greatest blows came in 447, when the Huns, under Attila, went on a rampage of destruction, virtually wiping it off the map. A Byzantine emperor, Justinian, subsequently rebuilt it in the sixth century, and one of his monuments was the Church of Saint Sofia, from which the city took its name much later, in the fourteenth century.

The church still stands, in the city's heart, wearing its antiquity with unpretentious ease. Some hip-looking youths are doing a credible rendition of the Beatles nearby, and peacock-colorful Gypsies offer to tell your fortune. Right next to the entrance, somebody is distributing free food, for which people line up quietly. Inside the large space, there are no postcard stands, or posters detailing the church's history, or any other signposts announcing that this is important and historical. No ornament graces the church's darkened brick, no statues, pillars, or sacred bric-à-brac; there are only the perfect proportions of the low dome, the Romanesque arches, and the three naves to create the effect of simple, achieved wisdom. We need nothing but this, this interior seems to say, nothing but this emptiness and this perfection. The great, domed rotunda is sunk in consoling darkness; pigeons fly in and waddle about on the threadbare carpet; people walk in and out casually, stopping for a brief moment of contemplation.

Not far from this venerable structure—since nothing is very far in Sofia—is a landmark more overtly spectacular, though less deeply affecting. This is the Alexander Nevski Memorial Cathedral, whose bulbous, golden onion domes and splendidly gilded interior invoke the Russian manner. The occasion of its building points to the genesis of the special Russian-Bulgarian relationship, since the church was conceived as a symbol of gratitude to the Russians for helping the Bulgarians gain independence from the Turks. The Turkish Yoke, as the Ottoman domination was called here, lasted for five hundred years, and was unrelentingly harsh, perhaps because the Bulgarians never stopped chafing violently against it. Still, neither the partisan subversions nor attempts at full uprisings by a small nation could hope to do effective battle against the Turkish empire—and it was not until another empire, the Russian one, declared war against the Ottomans in 1887 that Bulgaria's freedom was gained. These events, as much as the closeness of language, alphabet, and religion, were the cause of Bulgaria's friendship toward the Russians—a friendship that, to some extent, persisted even through the hypocrisies of the "fraternal" Soviet period.

The changes have come a few months later to Bulgaria than to the other countries I've visited, which means that I've come here at the very turning point, at the sharp and sudden corner. This is the stage at which the economy, caught between a collapsing centralized system and a new order as yet unknown, suffers a breakdown of all its production and distribution mechanisms, in a material equivalent to massive cardiac arrest. In terms of pure consumerism—though, oh, how far that word is removed from any reality!—Sofia, no less than Bucharest, offers a spectacle of almost pure nothingness. As far as I can tell, the entire stock in a big supermarket within the central department store consists of a few wan boxes of cookies and tea bags. I've seen long queues for washing soap. There are fears of severe oil and electricity shortages, of a dark, chilly winter.

A few days after I arrive, I go to a "café," in an underground passage close to the center of town, with Deyan Kiuranov, one of the founders of the Bulgarian opposition. There, the waitress brings us a sad imitation of a sandwich and tells us there's no mineral water, no sugar, no milk, no salad.

"Oh, yes, we're in for it," Deyan says briskly. "We're going to surpass Poland in 1980. We'd better prepare ourselves; we're in for it."

I've just met Deyan for the first time through a mutual friend, but we fall into instant, lively conversation, as if it didn't matter that we have different backgrounds, points of reference, and education. I later realize it doesn't matter because Deyan's education seems to be just about universal. But he also has a directness of manner that makes rapport seem natural. He wears very thick glasses and a sort of white sleeveless Nehru jacket; he's slightly pudgy, and emanates irresistible intelligence and energy.

Deyan reminds me that, in the not-very-distant past, it was Poland that was the measure of poverty, and Bulgaria a relative standard of regional prosperity. Now that's turned around abruptly. But the economic blues haven't stopped the Bulgarians from tackling the new politics with enormous zest. The political scene in Bulgaria, in these first stages of post-Communism, is a dizzying inverse of the Romanian one, featuring a veritable orgy of new political bodies. After declaring myself confused, I ask Deyan to enumerate the new parties for me, on the spectrum from left to right.

"Do you mean the prewar left and right? Postwar? Communist? Post-Communist?" Deyan asks, a flicker of ironical amusement appearing behind his thick glasses. I throw up my hands;

temporarily at least, Eastern Europe has made mincemeat of these categories. So we decide to dispense with the spectrum, and Deyan tells me that, in this country of not quite nine million people, there are sixteen parties united under one oppositional umbrella, called the United Democratic Front, or UDF. There are also several extraparliamentary formations that don't have enough votes to qualify as full members of the new democracy club; also, a brand-new Communist Party rather close to the lunatic fringe and two ecological parties. Completely outside the usual categories, there's the Human Rights Movement, which represents the large Turkish minority, although non-Turkish Bulgarians are beginning to join it as well.

Aside from this democratic profligacy, there was a strain of an almost fantastical imagination in the first days of free politics, which seemed peculiar to Bulgaria. During the three months before the elections, for example, a tent city appeared rather mysteriously in one of Sofia's main squares; it was supposed to serve as a living microcosm of an egalitarian society. Several hundred people lived in this independent community, which ran its own city services and free medical services for all. Perhaps this quirky, utopian idea drew on a deep and old communitarian strain in Bulgarian culture. Foreign travelers from very early times observed the communitarian and egalitarian tendencies in Slav social organization; and Bulgaria was the country that, in the tenth century, proposed something called the Bogomil Heresy—a radical system of belief that tried to abolish all hierarchy and inequality in the church, including the inequities between men and women. Bulgaria remained largely rural, and quite unindustrialized, until recently; and some of the old habits of sharing food, or ferrying children among friends and relatives, have survived to this day.

Deyan was instrumental in all the initial stages of the dissident movement, and in the founding of Eco-Glasnost, which now forms the core of the parliamentary opposition. But he has dropped out of official politics quickly; he was disillusioned by the power plays and intrigues that started dividing his dissident comrades-in-arms as soon as they gained some power. He's worried that they're nurturing a new elitism among themselves and turning into a *nomenklatura.*

Deyan's disenchantment, I sense, is commensurate with his high ethical expectations. But as it happens, he has just received a job offer about which he's clearly excited—to become the editor of a just-launched "antipartisan" newspaper, *Geopolitika.* (I think I hear him say "anti-antipartisan," but he says, "No, we haven't yet reached the stage at which we need an anti-antipartisan paper. We may, but we have to wait for that. For now, we have partisanship up to here.")

The new job carries with it its own brand-new ethical problems. For example, Deyan wonders whether, in his new post, he should continue to act as an informal consultant to Zhelyu Zhelev, Bulgaria's new president and his old friend. By the still-reigning Bulgarian standards, such an arrangement is entirely acceptable; but Deyan wants to be above suspicion, not only by Bulgarian, but by any standards.

"One thing is sure, though," Deyan says. "If I continue to advise him, I would want to be paid." Then he goes on to explain that, paradoxical though it may seem, money has become a guarantee of moral neutrality in the new Bulgaria. Money is somehow American and anti-Communist; and a financial transaction is different from the Communist ways of exercising influence, which were personal and whispered behind the arras.

"We have a saying nowadays," Deyan says with amusement, "that money is clean."

I laugh. It's taken many twists of the dialectic to come to the point at which getting paid is a sign that you're not being bought off.

We stroll around after our snack, and Deyan points out some of the sights: an old mosque within which a caretaker is sitting on the floor, reading his Koran; Turkish baths closed for repairs; a few stands, selling flowers and sunflower seeds, from which Oriental music emanates. We talk about Saul Bellow, whom Deyan is rereading, and Hemingway's *A Moveable Feast,* which

I've just bought from the Sheraton Hotel—one of the three English titles I could find in Sofia—and which Deyan, of course,
has read.

As so often in these travels, I feel myself enclosed by two levels of reality simultaneously: on one level, the stunning material
destitution that makes a cube of sugar unavailable in a restaurant; on the other, Deyan's sharp merriment, the gusto of his
mind, the excitement of new possibilities. Like every one of the
newly decolonized countries, except maybe more so, Bulgaria
seems poised between the moral fact of its new freedom and the
brute reality of its material crisis. Brute reality, at this moment,
looks overwhelming, a Sisyphean weight on the mountain of
democratic uplift. And yet, the X-factor of human energy and intelligence can, I think, start rolling even a large rock upward.

Several days into my stay in Sofia, I make contact with Dimitrina
Petrova, another founder of Eco-Glasnost. I had met Dimitrina
briefly in New York, where she had been invited to speak to a
distinguished group of academics, and I was instantly curious
about an environment that could have produced so formidable a
figure. In a roomful of strange people, in a city she didn't know,
in a language she had learned catch-as-catch-can, Dimitrina par-
ried her interlocutors' questions with a daunting intelligence,
confidence, and charm. Her answers and explications rose
through crescendos of theoretical complexity into perfectly
rounded, nearly symphonic arguments. It was an impressive performance.

Now she has returned from one of those generic conferences
on "the transition," held somewhere in Yugoslavia, and we make
contact through the very efficient Sofia grapevine. Dimitrina is
a beautiful woman in her thirties, with a smooth oval face, and
an animal surety of movements that stood out almost eerily in
nervous New York. Here, I see this contained steadiness
everywhere—a physical composure, a concentration that could
come from the habit of walking on mountainous terrain, perhaps, or from a straightforward relation to oneself.

In the months between our two meetings, Dimitrina has changed her hairstyle from a short, pixyish cut to a ponytail, and she has become a member of Parliament. And so the Parliament is the first place she takes me, with the quick decisiveness so characteristic of her; she's opposed to my wasting time. Once there, she picks out some representative types for me: there's one of the new technocrats, there an earnest ecologist, there a philosophical Communist. She introduces me to the latter, saying, "I'm introducing you to Ms. Hoffman because I wanted her to meet a real Communist."

"Socialist," he corrects, finger raised in playful warning.

"Words." She laughs.

"Ah, Dimitrina, as a politician you'll have to learn about the importance of words," he says in mock sadness. But I'm struck by the cordiality of their exchange.

During the next few days, I spend quite a bit of time in the airy, pleasant spaces of the Parliament, chatting with representatives of a bewildering array of parties, all of whom appear to maintain relations of easy amiability with each other. This is one of those rare moments when politics doesn't belong to career politicians, and the members of the opposition come from the cream of professions and arts and letters. They're a vibrant gathering of people, and something of the atmosphere of an animated literary club prevails in the lounges and hallways, with the added zest of a revolutionary enterprise.

There are several women among the parliamentarians, and I spend some time talking with some of them. One of them is Elena Konstantinova, a founder of a liberal party. She's a middle-aged, matronly-looking woman, with one of those honest, unmade-up, good-as-gold faces that one doesn't usually associate with leaders of movements. She seems perfectly comfortable in her role, though she is a literary critic by profession, and hadn't been remotely involved in politics before the changes. She'd spent some time in Poland, studying Polish literature, and admired Solidarity, but that was about as much of an initiation into political life as she had received. Then, when the changes began, she decided "it might be worth it" to restore the prewar Radical Democratic Party, in which her father had been very active, and which was a liberal party of the intelligentsia. Once this idea took root in her head, she discovered that some of the original members of the party were still alive. They got together, decided that their old idea was worth reviving, and presto! they had a little party once again, risen from its past incarnation. Sometimes, the return of the past in Eastern Europe is very literal.

Another woman to whom Dimitrina introduces me is Irina Bokova, a Communist MP who seems like Dimitrina's worthy counterpoint on the other side. Bokova is also beautiful, with dark, casually coiffed hair and prominent cheekbones, and she's dressed in an elegant navy-blue jacket and an Hermès scarf. The stylishness comes from abroad; like so many *nomenklatura* people, she had the advantage of traveling in the West, and for a while, she was attached to the Bulgarian mission at the United Nations. She also worked as a journalist, and she has written a number of feminist articles to which the party took exception.

Indeed, Irina thinks of herself as a feminist and she has tried to bring together the women in Parliament in a bipartisan alliance. The alliance hasn't panned out so far, but this afternoon, I saw Dimitrina and Irina caucusing in the hallway in perfect complicity, after an MP called the women in the assembly chatterboxes. The hapless MP was made to apologize, though Dimitrina told me, with some amusement, that he used that occasion to put his foot in his mouth again, and to say that women were "the ornament" of the Parliament.

Oddly enough, Bulgaria is the only country in my travels where I've heard feminism discussed seriously; perhaps this is in line with a certain undefensive openness I've sensed in people here. In this, and in other ways, Irina and Dimitrina seem so close, so much of a certain irrevocably postmodern type, that it's difficult for me to place Irina within a group that has been identified as the force of reaction. At some point, I can't refrain from asking her whether she has thought of crossing what's clearly a very thin line, and becoming a member of the opposition.

"I would never think of that," she answers quite heatedly. "I wouldn't leave the party now, when it has become weaker and is struggling to reform itself." What she particularly hates, she says, are the opportunists who pretended to be devoted Communists until a year ago, and who are suddenly spouting all the correct democratic slogans. How can you trust such people? No, she has grown up with the party, she owes it a lot, and she's staying with it; she'll try to change it from the inside.

Undoubtedly, the division between opportunists and those with a certain integrity of conviction is as deep as rifts between ideologies, and it's proving particularly telling now. Dimitrina has introduced me briefly to a prominent Communist MP whose son is an equally prominent dissident. "What I like about both of them is that they strongly feel—and I mean, precisely, feel—about their beliefs, and that their ideas come out of these feelings," she said appreciatively. Feeling as a guarantee of honesty; an oddly old-fashioned and appealing idea to apply to political life. She herself is friendly with several older Communists—for example, Boris Spassov, a breezy, humorous, suave man with whom I talk for a while in the Parliament's lounge. Aside from being an MP, he is a philosopher interested in logic and positivism. He was one of Dimitrina's mentors at the University of Sofia, as well as an influential teacher for many engaged activists of her generation. In those days, he was a critical Marxist, and now he considers himself something like a liberal Communist—but definitely a Communist, no bones about it.

Spassov is delighted to converse in English, which he pretty much learned on his own, and which he speaks flawlessly. "The situation is hopeless, but not serious," he says of his party, with gusto. Then he discourses bouncily about the main cause of the party's failure, which, in his view, was that it couldn't make the shift from an industrial to postindustrial mode of technology. But he thinks the party is not only salvageable but reformable. And he still believes—he goes on cheerfully—that Marx had the most sophisticated ideas about social change and the behavior of social groups. Here Spassov cites an article he read recently in the

English periodical *The Marxist Review,* and asks me whether I've read the latest *New Republic.* He probably gets them at his Party headquarters; but Western publications have always been more readily available here than in Romania or Czechoslovakia, and their accessibility may account in part for the lively, urbane intelligentsia I find here.

"The thing is," he says, and bends toward me confidentially, "the thing is that, frankly speaking, the Communists in Bulgaria have better intellectuals than the opposition. They'll come up with better theoretical models. They are even better social democrats." Here he gives me an intelligent look, to see if I appreciate this twist, and then floats away to be present at some important vote.

I do appreciate it. I've heard Spassov's analysis of the party's fall from other Communists, and it strikes me as self-servingly neutral; but I find it interesting that today's Bulgarian Communists would vie with the opposition for the honor of being better social democrats—in the Western sense of this term. Perhaps there is an emerging consensus on what might constitute a good society—on the basic aims of the game, if not on the particular moves required to play it properly.

Not that the Parliament *is* a literary club, of course, or that all disagreement in it is amiable. In the assembly hall there are conflict, bad blood, passionate shouting. Just now, temperatures are running high because of the attack on the Communist Party headquarters a few days ago. Neither side has wasted any time before accusing the other of instigating the riot. In such political contretemps, the Socialists, a.k.a. Communists, have a considerable advantage. Not only are they the majority, but also they are fighting an opposition barely in its salad days and still almost touchingly idealistic about the political process. Dimitrina tells me that it is impossible to figure out strategy in the United Democratic Front, because the group ethos dictates complete sincerity, both among themselves and in the Parliament.

In the meantime, the attack on the party headquarters has thoroughly confused at least one group—the policemen who were supposed to protect it. Or were they? This morning they staged a sit-down strike to demand, or plead for, some guidance as to their role in the new order. They are being blamed for their slow and halfhearted response to the vandalism of the headquarters. But they were understandably wary of resorting to quick violence. If everybody is all of a sudden on the side of the people, what are they—the policemen—supposed to do when the people, of their seemingly spontaneous general will, are attacking the symbols of their former oppression? And who are they supposed to take their orders from? It was surely much easier to be a policeman when they had one master, and everybody understood that the people were supposed to be kept in their place by firm and unambivalent authorities.

One of my parliamentary conversations, with an MP concerned with Turkish rights, has several twists. It takes place in a private lounge, because, he says meaningfully, "The walls still have ears." He seems uneasy even so, and once points his finger to the ceiling to let me understand that he's restraining himself from saying something because of the invisible listeners.

I can't tell whether this is justified caution or post-Communist paranoia—but I am touched by this man's gentle demeanor, his soft voice, his sympathy for the Turks. It has been the lot of the Turks in Bulgaria to play the unhappy role either of savage oppressor or the savagely oppressed. When Bulgaria freed itself from the Turkish yoke, some of the Turks—usually the poorest and least-educated ones—decided to stay. They had been in Bulgaria for many generations, after all; most of them were farmers. But the feelings against them have run deep. The latest round of persecutions against the Turks was launched in 1985, and was fueled not so much by folk prejudice as by the Communist animus against ethnic identity. The Turks, to some extent, had kept their separateness—and the Turks would be punished. The persecution took a rather bizarre, but psychologically cruel, form of requiring the Turks to take on Bulgarian names. And, in a living proof that what's in a name is the stuff of our essence, the Turks submitted to beatings, jail, and exile, rather than participate in this act of self-betrayal. Some who did submit felt it as so profound a loss of selfhood that they committed suicide. More than 300,000 people fled to Turkey, to an uncertain fate.

These persecutions were the chafing grain of sand around which the germ of the Bulgarian opposition was formed. Since the changes, more than 200,000 Turks came back—and now their lot is, legally at least, improved, though many returned to find their homes and their jobs gone. The MP to whom I'm talking has started a commission to investigate the treatment of the Turks, and to make sure that their rights are properly respected.

He talks to me about this painful subject in tones of saddened, personally felt sympathy. And so I am literally stopped in my tracks when I hear, several days later, that the same man was active in the persecutions of the Turks. I feel the sort of confusion—a quick somersault of one's assumptions—that Eastern Europeans must have experienced thousands of times, and are experiencing daily still. The sharp shock comes not only from the discovery that an ostensibly moral man could have commmitted immoral acts but also from the discovery of the utter treacherousness of one's own perceptions. It is unpleasant, it undermines one's trust in the world, to know that one can be lied to so touchingly and effectively, and I can see why political sincerity has become such an important virtue to profess, if not always, of course, to practice.

In each city I've traveled through, I've counted on the local literary club, or the literary café, for a bit of assured coziness and familiar gossip. But the tiny café in the writers' club in Sofia is so hot, so crowded, so thick with cigarette smoke that even after all the Eastern European smoke-filled rooms I find it hard to breathe there. Boris Christov, a poet whom I'm meeting, can see my difficulty, and we move to an airier space in the upstairs bookstore. Christov is one of Bulgaria's leading poets, a tall man with one of those Byzantine, long faces, a graying beard, and deep-set, serious gray eyes. He dresses in Indian shirts and sneakers, and walks as lightly as a big cat.

In our lighter space, we're joined by Blaga Dimitrova, who is also a poet and novelist, and perhaps Bulgaria's best-known literary figure. She doesn't speak much English, but something large and lovely about her personality is conveyed even across the language barrier. There is her voice, deep and deeply relaxed, with lots of air around it, as if she were playing a particularly smooth reed. It's a resonance one often hears in Bulgarian voices, which makes it less surprising that so many great operatic singers have come from here. There is also her beautiful, full smile, and a face about which there's no affectation or self-importance, but only warm responsiveness. Blaga Dimitrova is in her sixties, and she is widely learned—one of the polymaths whom one finds with unexpected frequency in Eastern Europe, perhaps because there was less pressure here to have a specialized, upward-moving career, or because, somehow, there was more time. I've read some of her writing translated into English: her poetry, which combines sensuality with an intense, meditative thoughtfulness, and one of her novels, which was daringly subversive for its time when it was published here. During those periods when to write freely was impossible, she occupied herself with translations from German, Russian, Polish, and ancient Greek.

Boris Christov had time on his hands, because he was employed by a film office on the condition that he do nothing in his "job." But he doesn't complain about this; he kept writing his poetry, and he's one of those who admits that, from a writer's point of view, this situation had its perverse merit. "We writers here were not distracted," he says. "Writing is about concentration. It needs lots of concentration and a little talent. When you're in a cell, as we were, you have the chance to concentrate." Then he changes his metaphor to explain himself better and says that writing is a form of contemplation, and writers here were "as in a rocket"—and he makes a gesture of going narrowly upward.

And in their narrow rocket, or cell, they sometimes traveled back into the deep past. Boris's own poetry—I've read some of it in English as well—pulses with surreal, pantheistic imagery, natural and religious and wild at once, full of country people and half-human beasts, and a sense of a whirling cosmos in which infinite spaces and microcosmal events are brought close together. The poems put me in mind of Bulgarian folktales, which are earthy and fantastical at once.

Both Boris and Blaga love the Bulgarian folk tradition, and they tell me about oral poetry recited in villages, which is complex and deep. Blaga talks about ancient Bulgarian myths, in which the gods are very remote—far more remote than in the Greek myths—and therefore nature is very important, because it mediates between these distant deities and the world of humans.

"If you understand these stories," Boris says rather mystically, "you'll understand our abyss."

"An abyss?" I ask. "Yes," he says, "I propose you this metaphor: an abyss, with a maze at the bottom."

I am out of my depth with this; our linguistic communication is less than perfect. But I'm struck by these two writers' appreciation of their own culture. In Bulgarian conversations, I've noticed little of that inferiority complex that is so marked in other Eastern European countries. Perhaps it's Bulgaria's geographical location, self-contained and tucked far away from the contemporary main drags; or perhaps it is the ancientness of its culture and the cultural "sense of self" that has acccumulated over centuries. Whatever the reasons, Bulgarians move in the world of ideas with the openness and ease of anybody's peers. Bulgarian intelligentsia is amazingly well informed about all manner of things Western; but their receptivity seems to come not so much from bedazzlement with the center's glitter, as from something precisely the opposite—a sense of their own, independent sufficiency.

I ask Boris and Blaga whether they ever thought of emigrating. Boris, in response, tells me of a conversation he had with a man from the University of Iowa, who tried to offer him a job there and a big, rent-free house. Boris said, "A man needs his own house, and his friends. His water and his apple tree."

"And his problems," Blaga adds, smiling her lovely smile.

"And his enemies," Boris clinches. "I said to the man in Iowa, I'll come if you can surround my house with my enemies. What can a man do without his enemies?"

And then Boris speaks about how Sofia is the middle of the world, and of the wonderful faces one sees here, created by centuries of cultural intermingling. He talks about how you can trace the continuity of culture from India to here in the various shades of blue along the old silk road; and how you can follow the movement of cultures in the human smile, which becomes more open as you go West.

And what about the road to Europe? I ask, using the trope of the season.

"The road to Europe?" he repeats skeptically, as if it weren't the most important thing. "I think the road to Europe is inside us."

"And maybe around us," Blaga says. This is a conception I've only met with here.

Taxis in Sofia have no meters, and for the same ride they can charge anywhere from three to thirty *leva,* which at the moment translates to a range of forty cents to a bit over four dollars. Almost all of them, however, have mawkish erotic postcards affixed to the windshield. Even the one woman driver I encounter has one, as if such a picture were the badge of her profession.

Krassi, exceptionally, doesn't have one. Instead, he has a fuzzy yellow animal and a holy picture suspended above his dashboard. Krassi is Boris's friend, and he's taking me to a gathering at Boris's house. On the way, he keeps making metaphorical observations.

"That's how we were under Communism," he says, pointing to a rather unusual sight—a pitiable-looking bear being led on a leash by a shabbily dressed Gypsy. "We were like this poor animal led by a beggar who pretended to be a master."

Or, noticing a bench hobbled by a caved-in leg: "That's how Communism is right now. We've broken one of its legs. Now we have to break the other ones."

Finally, I become impressed enough by the concreteness of his rage so that I ask him why he hates Communism so much. "Because it restricted the answers to all civilized questions," he answers.

So much for my expectations of naïveté. Moreover, for him, too, the "civilized answers" seem to lie right here, in Bulgaria. At some point, he plays a jazz tape, and when I say I've never heard Bulgarian jazz, he responds proudly, "Oh, yes, we have everything here. And now the world is going to know about it."

Krassi has just returned from Sweden, where he tried to be a guest worker, but he could rarely find any work; and now he has no job here, except this highly unreliable taxi business. He is Boris's neighbor in a block on the periphery of Sofia. "Our jail," he says as we approach the gigantic project, making a smiling bow in its direction. Indeed, these collectivist blocks are enormous, and their sprawling unendingness multiplies the sense of anonymity and human reduction.

Boris, however, is in an expansive, grand-vizier mood and greets everyone with formal graciousness. "You are welcome here, in my home, in Bulgaria, as long as I live," he declares, raising his glass to me and another American, a poet who is his English translator.

A friend, just returned to Bulgaria after thirty-two years' absence, arrives. "He's one of our most real, greatest writers," Boris announces. "And this—" pointing to me and the translator—"is my favorite prose writer and my favorite poet from America."

"Bulgarians use only heavy words," the new arrival says. He has lived in the West and he knows that this sort of hyperbole wouldn't go over there.

Others come in, one of them, or perhaps both, the greatest, the very greatest filmmaker in Bulgaria. They're supposed to be in trouble these days—their subsidies have been cut off, after all—but their mood seems excellent. One is making a film about their friend's return after thirty-two years. "It's just for us, for our friends," he explains. The exile, in turn, says that he and Boris are working on "a small program, just for our friends. He's going to play the trumpet, and I'll sing, and maybe write some new poetry, and we'll go and serenade our friends."

"This is how we like to do things," someone throws in. "For our friends." They really don't seem to care whether the world is watching.

"We prefer this language of music," the exile tells me. "Did you know that ninety percent of conversation is nonverbal? And the other ten percent is disinformation."

Music is the aspect of Bulgarian culture that Boris loves above all. He often gets together with village musicians for jam sessions, and he has a wonderful collection of folk instruments, most of them of ancient provenance: a wooden, flat block, with two pipes within it called *dvoyanka,* and another one with three pipes. There is also an instrument Boris devised to symbolize the possibility of Turkish-Bulgarian coexistence, which combines the Turkish *zurna* and the Bulgarian *duduk.*

Several of these instruments are capable of producing double lines of music and the complex harmonics required for the extraordinary music of Balkan peasants and shepherds. This is music whose wild, errant rhythms have an almost ungraspable intricacy, and whose sonorities and open fifth harmonies breathe enormous spaces. The alternately piercing and watery timbres of the instruments seem to come from across the mountains, or perhaps from somewhere further still; the jagged, circling, complicated patterns break out and then wind in on themselves like tautologies of longing.

"If you listen to this music, you'll know too much about our people," Boris says, meaning that I'll know quite a bit. "Every country has its blues and these are our Balkan blues."

We sit quietly for a while after Boris finishes, and then the American poet recites some child's verses he has memorized in Bulgarian, and everyone breaks into a noise of big-worded, highly gratifying appreciation. Throughout my travels, I've looked for living "authentic" folklore, and each time it has eluded me. The authentic is almost never found by being pursued; but there is no missing it when you are in its presence.

Indefatigable Dimitrina has introduced me to several university students who belong to a group, hitherto clandestine, called Praxis. They are a lively, vigorous bunch, whose ambition is nothing less than to embrace and practice all the arts. They write poems and novels, compose, paint, and they've even managed, in very unpropitious pre-1989 conditions, to make short movies.

As a sort of explanation of their origins, one of the Praxis members takes me to a place they call the Fantasy Club—though the full name of this organization, which by now strikes me as very Bulgarian, is the Integrative Club of Science Fiction, Heuristics, and Prognostics. It is located right in the official Culture Center, but until recently, the club was one of those interstitial institutions that existed in all Eastern European countries, and where, under the cover of eccentricity, or marginality, unofficial ideas could be discussed. I meet the club's founder, a pale middle-aged man with longish hair, in a dim room painted over by swirling images of mythical beasts and intergalactic spaces. He has had something of a guru status among the creative young, and he considers science fiction a high form, a way of thinking about the future, which is also a way of thinking about moral problems. In the club, they discussed not only the works of Stanislaw Lem and Isaac Asimov, but also such matters as "national problems and global problems," "Western and Eastern styles of thinking," "the future of the sub and contracultures," not to speak of "the syndrome of Oedipus" or "the future of sex relations."

The creative products of the Praxis group show definite marks of these influences. I meet with several of them again, in the inevitable dismal box apartment, which, however, becomes kinetic from the sheer vivacity of the people gathered there. The evident leader of the group is a long-haired, robust young man, whose artistic appetites are omnivorous. A beautiful Afghan dog, who shows an almost perfect morphological resemblance to the long-legged, thin hostess, bounds around the tiny living room. Her husband is a serious young man with a direct manner, and, like all of them, a background in philosophy. After spending some time in Sofia, I'm quite convinced that the city has more philosophers per capita than Harvard or the Sorbonne.

The friendship between the host and the leader of the group was cemented during a sort of exile in Libya, where their parents worked for an oil company. Libya seems like a strange window on the world, but it was there, though they felt isolated and unhappy, that they discovered the world didn't consist only of actually existing socialism, and there, that their rebellion began. Their works are supposed to be an expression of that rebellion, though to me, they seem a curious mix of high intellectuality and profound kitschiness. I'm shown lengthy poems, badly translated into English, about quests in fantastical worlds, featuring chalices, priestly figures, and other allegorical items. Then somebody plays a tape of their songs on the stereo—they're very proud of their mixing technology, though, truth to tell, the music sounds to me like a rather awful concoction of New Age mysticism and aleatory amorphousness sprawl.

Still, the peculiarity of the creations notwithstanding, there is something appealing about the creators, with their crackling energy, their forthrightness, and the unaffected sense of their own legitimacy, which has allowed them to hatch all these projects entirely on their own resources, and without any hope of reward or even acknowledgment. They seem to regard themselves as capable of almost anything; or rather, they do not seem to recognize the notion of difficulty. Their latest project is no less than a draft for a new Bulgarian constitution. They show me this thick document, which has also been translated into English. It's a detailed, well-thought-out proposal, and they tell me that in preparation for it they studied many countries' constitutions and held discussions about their political philosophy late into the night.

It's a measure of their strong sense of themselves that they thought their draft should be taken up by the government for discussion directly; and they're frustrated by having been made to wait. I am, again, impressed by the seriousness of their intentions. Although they're only in their early twenties, they evidently do not think of themselves as "young adults" still experimenting with life, but as people with fully mature purposes. But for the leader of the group, who's not only an extremely nice young man, but an angry young man as well, the disappointment of being ignored by the government is yet another spark fanning his fury at the limits imposed on him. He wants to break out of these limits; he wants to emigrate.

On the subject of emigration, I've become like Hamlet on marriages: I want to let us have no more of it. I understand the irony of this, of course; but the costs of uprooting and the relentless migrating urge—propelling whole populations westward and northward, as if by some bent heliotropic force—have begun to seem despairing and desperate to me. Why does hope always travel in one direction? And is it not going to become diminished everywhere, if we always pursue it elsewhere? And so I launch into my antiemigration diatribe: If you go to a new country, you're bound to have at least ten hard years before finding your footing; why not have ten hard years here, where you can participate in building a new world?

But the long-haired artist bridles at this, and bristles with impatience. He'll do any job in America, any at all. He'd rather meet with hardship there than be treated like a slave in his own country. "They didn't respect their own people," he says passionately, still referring to the old Them. "Do you know what that means?"

"That may may have been true until now, but it's about to change, isn't it?" I ask.

"Yes, but I have only my life," he says. "I don't want to be a member of another lost generation; there've been enough of those."

The host concurs, though his wife is less sure. She's content to finish her philosophy degree here, and she thinks that her husband's stories, which try to combine science fiction with political satire, will be published soon. But the young men struggle with the great temptation of a better place. In their minds, "better" seems to have to do not so much with greater prosperity as with more dignity. Their standard of dignity is wonderfully high; and it is just that dignity, the proud sense of their human worth, that would doubtless suffer injuries wherever they emigrated to. But of this they cannot be convinced; they are young, and they want to catch their fate like a bull by the horns, strongly, decisively, and right now.

I am to meet a group of psychologists from the Kliment Ohridsky University at the Kristal café, right next to a little park that has become the center of the new bohemian commerce— this being the first kind of commerce to appear after the break- down. As in most such places springing up instantly all over Eastern Europe, the quality of the wares displayed is frankly hid- eous, making Telegraph Avenue in Berkeley look like a haven of high design. Icon reproductions of unbelievable crudeness pre- dominate. When I inquire about the prices at a stand, the seller assures me, "They're expensive, very expensive." Bulgarian frankness may be quite unsuited to the ways of capitalism. Fur- ther on, several young men are prancing with wild energy on an outdoor stage, singing hard rock and trying to sound hoarse, though failing to disguise completely their beautiful, resonant voices.

At the Kristal café, I sit with the newly-met psychologists in a sweltering, smoke-filled room, and wait for coffee quite hope- lessly. We talk about the projects they are engaged in, the con- tacts they've made in the West. Once again, I'm struck by their resourcefulness: just as soon as the opening came, they started organizing conferences, international research projects, compara- tive studies. Nothing seems out of reach to them. At some point, I mention casually that I'd like to make some out-of-town excursions. No problem, they say—no problem at all. They'll or- ganize a trip for me to Plovdiv, one of Bulgaria's most historic cities. But how? why? I protest. "We like to do this," they assure me. "We like to help our guests." They quickly decide that Nadja, whom I haven't yet met, is the one to guide me. Someone gets up to make a phone call, and comes back to announce that Nadja will be happy to take me to Plovdiv. Presto—it's done. This is how things seem to happen in Bulgaria, quickly and simply, as if it were easier to take action than not to.

The next day I meet Nadja at an appointed place, and she assures me, with convincing enthusiasm, that going to Plovdiv is just what she'd like to do. It's no problem, her husband will drive us in their car. The only thing is that, in order to go, we need gas; and whether we can get it is not at all certain. But her husband will try a gas station this evening; sometimes you can get into an all-night queue, and buy gas in the morning. All night? I say incredulously. Oh, yes, Nadja says smiling. He's used to it.

Ultimately, Nadja's husband buys gas with my dollars, at a special foreign-currency station where the wait is only something like three hours, instead of the usual twelve or fifteen, and on a shimmering, sunny morning we set out on the highway to Plovdiv. The landscape, as we come out of the low Ljulin Mountains, is arid and harsh, alternating dry green and yellow stubble; this has been a summer of droughts and fires all over Eastern Europe. As we bear south, the scrubby brush begins to resemble northern parts of Greece, to which we are quite close. But this is also the route to Istanbul, traversed by successions of merchants and armies, by the Thracians and the Macedonians, the Romans and the Byzantines, the Crusaders and the Turks.

No signs are left, however, of this rich history. The only landmark in the bare hills is a one-story cement box that is a roadside café. Since it's actually open, and since it actually serves strong Turkish coffee, I'm as happy to have come upon this rather unsightly place as upon any noble monument; for the last few mornings, I've been suffering serious coffee withdrawal from the tepid brew served in my hotel.

Nadja is a lovely-looking woman in her early twenties, very tall, olive-skinned, with a stylish mane of black hair, doe-soft black eyes, and a fresh, melodious laugh. Demian, her husband, seems to be in the first stages of a summer flu, and he fusses with a thermometer and tea, while she teases him good-naturedly about pampering himself. "But I like being pampered," he declares. I happen to have some aspirin in my handbag, in which all of us invest great hope; aspirin is rare here, and therefore its powers seem more magical.

Plovdiv itself is one of those schizophrenic cities in which the disparity between the old and the new is particularly jarring, because the new is so unsightly: on the outskirts, factories producing computer parts; further in, the sprawling inhuman blocks and the soc-realist hotels.

But the other part—well, it has all the charm of the unclassifiable and the unfamiliar. "The Old Town meets us with its odour of basil and ancient woodwork parching in the sun. Short and narrow winding streets with their multicoloured clusters of houses and their perching in top of each other oriels and bay windows huddled up as if breathlessly whispering in each other's ears pour out relaxing silence and quiet beauty." Thus raves one Plovdiv brochure, trying to make up with poetic suggestiveness what it lacks in grammar.

The cobbled streets of the Old Town are very steep and exceedingly narrow, and the houses are built in what is known as the National Revival style of architecture. This esthetic was a rather self-conscious child of the late eighteenth and early nineteenth centuries and the reawakening of Bulgarian identity, after its long dormancy. And since Bulgarian identity didn't have many avenues of expression aside from the arts, these became infused with all kinds of folk-national implications. The National Revival houses, usually built by wealthy merchants, tried to synthesize various elements of native arts and crafts. The results are quite specifically Bulgarian and very beautiful. The Old Town houses have upper stories that are broader than the bases, thus reversing our usual expectations—though not so much as to violate our sense of balance. Outside, they are painted in pastel colors, accentuated by dark wood borders. Inside—for several of them are preserved as museums—they are an enchanting mix of indigenous crafts and cosmopolitan fashions. The owners of these houses could afford to bring back delicate French bureaus and satin-upholstered chaises longues from their travels; but for the structural work, they hired local woodworkers, who plied their craft with great refinement and subtlety. The ceilings, doorways, and shutters in these houses are made of light, almost white wood, and carved with beautiful, simple patterns that transpose traditional folk motifs into a slightly more elegant vein. No patterns, from room to room, are alike, since the rich merchants considered it shameful to resort to repetition, and thus reveal either inadequate imagination or insufficient funds. The guest quarters in these houses are by far the most sumptuous; these houses date from a time when hospitality was also a form of conspicuous display. In the center of the main salon's ceiling, there is usually a delicately carved rosette serving as a symbol of abundance.

One of the larger houses in town used to belong to a painter, Zlatin Bojadzev, and on entering it, I find that I'm faced yet again with that rarest of rarities—something for which neither my expectations nor my esthetic categories have prepared me. The house is now a museum devoted to Bojadzev's work, and it is divided into two distinct parts, just as his life, was distinctly divided. Bojadzev surely had one of the more unusual careers in the annals of art: he spent the first half of his years painting with his right hand, and the second half—after an early stroke—with his left. With both, he was very good, though it was only after the stroke that he seemed to find his full style and power. In his early, right-handed paintings, deep Dutch earth tones and blocky forms are applied to rather conventional scenes of peasant life. The later canvases are bigger, the painting looser and wilder. Most of them are also scenes of local village life, but they express more of the local tone, the simultaneous earthiness and fantasy that can be felt in Bulgarian fairy tales or poems. There are broad figures of peasants and vinegar merchants reminiscent of the surrealism of Botero; there are Chagall-like gatherings of dreamers in magic village streets, and circles of peasants prostrating themselves in prayers for rain. There is a group portrait of Bojadzev's family, in which the painter himself, bearded, suited, and pensive, is clearly the first "intelligent." His grandmother looks like a malicious witch, about to fly off on the missile of her elongated nose, and in the front row, there's a man who has just slit the throat of a very large, profusely bleeding pig. The position of being the first intellectual has its richness—and it's a richness characteristic of Eastern Europe, where peasant culture and modernity clashed and converged with abrupt, contradictory, fertile proximity.

I want to find out more about Bojadzev's life and influences, but the museum guide has just enough English, or perhaps just enough knowledge, to talk like a guidebook parrot. "He was a master," she keeps repeating in a twittering tone, as if that should satisfy me. "Master" seems to be not only a description of greatness but a professional category, as in "master craftsman." I like the idea of professional gradings for artists—why should they be exempt from sensible judgment more than anyone else?—but for the guide, this seems to imply that Bojadzev is beyond human judgment or explanation. And so there he remains, hermetically enclosed in his one museum, unexplained, unknown beyond Bulgaria—and in himself quite complete.

Throughout the day's vicissitudes, Nadja has retained her unflappable, mild good humor, and her easy command of what needs to be done. So when she declares a lunch break, we follow her happily to a restaurant, where we get a fresh, acceptable meal, served on a sunny terrace under umbrellas.

It transpires, during our lunchtime conversation, that Nadja and Demian hold somewhat different views of the changes. Nadja, who is in her early twenties, was described by one of her psychology colleagues as "one of our most fighting students." I find this hard to reconcile with her very gentle manner, but certainly the recent events have been the centerpiece of her young life. She has a characteristic gesture—a sort of triple shake of the hand, both delicate and defiant, which indicates that something is "really something," and that's what she resorts to as she talks about what has happened in her country. "When we heard that people were getting together, and we went to those meetings of Eco-Glasnost—oh, it was such a feeling of freedom!" she says. "It was the first time we could talk about so many things publicly, and we saw that others felt the same way. Everything changed then."

Not that everything has become easier; far from it. Nadja spends long hours in queues in order to get a few items for dinner; the money that she makes as a graduate teaching assistant and Demian's salary as a beginning architect-engineer barely cover the rent. But I can sense her excitement about the adventure of living in a changed country; her life has become bound up with this.

Demian is more of an angry young man—angry about what the Communists have done and what they're doing still, angry about being held back in his job by the lack of technology and money. He wants to leave—maybe for Canada, maybe for Greece, where Nadja has some relatives—anywhere but here.

In the meantime, Demian isn't standing still. He is developing new irrigation techniques for the dry Bulgarian fields, and he has written an American firm specializing in the necessary equipment, suggesting some form of cooperation. He speaks about this with the ease to which I'm becoming accustomed in his countrymen. His enterprise seems to him quite natural; and I can't help but think that if this kind of energy is applied right here, in Bulgaria, then Bulgaria is bound to get itself out of its doldrums.

We're getting ready to leave the restaurant when an elderly, soft-spoken man seated in the corridor asks us in a somewhat mysterious voice if we would like to see something interesting. Of course we would. What follows is a tour through the restaurant building. It turns out that in the early nineteenth century, this used to be the home of a Turkish merchant, and it has a genuine seraglio room, a beautiful, circular space with a bright blue tiled ceiling, copper-topped coffee tables next to red plush benches, and a little voyeuristic balcony from which the owner watched his concubines disporting below. But that's not all. Our guide next leads us, with proprietorial pride, to a lower level, where there are the remains of a Turkish bath, which had been built on still visible remains of a Roman floor. On the steps leading to the small bathing pit, there are several large, curvaceous earthen pots, from which water was poured on the bathers.

The guide resolutely refuses to take any money for this condensed demonstration of Plovdiv's antiquity. We stroll about, finding evidence of that antiquity everywhere. I never fail to be moved by knowing that the ground on which I walk is layered with the past—with achievement and strife and the repeated passions and conflicts of the human creature, always changing, always the same. Generations passing like grass. There was a town here in Thracian times, called Pulpudeva, which was renamed Philippopolis by Philip II of Macedonia, and Trimontium by the Romans and Filipe by the Turks. And, at the foot of one of Plovdiv's several hills, there stand, still dazzling in their white proportions, the remaining columns and seats of a Roman amphitheater, very much resembling the fragments in Aix-en-Provence. Trajan built this one in A.D. 114–117, and Attila nearly smashed it. The surprise of seeing it here is wonderful, for walking along its semicircled stone benches, one could be anywhere in Europe, and the distances and boundaries between Bulgaria and France, or Italy, or England, dissolve, and so do enormous distances of time, until one is simply in Europe, and Europe's history itself, if only for the briefest moment, becomes a transcendent, unifying force.

The unexpected, ah, the unexpected, I have found you in this strangely familiar guise, at last.

The next day we drive on steeply climbing roads, to Dolny Vidin, a village near Plovdiv with a part-Bulgarian, part-Turkish population. It's a hilly place, harsh with stone; the stone is everywhere, crumbled into small sharp pieces on the paths, piled up in hillocks, serving for rough stairs to the ungainly, boxlike houses, many of them built of stone as well. In the small central square, several men are sitting on a bench, fingering oblong prayer beads the color of dark amber. We sit chatting with them; their manner is subdued; they look at the ground. They all agree that the person we should meet is the schoolteacher; he'll tell us everything we want to know. Within a few minutes, this personage appears—he has clearly heard that there are foreigners in town. His manner is sharp and authoritative, and he questions us suspiciously about who we are. Once Nadja reassures him—she's translating—he wants to show us the local mosque. On the outside, the mosque is simply another ugly cement house. Here, the devout used to gather for prayers in secret; the Turks in the village haven't been allowed to build a real mosque, to offend with mosaic and minaret. Inside, some of the elements of a real mosque have been rather forlornly replicated: in a square room, the walls are multicolored, the floors are covered with layers of rugs; in one wall, a niche is filled with strings of beads and flowers. But the building lacks some details essential to the practice of the Muslim faith, the schoolteacher says—for example, the minaret. Now, at last, the Turks of Dolny Vidin are hoping to build a real mosque.

Several other men have followed us inside, and they stand about silently, their manner timid, even deferential. They couldn't be further removed from the fierce Turk of popular stereotype; they are men whose heads seem habitually lowered, who evidently don't think of themselves as people who can speak. They emanate an ineffably depressed air.

As the schoolteacher unfolds his story, Nadja gives her triple shake of the hand. It turns out that the mad policy of name-changing began right here, in Dolny Vidin, and the teacher was among those who were harshly persecuted. He spent a few months in a prison camp nearby, which had fallen into disuse since the Stalinist fifties, but was reactivated in 1985 for this new group of inmates. Eventually, like most people from the village, he fled to Turkey; then, like many, he came back, though his wife and child have stayed behind. "Many of us didn't like the style of life in Turkey," he says, "and there were no jobs. Bulgaria is our home, we've been here for centuries. But some of us are still afraid to come back. The *nomenklatura* is still here, the people who beat us and drove us out."

"It's very heavy for them, very heavy," Nadja says as we come out. Indeed, it looks so. The schoolteacher takes us to his house. It's a melancholy place. The outside is overgrown with weeds, the stairs consist of a few stones unevenly piled on each other. Inside, one small room is relatively neat; that's where he really lives, with his bed and bare table. The rest of the rooms look as though a hurricane or an invading army had passed through just yesterday. There are pieces of glass on the floor, sacks of spilled onions, and the pathetic innards of closets and drawers—shoes, pots, rags, all thrown about pell-mell, in that desolate scene of our times, the scene of chaos and flight. People often had only a few hours to pack their belongings and leave and he has kept the evidence intact, perhaps as a demonstration, or a kind of memento. In a neighboring apartment, a mattress, still in its plastic wrapping, leans against a wall. The owners have that habitually frightened, burdened expression. "They're ready to leave any time," the teacher says. "We're still not sure if we're safe. That's why they don't unwrap the mattress."

In another apartment, we're invited to stay for coffee, which is served by the wife, while the husband, a rather Western-looking person with ambitions in local politics, talks to us about the issues of village life. The wife is about to retreat to the kitchen but we encourage her to stay. She consents, but I can see that it's painful for her to face strangers in this unaccustomed way. She sits with her eyes cast down, clearly assuming that her husband will answer all the questions for her. She's pretty and dressed as an unpretentious young woman in any Eastern European small town might dress, rather than in the traditional harem pants I'd seen on older Turkish women. But I've become so accustomed to the feisty, fully emancipated and articulate women I've been meeting in Bulgaria that this shy, diffident creature seems to come from another epoch. I find myself observing her with too much anthropological curiosity; she is, after all, an incarnation of that silent Woman whom I've always thought somewhat mythical; and I keep wondering what it might be like to be her. She doesn't, to be accurate, look at all unhappy. Nadja tries to draw her out, but she's clearly relieved when we divert our attention from her and slips away quietly when she thinks we aren't paying attention. "Yes, there's an Oriental element to all this," the husband says, to show us that he is a modern man, and understands how his wife's behavior might appear to us.

Out on the stony street, we are approached by a young man with sandy hair and sad blue eyes, who introduces himself as a sort of village representative, and who offers to escort us around Dolny Vidin. His name is Ahmed, and he is the local secretary of the Movement for Human Rights and Freedoms, as well as an "artist"—though from the vague way he says that, smiling wanly, it's hard to tell of what kind, or even what the word means to him. Ahmed has a face that easily fills with feeling, especially sadness, and a wistful, philosophical way of talking. He takes us to his "office" at the edge of the village; it's nothing but a bare, unpainted space with a dented desk in the middle, but Ahmed sits behind it with the dignity of his position, and he tells us that this room has become important in the village. People come in all the time to ask for advice on their affairs. Many of them hardly know what their new rights are, or how to go about getting a job—and it's part of the continuing prejudice that, in a time of economic hardship, the Turks are the first to be fired. Ahmed skirts the question of his own employment; he seems to be ashamed of having no work. He talks instead about how hurt the Turks still are, in the aftermath of the persecutions. The worst thing is that they didn't get even a simple "I'm sorry" from those who wounded them. Still, Ahmed believes that if it weren't for "politics," the people in the village could live in friendship and love. Today is a holiday, during which a lamb will be slaughtered in sacrifice; but in his mind, the sacrifice is not to an Islamic deity, but to love, because only love among people is important. His eyes fill with emotion.

"Maybe I'm a romantic," he says, smiling sadly—and that's just what he seems to be. He puts me in mind of the village romantics often met in Russian, and for that matter in Bulgarian, novels of an earlier time—gentle souls who, from their small spots in the world, dream grand, melancholy dreams of universal harmony.

We meet another kind of romantic later in the day, an old farmer who is a friend of Ahmed's and who just got his land back, after thirty-five years. His farm, climbing up a hill, has plots of maize and onions, and a lovely orchard. He is working up in a cherry tree when we come by, and when he gets down from his ladder, I tell him that life can't be all bad when one has such beautiful cherries.

"Ah, but we don't live by cherries alone," he responds sadly. He's a truly beautiful old man, small and lean, with a finely lined, sensitive face. His hands are deeply stained with cherry juice.

His land, like all the farms around here, was taken away from him and collectivized in 1956. But he himself wouldn't work for the collective, and as a result, he got beat up and then imprisoned. It may have been particularly bitter for Bulgarian peasants to accept collectivization, since they considered themselves higher in the social hierarchy than the "workers"—the putative aristocrats of the Soviet system—who now came to run the villages. Aside from its priestly elite, Bulgaria has never had an aristocracy, and the peasants constituted the backbone of the nation, a sort of natural aristocracy. Being evicted from their land was, aside from all else, a great blow to their status and self-esteem.

After coming out of prison, the farmer tried to work on the collectivized land for several years; but that was more painful still. The people brought in from the outside, in lieu of the rebelling peasants, didn't know how to treat the land—his land. He found it unbearable to look at this, so he went to work in the zinc factory down below—even though he hates it, because it's poisoning the soil around here. He wants it shut down.

"But now I can finally work my land again," he says. "That's all I want." We are sitting directly on the parched, hard ground, and he takes some of the soil in his hands to show me that this, this is what it is all about—and quite unexpectedly, a dry sob contorts his face.

For a few moments, he sits very upright, his face fully exposed to us, sobbing. I think of old Bulgarian stories in which love of land is the predominant passion, moving human souls to greed as well as rootedness, and to murderous conflict. Still, I can't help being moved by such strength of attachment to a place, a particular plot of earth, and by the ability to cry at this age for something loved and lost and regained so late. The past redeemed is never redeemed entirely, or at least it comes accompanied by this knowledge of what might have been possible, of the years that will not come back.

"The Communists," Demian says angrily as we walk back, and he kicks a tree. Ahmed, who is carrying a bucket of cherries he picked while we were talking, tells us that the farmer was someone the Turks felt they could trust. "We always knew who was a good person," he says. "He was solitary and didn't say much, but there was something we knew was good. Something inward."

The Turks rarely owned land, so they have nothing to reclaim. They work in the zinc factory, and at low-skilled jobs; some of them find seasonal employment in the nearby tobacco fields. Ahmed, who has plenty of time on his hands, offers to take us there, and we drive along a stony, dusty road till we come to a field of plastic tents, in which the tobacco leaves have been hung to dry. There is nobody here. In the tents, the merciless sun and the overpowering smell of tobacco blend into something so suffocating that none of us can bear to stay inside for more than a few seconds. But the people who work here—mostly women, it seems—stay in the tents for long hours. Demian looks faint; Nadja gives her "it's really something" shake of the hand.

On the way back, Ahmed shows us a mural painted on the side of a prosperous Bulgarian house, and tells us that it was done by him, on the owner's commission. I am surprised by its competence, but Ahmed says he got into trouble because of it. The mural shows a very stylized, long-robed woman who looks closer to an abstract pattern than a realistic figure, and what got Ahmed into trouble was her breasts. These breasts, if you look closely, are indicated by Turkish crescent moons, and someone perceived nationalist sentiment in them; as a result, Ahmed was asked to leave his job. Or so he says. His manner is so softly evasive that it leaves me in some doubt of his veracity. Did he, in fact, paint the mural himself?

The evening falls pinkly in Dolny Vidin. We're ready to leave the village, but Ahmed pauses in a street, and, his manner suddenly turning very formal, invites us to be "guests in his house." Nadja quickly tells me this is a matter of honor, and so, with some formality, we accept. The entrance to his apartment building has the curious disorderliness that seems to prevail at the thresholds of the village houses. A door has been ripped out, and there are fragments of glass and pieces of sharp wire strewn about. It's as if the outside didn't count in the mentality of these house dwellers—as if the separation between the inside and the outside were abrupt and total.

But inside there's a decent room—two bunk beds, neatly made, a long table covered with a tablecloth. A quiet young man, Ahmed's roommate, brings us wonderful coffee and delicious halvah of great density. Ahmed talks dreamily of California, where he has an uncle who has promised to invite him, so he can take a course in an art school there, and become a "real artist.". . . Then he turns his hopes to his grandfather, who is a sage and respected healer, and who may get rich if he cures a young boy of epilepsy, which he's trying to do with a special medicine, involving a frog swallowed by a snake and injected with the snake's poison juices. . . .

At some point in our conversation, Ahmed brings out a drawing of a mosque, which he would like to design for the vil-

lage. Now I am ashamed of my suspicions. The drawing is surprisingly good, executed with precise detail and a touch of
Piranesi picturesqueness. I ask him how much he knows of the
Turkish, or the Islamic, tradition. Not very much, it seems. The
Turks in the village go to the hidden mosque and celebrate most
of the holidays, and sometimes they pray for rain. But the Koran
was forbidden reading, and most younger people know it only
through oral stories of the elders. "The Bulgarians were worried
we would become fanatics, fundamentalists, like the Shiites," he
says, smiling. "But we are not. We are like other Bulgarians. We
are modern people."

Modern and premodern, it seems to me—blended in a curious, baffling mix. During part of our conversation, Ahmed has
been making laborious strokes on a piece of paper with a thick
pencil, and before we leave, he gives me his handiwork—again,
a well-crafted drawing of a generic Turk, with a message in Bulgarian, which resembles Russian enough so I can read it. It expresses his fraternal feelings, and his hope for understanding
between all people in the world.

But as we say good-bye, his mood changes, becomes more
melancholy. "If you write a book about all this, I have a title for
you," he says as we shake hands. "I think you should call it *The
Year After the Hope.*" And so we leave him, looking now not
only wistful but downcast, depressed. He has told us his dreams,
his ideas and visions, and now he has to go right back into his
ordinary life, which remains just the same as it was yesterday.

The next morning, we veer south into the Rhodope Mountains,
to stop at the ancient Bačkovo monastery. The mountains here
rise in dramatic, flat walls of rock, and fall into deep gorges, cut
by foaming, wild streams. The monastery emerges at the top like
yet another, particularly regular, rock formation.

There are many of these fortress monasteries in Bulgaria,
some of them more than a thousand years old, and they were
crucial to the survival of Bulgarian culture. Here, learning and
literature were preserved when they were extinguished else-

where, and national sentiments could be expressed freely. As it happens, Bačkovo had to be abandoned when the Turks came in, and the monks came back only in the seventh century. But many monasteries were centers not only of contemplation but also of subversive activity. They often sheltered the *hajduks,* or peasant partisans, who roamed the mountains trying to wrest concessions from the Turkish occupants, or take revenge for extortionary taxation and plain robbery of Bulgarian households. Among the *hajduks,* there were quite a few women, including leaders of guerrilla units. Centuries of costly, unsubdued rebellion: the Bulgarian, no less than the Polish, or the Hungarian pattern.

Aside from offering refuge to the *hajduks,* the monasteries were part of ordinary life in Bulgaria, and the monks rarely indulged in the excesses of ascetic piety practiced by their Catholic counterparts. In Bulgarian folktales and stories, the priest is often a sinning sort of mortal, more a figure of fun than of reverence. And the literature preserved in the monasteries included bawdy, realistic descriptions of daily life. I've been told about a priestly glossary of obscene verses and words, in which the Bulgarian language is apparently very rich.

Bačkovo is approached on foot by a long, steep road, and preceded by a Balkan bazaar with stands selling ground nuts and raisins, odd pieces of discarded clothing, and the usual array of new, badly-painted icons. The monastery itself is a beautiful place, combining the richness of old architecture and ornament with the unharnessed freshness of the natural setting. Its founding structures date all the way back to 1083, the height of the Second Bulgarian Empire, and it consists of several chapels, churches, and dormitories, connected by arched walkways and courtyards. By now, I recognize with satisfaction some of its architectural elements from the National Revival houses, in which they were later repeated; each culture seems to have these signature forms, clues to its vision of the world. There are ornamented wooden balconies attached to brick buildings, jutting top stories, and, as in Romanian monasteries, gorgeous external frescoes.

At the entry to one of the churches, a group of people are waiting for a baptism. A deacon beckons us inside, and we walk into that other kind of slow, untargeted time. It's dim and cool in the tiny chapel, and the twelfth-century frescoes, covering the walls from floor to the high, cylindrical dome, create the sense of plenitude in miniature. The deacon and Demian sit in the recessed side pews, and talk in low voices across the high dividers. Perhaps because they've arranged themselves into a perfect photograph—an image by Kertesz or Cartier-Bresson—I have the impression that the deacon, in his spacious black soutane with stained sleeves, and his white, uncombed beard, and his twisted, disaffected lip, has spent his whole life thus, in the recess of the bench, whispering. At one point, Demian shows him a cigarette lighter; the deacon has never seen one, and tries futilely to make it light up.

We wait. After forty-five minutes or so, the deacon gets up reluctantly, lights a few candles, and picks up some buckets leaning against the ancient frescoes, to fill them with water for the baptism. "Once it begins, it'll be over in fifteen minutes," he assures us. "This priest doesn't waste any time on these things."

Finally, the priest, in a resplendent robe decorated with a gold-embroidered blue satin sash, comes in, followed by the waiting throng. Immediately, the small interior is filled with a cheerful hubbub. The infants wail, their mothers smile. The ceremony itself is indeed as efficient as the stamping of a document. Each infant has water poured over it three times, the sign of a cross is made over its forehead, and the baby is then quickly bundled up in a towel brought by some attending relative. Two adolescent boys and two grown men are going through the rite as well. "Communists," Demian whispers vindictively, for the former *nomenklatura* is getting religion fast these days, to show that they are truly of the people. Communists or not, the men and the boys smile enormous, happy smiles at the few drops of water poured over their bare backs, and then everyone joins hands and walks around in a circle, while the priest makes rather perfunctory gestures of blessing. Then everyone breaks up in chatter and laughter. There's nothing reverent in the atmosphere of the little chapel, least of all the quick-moving priest and the sour deacon. But then, despite the current fashion for religion, the Bulgarians on the whole are a resiliently secular people, I've been often told, attached to what they can see and touch and feel, rather than to extraterrestrial beliefs. I've heard this tendency bemoaned by some, who think that a stronger church and stronger religious feelings, such as prevail in Poland, would have been an antidote to Communism. But perhaps the earthy empiricism has something to do with that health of personality I've sensed here, with that lack of self-consciousness and self-contortion and self-doubt. Later in the day, I ask Nadja, who has studied the subject of loneliness, what the acknowledged social pathologies in Bulgaria are. Well—loneliness is one; then, after thinking some more, she comes up with smoking. On the whole, this seems like a fairly bucolic state of affairs.

From Bačkovo, we drive straight to the Plovdiv train station, from which I'll travel on my own to Burgas, a city on the Black Sea coast. In its blithe way, the Bulgarian network has coordinated my trip, so that I'll be met by Dimitrina, who comes from Burgas, and who is visiting her parents there. It's a burning hot day, and just standing at the Plovdiv station in the exposed sun is uncomfortable. Demian complains of feeling unwell, and both Nadja and he worry about the conditions on the train. In fact, the train is a nightmare. The temperature within it must be well over 100 degrees, and it's full to the gills, with people as crowded in the corridors as they are in the compartments. The cigarette smoke travels through the air in wavy curlicues. Fortunately, I spot a narrow slice of unoccupied seat, and indicate by a gesture my desire to sit down. Immediately, the other people in the compartment squeeze closer together, one sits on another's knee, and a larger space is cleared for me. It's only after I sit down that I realize the compartment is occupied by a group of young men, or boys rather, who are speaking Russian. They're all from Siberia—we communicate in my elementary Russian and some general pan-Slav mix—and throughout the four-hour trip, they laud the virtues of Siberian culture, insofar as I can understand. They also pass a bottle of foul-looking liquor around, play cards, smoke many cigarettes, and fall asleep on each other's shoulders in a perfectly unselfconscious way. Although they get rowdy occasionally, they maintain faultless courtesy toward me; only once does one of them say something in a provocative tone—but the others quickly silence him. Then, in about the third hour, they take a guitar off the overhead shelf, and begin to sing.

And good God, how they sing! They sing ballads that start in a rhythmical recitation and rise into music from the sheer eloquence of feeling that drives them. They sing with a steady fierceness that seems to cut right through to the core of human pride. Even the most unappealing member of the group—the hooligan, who has shouted insults at others and has been on the verge of a fistfight—is lit by the straight-out, furious lyricism of his singing. I can forgive him a lot for this, this Russian gift. What is it they have access to that enables them to sing like this?

Then the guitar is put away, everyone reverts to the horrid-looking liquor—they tell me they haven't eaten since the morning, and it's now midevening—and to general boisterousness. They've been on a sort of "working holiday" in Bulgaria; they're rather vague about what they've been doing. Before I leave the train, they tell me I should visit their country; that I would find a beautiful and civilized culture in Siberia. I disembark a bit woozy from heat and smoke fumes, and with several Siberian addresses scribbled in my notebook.

The air in Burgas, blessedly cool, with a mild, salty breeze, immediately announces a seaside city. Dimitrina is waiting for me at the train station with several friends. They're already in the middle of their evening, and they incorporate me into their group with the utmost simplicity. We walk down a pleasant, tree-lined promenade back to the cultural club that is their regular hangout, and from where they've come to fetch me at the station.

Burgas is one of those Eastern European cities, like Zakopane in Poland, or Szentendre in Hungary, where the bohemian tradition has persisted through everything, and the club has been a combination of salon and shelter for artists and literati. It's composed of several rooms, decorated in the Bulgarian folkloric style, lively with conversation and people moving from table to table to greet their friends.

Though she lives in Sofia, Dimitrina was elected to Parliament from Burgas, so she's something of a visiting dignitary; but she's mainly an old friend, and the mood at her table is convivial. Like all such clubs, this one has its presiding personalities, and one of them is Stoicho, a freelance philosopher and a guru to students who have come from all over the country to take ex officio courses from him. Stoicho is a bearish, corpulent man, full of energy, friendliness, and observations on many subjects—the kind of intellectual produced in Eastern Europe by a mix of political involvement, voluminous curiosity, and ideas with a *frisson* of the forbidden.

At the moment, Stoicho is thinking about the essence of cultural differences—a highly contemporary subject, to which, however, he brings an original, local twist. Each culture, he thinks, has its form of conversation, whose concerns and interests are different from the subjects of conversation in other cultures. Moreover—so Stoicho thinks—each culture's conversation has a specific, unique rhythm, which is the primal rhythm of a cultural sensibility. The rhythms of Bulgarian culture are caught in its music; three against four in each bar and three against four from bar to bar, and this slippage, this strong uncertainty, is a fundament of something in Bulgarian character—an acceptance of ambiguity, of the way things are.

Acceptance of ambiguity; I've heard Hungarians talk about this, and Romanians, too. Perhaps such acceptance is characteristic of these regions, which are closer to the Oriental East, after all. But the musical part of this theory, I think, could only be born in Bulgaria, where musical rhythms are so old and powerful, where Orpheus's lyre still speaks with eloquent meaning.

Then Stoicho tells us, with great vivacity, about international conversations that resulted in some misunderstandings. There was a recent philosophy conference in Burgas during which the English and American philosophers wanted to talk about nothing but politics and were disappointed that the Bulgarians wanted to talk about the pre-Socratics. Stoicho, in turn, thought the Westerners were "ridiculous"; this was a philosophy conference after all—and in any case, he doesn't want his students to follow fashions, however international they are; he wants them to follow their own gods. "You've got to have your own face," he says.

I am struck, again, by the self-confidence of this, the insistence on one's own integrity. Stoicho follows this with another anecdote about foreigners: "There were these American consultants who came to advise us on how to conduct election campaigns; and they seemed to have this extreme sense of separation between reality and public image. So finally I asked them, which should we emphasize? Image, they said. Always image."

"I'm not surprised," I say, too wisely by half.

"Yes, but it was a complete misunderstanding of people's mentality here," Stoicho says. "They're tired of lies, they want something real."

Oh, good for them, I think—but immediately, the Bulgarian penchant for reality, and for sincerity, redounds back on me.

A tall theater producer leans toward me across the table, and looking at me earnestly, asks, "Right now, are you doing business, or are you enjoying yourself?"

It's a question that has the power to confound me, because it has never been far from my mind in my travels. There is an element of a complicated doubleness, or near-inauthenticity, of which every writer engaged in an enterprise such as mine is guilty. I like all the people around this table; I am, in point of fact, enjoying myself very much. But there's no denying that out of a corner of my mind I'm observing what's going on from a slight observer's distance.

Kindly, the others at the table try to hush my interlocutor up.

"I dissociate myself from this question," they say, one by one, repeating a phrase that was apparently a political slogan in the elections. They can see exactly why this earnest inquiry would be discomfiting to me.

"You see, this is the preoccupation with image," Stoicho says. "They want to know whether something real is happening here."

I rather anxiously say something about how writing is an occupation in which there is little disparity between work and ordinary experience—something as close to the truth as I can make it. We talk about this for a while. I can see that everyone at this table understands the intricacies of our momentary relationship and its possible misunderstandings so well that the oppositions, the putative inequities, between the observer and the observed, the interviewer and the interviewed, in effect vanish. I am hardly the coldly objective researcher; they are hardly the unconscious material. We share the minor dilemma of this moment in common; when all is said and done, we are having an ordinary, real conversation.

Dimitrina has invited me to stay in her parents' house, and we make our way through the pleasantly breezy streets, accompanied by all the others, to a standard Eastern European apartment building, made less dismal only by its smaller, provincial scale. Dimitrina's parents greet me with that unaffected directness to which I'm becoming accustomed. Her father shakes my hand robustly; her mother gives a big welcoming smile. Dimitrina's father is a factory worker and an old-style, working-class Communist—the sort of person who now forms the backbone of support for the new Socialist Party. Although he disagrees with his daughter on many matters, their relations are affectionate and respectful; a big campaign poster of Dimitrina hangs proudly in the living room. Dimitrina's mother is a Greek Bulgarian—there is a large Greek community in this part of the country—and she is the neighborhood healer. Just this morning, Dimitrina tells me, she was summoned to advise a downstairs neighbor who is very ill. Her prescription in this case was an interval of near-starvation diet, though she has a repertory of other remedies as well, which Dimitrina assures me, have worked magic, even on very serious diseases.

In Burgas this summer, there is no running water except for a few hours each day. One never quite knows when it will come on, but when it does, the news spreads through the town immediately. Everyone runs home to take a shower and to fill up buckets for the next day. There have been rumors that the water will materialize later that night. In the meantime, Dimitrina's father brings out an excellent supper of bean soup—a staple of Bulgarian diet—sardines, and tomato salad. Dimitrina reminisces about growing up here and wanting to know, to master, everything. She still has a great self-perfecting urge, and tries to make time for reading and writing within her parliamentary schedule. Then there are her two small daughters—though when I've asked her about the difficulties of bringing up children in Bulgarian conditions, she said, "Oh, it isn't hard. They just grow near you. You just let them grow." Her husband, Krassi, takes care of them in her absence—actually, she says, he's the more patient one; and when both of them get very busy, the children spend long intervals with Krassi's parents, who have a cottage in the country.

Late at night, the water does come on, and we take our turns making the most of it. In the small apartment, everyone negotiates my presence so gracefully that these vicissitudes seem perfectly ordinary to me. Either I'm becoming used, once again, to the greater human proximity I knew in my childhood, or the Bulgarian gift for cutting through difficulty is catching.

Dimitrina and her friends tend to travel in a group, and in the next few days, I join them in their loose peregrinations in and around Burgas. During the Cold War, the Bulgarian Black Sea coast was to the Eastern Bloc what the Riviera has been to the West. A summer vacation on the Black Sea was the great romantic adventure for thousands of young people from Poland and

Czechoslovakia and Hungary. The *nomenklatura* had its designated beaches here, and so did university students. Part of the coast's appeal was that one could encounter Western tourists here as well, and many young women came with the more pragmatic than romantic hope of meeting somebody who might whisk them off to "the other side." Often they did, and the beaches were famous for the many romances and marriages contracted here. These days, mostly Austrians come, to take advantage of their still-hefty currency advantage; as for the rest of Eastern Europe, now that the Iron Curtain is down, it's going West, by hook or crook, on night trains and rattling buses.

We spend some time on the beach in Slâncěv Brjag, or Sunny Shore, a rather good resort town. The hotels jut out too aggressively onto the white sand, but the beach is uncrowded, the habits unpuritanical: people step in and out of their bathing suits quite casually and in full view. The water looks wonderfully clear to me, but I'm assured that it's not what it used to be, because the Burgas industry causes massive pollution. Oh, the sameness of issues all over the world!

Dimitrina and her friend Anelia, however, talk of what is always most important, of their personal lives. Anelia is divorced and involved with a younger man, about whom she talks in a way that's intensely romantic, and almost starkly frank. She wants to have a child by him; she's afraid he'll leave her. Dimitrina, with her strong view of things, wonders what Anelia needs him *for.* But Anelia is not about to question her emotions; she's another romantic, and she's giving herself over wholly to her feelings. "What do you think about love?" she asks me at one point dreamily, but very earnestly, as if there were an answer to such a question, and as if somebody could provide some final enlightenment; but I tell her, I'm no more enlightened on this subject than she. . . .

And yet Anelia's behavior with her lover is discreet in the extreme. On our common excursions, they act as though they barely know each other. The distinction between public and private seems to be absolute for them, and dignity inheres in keep-

ing your private affairs very private. But among those admitted
to the trusted circle—as I've been admitted either by virtue of
being Dimitrina's friend or perhaps a foreigner—you hold nothing back.

After Slâncěv Brjag, we make our way to Sozopol, a town on
a small cape south of Burgas. After having stumbled upon the
unexpected in Plovdiv, in Sozopol I feel I have come upon the
exotic. This quite enchanting town used to be the ancient
Apollonia, the oldest of all the Greek colonies, and had an enormous statue of Apollo, which was transported to Rome after the
town was sacked. Now, it's a small, unique gem of a place, consisting almost entirely of old National Revival houses, built of tan
wood that emits a faint odor of heated sea water. The whole
town is permeated by this tan color, belonging to a more northern earth, by the fragrance, and a southern sun. Sozopol has become a rather hip resort for the cognoscenti, and various cultural
events are amply advertised. On one side of the cape, the sea
beats against the rocky shore in brilliant blue and foaming white;
on another, there's a winding promenade, lined with fig trees that
bend almost at a right angle toward the sea, as if they wanted to
touch the tips of their large leaves to the water. On this beautiful, winding walk, the heated, elusive fragrance of the trees, mingled with the sea and the sun, speaks of a mythical southernness,
a sensuous completeness.

In the evening, a member of our little group—a journalist who
writes for a local newspaper—declares that he would like to interview me. The world is becoming a sort of Möbius strip of interviews, in which the interviewers and the interviewed exchange
places and blend into each other quite seamlessly. Mostly, the
journalist wants to know what I think of his country; but somehow the inevitable subject of Eastern European anti-Semitism
makes its way into our conversation. The journalist says he can't
understand why, for example, there was anti-Semitism in Poland,
"since there were so many Jews" there.

This must be a uniquely Bulgarian perspective—for Bulgaria

seems to be a country unusually innocent of anti-Semitism. The preservation of Bulgarian Jewry during World War II is one of the great, largely unsung stories of that dark time. Bulgaria entered the war on the German side; and there were, of course, enormous pressures on the government to deport the more than 200,000 Jews living in the country. The authorities resisted with great determination. King Boris sent many Sofia Jews to the countryside, where they would be safer; there were vocal protests against the German demands in the Parliament; and the Orthodox Patriarch of Bulgaria passionately declared that if deportation trains started moving through his country, he would personally throw himself on the rails in front of the first one. In the end, almost all Bulgarian Jews were saved.

I tell them how moved I was when I first heard these facts—and they agree that this is one deed of which their country can be proud. Then they shift conversational pitch and ask me whether I got my job at *The New York Times* because I'm an attractive woman. I'm flattered by their compliment, of course, but I try to explain that one doesn't get hired on such grounds, and it wouldn't really be a compliment if one did. . . .

Explanations, mutual explanations; and sometimes, when I have glimpses of minute, telling differences, I wonder how fully we can explain ourselves to each other after all.

Dimitrina, Anelia, and I go back to the cultural center in Burgas once more, not only because it offers a guaranteed cup of coffee, but also to meet a woman who is known as a sort of "muse" to many Burgas artists. She is thought to be unusually elegant and charming—a "sophisticated woman," Dimitrina underlines. When I meet her, the "muse" is more carefully made up than anyone I've met here, and there's an element of coquettishness in her manner, an aspiration to a certain kind of charm. She views herself as a romantic figure, and she tells us, somewhat affectedly, of the poetry she's writing, and of letters she exchanges with a man whom she sees every day, because there are certain things that can only be said in writing. The others clearly admire

her, and think her very feminine, though to me, their own directness, so without coyness or mannerisms, seems a more powerful
expression of femininity.

Eventually, the conversation turns to politics, and the three
women—all of whom exercise some influence in Burgas—
speculate about who should run for office in the upcoming local
elections. They mention several names and dismiss them: these
people want power too much.

But in order to be in politics, don't you have to want power,
or at least know how to wield it, to some extent? I ask.

Yes, the muse says, but she can tell who wants it in order to
do some good and who craves it just for personal ambition. The
person she's thinking of—well, he runs around too busily, pro-
moting himself, he tries to please everyone too much. No, they
want somebody who at least has the good taste not to show that
he—she—wants to hold office.

Could you or Anelia run for something? I ask.

Both women shake their heads. We're too aristocratic for
that, the muse finally says, with a slight pout. Too aristocratic to
put ourselves up for something we may not get, or may not do
well enough. It's part of dignity not to try too hard, to know
your limits.

This has become a familiar theme from my Eastern European
conversations—a new puritanism about power, bred partly from
the revulsion developed in the last decades, and partly from
some older mistrust of ambition. Under the presumption inherited from the Communist dispensation, people who agree to play
the power game are almost automatically suspect. And under the
older ethos carried over from a feudal, more settled, society,
those who try to climb the social ladder, to outdo themselves or
reach beyond their limits, are likely to be unsavory characters, or
fools.

By this logic, decent politicians are an oxymoron, and honest
governance is impossible to conceive. Though most of the time,
the practice of politics conforms to this sorry premise, nevertheless, I've often thought during these travels that somewhere in
our scheme of things we need to allow for the art of possible

politics—and for politics as the art of the possible, rather than the ideal or the demonic.

As it happens, later in the evening, I witness a small incident that to me is a credible illustration of what good politics may look like. At supper, a merry group gathers in a restaurant, and Dimitrina, before leaving Burgas, decides to update her friends about recent events in Parliament. She begins to speak softly, but her voice, her face, gather power as she goes on, a vertical line forming in her forehead, expressing that enormous concentration that is a form of charisma. She's not playing to her audience, but everyone listens to her with absolute attention. She is, after all, someone utterly to be trusted, and there seems to be no discontinuity between the person they know and the politician. "Excuse me for speaking Bulgarian," she says, turning to me at one point, "but I want my friends to know what's going on." That's all; she wants them to know what's going on. Then she picks up her theme and goes on, building, I can tell, the different blocks of her explanation, until everything is coherent and clear.

▌keep thinking of Rebecca West in Bulgaria, and her great book *Grey Lamb and Black Falcon*. The book is about Yugoslavia and not Bulgaria, and yet many of Rebecca West's perceptions come alive for me here. In 1936, West made a trip to Yugoslavia on what was meant to be a purely professional occasion, and instead, she fell in love with what she found. In 1937, she returned to Yugoslavia, to follow up on her initial infatuation and intuition—to find out what she had fallen in love with. When her husband presses her to explain why she insists on going back there, she sounds almost inarticulate, or mystical. Yugoslavia, she tells him, is "a land where everything was comprehensible, where the mode of life was so honest that it put an end to perplexity." And she tries to communicate to him, not very successfully, something about an ineffable sense of completeness, of sufficiency, that she had felt there. When he asks just where it comes from, she says, "Well, there is everything there. Except what we have. But that seems very little." "Do you mean that the English have very little," he presses, "or the whole of the West?" And she replies, boldly courting implausibility, "The whole of the West."

That was Yugoslavia before it exploded in fraternal violence during World War II; before the orgy of recent atrocities. But I keep thinking of what she found there, because it's some such ineffable completeness that I sense in Yugoslavia's neighboring Balkan country. I sense it through all the glaring incompleteness, shortages, young people's anger—Rebecca West found lots of anger in Yugoslavia—and the sound and fury of politics. I sense it in the frankness of people's faces and in the dignity that inheres in not comparing themselves to anybody else. I intuit it in the ease with which everything is settled and done, without fuss or anticipatory anxiety. They seem to have eliminated much of the tension between intention and action.

Of course, Yugoslavia couldn't be anybody's political model even in the 1930s, as Rebecca West fully understood; and Bulgaria, judging by any of the cruder criteria, is nobody's earthly paradise. And yet the straight relation to themselves and the world that I sense in so many people here, and the straightforward energy that seems to be released by it, seems to me an important, indeed a profound, form of liberty.

To the uninitiated eye, Sofia in the summer of 1991 might seem a materially desolate place, but on my second visit, it is marks of progress that I notice. During an evening walk through quiet, backwater streets, Deyan points out new private shops, and I gape at rows of shampoo bottles in a cosmetics store; where previously there was no shampoo, shampoo can seem quite magical—the very illustration of the new, and still extremely modest, Eastern European materialism.

"We are fast attaining the postmodern condition," Deyan says, taking me through an outdoor market. The ramshackle area of wooden shacks and improvised counters features an eclectic, if very unprepossessing, mélange of objects, modes, and time zones. Handmade pottery competes for counter space with packs of Marlboros, and sunflower seeds are set out on a newspaper next to sophisticated electrical tools. On an overturned garbage bin, a gambling game is going on, culminating in a brief scuffle and the intervention of a genial policeman. The gamblers disperse, to return as soon as the policeman turns his back. Further on, an Orthodox priest with a briefcase stares at another group of gamblers with great interest, hardly bothering to set an example.

Of course, postmodernism—if it's defined as a jumbled juxtaposition of heterogenous elements—is always with us, and it has even existed in Eastern Europe during the ostensibly most monochromatic of times. There have always been Jews, Gypsies, and Turks, and a mixture of languages and traces of other eras; they have even been visible to those who lived here. It's just that they are now acknowledged, and it is this acknowledgment, the noticing of discontinuities and distinctions rather than stabilities and homogeneity, that marks Eastern Europe's entry into our—sufficiently heterogenous—world.

Deyan has had some disappointments during the past year, a year into which at least a decade's worth of euphoric hopes and dashed expectations got confusingly compressed. The newspaper he was to edit never got off the ground; no funds. He now works for the Center for Democracy—a new institute for the study and development of democratic habits—and one morning I find him there, receiving a Chinese delegation, closely followed by a group from Denmark. The world is becoming curious about Eastern Europe's versions of the democratic experiment.

He has traveled in the past year as well. He made a brief visit to America, the capital of postmodern, and he was fascinated by all that pop culture everywhere—"a culture for everybody"—and also by a particular kind of freedom, derived from the sense that your actions aren't perpetually and vigilantly registered on a set of coordinates. "I had this feeling there that you could just walk out of the house and vanish," Deyan says somewhat dreamily. I tell him that from my point of view there are pitfalls to uncharted freedom as well. Just as we can suffer from an overdetermination of coordinates and of symbolism, so we can feel an anomie from their lack. Perhaps finding a happy symbolic balance is one meaning of a useful freedom, and of a good society.

Dimitrina, when I meet her this time, sounds uncharacteristically impatient, even harassed. It had been a hard fall and winter, before the economy started picking up a bit, and there was so little aEfoodin Sofia that she sent her younger daughter to spend some time in the country with her grandmother. She's also thinking of quitting the Parliament, which has become too intrigue-laden to provide the sense that she's doing something useful. The oppositional UDF is becoming too conservative for her taste; there is already an inner clique, she says with her usual analytic acuity, who work not for any aim, but only "for the perpetuation of the apparatus." The brief moment when the sense of common cause was more important than the maintenance of careers or the bureaucracy is over, she feels; from now on, it is politics as usual and the only marker of difference is the high level of disillusionment with that state of affairs.

But mostly Dimitrina suffers from the lack of time. She would like to spend more time with her daughters, but she's all of a sudden busier than ever before. The journal she wants to start isn't getting off the ground easily. There's fund raising to do, and then there's the Parliament work, and Dimitrina feels as though she isn't doing anything right, as though, she says, illustrating this with a gesture, she's carrying too many watermelons, and they're all tumbling out from under her arms—the Bulgarian equivalent, I suppose, of juggling too many balls in the air. "I could use some psychoanalysis," she says. "Many of us could."

"Welcome to postmodern time," I say. "The shrinks will surely follow."

By the time I hear Deyan's story fully, the surprise is how well I know its outlines: the stamp of a common history on the Eastern Europeans of his generation has been remarkably strong. Like so many leading Eastern European dissidents, he's the son of early, idealistic Communists who stayed in the Party despite their various doubts and disillusionments. In his specific way, Deyan has gone through the stages of belief, revisionism, doubt, despair, and dissidence that I well recognize.

But there is a Bulgarian difference in Deyan's narrative, and it lies in its relationship to the story of his parents. Oppositional activity didn't start in Bulgaria until the mid-1980s, and Deyan was pivotally involved in all its stages. But one of the headiest surprises of that period was that, after a period of painful ruptures, he and his parents were, if only briefly, on the same side. Both parents and son, unbeknownst to each other, joined the Club for Glasnost and Perestroika—the germ of the later opposition. It was only on the way to the first meeting that they discovered they were going to the same place. For the parents, who were still in the Party, this was a risky step; but quite a few of their Communist colleagues were there as well.

It is another important Bulgarian difference that Deyan's parents decided to rejoin the party after the changes. When Todor Zhivkov, who happened to be the longest-ruling Communist dictator, stepped down in 1989, and the party declared its reformist intentions, Deyan's father, who had been recently expelled for his dissident activity, was not only asked to resume his membership, but was nominated to the Politburo. Surprisingly, Deyan's advice was to accept. "We thought about these things very consciously," he says. "I told him—go on, that's where you started; do your best." Apparently, there was enough reason even for Deyan to believe that the Party could change for the better.

In the last year, Deyan's attitude toward his parents' renewed role in the party has become much more complicated. "His best wasn't good enough for me," he says about his father, with an unexpected toughness. Still, the one thing he never accuses his parents of is bad faith. There is a certain tone he adopts when he speaks about them—especially, perhaps, about his mother—made up equally of frank disagreement, deep respect, and the kind of uncompromising judgment one reserves for people whom one holds to the highest standards. The son paints his mother as a figure of "radical" independence and integrity. These days, he holds it against her that for the first time in her life she's becoming "the American wife"—that is, a wife who supports her husband no matter what. Still, it's a criticism that gives me a glimpse of how much he expects of her. "She's all right," Deyan says, as if wanting to suppress by understatement an excess of pride, "I think you'll see that she's all right."

Deyan is not the only one who holds his mother in high esteem. Iskra Panova—she has always kept her own name—has an almost cultish reputation in Sofia. People speak of her as a charismatic teacher—she taught French literature at the University of Sofia for a while—as someone of legendary courage and compassion; as one of the few untouchables, the ones above suspicion.

In the first few minutes of our meeting, though, Panova might well be mistaken for a kindly hausfrau, who is a bit worried about the neatness of her house. In fact, her apartment is neat as a pin, and filled with wood objects and furniture from the nineteenth century carved in the wonderful indigenous style. Panova herself is a tiny woman in her seventies, with a pretty, mild face, a deep dimple in one of her cheeks, and enormous eyes which look out from behind her glasses with great kindness and penetration. It is her voice, however, much larger and deeper than one might expect, that is the first clue to the strength of her personality. She was reluctant to talk to me at first; but once she agreed, she talks with an unreserved frankness and generosity.

She also speaks with that tremendous rhetorical energy that I have noticed in Communists of her generation—the energy of conviction, perhaps, and of a mind directed toward action and the external world, rather than toward the self and self-doubt. Like many Communists, she has an extraordinary historical memory; and in her account, the vicissitudes of the Communist Party in Bulgaria fifty years ago are as alive as the events of her own life—and coterminous with it.

Her biography also falls into familiar, turbulent patterns; by now, I recognize most of its elements. There was her father, who was an early Communist activist; there was her own formative experience of prison and labor camp. At the beginning of the war, she received a death sentence for her anti-Fascist activities. She had the Dostoevskian experience of waiting for her execution—but at the last moment, the sentence was commuted to life imprisonment. Only the end of the war released her. In her confinement, she drew conclusions more basic than ideology. "I myself am a kind of individualist," she says. "But living in an overpopulated cell, you start thinking, Is it better to be among people, or alone? I decided I preferred to be among people. These may be simple questions, but they're profound as well. Prison was a school for friendship, for solidarity. There were so many human fates right there—and the necessity of mutual help. We knew, for example, when executions were to take place, and we saw people who were waiting for executions. We learned how to be with them. Despite everything, human beings are capable of making profound conclusions, of discovering values, and these values stay inside you."

There was the period of an official party career, and the intrusion of the worm of doubt: she worked as an editor of a youth magazine after the war, but resigned from it on a matter of principle, became a director at the Ministry of Culture, and married her deputy. "I made the theories, and he did the organization," she says good-humoredly. There was her decision to turn to "real science"—that is, linguistics—which she studied in Moscow. It gives me a glimpse of the complications of intellectual life here that later Panova got into trouble for preferring the early Russian structuralists to linguistics of the Stalinist stripe. There was a stint in the United Nations in Geneva with her husband, where the "darkness" of the invasion of Czechoslovakia came upon them, and a decision to remove herself from the central activities of the party to become a sort of solo gadfly at the literary institute.

The Bulgarian twist comes in the recent stages. It may go some way to explain the Bulgarian climate right now—the relative absence of revanchist hatred—that a number of reformist Communists were involved in the opposition movement from the very start. The Club for Glasnost and Perestroika was initiated by Zhelyu Zhelev, Bulgaria's first post-Communist president, and by five party members. Panova doesn't find this at all surprising:

"The party gave them materials with which to change their opinions," she says, "partly because it taught them to think politically, and partly through the awful things it did."

But she does find it "in a way miraculous" that when the rebellious party members were given an ultimatum—to choose between the party and the club—everyone chose the club.

The next twist came after the changes, when, with a group of other Communists, she broke with the new oppositional coalition after all and decided to return to the party. Why?

"There were puzzling tendencies in the first Round Table discussions," she remembers. "There was a primitive anticommunism, an antisocialism that is a kind of antidemocratism. I have long political experience, you see, and I know how tendencies develop. I can see that they're coming to fruition even now—I can see the embryos of reactionary tendencies."

In this perception, she is quite close to Deyan; he worries about the very same tendencies as well. He has opted out of direct political action. She has decided to reenter the fray, to fight the new battles in her old arena. Somehow, the party in Bulgaria has retained enough credibility to command the passionate loyalty of someone like her. Perhaps this is because the party here "was not imported," as Panova says; it had indigenous roots. And, although it committed its full share of atrocities, it did not ruin the country economically; Bulgaria was the only country in the Eastern Bloc whose economy improved under the Communists.

In any case, Panova, like other liberal Communists who have taken the same route, is fervently convinced that the party can be reformed and become a force for good; that after its last Congress "it has taken a walk away from its past."

What she hopes is that the party, by walking away from its actual past, will return to that old kernel of idealism that drew her to it in the first place. But her loyalties are to the actual past as well, for all its wrenching complexities. "Our history, our long past," she says, her voice rising in a crescendo, "this is one of the strings that keeps us together now—the old Communists who were in these camps, who saw people killed in prisons. Though the bitter thing is that so many of the people who were in prison are against each other now. I cannot talk anymore with many of the women I knew there. And many of the comrades who were executed in the 1940s would have turned into people with whom I could not agree. Heroes became killers—but those who were killed gave their lives nevertheless. These are the deep structures, the deep relations between us.

"Some years ago," she recalls, "Deyan said to me that I'd accomplished my mission; that I should hand my ideas over to him. Well, I don't want to pass on my ideas—I rejected the old banners, but the idea of the old movement is still mine. It's something we have to preserve, but not as relics of the past, not as the Old Red Women, but as a kind of seed that could be cultivated."

I am impressed by the fierceness of this; but though she hasn't passed on "the movement" to Deyan, she has passed on something perhaps even deeper. At some point, I tell her that I admire the energy of hope that has enabled her, in effect, to start again, and she answers readily that she needs, wants, energy— precisely because experience shows that hopes are mostly disappointed. "I have a kind of calculation," she says, "that to achieve three percent of what you hope, you have to have three hundred percent energy. But I also have a rule, which might sound irrational at first, but which has helped me, that it is not good for a person to start doing something if one has a guarantee that it'll be accomplished. There's a moral imperative that goes with this: if you make your analysis, good or bad, you have to follow it, even if you have no idea what will happen, where it will lead."

Acting on moral imperatives; living with the consequences of one's analysis: this version of the examined life the mother and the son have in common. His analysis right now leads him to very different conclusions. "We have lost one set of coordinates," he says, "and if I'm doing anything intellectually, it's trying to elaborate a new set of coordinates."

He is moving, in other words, to a more individualistic, more multivalent world—the way his mother will probably never be willing to do. In making this leap, what he wishes is a complete break with the past. "Let's forget about it," he says with something like anger. "Let's get on. It cannot help us. I wouldn't like my grandchildren to know about it—not even my children. Looking back will give us a false sense that we know what we're doing—when we don't. Oh, yes, we tried to analyze it every which way, we had mathematical models, we tried everything. We had time for that. But none of it can help us in this new situation."

It is a strong response to radical change—and a very postmodern vision of history. Sometimes, the past doesn't move logically into the present; sometimes, the "lessons" of experience are misleading precisely because history doesn't repeat itself. As strong a response, in its way, as his mother's. They have diverged vastly in their paths; but there's the connective of a powerful consciousness, and integrity; a form of continuity that may be useful in the future, and that may—in the specific Bulgarian climate—make going on without excessive bitterness possible.

In my neat and neutral hotel room at the Sofia Novotel, I curl up with an Iris Murdoch novel I bought at the Budapest bookstore. I got it for pure escape—I can't think of a universe further removed from Eastern Europe than Iris Murdoch's fiction—but as usual, it turns out that one's reading informs the occasion, or else is informed by it. The novel, *The Sacred and Profane Love Machine,* is a sort of argument against "the dreary fiction of historical character," as the narrative voice puts it. The characters' lives go through wild somersaults of unpredictable events; anything can happen next, and does: shocking discoveries of adultery in a perfect marriage, partings, reconnections, coincidences, and accidents. Much as the characters would like to impose some control and order on their tastes, the events have a sort of independent life. The present simply doesn't follow from the past. Character isn't fate.

Well, yes; there could be no better illustration of this than the recent history of Eastern Europe. Who could have inferred 1989, the *annus mirabilis,* from 1979, or even 1988? And yet I wonder if we can live with the sense of utter fortuitousness; without some belief in a profounder connective tissue, even if it's just ourselves. "The dreary fiction of historical character." Yes, it can be dreary, if it's reductively overdetermined: I have a cat phobia because my mother spanked me, and love sunsets because that was the hour when daddy came home. But an existence in a sequence of disconnected moments can lead to a different kind of fatalism: Why do anything if our lives are just one damn thing after another? I can see why so many people in Eastern Europe are scrambling for some alternative system of belief; it's so hard to shape one's life without one, without some hope in the future; without some perhaps illusory, but necessary, fiction.

An evening with several members of the Alternative Socialist Party, a small, extra-parliamentary body whose motto—"Make politics in a good mood"—should, I think, be taken to heart by political parties everywhere. The mood is certainly excellent on this occasion. One of the group's founders asks me if I think their party would do well in the United States. "Perhaps if you dropped the middle term," I suggest.

Davidov Assen, a wry, jocular man, who has just become the chairman of the philosophy department at the Kliment Ohridsky University, reminisces about his grandfather, who was the official philosopher of the Communist Party, but who, early in his career, got into trouble for "emulating" Lenin in his writing.

"But what were you supposed to do with Lenin, if not emulate him?" I ask, truly perplexed by this new refinement in the intellectual etiquette of tyranny.

"Study and revere him, of course," Assen replies.

This leads somebody else to remember about how their "cell," composed largely of philosophers, defended Zhelyu Zhelev, who is now the country's president, but who then had written a book on fascism that had become a cause célèbre. And someone else brings up the time when they got into real trouble, because they hadn't praised a book by Todor Zhivkov's daughter sufficiently. This daughter, in their view, was clinically schizophrenic, but for Todor Zhivkov she was "the holy of holies," and more untouchable than the ten basic tenets of Marxism.

War stories, which can now be told with the zest of still-fresh farce.

Assen then gives a bemused thumbnail sketch of his own ideological odyssey: from a Young Pioneer brought up in Moscow, to an Orthodox seminarian—though he's Jewish—to a revisionist Marxist, and then a skeptic fighting the system from within.

And now? "Ah, it's harder now," he admits. "Now, there are real choices. Before, you couldn't even choose to be hero or victim. There was a man I knew whose writings got him into great trouble—he was a hero for a while. But then he was summoned back by the party and was elevated—and proceeded to become a more and more horrible person.

"But it wasn't unmanageable. Totalitarianism is total—that's why it's totalitarianism. There's no way to wedge it from the inside. So you live with it.

"Now everything is a decision and a symptom of character. There's a possibility of sending my daughter abroad to school. There are questions about whether to fire a former *nomenklatura* in my department, and hire a well-meaning but less competent person. Real free choice."

On a large scale and a small, on the personal level and the political, this is the simple essence of what has changed in these unprecedented, slow, dramatic, and elusive changes. And among all the possible variants of regret, nostalgia, bitterness, vengefulness, obsessive remembering, and self-deceiving forgetfulness, Davidov Assen has found a way to connect the past and the present in a way that seems most truly free, and truly liberating.

Was his former experience, I ask him, useful for dealing with the present?

"Ah, I don't regret any of it for a minute," he answers. "For one thing, it was such an active experience of politics and of human nature. But I'm reminded of Nietzsche," he continues, "who said 'Was that life? Was that really life? Let it begin!' So I say," he wraps up, his eyes sparkling, "I say, Let it begin!"

← ← ← ←

AFTERWORD

On the way back from Sofia, the plane makes a stop at the Belgrade airport. Clusters of people are watching news attentively on the TV sets overhead, but I'm distracted by the shiny boutiques lining the lobby. Chrome, clean glass, glistening goods! I don't think of myself as a person seduced by shopping, but after several months without this simple pleasure, it appears that I've felt deeply deprived of my right to exercise consumer choice. I press my nose to the various vitrines like a child hungry for candy, and buy a dress without trying it on, just to buy *something,* for heaven's sake. The dress turns out to be unwearable.

The next day, I find out why those people were watching television so intently: fighting had just broken out in Yugoslavia. A moment of guilt for my moment of frivolity. But I can hardly credit the news; in the parts of Eastern Europe through which I traveled, the controls—of experience, of wartime memory, of the desire for normalcy—seemed to me firm enough to temper the more angry passions. In Yugoslavia, the passions have followed a different logic, developing one strand of awful possibility.

When I get back, New York seems more extreme than before. Glitz and degradation, both at a pitch rare in Eastern Europe. In the months following my reentry to New York, Eastern European voices wake me in the night. A Romanian economist phones from Harvard to tell me in a voice subdued by intensity how much he wants to prove himself, to do well. . . . "There are so many great people here," he says almost despairingly. "I'm sure you'll do fine," I say encouragingly. "Oh, thank you, thank you for saying that!" he brings out, as if I've just thrown him a lifeline. A young Bulgarian woman calls from the University of Iowa, and in a soft, breathless voice tells me about murders that took place on campus a few days before. "I'm sorry to bother you, but I can't just call somebody in Bulgaria to tell them that these people were killed while I was practically in the room," she apologizes. "They wouldn't understand."

On the streets of New York, Polish is one of the seven or so languages routinely spoken. They're coming, the Eastern Europeans are coming, to inspect us from close up as we can now inspect them. The world is becoming utterly nomadic and interpenetrated, even while it becomes more separatist. Perhaps it is precisely the interpenetrations that breed the separatist urge. The odd, reiterated hypernationalism being enacted in some parts of Eastern Europe may be national identity's last stand, before it gives way to the intermixed realities of our world.

Those realities are still, in Eastern Europe, in transition and in flux. Since I traveled there, Czechoslovakia has split into two countries; the Polish parliament has passed a retrograde anti-abortion law; the embers of anti-Semitism in Hungary continue to be stirred. At the same time, the basic economic trend in most places is definitely upward, and unemployment has been much less massive than has been expected; with the exception of Romania, where miners were summoned once again to the government's aid, there have not been any dramatic abuses of democracy, and in most of the countries I visited, the social safety structures—free education, free health services—have remained in place, whatever their quality. In other words, the news is both better and worse than was hoped and feared. After their initial moment of euphoria, Eastern Europeans themselves have become acutely aware of the limits of their situation: the limits of social change, and of most tried and true social systems; the limitations, also, imposed by the economic devastation of their countries, by that hardness of the material world which cannot be deconstructed or reconstructed by good intentions alone. If the changes are partly retro revolutions, they are also skeptical revolutions, revolutions minus apocalyptic hope.

In this absence of utopian ideology, in their mix of professed liberal norms and conservative pulls, these more moderate Eastern European societies are coming to resemble our own contemporary, "normal" world—which they happen to be rejoining at a time when the shortcomings of our social arrangements are becoming all too evident as well. From our side, the temptation to continue seeing Eastern Europe as a screen for our projections— a wild region still, or a sort of moral wilderness reservation which ought to be innocent of the deeper corruptions of the West—remains powerful. The Iron Curtain has lifted, but imaginative curtains take longer to remove, and I would not be surprised if we became prone to Cold War nostalgia just for that reason, if we felt secretly disappointed should Eastern Europeans turn out to resemble us too closely. But at best I think that Eastern Europe should be an occasion not for projection, but for its reverse—for self-reflection. Insofar as it is trying to become more like us, Eastern Europe is partly a test of what we stand for. The societies there are at present a sort of laboratory in which everything is being redefined from the ground up—redefined in the context and terms of our world. Therefore, they challenge us, indirectly, to think afresh about what our world is and what we would like to make of it; what is worthwhile in it and what reprehensible; what we would advise people we feel friendly toward to take on, and what to discard. Do we really want to counsel a purity of materialism that some of us seem to wish for Eastern Europeans? Or, for that matter, the purity of non-materialism? For me, one of the potentially invigorating effects of the changes is that they clearly confound the outmoded, often mind-stifling categories through which we are accustomed to position ourselves in social debate.

Indeed, one of the challenges facing Eastern Europeans themselves right now, as well as those who would understand them, is to adjust the categories, lenses—even the emotions—through which to comprehend their experience in order to keep up with the changing experience itself. But coming late to the scene might have certain advantages. Gertrude Stein once said that America was the oldest country in the world, because it was the first to come to modernism—and it is possible that Eastern Europe might be in the vanguard of *something*: a "third way" different from what we have yet conceived. Like all experiments in reality, the grand, complex Eastern European experiment is both determined and utterly fluid; its results can only be shown in time, and they can—perhaps fortunately—never be finally declared.

—New York,
April 1993